Gender, Class, and Shelter

Gender, Class, and Shelter

PERSPECTIVES IN VERNACULAR ARCHITECTURE, V

Edited by
Elizabeth Collins Cromley
and
Carter L. Hudgins

The University of Tennessee Press
Knoxville

Library of Congress Cataloging in Publication Data

Gender, class, and shelter/edited by Elizabeth Collins Cromley and Carter L. Hudgins.—1st ed.
    p. cm.—(Perspectives in vernacular architecture; 5)
Includes bibliographical references and index.
ISBN 0-87049-872-X (pbk.: alk paper)
1. Vernacular architecture—United States.
2. Architecture and society—United States.
I. Cromley, Elizabeth C. II. Hudgins, Carter L.
III. Series: Perspectives in vernacular architecture (Knoxville, Tenn.); 5.
    NA705. G36 1995   94-18715
    720' .1'060973—dc20   CIP

Contents

Illustrations

FIGURES

TABLES

Preface

The study of vernacular architecture has been the special focus of members of the Vernacular Architecture Forum, a group founded in 1980. For us, the term "vernacular" points to both a subject matter and a mode of study. The vernacular is the language spoken at home: it is informal and intimate. When applied to architectural objects, it identifies that body of buildings and landscapes made for everyday use. When used to identify a method, "vernacular" studies suggest an analysis of everyday qualities: common uses for buildings, the ethnic traditions of builders and building users, or the meanings embodied in buildings and landscapes that preserve and convey cultural knowledge to the next generation.

For fourteen years the Vernacular Architecture Forum has sponsored an annual conference at which scholars from a wide range of disciplines have explored the field of vernacular architecture, both as a corpus of buildings and as an evolving method. With the help of seasoned local scholars, these meetings have provided unsurpassed opportunities to analyze the commonplace buildings that dot the landscape. Forum members have met in New England and on the West Coast, at two sites on the Mississippi, in the upper Midwest and the Southwest, and places in between. They have investigated attics and basements, floor plans and room uses, framing systems and circulation patterns, and have asked the legion of questions that old buildings invite.

As important as these field studies have been, however, it is the presentation of the results of scholarly research at these conferences that has held the most significant intellectual consequences for vernacular architecture studies. The first four volumes of *Perspectives in Vernacular Architecture* preserve the research endeavors of conference participants in the form of papers selected from those presented at the 1980 through 1989 conferences. This volume, the fifth in the series which began in 1982, presents papers selected from the 1990 meeting in Kentucky, the 1991 meeting in New Mexico, and the 1992 meeting in New Hampshire. The purpose of this fifth volume of *Perspectives* is the same as it was for its four predecessors—to present expanded versions of the best papers delivered at the Vernacular Architecture Forum's annual meetings and to capture the range of topics and methods covered.

This volume of *Perspectives* is in many ways like its predecessors, but it also contains clear evidence that our discipline is changing. Traditionally, vernacular architecture studies have focused on certain types of buildings and landscapes—those buildings and places produced by "folk" builders. The objects and places that fit under this definition seemed to have been found especially in pre-industrial times and locations. Although this analytical stance was shaped by folklorists and ethnologists, scholars from many disciplines shared its premises. The vernacular process and its products were seen as governed by tradition, with skills learned and passed from one generation to another. Its artifacts were strongly characterized by regional differences, flavored by ethnically derived rules, and its locale was almost always rural. The analytic perspective of vernacular architecture scholars assumed a built environment shaped by peoples who raised buildings long ago and who were simply "not us."

However, growing awareness of the repertoire of vernacular buildings has encouraged scholars to embrace a broader research agenda. New perspectives that can be observed in recent vernacular architecture research reflect the redefinition of the scholar's relationship to peoples, places, and times that are "not us." What once seemed delimited areas of inquiry—others' ethnic traditions, appropriately distant time periods, remote geographical areas—came in for questioning. It soon became evident that buildings and landscapes of more recent times shared "vernacular" properties. As scholars expanded the scope of their analyses beyond the pre-industrial timescape, they embraced a much wider range of architectural and analytic issues.

Those who are new to vernacular architecture studies may trace the changed attitudes toward our field of study in past issues of *Perspectives in Vernacular Architecture*. Students of common buildings have often been attracted by resilient craft traditions and by ethnic architectural templates. Initially, these ethnic characteristics were identified with the first Anglo, French, or Hispanic colonial settlers or with the nineteenth-century European and Asian immigrants who arrived on both coasts. The ethnic stamp was indeed indelible on those structures built by first-generation immigrants, but neither industrialization nor "Americanization" eroded the vitality of ethnic building traditions. For one thing, immigrant groups kept arriving and reinvigorating implanted ethnic traditions. Indeed, new immigrant groups continue to add to America's ethnic mix. Caribbean immigrants who arrived during the 1970s in Brooklyn, for example, continued to make and shape landscapes and buildings to suit their specific needs and to express differences that, in part, defined their culture and their identity.

Similarly, the geographical and temporal limits of our objects of study have expanded. Early vernacular architecture studies focused on individual buildings in rural or village settings and on agricultural or small-town landscapes and architectural assemblages. Not long ago it might have been argued that the vernacular boundary was the line that separated pre-industrial and post-industrial America. The knowledge gained from and methods developed for those rural studies, however, proved to be equally fruitful when applied to urban landscapes, city dwellings, and modern institutional spaces. Thus, studies of the villages built by French settlers in the Mississippi valley are now complemented by studies of the towns created under federal sponsorship in California in the 1930s. Vernacular architecture scholars still study how the rooms were distributed in a circa 1800 Shenandoah Valley German *Flurkuchenhaus,* but they also apply vernacular methods to understand how the family rooms in 1970s suburban houses worked.

In addition to the expansion of the limits of time, ethnicity, and region, vernacular architecture studies have adopted new concerns and have added new methods. Like scholars in a number of disciplines, some vernacular architecture scholars have begun to look at the ways that gender differences structure the world. Inquiry into the effects of America's gender-bifurcated culture has opened up useful new questions about buildings, from the gender mapping of farmsteads in Tom Hubka's *Big House, Little House, Back House, Barn* to Michael Ann William's interviews with women of Appalachia who grew up in single-pen houses.

The expanded terrain encompassed by vernacular architecture studies has had implications for other fields as well, in part because our members belong to so many professional and academic fields. Architectural history—with its traditional emphasis on high style and artistic matters—shows signs of opening up to the social and cultural issues uncovered by vernacular architecture studies. Historic preservationists sometimes work to preserve common and popular-culture landmarks as well as costly and refined monuments. Interpretive strategies used at historic sites benefit from the multi-disciplinary research models of vernacular scholars. Even the practices of recent architects have been influenced by what has been discovered about vernacular architecture: the vernacular's responsiveness to climate and its vocabulary of regionally appropriate forms have especially captivated present-day architects.

The essays in this volume of *Perspectives* demonstrate that the definition of "vernacular" continues to expand, and that the methods applied to the study of vernacular spaces and places are increasingly wide ranging and fruitful. Three themes especially—an increasing interest in the architecture of this century, new attention to the analysis and interpretation of gender, and the emergence of methodologically innovative studies of urban building forms and neighborhoods—bear close watching. The work included in this volume is likely to change the way these themes are interpreted in the future.

The essays tackle a diverse range of sites and issues, but group themselves loosely around five topics: gender, institutions, ethnicity and race, popular culture, and rural and urban geographies. In the opening section, "Architecture and Difference," the essays use gender as an analytical category in vernacular architecture studies. The two essays by Deryck Holdsworth and Angel Kwolek-Folland originally constituted the 1992 methods session on this topic at the New Hampshire meeting. Kwolek-Folland argues that vernacular architecture specialists in the 1980s often failed to incorporate the category of gender in their analyses, missing important opportunities for deeper insights into the work they examined. The Holdsworth essay identifies numerous male-associated building forms, such as sailors' housing or logging camps, that have not been examined by architecture scholars before. William D. Moore demonstrates that sensitivity to the nuances of gender in architecture—he examines the Masonic lodge—will yield important new knowledge. In the essay by Jane Young and Michael Ann Williams, their critique of scholars' dependence on lin-

guistic theory (and its universalizing tendency) is in part motivated by Young and Williams's efforts to incorporate women's insights (with the authors' insistence on differences, not universals, of experience) into their analyses of vernacular architecture.

A second group of essays, "Architecture and the Meaning of Institutions," examines the architecture of churches and schools. Institutional architecture is a topic more often explored by historians of high-style architecture, although Dell Upton's book *Holy Things and Profane* provides a model analysis of churches using vernacular methods. The authors of these essays, Peter Kurtze, Susan Garfinkel, and Diane Shaw, develop methods of understanding institutional architecture in an urban context. Kurtze follows the development of a Baltimore school form based on Joseph Lancaster's design, originally for the London poor. Garfinkel explores the ways that Philadelphia Friends' meetinghouses acknowledged the pressures of the outside world while resisting worldliness. Shaw's study shows how the location and relocation of churches helped form the character of Frederick, Maryland. These essays suggest that the kinds of interpretive strategies devised a decade and more ago for rural areas hold great potential for the analysis of architectural forms in urban communities.

The next section, "Architecture, Ethnicity, and Race," assesses the effects of Hispanic, Chinese, and African-American traditions on architectural forms and building types. Abigail Van Slyck's essay on the revival of the Southwest's Hispanic colonial architecture examines the appropriation of ethnic traditions to modern market needs. In her analysis, an elite's desire for a more artistic architecture was shadowed by the racism of the early twentieth century. Christopher Yip identifies a building type common to West Coast Chinatowns, the association building. He examines the ways that the tradition of urban, commercial-block architecture intersect with the specific symbolic and practical needs of Chinese communities. John Michael Vlach's essay grows out of an ambitious re-evaluation of information on slave housing collected—beginning a half-century ago—by the Historic American Buildings Survey. He suggests an interpretation for slave housing that is more varied and more complex than the canonical reading of impoverished African-American dwelling forms.

The next group of essays, "Architecture and Popular Culture," takes up the relation of popular culture's products to buildings. Studying the nineteenth-century arrival of mass-produced architectural products and designs forces scholars to reconsider the relation of "high-style" design to popular audiences, as they observe breaks in the boundaries that once divided rural from urban, handmade from factory-made, traditional from mass culture. Jan Jennings explores the way popular architectural advice was disseminated through the magazine *Carpentry and Building,* sometimes blurring distinctions between the professional builder and the client or amateur. Pamela Simpson traces the history of a new product available to the modern builder or client—the pressed metal ceiling. Her study is part of a forthcoming longer work on new nineteenth- and twentieth-century building materials and products. Susan Chase takes a popular dwelling type—the twentieth-century bungalow—and overturns canonical interpretations of it. Her treatment of bungalows in Delaware is an example of how the close analysis of commonplace buildings from our own century can reveal unexpected links to the past. Annmarie Adams's essay on the Eichler homes of 1950s California positions the developer's intentions for the house against an actual family's use of the house, identifying some disjunctions between the prescribed and the lived architectural experience.

The four essays in the concluding section of this volume, "Architecture in Rural and Urban Geographies," are devoted to the study of the way architecture mediates the larger-scale forms of the landscape. The geographic scale of landscape studies has claimed attention at all Vernacular Architec-

ture Forum tours and paper sessions. The methods session at the Kentucky meeting, for example, was devoted to issues in the interpretation of gardens and plant usages, and the New Mexico meeting included an address by the doyen of cultural landscape scholars, geographer J. B. Jackson. Warren Hofstra and Karen Koegler reflect the continuing scholarly use of architectural evidence to elicit understanding of rural landscapes. Both use buildings as a way to understand how the social organization of a region, once settled, changed as the initial immigrant population and its progeny created stable agrarian communities from frontier settlements. Hofstra accounts for a re-mapping of community structures, rural movement paths, and settlement patterns in the Shenandoah Valley. Koegler uses stone house-building techniques as evidence to map the distribution of wealth in southwestern Pennsylvania. Bernard Herman portrays the class-charged townscape of Portsmouth, New Hampshire, through the experience of a workman's path from home to work. His analysis illuminates distribution patterns of rank, wealth, and building type in the colonial city. Greg Hise is interested in a more recent kind of townscape built for those men and women who migrated from the interior toward the West Coast during the middle decades of this century. His essay on Depression-era farm camps imaginatively treats an overlooked topic and brings some of America's forgotten workers back into historical focus.

As a group, the essays in *Perspectives V* reflect the continuing expansion of the vernacular architecture agenda. They are different from earlier generations of essays for what they have to say about gender, urban communities, and the recent past. Like their predecessors in *Perspectives I–IV,* they represent the multidisciplinary and interdisciplinary approaches to the analysis of buildings and places that have characterized vernacular architecture studies from the beginning and that assure its continuing vitality.

Acknowledgments

This volume marks the debut of our working together as co-editors of *Perspectives in Vernacular Architecture*. Our task was made easier by the support we received from the officers and directors of the Vernacular Architecture Forum. When they entrusted us with this volume, they could not have guessed that it would take so long to bring it to publication. We are grateful for their patience and good cheer. We also thank the authors of the essays that appear in this volume. Patience is a quality that they too have in good store, and we thank them for that as well as for their contributions to this volume.

Like all the editors who preceded us, we have sought advice and assistance from many members of the Vernacular Architecture Forum. The editorial board for this volume of *Perspectives* consisted of David Ames, Catherine Bishir, Richard Candee, Edward Chappell, Paul Groth, Kim Hoagland, Neil Larson, Ruth Ann Little, Richard Longstreth, Carl Lounsbury, Sally McMurry, John Pearce, Julie Riesenweber, Gary Stanton, Dell Upton, Camille Wells, Chris Wilson, and Mark Wenger. Their willingness to help us reaffirmed our sense that we are fortunate to have them as friends and colleagues. Their sage comments and advice brought clarity and strength to the essays collected in this volume.

At Mary Washington College, our work was assisted by Kelly Lafollette and Jeanette Richards and Provost Philip L. Hall who provided both encouragement and moral support. At SUNY-Buffalo, Debbi Smith and Sue McDonald helped with mailings and typing. At Historic Charleston Foundation, Betty Guerrard and M. E. Van Dyke cheerfully helped bring the project to completion. Finally, Meredith Morris-Babb at the University of Tennessee Press helped us through a period of transition and made it possible for us to transform oral performances into a more permanent record of the intellectual contributions members of the Vernacular Architecture Forum make to American architectural history.

Elizabeth Collins Cromley
State University of New York at Buffalo

Carter L. Hudgins
Historic Charleston Foundation

Part I
Architecture and Difference:
Theories and Case Studies Instigated
by Gender as a Category of Analysis

Chapter 1

Gender as a Category of Analysis in Vernacular Architecture Studies

Angel Kwolek-Folland

There is a growing awareness among scholars in many fields that gender is an important area for study. Most now agree that gender is an experiential and analytical category as fundamental as class or race.[1] Therefore, my purpose in this essay is not to suggest ways to "add women and stir" in order to arrive at some more fair version of experience that incorporates women's lives into a history written in male terms. Rather, I want to move directly to the issue of how we can make gender an integral part of our research. In this essay, I shall focus on some ways I think gender can open up new avenues for understanding the history of the design and experience of vernacular environments. My task here is to challenge and to encourage—and perhaps to provoke—further discussion of this issue by providing some approaches to using gender as a category of analysis.

When new topics or issues are introduced into the scholarly debate, the need for new methods often seems imperative. And indeed new methods can be helpful in getting at difficult research problems. Sometimes, however, the call for new methods can become a way to avoid the issues. In that light, I would like to take a position that runs counter to the usual academic notion that new problems need new methods and argue that in order to incorporate gender we do not need any new methods. Vernacular architecture studies already have borrowed just about every useful method that is available. It seems to me, however, that while we do not need new tools, we could use some different blueprints. It is not *what* we use to build,

in other words, but *how* we conceptualize our research problems that needs to be redesigned if gender is to be a revealing category of analysis in understanding vernacular architecture. Just for the record, no one, to my knowledge, has ever claimed that using gender as a category of historical analysis would be easy.

I should begin with a definition. By "gender" I do not mean "women," although the term is often used that way as a kind of politically neutral shorthand. By gender I refer instead to a set of abstractions rooted in biology and expressed in social, cultural, and historical terms.[2] Gender differences build on the biological fact that males and females have different sex organs and different reproductive functions. This biology inherently has no history: the existence of reproductive organs is timeless. They were present in prehistory (or we would not be here), and they have been with us ever since. Unlike biological sex differences, however, gender *does* have a history because it is a social creation that changes according to ethnic, cultural, religious, economic, national, racial, and temporal differences, among others. Gender, then, is a system of interrelated ideas about men's and women's social roles, self-definition, and cultural experience that is grounded in the historical process. It is closest to class as a socially constructed category of human experience, but it is also like race in that it is based in biological fact but expressed in cultural terms.

Gender is a concept that includes both men and women, manhood and womanhood, and other definitions of self that build on biological sex. We have two genders; some cultures have three and even four. We have heterosexual dominance, but we also have gay and lesbian people who have historically used manhood and womanhood to define a non-heterosexual cultural experience.[3] There are people, such as a student at the University of Kansas in the late 1980s, who insist they are sexually neutral and refer to themselves as "it." While the biological is embedded in the cultural aspects of gender, it is the cultural expressions of gender that have the most bearing on the study of vernacular architecture, since it is in culture that human choice and creativity are found.

With this definition of gender in mind, I would like to describe briefly four ways of thinking about gender that I believe would be useful to research on the gendered dimensions of vernacular architecture. I then will provide several specific examples in which I see gender operating in ways that force us to modify our interpretations of vernacular architecture. These are neither exclusive nor definitive; I offer them here simply as a basis for discussion.

First, gender is a structural category. It encompasses the underlying notions of manhood, womanhood, and/or other gender divisions in social, economic, and ideological systems. In our western, Anglo-dominated society, patriarchal structure is both idealized and a reality. It appears in the labor market, where women continue to earn sixty cents for every dollar a man earns. It appears in ritual, where brides are still "given away" by their fathers. Men give women engagement rings to cement their property rights against the claims of other men. Men, however, do not themselves accept a similar token of exclusive rights.

Reality does not always conform to ideal, however. Despite assertions of male dominance, for example, recent literature on business management has argued that male managers should learn their interpersonal skills from women, who, some claim, are more empathetic and other-directed than men.[4]

Some claim that the recent appearance of a "men's movement" grows out of men's sense of their economic and social subordination.[5] Finally, there are those who believe that social gender is *directly* linked to biology. Some people on both the right and left of the political spectrum claim that women's hormones dictate a predisposition to nurturance and empathy and men's hormones a tendency to violence and insularity.[6]

Structural patriarchy also must acknowledge racial, sexual, and ethnic differences. Right now, unemployment levels are high for everyone, but highest for black men, who consistently have higher unemployment levels than any other group. Gay men are subject to beatings by gangs of "straight" thugs. This theme, I might add, is often couched in spatial terms: for example, the city streets of Rod Stewart's song "Georgie Boy" or the playground violence that ends the life of Matthew Broderick's character in the film *Torch Song Trilogy.*[7] Not all men, in other words, benefit equally from structural patriarchy. Any gender system, therefore, will have both dominant and contested meanings: ideals that are held as culturally important and challenges to those ideals that complicate the dominant structure.

Second, gender is a chronological category. Gender systems are subject to historical flux and perhaps can themselves stimulate change. For example, the notion of "separate spheres," which has guided so much of the research in women's history and shaped gender studies, grew out of trying to understand the nature of patriarchy. It has, however, proved too simple as an overall organizing principle for the study of women, men, or gender because it is specific to a particular time—the nineteenth century—a particular class—the middle class—and a particular racial group—whites. While that group has had power to impose its own gender norms on others in the form of laws and regulations, "separate spheres" is neither a description nor an organizing assumption that has proven universally useful.[8]

Sally McMurry's work on the evolution of farm family dwellings in the nineteenth century provides an excellent critique of the separate spheres notion and modifies it in useful ways. She emphasizes the economic distinctions of separate gender spheres in urban and rural life, and she shows the ways rural men and women defined their economic, social, and familial positions first in contradiction to and then in subversion of urban gender roles. In McMurry's work, separate spheres is a complex set of relationships between men and women, work and home, farm and family space, and urban and rural experience that simultaneously highlights the connections as well as the conflicts between men's and women's worlds.[9]

Race and class also complicate the model of separate spheres over time. In the seventeenth and eighteenth centuries, ideas about manhood and womanhood stressed social and legal differences, but emphasized sexual, racial, and class similarities. In the nineteenth century, with the evolution of the white, middle-class notion of separate spheres, white men's and women's economic, social, and sexual roles sharply diverged in both theory and practice, even as differences of class and race developed that created complex gender categories. The sexuality of white men, lower-class women, and men and women of color recalled the earlier seventeenth- and eighteenth-century emphasis on human sexuality as based on uncontrollable and animalistic urges, while middle-class white men and women defined the sexuality of white middle-class women as pure, passionless, and reproductive.[10]

Third, gender is a fragmented category. Any dominant gender system will engage different people in different ways and will create multiple layers of experience. One of the best examples of this is the way in which gender complicates the history of the family. The family is not and never has been an emotional or experiential unit, despite its predominately patriarchal structure. Men and women, children and adults, boys and girls, and parents and siblings are not necessarily vested in the family in the same way. Some historians, in fact, see the family as the basic unit of social and political struggle over allocation of resources, control over reproductive issues, and the sexual division of labor.[11] Thus, to talk about a "house" or even a farmstead as a single unit of construction and experience is inaccurate, since men, women, and children make different contributions to the shape of family life. It is especially inaccurate if the paradigm of that experience is male, since women's predominant place of work throughout our history has been within the household. Joan Jensen's research on early-nineteenth-century rural Pennsylvania, for example, demonstrates women's critical economic and technological role as butter makers. Not only did women's butter making help bring the farm family into the national market economy and represent a crucial gender-linked set of skills and interests, but it also reshaped the material technology of butter making as women adapted boards and churns to increase their production.[12]

Fourth, gender is an experiential category. Individuals and groups, variously constituted and acting in various capacities, may experience gender in different ways. Like race but unlike class, gender is simultaneously a private, intimate, personal category and a public, communal, social expression of self. Like class and race, gender can link the individual to society in personal, forceful ways.

For example, the history of the nineteenth- and twentieth-century city will be forever incomplete without a comprehensive treatment of the rise of gay and lesbian urban culture. In the cities, gender became a way to define the self *against* the dominant culture's expectations for individual behavior. In turn, this complex play of self-defined and culturally imposed "deviance" became the foundation for urban spaces, which acted as "bohemian zones": places where gay and lesbian men and women led the way in creating alternative identities, economies, and communities. These urban bohemian zones reached both inward—to provide safe and economically viable places for a persecuted minority—and outward—to the possibilities for self-definition those urban spaces helped present and embody for *all* city dwellers.

Thus gender as a category of analysis is as complex as race or class, and as useful as race or class to understanding historical change. Gender analysis demands no methodology vastly different from any used in historical study. One of the most revealing discussions of gender in Native-American workplaces, for example, used time-honored archaeological fieldwork techniques to uncover task differentiation among the Hidatsa Indians.[13] A recent book on Native-American architecture uses photographs, drawings, paintings, oral histories, and the written records of anthropologists—all traditional historical documents—to link gender to housing construction. In the latter book, understanding gender was not the primary aim; rather, an awareness of the ways dwellings, work, and cosmology were gendered simply was part of the overall analysis.[14]

What *is* different in using gender as a category of analysis is the level of awareness and the added complexity that gender demands of historical reconstruction. What, then, should be kept in mind about gender when studying vernacular architecture? What can using gender as a category of analysis tell us about the built environment? Let me suggest four areas in which I think gender would be useful in reconceptualizing vernacular architecture. As my examples, I will interpolate some well-known essays in the field of vernacular architecture studies. In doing so, my intent is not to castigate any of the authors for essays they did not write. Rather, I am using them because they are exemplary essays by prominent and well-known experts in the field, and therefore pieces with which most students of vernacular architecture are already familiar. I would like to use them to think about ways we might push our usual methods, and what we already know, a step or two closer to a gendered analysis.

First, the study of vernacular architecture will have to be very inclusive of subject material if the gender of environments is to be understood. Many contributions to vernacular architecture are ephemeral, a fact particularly true in the case of women. In our historical experience of gender, the trappings and interior decorations of buildings, some of which are seasonal, are important to the meaning and experience of vernacular space.[15] To understand gender in everyday spatial expression, we may have to go to artifacts other than the building to understand the building as an environment.

To suggest some ways the inclusion of gendered ephemera would expand our understanding of vernacular space, I would like to build on Dell Upton's famous study of Anglican parish churches. Upton found women acting as sextons (or janitors), as wives and daughters of elite men, and they were segregated in the lower-status seating areas of the church.[16] Thus, Upton's portrait of women's participation in vernacular space emphasizes their subordination to men's definitions of that space. We know, however, that it was women's work as seamstresses to provide special vestments, robes, and other ornamental elements for church worship. A study that included these ephemera would throw the status implications of church participation into a different and more complexly gendered light.

Official positions within the parish church may not, in fact, exhaust the gendered experience of eighteenth-century church going in Virginia. Laurel Ulrich has argued that New England women also *took part in* status definitions through their struggles over seating space in church. Further, both men and women contributed in different ways to the status of a family. A man might have the trappings of wealth, but it was his wife who cemented elite status through careful management of household goods, servants, and children.[17] In other words, although the cultural *ideal* of seventeenth-century Anglo-America was female submission and male dominance, the *reality* seems to have been much more contested and open to interpretation.

Second, attention to gender suggests that the same places and social messages may be interpreted by men and women in different ways. Carol Gardner tested Erving Goffman's sociology of public place by subjecting it to gender variables.[18] Gardner's findings suggest men and women approach public space very differently. Using standard anthropological field study techniques and oral interviews, Gardner found that women were not at ease with social interactions such as wolf whistles or even asking a stranger the time of day in a public place. For men, these activities signaled openings for encounters; for women, they could be threatening. This fear of public places led women to invent complex imaginary identities that included pretending they were waiting for a man when they were not. What Goffman took for granted in public space—that male experience defined public encounters and that those encounters were experienced in the same way by men and women—turned out not to be true. Gardner used no innovative new methods to gain these insights; she merely approached her study with an eye to gender differences between men and women.

Third, gender ideologies can have an impact on the experience and definition of space that can complicate or add to other meanings. Here I would like to use Robert Blair St. George's fascinating essay "Set Thine House in Order" about the changes in domestic space that took place in seventeenth-century New England.[19] Leaving aside the fact that St. George treated both the barn and house as male space (an unrealistic assessment given the work roles of seventeenth-century New England women), let me point to his intriguing insight about the spatial attitudes of one New England farmer, William Morse of Newbury, Massachusetts. Morse, he observes, experienced the walls of the house as a thin membrane separating the rational, domestic order from the irrational, supernatural tumult of nature. For Morse, St. George argues, the world outside the house was filled with spirits, with witches, with all the wild and uncontrolled urges of the devil's company.

What happens to this sense of clear boundaries, however, if we add that in seventeenth-century New England, as Carol Karlsen has demonstrated, witchcraft and the supernatural were gendered?[20] Most witches were *women,* and it was women's proximity to nature and the animal world that allowed them to make cows go dry and children to be born with deformities. This is not to say St. George was wrong about Morse; perhaps house walls *were* boundaries. But Morse also *lived with* the supernatural world in the form of his mother, his wife, his sisters, and his daughters. The supernatural was both outside and inside, although in different forms. Was there a way that the houses and barns, the steads and lofts, the workplaces and living spaces were divided to keep out the darkness outside and also to keep the darkness within the family—in the form of women—contained? I do not propose to answer these questions; I merely raise them to suggest that while St. George was onto something, his interpretation of the meaning of house walls could be enriched by the dimension of gender.

Fourth, gender can add to our understanding of the transmission of dwelling types and other built forms and to our understanding of the way culture and history modify those types. Dominant gender systems never stand alone in any social or temporal context, but rather play against multiple systems that may involve different classes, ethnicities, and races, and may take us beyond national boundaries.

Another familiar essay can elaborate this point. John Michael Vlach's path-breaking study of the shotgun house is an eclectic bit of detective work that clearly ranged far from the national, ethnic, regional, and racial boundaries initially set for this well-known southern housing form.[21] From New Orleans to Haiti to the Arawak Caribbean to Nigeria, Vlach traced the development of this architectural type through the slave trade. This essay is a model for precisely the kind of informed, creative approach we must have to understand gender and vernacular architecture. I would like to use Vlach's method as a pattern and merely approach the shotgun from a slightly different direction.

The famous Nigerian novelist, Buchi Emecheta, has written extensively on the role of women and the family in Yoruba and Ibo tribal experience.[22] Her books contain vivid fictionalized portrayals of the social life of family compounds and the spatial uses of the twentieth-century Ibo equivalent of the shotgun dwelling. Where Vlach traces a housing type and makes a point about slavery, Emecheta's stories suggest questions about the *social* functions of this housing type, and specifically the role of the compound in defining and shaping men's and women's cultures. Combined with what we know about the gender divisions of slavery—the ways in which African and African-American slaves created extended families, non-exclusive parenting, and communal living spaces—we could reveal not only the continuation of a particular architectural

form but also the ways that form supported particular cultural constructions of manhood, womanhood, family, and communal experience.

Again, I do not intend to make all these connections in this essay. Rather, I raise these examples to suggest that the lack of a method for incorporating gender is not the problem. We have the methods; we even have as precedent the thoughtful, nuanced work of scholars like Upton, Gardner, St. George, Vlach, and others. What is needed is the sense that gender *matters,* that it acts in powerful and compelling ways, that it can reveal important aspects of the history of the built environment that otherwise would go unexplored. For the sake of discussion, I would argue that gender is not an optional category, any more than race or class are optional, if we are to reconstruct the story of the ways humans have created and experienced their built environments.

Notes

1. For a review of literature on women and vernacular architecture, see Sally McMurry, "Women in the American Vernacular Landscape," *Material Culture* 20 (1) (1988): 33–49. In 1989, the Winterthur Museum took as the theme of its annual conference the intersection of gender and material culture. See Kenneth L. Ames and Katharine Martinez, eds., *The Material Culture of Gender/The Gender of Material Culture* (New York: W. W. Norton, forthcoming). On gender, see Joan W. Scott, "Gender: A Useful Category of Historical Analysis," *Gender and the Politics of History* (New York: Columbia University Press, 1988), 28–50, and Peggy Sanday, *Female Power and Male Dominance: On the Origins of Sexual Inequality* (New York: Cambridge University Press, 1981).

2. On the social construction of gender, see Suzanne Kesseler and Wendy McKenna, *Gender: An Ethnomethodological Approach* (New York: John Wiley, 1978), 1–20, and Sherry B. Ortner and Harriet Whitehead, *Sexual Meanings: The Cultural Construction of Gender and Sexuality* (New York: Cambridge University Press, 1981).

3. See, for example, Elizabeth Kennedy and Madeline David, "The Reproduction of Butch-Fem Roles: A Social Constructionist Approach," in *Passion and Power: Sexuality in History,* ed. Kathy Peiss and Christina Simmons (Philadelphia: Temple University Press, 1989), 241–56.

4. See, for example, Margaret Hennig and Anne Jardim, *The Managerial Woman* (New York: Simon & Schuster, 1978); Margaret Laws, "The Superior Sex," *Working Woman* 9 (Mar. 1984): 16; Ann Hughey and Eric Gelman, "Managing the Woman's Way," *Newsweek* (Mar. 17, 1986): 46–47; and Angel Kwolek-Folland, "The Female Management Style: The Cultural Construction of Gender in Offices, 1960–1989," paper presented to the American Studies Association Annual Meeting, Nov. 1989. For the historical development of gendered work definitions in

offices, see Angel Kwolek-Folland, *Engendering Business: Men and Women in the Corporate Office, 1870–1930* (Baltimore: Johns Hopkins University Press, forthcoming).

5. See Robert Bly, *Iron John: A Book About Men* (Reading, Mass.: Addison-Wesley, 1990), and the "Epilogue" in E. Anthony Rotundo, *American Manhood: Transformations in Masculinity from the Revolution to the Modern Era* (New York: Basic Books, 1993), 284–93.

6. On the links between definitions of maleness and femaleness and the development of modern science, see Evelyn Fox Keller, *Reflections on Gender and Science* (New Haven: Yale University Press, 1985); Cynthia Russett, *Sexual Science: The Victorian Construction of Womanhood* (Cambridge, Mass.: Harvard University Press, 1989); and Londa Schiebinger, *The Mind Has No Sex?: Women in the Origins of Modern Science* (Cambridge, Mass.: Harvard University Press, 1989).

7. For historical works that focus on the importance of urban space for the gay and lesbian community, see Jeffrey Weeks, *Coming Out: Homosexual Politics in Britain from the Nineteenth Century to the Present* (New York: Quartet Books, 1990), and Joanne Meyerowitz, *Women Adrift: Independent Wage Earners in Chicago, 1880–1930* (Chicago: University of Chicago Press, 1988). For a brief review of literature on urban space and women's culture, see Linda Kerber, "Separate Spheres, Female Worlds, Woman's Place: The Rhetoric of Women's History," *Journal of American History* 75 (1) (June 1988): 32–37.

8. Kerber, "Separate Spheres," 9–39.

9. Sally McMurry, *Families and Farmhouses in Nineteenth Century America: Vernacular Design and Social Change* (New York: Oxford University Press, 1988). On women's contributions to the built rural environment, see Rebecca Sample Bernstein and Carolyn Torma's "Exploring the Role of Women in the Creation of Vernacular Architecture," in *Perspectives in Vernacular Architecture IV,* ed. Thomas Carter and Bernard L. Herman (Columbia: University of Missouri Press, 1991), 64–72.

10. The literature on these shifts is voluminous. A good summary can be found in Estelle Freedman and John D'Emilio, *Intimate Matters* (New York: Harper & Row, 1988).

11. Tamara K. Haraven, "The History of the Family and the Complexity of Social Change," *American Historical Review* 96 (1) (Feb. 1991): 95–124; Rayna Rapp, Ellen Ross, and Renate Bridenthal, "Examining Family History," *Feminist Studies* 5 (1) (Spring 1979): 174–200; and Heidi I. Hartmann, "The Family as the Locus of Gender, Class and Political Struggle: The Example of Housework," *Signs* 6 (31) (1981): 366–94.

12. Joan Jensen, *Loosening the Bonds: Mid-Atlantic Farm Women, 1750–1850* (New Haven: Yale University Press, 1986).

13. Janet D. Spector, "Male/Female Task Differentiation Among the Hidatsa: Toward the Development of an Archeological Approach to the Study of Gender," in *The Hidden Half: Studies of Plains Indian Women,* ed. Patricia Albers and Beatrice Medicine (New York: University Press of America, 1983), 77–97.

14. Peter Nabokov and Robert Easton, *Native American Architecture* (New York: Oxford University Press, 1989).

15. See, for example, Angel Kwolek-Folland, "The Useful What-Not and the Ideal of 'Domestic Decoration,'" *Helicon Nine* 8 (1983): 72–82, and Angel Kwolek-Folland, "The Elegant Dugout: Domesticity and Moveable Culture in the United States, 1870–1900," *American Studies* (Fall 1984): 21–37.

16. Dell Upton, *Holy Things and Profane: Anglican Parish Churches in Colonial Virginia* (Cambridge, Mass.: MIT Press, 1986), 7, 186, 188, 194.

17. Laurel Thatcher Ulrich, *Good Wives: Image & Reality in the Lives of Northern New England Women, 1650–1750* (New York: Knopf, 1982).

18. Carol Brooks Gardner, "Analyzing Gender in Public Places: Rethinking Goffman's Vision of Everyday Life," *The American Sociologist* (Spring 1989): 42–56.

19. Robert Blair St. George, "'Set Thine House in Order': The Domestication of the Yeomanry in Seventeenth-Century New England," in *Common Places,* ed. Dell Upton and John Michael Vlach (Athens: University of Georgia Press, 1983), 336–64.

20. Carol Karlsen, *The Devil in the Shape of a Woman* (New York: W. W. Norton, 1987).

21. John Michael Vlach, "The Shotgun House: An African Architectural Legacy," in *Common Places,* 58–78.

22. See, for example, Buchi Emecheta, *The Slave Girl* (New York: Braziller, 1977), and *The Bride Price* (New York: Braziller, 1976).

Chapter 2

"I'm a Lumberjack and I'm OK": The Built Environment and Varied Masculinities in the Industrial Age

Deryck W. Holdsworth

Recent scholarship that has focused on women, which reflects a concern for gender issues, has successfully challenged assumptions that construct insights only from the performance, participation, or perceptions of men. The search for a balanced view, however, needs to broaden the gender focus beyond just women and consider instead the whole continuum of femininities and masculinities that inform understanding of people and places. My emphasis here on masculinity and the built environment does not mean that I am writing in opposition to recent writing on feminist perspectives, nor blinkering myself to a partial view of gender. Rather, in recognizing that gender labels have been historically constructed, and contested, and that gender labels have always existed across a spectrum of what we have come to regard as monolithically male and female, I seek to re-assess some of the reified views of "man's world."

My approach to the issue of gender as a category of analysis begins by critically reassessing how I might differently go about research on some of the rough-and-tough hardy structures associated with the resource frontier, those seemingly "natural" settings for masculine forms; such buildings often get sidelined in the emphasis on pioneer family housing. My title, though humorous, is deliberate. Fans of Michael Palin and Monty Python will know that the life of a particular lumberjack in British Columbia has a distinctly ambiguous meaning: a harried British retail clerk confesses he really wanted to be a lumberjack, and the scene shifts to a forest setting where he sings a stirring male song to his sweetheart, backed by a chorus of red-coated Mounties, only to have the song, his girlfriend, and the Mounties unravel as he confesses a preference for women's clothing.[1] As I have encountered recent literature on issues in gender identity, the first line of that Python song seemed appropriate as a heading under which I could explore a range of places and structures where male identities, straight and gay, have found expression. One set is on the resource frontier; the other in urban settings. The two worlds were connected, even if their built environments have considerable difference in their permanence, materials, and conscious design. The paper suggests new empirical foci in shelter research, but does not pretend to offer detailed empirical evidence; rather, it speculates on possibilities for new (gendered) perspectives on perhaps taken-for-granted built forms.

Gender as a Category of Analysis

The African-American feminist bell hooks recalls "spaces of silence" in her childhood, when the powerful creativity of adult women and young girls was vocal during the day, only to be marginalized in the evening when the male came home.[2] She also offers a sharp definition of male/female relations: "Sexism is unique. It is unlike other forms of domination—racism or classism—where the exploited and oppressed do not live in large numbers intimately with their oppressors or develop their primary love relationships (familial and/or romantic) with individuals who oppress and dominate or share in the privileges attained by domination."[3] Since our society is patriarchal, feminist discourse, by definition, often sees "sites for male domination and oppression of women" in every aspect of society. What sites for nonsexist male discourse are possible, if the male voice is eternally accented by its identity within patriarchal society, and the heritages of economic inequality and violence to women never fade away? The gay movement has gone some way toward identifying some of the strands of an oppressive masculinity in dominant, heterosexual culture. As David Jackson notes: "It is hierarchical, heterosexual masculinity, as the dominant form of varied masculinities, that imposes its stifling and brutalizing agenda onto women and other men."[4] The social geographer Peter Jackson observes that scholarship in cultural studies similarly has begun to explore "a plurality of masculinities, with their attendant instabilities and contradictions, rather than assuming a uniform and unitary pattern of masculinity."[5] Social historians, such as Peter Stearns, Harry Brod, and Michael Kimmel, have excavated settings and circumstances of maleness,[6] but rarely has there been an explicit consideration of built environment issues. Dolores Hayden offered a pioneering example in her work on feminist design,[7] and more recently Daphne Spain's *Gendered Spaces* offered "a topography of gender inequality,"[8] that forcefully documents historical continuities in the way that women have been the victims of physical (design) segregation.

Explanations of the production of the built environment often stress economic or sociocultural forces.[9] If economic forces are privileged, then structures associated with settings for work, residence, or consumption can be seen as varying according to the changing modes of production that accompany a shift from mercantile to industrial and corporate capital, or from an agrarian subsistence environment to a wage-labored urban industrial work force. Issues of masculinity (and femininity) and the built environment might reasonably reflect expressions of moments in that capital transformation. At different historical moments, Kimmel argues, crises in gender relations have spun out from transformations of the economy and the organization of work.[10] A second broad category of explanations have emphasized social or cultural forces—often, in the case of vernacular studies, issues around ethnicity.[11] It is increasingly clear that cultural politics aligned by gender issues is a possible framework for analysis. David Jackson argues there are "invisible, reproductive structures (that) work to secure men's domination over women. They do this through a complex of relationships in which men secure the sexual, child-rearing and labor services of women that benefit men every day of their lives."[12] The backcloth to this paper, accordingly, is framed by queries such as: in what ways does the built environment act to help secure these gender-specified services? And as we examine a range of masculinities—straight or gay, aggressively misogynic or homophobic, sporting or family oriented, for example—can we identify specific built environments that are associated with lifestyle options as well as production systems?

Shelter along Resource Frontiers

There are rich empirical veins, many as yet untapped by scholarship in vernacular architecture studies, that suggest—at first glance—distinctively masculine built environments. It is possible to accumulate evidence of folk and vernacular form for different resource sectors and periods, e.g., cookrooms that housed fifty or so men and boys who worked as seasonal labor in the offshore fisheries in seventeenth-century Newfoundland; the camboose shanties that housed up to eighty men in isolated winter camps for logging from Maine to Minnesota in the nineteenth century; the ephemeral line camps, more substantive drovers cottages, and other end-of-drive railhead hotels for cowboys on the western plains; the lodging shops and barracks of early mining activities in Pennine Britain; the bothies or boarding cars, the YMCA hostels, and dormitories used to house construction gangs, train drivers, firemen, and other railroad workers. This itself is an intriguing project that stretches the definitions of pioneer architecture away from the log-cabin forms that most often are seen as frontier environments for men and women.

Yet even these self-consciously gendered landscapes must be seen in the context of a broader gendered space economy where—for some men—wives, mothers, children, and widows occupied other spaces with invisible yet binding ties to these sites of resource exploitation. At a conceptual level,[13] one might envisage that household labor has gone through a variety of phases: a joint male and female preindustrial struggle for subsistence and surplus; a phase (for some) of an uncoupled household economy with men and boys off in male environments while women maintained the home base; a phase in which there was a conscious reuniting of male and female components of the household economy to maximize production systems, which might be called the domestication of still-male labor pools; and a phase of the explicit feminization of the labor force, a phase that sometimes undermines male labor value.[14]

The historical question here is what were the circumstances by which men and boys were employed and housed in seasonal resource extraction industries—such as fishing, logging, ranching, and mining—and, necessarily, what were the circumstances by which women were excluded from these industries? Moreover, having identified these various 'work' settings, are the changing built environments associated with capital and technological transformations in these industries, or with changing gender relations in society, or with a mixture of both?

Fishing and the Sea

The migratory fisheries from western Europe to the east coast of North America were an explicitly male world. Clark's account of the world of fishermen on the Isle of Shoals off Portsmouth in the 1670s includes a description of a rough fishing headquarters:

> On the island near the harbour, Winter's men, more accustomed to ships than houses, built what must have seemed to them an entirely logical kind of accommodation. Probably using boards they had brought from England, they put up a two-story wooden structure forty feet long and eighteen feet wide. The lower level, which contained a storeroom and a large kitchen "for our men to eat and drinke in", may have had walls of stone because it seems to have been partly underground. One can imagine the crew of boisterous bored young seamen spending the long winter evenings here by firelight around long dining tables, gulping down their home-brew beer, repeating endlessly the same repertory of bawdy songs and stories, and intensifying the constant battle of wits until a session of rough raillery ended in a fist-fight. When too sleepy or drunk to continue, they staggered upstairs to the upper level, which the builders probably thought of as the main deck. In one of the two second-story "Chambers", each man had his narrow bunk, boarded in to make a private sleeping compartment. The bunks, which Winter called "Close borded Cabbins" were ranged along one side of the sleeping room, one above the other.[15]

Similarly, the pioneer phase of Newfoundland settlement by masters and servants was explicitly dominated by *man*power. In 1684, a captain of the British Royal Navy, while discussing the large number of planters overwintering in what was supposed to be just a ship-based migratory fishery, commented, "Soe longe as there comes no women they are not fixed."[16] Handcock notes that there were some women working in Newfoundland in this period—they were hired as servants for the masters—but it was clear that a work force of seasonal male labor was seen as most efficient for both exploiting a resource in very hard physical conditions and in a volatile strategic environment constantly needing naval presence. One or more "cookrooms," where "the men slept in bunks, arranged around the cookroom like berths in a ship,"[17] were sufficient for shelter.

We know little of the everyday lives of wives, mothers, and widows in the West Country English or southwestern Irish farms and villages from whence these men and boys were drawn. Handcock describes a world where pauper boys were sent to the Newfoundland fishery by the overseers of the poor in each parish. A distinct element of the "Wessex region" of southwest England were "groups of individuals who used the fishery as their main means of livelihood, but who maintained their domiciles and families outside Poole."[18] Many mariners brought their wives and families to the port and rented rooms; the men on monthly wages made arrangements with merchants to pay their families, but death, desertion, or hard times often led to Poor Law removal orders for those women, and they were sent back to where they came from.[19] The lure of the sea for men and boys was economic necessity, an alternate to life as farm laborers in a world where neither farm tenancy nor ownership was a possibility.[20]

For sailors, the most noticeable land-based built environments associated with the "severe shipboard regimen of despotic authority, discipline and control" were the pubs, gin houses and taverns, brothels, crimping houses (where crews were gathered), and prisons in port neighborhoods on both sides of the Atlantic.[21] Hugill has assembled a composite picture of *sailortown:* "a Fiddler's Green of pubs, dance-halls, groggeries and brothels . . . its main thoroughfare was usually some Shit Street, an effluent maze of alleys."[22] Although the facades and interiors of sailortown would differ between London, Liverpool, Boston, Natchez-under-the-Hill, Havana, or Montevideo in reflecting local materials, climate or design, it is their commonality as masculine space that characterized this locale around the world. Changes came slowly in the nineteenth century as shifting morality, the temperance movement, and attempts to provide a more efficient labor force brought sailors' homes and Salvation army refuges into the landscape of port cities, such as Canadian examples in Halifax and Saint John.[23]

If the industrial era tried to reform sailors' land life—and this change was reflected in new designs for boardinghouses for marine wage-earners—then so too did the economic reorganizations of the fishery find reflection in the built environment. As the struggles between English, French, and Portuguese were settled and the English hegemony over the fishing banks were established, the fishery changed. By the early nineteenth century, economic sense dictated that people live in Newfoundland to better manage the fishery by having an overwintering population that could tend and mend the fisheries' infrastructure. English and Irish merchants established "outport" settlements, peopled with women as well as men. Nuclear families developed. Thus, the "united domestication" of the labor force began, instigated by mercantile capital interests that sought to more efficiently reproduce labor locally and minimize costs of provisioning, while maximizing the returns on their monopoly position in a trading system. Although it was entirely men and boys who were involved in the actual fishing, women participated in salting and drying, in the agricultural sector, as well as in the domestic sector.

Manifestations in the residential built environment thus are the transition from a cookroom (bunkhouse) complex to a wide array of shelters that included the master's house, rows of cottages, detached cottages, and the like, such as those in Ferryland, Newfoundland, by 1825.[24] Over the nineteenth century, house forms evolved in ways that kept many of the Old-World preferences for room arrangement.[25] In the late twentieth century, the fishing industry has become far more mechanized in the catching end of things (factory ships, etc.), and there has been a conscious feminization of the paid labor force—hundreds of women are involved in freezer, processing, and packing plants along the Atlantic shores.

Logging

A similar disconnected family environment was evident in the case of historical phases of the North American lumber economy. Shelter in remote logging camps was also male and minimal. The cookroom of the fishery—*kabenhuis* in Dutch—became the "camboose" of the forest. Camboose shanties housed up to eighty men around a central fire used for cooking, and men slept two to a bunk on two tiers. Accounts of the cramped quarters describe the collision and fusion of different cultures and temperaments; the expression "he's got a chip on his shoulder" dates back to when a man who was itching for a fight in the cabin-fever confines would put a wood chip on his shoulder and dare anyone to knock it off. These brutally strenuous winter logging camps stayed male throughout the nineteenth century, but they too were linked—for some married men—as a seasonal wage environment to pioneer farms: the husband left the wife to run the farm in winter while he gained money for seeds, implements, and building material for the expansion of the farm.[26]

Transitions of the shanty form through the nineteenth century, especially to the dingle shanty format with additional buildings for filers, foremen, and teamsters,[27] were a result of both technological developments (stoves instead of open fires) and a new division of labor in pulp camps that brought a more hierarchical and spatially distinct set of cabins for a differentiated labor force. When logging became year-round on the West Coast, loggers became more of an industrial proletariat, i.e., permanent labor rather than traversing seasonally between camp and farm; camps, now prefabricated bunkhouses, were still all male for many more decades. Only since the 1920s, when trucks and better roads improved accessibility to logging camps, did women become a presence, and then only as cooks (even though considerable mechanization of cutting and hauling might have made logging jobs accessible to women). At the same time, the logging frontier began to take on more of a suburban quality when company towns for processing logs into pulp and paper were established in these still-remote cutting areas. In such settings, Marchak observes that "women do the maintenance tasks in the homes and the service tasks in the offices, stores, shops, schools, and hospitals. In their absence, the forest company employers could not maintain company towns, and the overall cost of obtaining a male labor force would increase sharply."[28] Her research shows that "young married men with families" were the preferred labor force in instant towns.[29]

Mining

In other resource sectors, too, the domestication of labor involved the development of family environments to enhance the still-male labor tasks. The *lodging shops* that grimly housed male miners at the openings to lead mines in the English Pennines were only functional in relation to the presence, up to six miles away, of farms run by women. The men walked home, tired on a Saturday night, before heading back to the bunkhouse environments for Monday morning.[30]

Studies of early coal-mining environments are especially intriguing for students of vernacular architecture, since there is a slow folding in of folk-ways and agricultural social practices toward a more industrialized production environment. Often the same landlord provided row houses for agricultural estate workers and coal miners. Building practices from rural tradition were incorporated into materials and layouts for mining enterprises.[31] Although form and materials varied regionally, miners' housing soon became one of the most standardized types of shelter prior to the onset of suburbia. While some seams were opened by male gangs in barracks, the shift to "family" housing came fast. As Bill Williamson has observed: "Without women, mining communities would not exist: they would be labor camps."[32] Yet, as D. H. Lawrence has so vividly portrayed for us, that life for women was tough: "There was a big discrepancy, when I was a boy, between the collier who saw, at the best, only a few hours of daylight—often no daylight at all during the winter weeks—and the collier's wife, who had all day to herself when the man was down the pit. The great fallacy is, to pity the man."[33] Williamson concludes: "Women were left to bear the psychological risks of the pit and the precariousness of their own and their children's security."[34] The involvement of women as unpaid household labor was a conscious decision by capital to encourage a family environment—"home" would contain the militant, restless worker by instilling a stake in family and community, thus making him less likely to go on strike. At times, of course, this led to a further militancy, as the notion of a decent wage and minimal living conditions set demands that were supported by wives.

Migrancy

A final example of a predominantly male world is found in the circumstances of migrant workers. One distinctive group of such workers was the more than four hundred thousand Chinese men attracted or recruited to North American mining or cannery camps, railroad construction sites, and urban laundries between the 1850s and 1920s. They,

like the North Atlantic fishermen, had a spatial "distant intimacy" with their wives and families in south China.[35] Their "bachelor" existence at the ghettoized margins of the North American world stood in stark contrast to their periodic visits back home to father and occasionally see their children.[36] Whether these too are examples of patriarchal securing of women's services or heart-rending adjustments to economic survival in periods of turmoil is perhaps an ideological issue.[37] For all the intentions of short-term sojourning, racism and poverty prevented family unification in North America, and the consequent artificial world of tenements, tenderloins, opium dens, and gambling houses steepened racial stereotypes. This enforced bachelor world found concrete expression in several forms. Laundrymen often slept in the isolated suburban or small-town laundry setting and visited Chinatown on occasional weekends. For those who worked in the service sector of Chinatown itself, crowded rooming houses and tenements included the *gong si fang,* or "public room," where eight or ten men occupied cubicles and shared a kitchen and toilet.[38]

Cowboys and drovers were the emblematic Western male. They lived in bunkhouses at the home ranch, in line camps or under the stars during drives, and frequented saloons and drovers' cottages at the end of the trail in Kansas during the 1870s. As the railhead moved west, drovers' cottages, and even bagnios, were moved west on rail flatcars to the next place where dance houses and rooming houses were needed.[39]

Migrant agricultural workers, such as those hired by fruit and vegetable farmers in California's Central Valley, lived in labor camps that were provided with minimal facilities.[40] The seasonality of the migrant ranch/oil/lumber settlements, wherever they were built, meant that they had an urban counterpart, such as the *barrel-houses, flop-houses.* Later there were reformist lodging-house hotels (e.g., the Harvey-McGuire system) for itinerant unskilled labor that Andersen researched for Chicago.[41]

In all these resource-related built environments reviewed above, the morphology of dwellings varied by time period, economy, and social relations. In seeking a gendered perspective on such structures, my commentary assumed the norm as heterosexual, and gender relationships consequently linked males to wife and family or to dance-hall girls and prostitutes. Yet this was a world of gay as well as heterosexual maleness. The world of the migrant and the rooming house had its vocabulary for gay partners;[42] the land-side meeting places of sailors included gay centers, including the army and navy YMCAs—"one of the central institutions of gay male life" in Providence, Rhode Island, for example;[43] and the hotels around New York's Times Square were similarly settings for wartime soldiers and sailors seeking gay relationships.[44]

The current debate concerning gays in the military is often represented homophobically in the media, which uses images of men living in close quarters in ships and submarines or sharing communal showers. Yet, historically, "rugged" lumberjacks slept spoonlike two to a bed in the camboose shanties, but we have few references to homosexuality in accounts of early lumbering or the fur trade. Whether such accounts were censored or whether diaries just do not survive is an important point. Certainly, the human sex drive is strong, and in isolated environments, be they prisons, barracks, ships or on the road, opportunities for sexual outlet were constrained. Is it hegemony by a dominant masculinity that represents fighting, drunkenness, and whoring as "natural" lifestyle behaviors associated with these worlds?[45]

A second perspective on the multiplicities of resource-frontier shelter is to see them in the context of their metropolitan sites of management and control. Agents of this sort of metropolitan control in the frontier include such historically male environments as barracks and forts, both for the military and traders,[46] and, in imperial settings such as Indian structures, the inspection or "dak" bunga-lows that the English used to tour plantation districts.[47] Explicit urban settings for management include the merchant exchanges and coffeehouses of the eighteenth century and, since the late nineteenth century, the skyscrapers that housed head office and supporting corporate functions.[48] What associations between masculinities and built environments can be extracted from a review of urban case studies?

Some Male Sites
in Urban Space

In the transformation from the mercantile to the industrial city, downtown shifted from being a multifaceted place for residence, manufacture, office, retail, and public activities to more spatially distinct office environments, around which were separate industrial areas and suburban residences. Industrial zones became distinctly gendered spaces, especially in factories, where distinct skill tasks were assigned to men and women. Suburbia is perhaps the clearest focus for urban work on the patriarchal imposition of subordinate and powerless positions on women.[49] It is here, undoubtedly, that the richest writing in social geography on gender has occurred, mostly on experiences of women in recent decades and examining the everyday struggles to work and parent. Historical phases of the construction of "home" as a category have also been analyzed.[50] How might we view the worlds of men from a gendered perspective?

Office Buildings
Accompanying the structural and spatial transformation to the industrial city was the shift from a horizontal to vertical urban silhouette—with all its attendant masculinities. The most clichéd example is to see the skyscraper as a phallocratic landscape element—"my tower is bigger than yours"—whereby corporations, and especially centrally masculine CEO egos, sought to memorialize

their power and importance not just in relation to the city as a whole but also directly to their male competitors. There is also debate about the masculinity and femininity of buildings in the urban development of the turn of the century.

In one of the most famous parts of Louis Sullivan's *Kindergarten Chats* (1901–02), the Marshall Field Wholesale Store (1895–97) in Chicago is praised for its manliness: "Here is a man for you to look at . . . a real man, a manly man; a virile force—broad, vigorous and with a whelm of energy—an entire male."[51] The defining attributes of such maleness were its solid, block-like form, its rough surfaces, and its minimal ornamentation. O'Gorman's reading of the Field buildings sees gendered spaces: the retail store (on the other side of the Loop) "with a decidedly local and female appeal" and the wholesale store "as clearly territorial and masculine."[52] The elegant retail store catered to the fashionable ladies where "woman was queen"; the wholesale store "served the needs of the travelling man from the outlying towns . . . it was a matter-of-fact space."

The multiple readings of Richardson's design for Field is centrally connected to Sullivan's enthusiasm for the store, compounded by various interpretations of Sullivan's suppressed homosexuality. David Andrew writes about Sullivan's "deflected or sublimated autoeroticism,"[53] and Brendan Gill builds on this view in speculating about the ithyphallic nature of his designs and his poetry on ornament.[54] Narciso Menocal has also written about the sexual signification of the coloring of Sullivan's banks: greenish-gray for Newark, Ohio, and brown for Owatonna, Minnesota, were masculine, whereas creamy-white was gynecomorphic.[55] (This reader is left confused by creamy-white feminine skyscrapers on the one hand, yet skyscrapers as proud, soaring male things on the other.) Menocal sees the masculine and feminine mixed in Sullivan's prairie banks: "The large areas of mosaic, of terra-cotta ornamentation, and of artglass windows often gynecomorphize the brown,

masculine boxiness of the buildings."[56] This fascinating literature stretches, perhaps, the limits of a psychoanalytical approach to the analysis of buildings.

However, if one does go inside those prairie banks, they do record a shift in gendered space. The banks were constructed in an era of transition from a nineteenth-century view of finance as a male preserve (and so why would women want to enter a bank) to a period when women did work and have their own money that they wanted to deposit. Even so, in what was still regarded as a male building, whether brown or cream, banks often had a separate women's waiting room with its own teller's wicket to the savings department.[57] Craig Zabel argues that the transition from prairie bank as a Richardsonian male "strong box" to Sullivan's more feminine "jewel box" continued with Elmslie's "bank home," perhaps showing the further domestication of a previously male environment.[58]

The skyscraper, if seen as a cluster of office spaces rather than as a (gendered) facade, also reflects changing gender relations in the workplace. Secretarial work used to be male work, and indeed the title secretary-treasurer in many organizations continues to be a male power position. For Braverman, the deskilling of clerical work is associated with the femininization of the work force, and the remuneration and status afforded clerical work declined accordingly.[59] For the social historian Olivier Zunz, however, female participation in office work was also a transitional, part-time, waged convenience between girlhood and adult, married, nonwork status, and the class assumptions of respectable middle-class identity worked to transform and subtract from the female working class by the process of marriage.[60] Issues of gender and class are clearly intertwined. Zunz also provides examples of specifically gendered architectural features, such as separate elevators, women's as well as men's dining rooms, balconies on setbacks to provide respectable female fresh-air spaces away from the perceived (male, working class) raunchiness of the urban street below.

As noted earlier in the paper, it is in moments of economic transformation that some of these gender issues emerge most clearly. At the very end of the nineteenth century, Mr. Spencer, a real-estate leasing agent in New York, worked with designers in Cass Gilbert's office to suggest second, eighth, and fourteenth floor toilet rooms in the new Broadway Chambers be revised by taking out urinals and putting in water closets in their place. As the labor force began to include more women, agents were sensitive to the gendered implications of design: "Experience has taught them that where women's toilet rooms are placed in a building, the women should be furnished, each and every one, with a key and the toilet rooms not left open to the public. This is necessary to avoid certain indiscretions and annoyances by office boys and others. It is also noted that women do not like to have their toilet rooms all on one floor as is the case in this building, for the reason that every person doing business in the building knows the location of the toilet room, and when the women are using the elevators to this special floor they may be subjected to certain annoyances which are not desirable."[61]

Even if these new white-collar settings perpetuated the patriarchal power of men over women, office work presented a crisis in masculinity that found solutions in other settings. The social historian David Stearn has traced the emergence of a middle-class male identity during the period of industrialization. Before then, male identity was tied closely to manual labor, and pride came from strength and skill; a crisis of middle-class masculinity emerged for those whose work was not manual but deliberately set apart in an office.[62] For this new generation distanced from manual work, new constructions of manliness evolved around athletic and sporting activities. Prowess came in different forms, and these "new" male skills were marked, for the elite, in trophy rooms in big houses.

Here, then, is a focus for research on male "domestic" space. We can think of the pre-industrial "lord of the manor" mansions as explicit statements of status, with their distinct male quarters, such as the library, billiard room, smoking room, gun room.[63] Perhaps we can also think of the array of male fraternity houses near American campuses as "training sites" for that particularly dominant form of masculinity and for the later white-collar business world.[64] Spaces given over to the sale of and repairs of cars and guns have also been fused traditionally as male environments. Many readers might be familiar with the presence of pin-up images of women in such settings and the aggressively misogynist language addressed to parts of cars needing attention.

Leisure and Entertainment Spaces

To date, the most studied venues for the sexual/power desires of men undoubtedly are brothels.[65] A recent collection of essays on New York's Times Square point the way to possibilities for other places.[66] At the turn the century, lobster palaces developed where wealthy sports or playboys took playgirls for suppers.[67] Later, in the 1920s and 1930s, according to Tim Gilfoyle, heterosexual sporting males were attracted to the "rough masculinity" of the areas as settings for prize fighting, pugilism, and heavy drinking. Merchants and business clerks, bookkeepers, bank tellers, and insurance employees sought out sites for sporting male culture as an antidote to their more controlled business world.[68] As Forty-second Street in New York transformed from theaters to burlesque houses, the masculinization of the street was underlined by "strippers inside and semi-pornographic billboards and barkers announcing the show outside (that) contributed to the image of the street as a male domain, threatening to women."[69]

Yet, for all the dominant masculinity associated with downtown men's clubs, locker rooms,[70] and suburban golf and country clubs,[71] such clubs have historically also played a role as venues for other forms of masculinity. Accounts of molly houses in the eighteenth century,[72] the YMCA cited above for Providence (see note 43), London's Corinthian Club in Hollinghurst's fiction,[73] or gay sports clubs[74] present a more varied view of urban space. George Chauncey Jr. has shown that Times Square was "the site of multiple sexual systems, and each with its own cultural dynamics, semiotic codes, and territories."[75] For example, one side of the oval bar in the Hotel Astor at Seventh Avenue and Forty-fifth Street was a condoned gathering place for gay men,[76] and the Metropolitan Opera on Broadway at Fortieth was a standard meeting place.[77] Wayne Koestenbaum comments, "Two quintessentially queer sites at the opera are the line, and standing room: spaces of mobility, cruising, maximum attentiveness; spaces where one broadcasts commitment, desperation, patience, spaces where one meets other fanatics; spaces of rumor, dish, cabal."[78] The special attractiveness of opera divas to gay men extended to singers such as Judy Garland, and the memory of her continues in vernacular names for parks (such as the gay part of Philadelphia's Fairmount Park) and for gay bowling leagues. Research on gay cruising settings in different historical eras would also enrich our knowledge of male space. Park venues have been long established and well known, but they are also contested settings, as the numerous incidents of gay bashing and sometimes murder attest. More private settings, including steam baths and after-hours clubs, have also been the targets of raids. Ethical considerations in all likelihood mean that it is the historical rather than contemporary contours of gay urban space that will reach academic attention.

More recently, as a more open and confident gay community has become a force in urban politics and real estate, research into the gentrification process needs to pay far more attention to the role of gay males in the construction of revitalized urban environments. Whether there are different rehabilitation architectures or aesthetics between heterosexual or gay couples, as opposed to different rehabilitation structures between couples with families and childless couples, offers another research focus.[79]

Finally, the question of whether there are gendered layers in paternalistic environments needs to be raised. Attempts by industrialists to develop shelter for their workers and to contribute to places for social intercourse were often part and parcel of the notion that a happy work force is a productive work force. For example, the Pennsylvania Railroad provided YMCA dormitories—complete with reading rooms, gymnasiums, and the like—for its running-trades workers who had to be away from home for extended periods. Further, the railroad sponsored delegates to attend YMCA conferences on industrial health. The company also built bunkhouses for single men when needed and occasionally erected prefabricated industrial housing in an attempt to retain family (what they regarded as "good") labor.[80] A parallel example can be seen in the British tailoring chain Montague Burton, which provided Temperance Billiard Saloons above their High Street custom tailor shops (landmarks in interwar townscapes), as a respectable place for young men to spend their evenings off the street and out of pubs.[81]

Conclusion

The reviews of research on resource environments and urban spaces have underlined how issues of gender, particularly masculinity, might frame research on the built environment. In many cases, economic forces still provide persuasive conceptual frameworks. If so, debates still tug as to whether environments were structurally produced as the consequence of management decisions in mercantile and industrial enterprise or, alternatively, environments were produced by people coming to terms with their immediate circumstances in ways that demonstrate the agency of individuals and groups. As Peter Jackson has shown, images of racialized and gendered labor are not fixed. Criteria can be conveniently reconstructed; for example, a labor force of "female nimble fingers" in Bradford woolen mills gave way to "nimble male Asian fingers" once Pakistani men could be hired and paid less than local women.[82]

The environments that have been explored here suggest the duality of a gendered set of spaces, rarely monolithically masculine or feminine, and rarely just the dominant form at that. By making gender a more explicit focus, a richer array of settings, and multiple uses of settings once fused in imagination with single land uses, will broaden our understanding of the multiple meanings of environments—and provide an even richer research agenda for work on structures and spaces.

Being open to the possibilities of multiple interpretations of historical contexts often involves being able to reflect on one's own existential circumstances in everyday life. For me, it has been the struggle to co-parent in an economic and social order that still emphasizes resolute maleness at work; paternity leave takes on a dramatic meaning in its absence. Moreover, in the urgency of children's toilet needs, the gendered assumptions of parenting are irritatingly concretized in old-fashioned bathroom layouts. On a positive note, the increasing presence of diaper-changing stations in men's washrooms, both in restaurants and in interstate rest stops, are a sign of optimism.

Notes

I would like to thank Bob Clark, Gale Fenske, Sue Friedman, Tina Jacquette, Glenda Laws, Peter Jackson, Philip Jenkins, Larry McGlinn, Aiden McQuillan, Don Mitchell, and Craig Zabel for useful comments on earlier drafts of this paper.

1. The first line of the chorus is used as the title of my paper. For a discussion of the frontier image for British Victorian urbanites, see John A. Mackenzie, "The Imperial Pioneer and Hunter and the British Masculine Stereotype in Late Victorian and Edwardian Times," in *Manliness and Morality: Middle-Class Masculinity in Britain and America 1800–1940,* ed. J. A. Mangan and James Walvin (Manchester: Manchester University Press, 1987), 176–98.

2. bell hooks, *Talking Back. Thinking Feminist, Thinking Black* (Boston: South End Press, 1989), 128.

3. Ibid., 130.

4. David Jackson, *Unmasking Masculinity: A Critical Autobiography* (London: Unwin Hyman, 1990), 27–28.

5. Peter Jackson, "The Cultural Politics of Masculinity: Towards a Social Geography," *Transactions, Institute of British Geographers* N.S. 16 (1991): 199–213. See also Peter Jackson, *Maps of Meaning* (London: Unwin Hyman, 1989).

6. See, for example, Peter N. Stearns, *Be a Man! The Male in Modern Society* (New York: Holmes & Meier, 1979); Harry Brod, ed., *The Making of Masculinities* (Boston: Allen & Unwin, 1987); Michael S. Kimmel and Michael A. Messner, eds., *Men's Lives* (New York: Macmillan, 1989).

7. Dolores Hayden, *The Grand Domestic Revolution: A History of Feminist Designs for American Homes, Neighborhoods, and Cities* (Cambridge, Mass: MIT Press, 1981).

8. Daphne Spain, *Gendered Spaces* (Chapel Hill: University of North Carolina Press, 1992). The quote is from Michael Kimmel on the dust cover.

9. Anthony D. King, ed., *Buildings and Society: Essays on the Social Development of the Built Environment* (London: Routledge & Kegan Paul, 1980); *The Bungalow: The Production of a Global Culture* (London: Routledge & Kegan Paul, 1984).

10. Michael S. Kimmel, "The Contemporary 'Crisis' of Masculinity in Historical Perspective," in *The Making of Masculinities,* ed. H. Brod, (Boston: Allen & Unwin, 1987), 121–53.

11. Dell Upton, ed., *America's Architectural Roots: Ethnic Groups That Built America* (Washington, D.C.: National Trust For Historic Preservation, 1986).

12. David Jackson, *Unmasking Masculinity,* 12.

13. Note that the conceptual schema do not easily work if one moves away from initial assumptions about "ideal" heterosexual nuclear family relations.

14. One example is the development of clerical back–office functions in places such as Scranton, Pennsylvania, drawing on large pools of female labor in a region where historically male industries such as coal mining and iron making predominated.

15. Charles E. Clark, *The Eastern Frontier: The Settlement of Northern New England, 1610–1763* (Hanover, N.H.: University Press of New England, 1983), 22–23.

16. W. Gordon Handcock, *Soe longe as there comes noe women; Origins of English Settlement in Newfoundland* (St. Johns: Breakwater Books, 1989), 21.

17. D. W. Prowse, *A History of Newfoundland from the English, Colonial, and Foreign Records* (London: MacMillan, 1895), 450.

18. Handcock, *Soe longe as . . . ,* 186.

19. Ibid., 199.

20. In the 1740s, English merchant seamen were usually in their early twenties. "Some were the younger sons of yeomen and poor farmers, men who had migrated to the cities in search of work and finally found it in the docks. Some, perhaps, had been dispossessed of land by enclosure. . . . Economic necessity pushed many to the water's edge." Marcus Rediker, *Between the Devil and the Deep Blue Sea: Merchant Seamen, Pirates, and the Anglo–American Maritime World, 1700–1750* (New York: Cambridge University Press, 1987), 13.

21. Ibid., 159. For an account of the port neighborhoods of the Atlantic trade, see chap. 1, 10–76.

22. Stan Hugill, *Sailortown* (London: Routledge & Kegan Paul, 1967), 72.

23. Judith Fingard, *Jack in Port; Sailortowns in Eastern Canada* (Toronto: University of Toronto Press, 1982), 234–39.

24. G. Pocious, "Architecture on Newfoundland's Southern Shore: Diversity and the Emergence of New World Forms," in *Perspectives in Vernacular Architecture,* ed. C. Wells (Annapolis: Vernacular Architecture Forum, 1982), 217–32.

25. David S. Mills, "The Development of Folk Architecture in Trinity Bay," in *The Peopling of Newfoundland,* ed. J. J. Mannion (St. John's: Memorial University of Newfoundland, 1977), 77–101.

26. Carville Earle and R. Hoffman, "The Formation of the Modern Economy: Agriculture and the Costs of Labor in the United States and England, 1800–1860," *American Historical Review* 85 (5) (1980): 1055–94.

27. G. S. Kephart, "The Pulpwood Camps," *Forest History* 14 (2) (1970): 27–34.

28. Patricia Marchak, *Green Gold: The Forest Industry of British Columbia* (Vancouver: University of British Columbia Press, 1983), 213.

29. Ibid., 217.

30. Thomas Sopwith, *An Account of the Mining District of Alston Moor, Weardale and Teesdale* (Alnwick: Davison, 1833), 133; Barrie Trinder, *The Making of the Industrial Landscape* (London: Dent, 1982), 189–90.

31. Jeremy Lowe, *Welsh Industrial Workers Housing 1775–1875* (Cardiff: National Museum of Wales, 1977).

32. Bill Williamson, *Class, Culture and Community: A Biographical Study of Social Change in Mining* (London: Routledge & Kegan Paul, 1982), 118.

33. D. H. Lawrence, *Nottingham and the Mining Country,* quoted in Williamson, *Class, Culture and Community,* 118.

34. Williamson, *Class, Culture, and Community,* 118.

35. P. C. P. Siu, *The Chinese Laundryman: A Study of Social Isolation* (New York: New York University Press, 1987). I am grateful to Larry McGlinn for pointing out this reference, which discusses "money or men" letters sent by wives to Chinese laundrymen—"I need more money, or come on back home yourself."

36. Larry A. McGlinn, "Institutions and Individuals: Space and Power among Chinese in the Northeastern United States, 1870–1920," (Ph.D. diss., Pennsylvania State University, 1992).

37. A good place to start might be Marlon K. Hom, *Songs of Gold Mountain: Cantonese Rhymes from San Francisco Chinatown* (Berkeley: University of California Press, 1987), especially the sections "Lamentations of Stranded Sojourners," "Lamentations of Estranged Wives," and "Songs of the Hundred Men's Wife." Equally powerful is Maxine Hong Kingston, *China Men* (New York: Knopf, 1980).

38. Gwen Kinkead, *Chinatown: Portrait of a Closed Society* (New York: HarperCollins, 1991), 14–18, described visiting one such *gong si fang* in New York in the 1980s. Her descriptions are little different from those presented about housing circumstances in the Victoria and Vancouver, Canada Chinatowns to a Royal Commission on Chinese and Japanese Immigration in 1902, quoted in C. H. Young and H. R. Y. Reid, *The Japanese Canadians* (Toronto: University of Toronto Press, 1938), 222. A detailed analysis of the distinctive buildings and alleys of Canada's earliest Chinatown can be found in David Chuenyan Lai, *The Forbidden City within Victoria* (Victoria: Orca, 1991).

39. Robert R. Dykstra, *The Cattle Towns* (New York: Athenaeum, 1974), 96–107.

40. Carleton H. Parker, *The Casual Laborer and Other Essays* (New York: Harcourt, Brace and Howe, 1920).

41. Nels Andersen, *The Hobo: The Sociology of the Homeless Man* (Chicago: University of Chicago Press, 1923), 27–33.

42. Andersen's lexicon of tramps included a "jocker," who taught minors to beg and crook; "road kid or preshun," a boy held in bondage by a jocker; "punk," a boy discarded by a jocker; and "gonsil," a youth not yet adopted by a jocker. Ibid., 101.

43. George Chauncey Jr., "Christian Brotherhood or Sexual Perversion? Homosexual Identities and the Construction of Sexual Boundaries in the World War 1 Era," *Journal of Social History* 19 (Winter 1985):189–211. See also Jodi Vanderberg–Davies, "The Manly Pursuit of a Partnership Between the Sexes: The Debate Over YMCA Programs for Women and Girls, 1914–1933," *The Journal of American History* (Mar. 1992):1324–46.

44. George Chauncey Jr., "The Policed: Gay Men's Strategies of Everyday Resistance," in *Inventing Times Square: Commerce and Culture at the Crossroads of the World,* ed. W. R. Bender (New York: Russell Sage, 1991), 315–28.

45. A similar skewed representation is the way that Abraham Lincoln is always represented in movies and in Disneyland with a "manly" baritone, whereas in real life his voice was a high, shrill tenor. See Gary Wills, "The Words That Remade America: Lincoln at Gettysburg," *The Atlantic Monthly* 296 (6) (June 1992): 65.

46. See, for example, C. M. Whitfield, "Tommy Atkins: The British Soldier in Canada, 1759–1870," Ottawa: National Historic Sites, *History and Archeology* 56 (1981); D. Wayne Moodie and Victor P. Lytwyn, "Fur–Trade Settlements," Plate 64 in *Historical Atlas of Canada, Volume I,* ed. R. Cole Harris (Toronto: University of Toronto Press, 1987). The events of the Tailhook convention in Las Vegas underline the persistence of such dominant male worlds in the 1990s.

47. On dak and other bungalows, see Anthony D. King, *The Bungalow: The Production of a Global Culture* (London: Routledge & Kegan Paul, 1984), 44–45. The marginal (and often frustrated) position of European women in these male settings is aptly conveyed in the novels of Somerset Maugham.

48. Gunter Gad and Deryck W. Holdsworth, "Corporate Capitalism and the Emergence of the High–Rise Office Building," *Urban Geography* 8 (3) (1987): 212–31; Gail Fenske and Deryck W. Holdsworth, "Corporate Identity and the New York Office Building," in *The Landscape of Modernity: Essays on New York City, 1900–1940,* ed. D. Ward and O. Zunz (New York: Russell Sage, 1992), 129–59.

49. For a good overview, see Daphne Spain's essay "Space and Status," *Gendered Spaces,* 3–29.

50. Richard Sennett, "Middle–Class Families and Urban Violence: The Experience of a Chicago Community in the Nineteenth Century," in *Nineteenth–Century Cities: Essays in the New Urban History,* ed. S. Thernstrom and R. Sennett (New Haven: Yale University Press, 1969), 386–420; Gwendolyn Wright, *Building the Dream: A Social History of Housing in America* (New York: Pantheon, 1981), 240–61; W. Rybczynski, *Home: A Short History of an Idea* (New York: Viking, 1986).

51. Louis H. Sullivan, *Kindergarten Chats and Other Writings* (1901, 1917; reprint, New York: Dover Publications, 1979), 29.

52. James F. O'Gorman, "The Marshall Field Wholesale Store: Materials Towards a Monograph," *Journal of the Society of Architectural Historians* 37 (3) (Oct. 1978): 177.

53. David S. Andrew, *Louis Sullivan and the Polemics of Modern Architecture: The Present Against the Past* (Urbana: University of Illinois Press, 1985), 13.

54. Brendan Gill, *Many Masks: A Life of Frank Lloyd Wright* (New York: Putnam, 1987), 78–80.

55. Narciso G. Menocal, "Sullivan's Banks: A Reappraisal," in *The Midwest in American Architecture,* ed. John S. Garner (Urbana: University of Illinois Press, 1991), 120.

56. Ibid., 122.

57. Wim de Wit, "The Banks and the Image of Progressive Banking," in *Louis Sullivan, The Function of Ornament* (New York: W. W. Norton, 1986), 164–65.

58. Craig Zabel, "George Grant Elmslie: Turning the Jewel Box into a Bank Home," in *American Public Architecture: European Roots and Native Expression,* Papers in Art History from The Pennsylvania State University, Vol. V, ed. C. Zabel and S. S. Munshower (University Park, Pa.: 1989), 228–72.

59. Harry Braverman, *Labor and Monopoly Capital: The Degradation of Work in the Twentieth Century* (New York: Monthly Review Press, 1974).

60. Olivier Zunz, *Making America Corporate 1870–1920* (Chicago: University of Chicago Press, 1990), 116–24.

61. Samuel Stevens Haskell to Cass Gilbert, Dec. 18, 1899, Minnesota Historical Society, Cass Gilbert Papers, box 3. I am grateful to Gail Fenske for sharing this information with me.

62. Stearns, *Be a Man,* 79–112. Joy Parr has traced the way that this worked out for two generations of management in a Hanover, Ontario, furniture firm, where Daniel Knechtel had worked alongside the men, but his son J. S., a product of the age of Taylorism scientific efficiency, was separated from the men by layers of managers; Joy Parr, *The Gender of Breadwinners: Women, Men and Change in Two Industrial Towns, 1880–1950* (Toronto: University of Toronto Press, 1990), see especially chapter 7, "Manliness, Craftsmanship and Scientific Management," 140–64.

63. Mark Girouard, *The Victorian Country House* (New Haven: Yale University Press, 1979); Spain, *Gendered Spaces,* 112–15.

64. Evidence from campus rape crisis centers and the constant litany of complaints about boisterous noise, excess drinking, and predatory male behavior certainly make for a different reading of the revivalist architecture of fraternities. See Peter Lyman, "The Fraternal Bond as a Joking Relationship: A Case Study," in *Men's Lives,* 166–71.

65. See, for example, R. Symanski, *The Immoral Landscape: Female Prostitution in Western Society* (Toronto: Butterworths, 1981).

66. William R. Taylor, ed., *Inventing Times Square: Commerce and Culture at the Crossroads of the World* (New York: Russell Sage, 1991).

67. Lewis Erenburg, "Impressarios of Broadway Nightlife," in *Inventing Times Square,* 161–62.

68. Timothy J. Gilfoyle, "Policing of Sexuality," in *Inventing Times Square,* 301–3.

69. Chauncey, "The Policed," in *Inventing Time Square,* 322.

70. But reflect a moment on the orgasmic champagne shaken and spilled by and on men during championship celebrations in baseball, football, or basketball.

71. Golf and country clubs are not all–male spaces of course; rather, they are male dominated, with women part of that landscape, as service workers and secondary social members (sometimes labeled in society–page photographs with the "possessed" title, e.g.,. Mrs. John Smith).

72. Randolph Trumbach, "London's Sodomites: Homosexual Behavior and Western Culture in the Eighteenth Century," *Journal of Social History* 11 (1977): 1–33.

73. Alan Hollinghurst, *The Swimming–Pool Library* (New York: Vintage International, 1988).

74. Brian Pronger, *The Arena of Masculinity: Sports, Homosexuality, and the Meaning of Sex* (New York: St. Martin's Press, 1990).

75. Chauncey, "The Policed," 322.

76. Ibid., 326.

77. Ibid., 327.

78. Wayne Koestenbaum, *The Queen's Throat: Opera, Homosexuality and the Mystery of Desire* (New York: Poseidon, 1993), 46.

79. Manuel Castells, "Cultural Identity, Sexual Liberation and Urban Structure: The Gay Community in San Francisco," in *The City and the Grassroots* (Berkeley: University of California Press, 1983), 138–69; also Mickey Lauria and Lawrence Knopp, "Towards an Analysis of the Role of Gay Communities in the Urban Renaissance," *Urban Geography* 6 (2) (1985): 152–69.

80. Historical Collections and Labor Archives, Penn State University, Pennsylvania Railroad & New York Central Railroad Collection, box 78, file 98; box 89, file 160; box 95, file 160A.

81. Kenneth Hudson, *Food, Clothes and Shelter* (London: Baker, 1978), 81.

82. Peter Jackson, "The Racialization of Labour in Post–war Bradford," *Journal of Historical Geography* 18 (2) (1992): 190–209.

Chapter 3

The Masonic Lodge Room, 1870–1930:
A Sacred Space of Masculine Spiritual Hierarchy

William D. Moore

We have a holy house to build,
A temple splendid and divine,
To be with glorious memories filled,
Of right and truth, to be the shrine.
How shall we build it, strong and fair,
This holy house of praise and prayer . . .
This house, this place, this God's home,
This temple with a holy dome
Must be in all proportions fit,
That heavenly messengers may come
To dwell with those who meet in it . . .

Albert Pike, "The Mason's Holy House"

Freemasonry, a ritual-based fraternal brotherhood with roots stretching back to sixteenth-century Britain, reached its greatest strength in the United States, in both popularity and influence, in the last third of the nineteenth and first third of the twentieth centuries.[1] This period was contemporaneously called the "Golden Age of Fraternity."[2] Freemasonry was at the core of this golden age, as it was both the archetypical fraternal organization and the most successful one. In 1879 there were an estimated five hundred and fifty thousand Freemasons in the United States.[3] In 1896, membership was claimed to be seven hundred and fifty thousand, and by 1925 the number was reported at over three million.[4] By the 1920s most towns in the United States boasted a lodge of Freemasons, and every lodge had a room, a "Mason's Holy House,"[5] dedicated and set aside for the performance of the Masonic rituals.

The 1930s witnessed the collapse of this blossoming of interest in Freemasonry and, more generally, in fraternal societies. The movement suffered from what one commentator at the time called "The Tuberculosis of Fraternalism."[6] Masonic membership declined. Lodges went bankrupt. Freemasonry never regained the status it had attained in this golden sixty-year era.

By drawing upon architectural, diagrammatic, artifactual, and documentary evidence, this essay analyzes the spaces in which American Freemasons of this era practiced their rites. It will argue that these rooms served as both theaters and sites of worship, and that the concepts of hierarchy and incorporation were central to their function and design. Finally, the Masonic lodge room will be related to transformations occurring in American society at the time, with emphasis placed upon changes in American religion, economic structures, and conceptions of gender.[7]

Any building that held a Masonic meeting room became known as either a Masonic hall or a Masonic temple.[8] At the beginning of the time period under discussion, these structures were usually multiple-use buildings, like the Charlestown, Massachusetts, Masonic Hall, dedicated in 1876 (fig. 3.1). This hall was built by the Charlestown Savings Bank, which occupied the first two levels, while the Masons occupied the top floors.[9] By the 1910s and 1920s, Masonic temples were often devoted entirely to Masonic purposes. For example, the temple designed by J. William Beal, Sons, and built in Quincy, Massachusetts, in 1926 contained only spaces for the use of the fraternity (fig. 3.2).[10]

Fig. 3.1. Charlestown, Massachusetts, Masonic Hall, 1876. (Photograph by William D. Moore.)

While much could be written about the way in which Masonry was expressed on the exterior of these structures, this essay will concentrate on the lodge rooms within the buildings, for these spaces were of central importance to the Masonic character of the buildings.[11] In 1886, at the dedication of the Masonic temple in Waterbury, Connecticut, J. W. Richards called the lodge room "a soul within a tabernacle of clay." He said that it was here that "Masonic thought and activity are born; here that life courses which gives meaning to all the externals."[12] The lodge room was where Masonic rituals were enacted. It was where the abstract idea of a fraternity of men took concrete form, and where a lodge defined itself.

For these reasons, when Masons had institutional portraits made the photographs were often taken within the lodge room. In posing for their 1898 portrait, the identities of the officers of Mount Carmel Lodge of Lynn, Massachusetts, were en-

hanced by their presence within their institutional space (fig. 3.3). The lodge room and the members of the organization functioned within a dialectical relationship. The room had only the significance assigned to it by the Masonic membership; yet, by being present within this space, which they had set aside as different, the individual members' personal worth was elevated.[13] The room was shaped and decorated by the members of the lodge, but it simultaneously transformed the men that inhabited it. The grandeur of these men's surroundings transported them from their own particular locations in time and space and allowed them to occupy a grander, timeless role. Within this space, they were no longer merely nineteenth-century residents of Massachusetts, but had become part of the chain of Masonic officers, a chain which both their literature and ritual portrayed as being eternal.

Certain characteristics of the Masonic lodge room rarely varied. As a rule, the room was above street level, was longer than it was wide, had a high ceiling, symmetrically placed doors on one end, and an altar in its center.[14] These features are evident in the interior of the lodge room of Montgomery Lodge in Milford, Massachusetts, photographed in 1897, in a floor plan of the second floor of the Worcester, Massachusetts, Masonic

Fig. 3.2. Quincy, Massachusetts Masonic Temple, 1926, J. William Beal, Sons, Architects. (Photograph by William D. Moore.)

Fig. 3.3. Officers of Mount Carmel
Lodge, Lynn, Massachusetts, 1898.
(From *One Hundred Years, Mount
Carmel Lodge of Lynn, Massachusetts*
[Lynn, Mass.: Historical Committee
of the Lodge, 1905], opp. 14.
Courtesy of the Library of the
Grand Lodge, A.F.&A.M., of
Massachusetts, Boston.)

Fig. 3.4. Montgomery Lodge Room,
Milford, Massachusetts, 1897.
(From Clarence A. Sumner,
*Centennial History of Montgomery
Lodge, A.F.&A.M., Milford,
Massachusetts, U.S.A.*
[Boston: The Lodge, 1899], n.p.
Courtesy of the Library of the
Grand Lodge, A.F.&A.M., of
Massachusetts, Boston.)

Temple, designed by George C. Halcott and built
in 1914, and in a diagram from *Duncan's Masonic
Ritual and Monitor,* a guide to the Masonic ritual
from the second half of the nineteenth century.
From the latter diagram, space within the lodge
room can be understood as being ordered around
a pair of axes. The primary axis runs down the
center of the length of the room. Starting at the
letter G on the wall—a symbol denoting both God
and geometry—the axis runs through the master,

who wears a top hat, through the altar, and ends
with the senior warden, sitting with his back to
the viewer. The secondary axis is perpendicular
to the primary one, and runs from the junior warden on the right through the altar to the far wall
splitting the room in the other direction. In the
Milford lodge room, this axis terminates with a
large emblematic painting on the far wall (fig. 3.4).
In Halcott's floor plan, the presence of the axes is
indicated by the elevated platforms meant for the

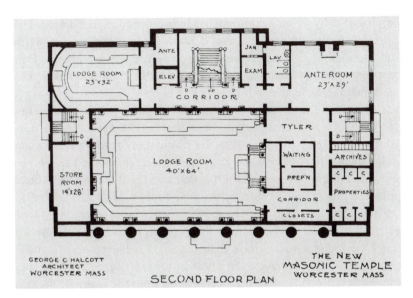

Fig. 3.5. Second Floor Plan, Masonic Temple, Worcester, Massachusetts, 1914, George C. Halcott, Architect. (From *Masonic Temple Worcester Massachusetts* [Worcester, Mass.: Worcester Masonic Charity and Educational Association, n.d.], n.p. Courtesy of the Library of the Grand Lodge, A.F.&A.M., of Massachusetts, Boston.)

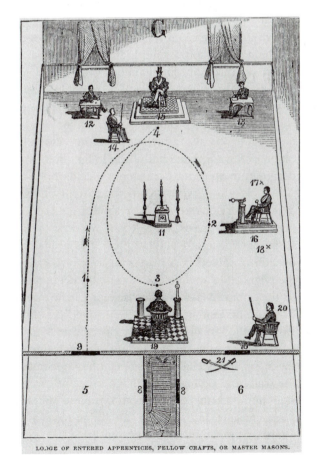

LODGE OF ENTERED APPRENTICES, FELLOW CRAFTS, OR MASTER MASONS.

Fig. 3.6. "Lodge of Entered Apprentices, Fellow Crafts, or Master Masons." (From Malcolm C. Duncan, *Duncan's Masonic Ritual and Monitor* [New York: Dick & Fitzgerald, 1866], 8.)

officers' chairs on three sides of the lodge rooms (fig. 3.5). Everything in the lodge room is organized around these two axes. A person's or an object's relative proximity to the axes was directly related to their ritual significance.

The axes terminate in the chairs of the officers, of the worshipful master, the senior warden, and the junior warden (fig. 3.6). These chairs both define the ends of the axes and ennoble the men who occupy them. This double function of the officers' chairs resulted in their assuming exaggerated proportions. The backs of these chairs, like the master's chair in the lodge room in Lynn, Massachusetts, often stretched to more than six feet in height. They took on monumental scale in order to attract attention, since their positioning identified the ends of the axes and defined the space within the room.[15] The importance of these seats and their occupants was further emphasized by their traditionally dictated location upon platforms that were raised a ritually significant number of steps above the main floor.[16] These exaggerated, elevated ornamental seats served as benchmarks by which members understood their positioning within the ritual space.

Just as the officers' chairs marked them as significant, the greater portion of the lodge members occupied seating furniture that indicated their identical organizational status. Members' settees, like those visible along the walls of the Milford lodge room, also would be located on the platforms located around the perimeters of the lodge rooms in Halcott's floor plan. These seats were the institutional equalizers, the material manifestations of the Masons' ideology of equality. Whether a brother was a bank president or a ditch digger, if he was not a lodge officer, he sat with the rest of his brethren on these settees.

Significantly, the members' seats faced the center of the room. This arrangement allowed the members of a lodge to see one another, to know who their brothers were, and to be witnesses of one another's presence. This seating formation is in direct contrast with that of the pews in a traditional Protestant church, where the pews were aligned in rows facing toward the altar and pulpit at the front of the sanctuary. Thus, the minister was the only person with whom a member of the congregation maintained eye contact during the service. A member of the congregation saw only the backs of the heads of their fellow parishioners. This type of seating promoted a one-on-one relationship with God and with His ministers. In Protestant churches, interpersonal interaction was stymied within the sanctuary by the individually isolated attitude dictated by the positioning of the pews.

The Masonic floor plan, in contrast to the Protestant one, assured the brethren that they were part of a group. It encouraged them to witness one another's presence and to conceive of the lodge

as a corporate body composed of individuals. Further, it arrayed them around the edges of the room, where they were roughly equidistant from the altar in the center of the floor where the axes crossed.

As ritual hierarchy of space was determined by proximity to the central axes of the room, the most ritually significant position in the room was located where the axes intersected. This sacred space was reserved for the altar and the Bible. All seats faced this spot, which was further differentiated by being ceremonially lit, either by candles or by spotlights. This is the position in the room where initiates took their oaths, as is illustrated in another image from *Duncan's Ritual* (fig. 3.7). At the altar individuals were raised from the realm of the profane, status was conferred, liminality was resolved, and incorporation was enacted.[17] This was the location and these were the activities that the architecture of the lodge room was designed to privilege.

The act of incorporating individuals into a fraternal organization simultaneously excluded all others. Inclusion and exclusion were complementary effects of the same action. The lodge room was organized to promote the act of incorporation, but it was also arrayed to reinforce the definition of the corporate body. The lodge room was designed to shut out the exterior world and outsiders. Windows were either nonexistent or rendered impervious to vision by shutters or stained glass. In most cases, lodge-room windows were so far above street level that there was no risk of outside observers.[18] A man with a sword, called the tyler, sat in an anteroom to guard the entrance to the room. A set of stairs separated the room from the pedestrian realm. Often, sound proofing was installed in the walls of lodge rooms.[19] Esoteric symbols, the understanding of which united members and excluded outsiders, often decorated the walls and ceiling of the lodge room, as can be seen in the examples from both Lynn and Milford, Massachusetts. In its totality, the lodge room was a fantastic realm in which the power of the orga-

Fig. 3.7. "Candidate Taking the Oath of a Master Mason." (From Malcolm C. Duncan, *Duncan's Masonic Ritual and Monitor* [New York: Dick and Fitzgerald], 1866, 94.)

nization was emphasized and outside reality was consciously abrogated.

As fantastic realms, lodge rooms were often decorated in historical motifs so that the Masons could separate themselves temporally, as well as spatially, from the ordinary world. Revivalist styles presented on furniture and wall decorations allowed the Masons to leave the present and lose themselves in a romanticized past. Some of the most outstanding uses of revivalist decoration are found in the temple of the Grand Lodge of Pennsylvania in Philadelphia. The Egyptian room of this temple was decorated in 1889 (fig. 3.8). The design of the lavishly decorated interior of this hall was the work of George Herzog, one of Philadelphia's most prominent interior designers of the time.[20] While Herzog was responsible for the design of the temple's rooms, he was supported by the Masonic Temple Art Association, which included among its membership the important American engraver John Sartain, who was a thirty-third degree Mason.[21]

The lodge room, then, was a space designed to fulfill specific functions. First, by placing certain important people in ritually and physically elevated positions in furniture that attracted attention, it emphasized hierarchy. Second, it privileged incorporation by centrally locating the site where vows of membership were taken. Finally, it reinforced corporate definition by placing the membership in positions where they could witness the presence of their brothers and by distancing the exterior spatial and temporal world.[22]

How did these fantastic spaces function culturally? Why was such a large portion of the American male population drawn to use these elaborate rooms? One key to this puzzle lies in perceiving the floor of the lodge room as a stage and understanding the rituals enacted there as popular participatory theater.[23] The evenings of ritual in the lodge room were community dramatics with which Masons entertained themselves in an America without movies, radio, television, or any of the other forms of today's modern entertainment. Masonic literature of the period supports such an understanding of Masonic ritual as theater. H. R. Evans, a thirty-third degree Mason in the Scottish Rite, writing in 1916, stated this reading succinctly. "The Masonic degrees," he wrote, "from Entered Apprentice to Sublime Prince of the Royal Secret [the thirty-second degree], are dramas, and should be so regarded by Masons."[24] Similarly, the nineteenth-century actor Edwin Booth, also a member of the fraternity, while referring to the central legend of the Masonic ritual, wrote, "In all my research and study, in all my close study of the masterpieces of Shakespeare . . . I have never, and nowhere, met tragedy so real, so sublime, so magnificent as the legend of Hiram. . . . To be a Worshipful Master, and to throw my whole soul into that work, with the candidate for my audience and the Lodge for my stage, would be a greater personal distinction than to receive the plaudits of people in the theaters of the world."[25]

Many of the Masonic rituals were participatory enactments structured around memorized dialogue and standardized floor movements. Initiates, who

Fig. 3.8. Egyptian Hall, Philadelphia Masonic Temple, Philadelphia, Pennsylvania. Interior design by George Herzog, 1889. (Courtesy of the Masonic Library & Museum of Pennsylvania, Philadelphia.)

could not be expected to know the plot or dialogue of a drama they had never witnessed, were assigned a guide and spokesman who responded for them when they were ritually challenged.

Other Masonic rituals, like those of the Scottish Rite of Freemasonry, were not participated in by the initiates, but were performed by members of the organization for their edification. In these instances, just as the characteristics of theatrical production and ritual enactment were merged in the actions of the participants, the formal qualities of the lodge room and the theater were synthesized. In the 1910s, Kenwood Lodge No. 303 of Milwaukee, Wisconsin, built a new temple, designed by the architects Leenhouts and Guthrie, that emphasized the connection between lodge room and theater.[26] The floor plan of the lodge room met all the requirements of the Masonic ritual (fig. 3.9). There is an altar at the center of the room. Members' seating is located around the perimeter of the room, the doors are symmetrically arranged at one end, and the officers' chairs are in their ritually prescribed positions. This particular room, though, is worth noting because the space behind the

master's chair is separated from the main area of the lodge room by a line representing a curtain and is clearly labeled "Stage."

An understanding of the lodge room as theater is further advanced when it is realized that the rituals often were performed by members in elaborate costumes and makeup. In performing the fellowcraft ritual of the second degree in 1928, for example, Pacific Lodge No. 233 of New York City utilized a team of thirty-one members in full costume, representing a wide range of characters.[27] At the height of the blossoming of the golden age of fraternalism between 1870 and 1930, scores of companies provided costumes and props for these productions. Among the largest of these firms were the Pettibone Brothers Manufacturing Company of Cincinnati, Ohio, the Ward-Stilson Company of Anderson, Indiana, the Henderson-Ames Company of Kalamazoo, Michigan, and M. C. Lilley & Company of Columbus, Ohio.[28]

The first three degrees of Masonry in this period, called the Blue Lodge degrees, culminated with raising an initiate to the status of Master Mason, and comprised the most commonly performed

Masonic rituals. In these degrees, the master of the lodge played the role of King Solomon. More accurately, the master of the lodge did not play King Solomon; he metaphorically became King Solomon, and the lodge room became Solomon's temple. In many cases, the master would don an elaborate robe and crown to signal this transformation.

Writing in 1886, Arthur W. Clark of Michigan, discussed the rationale for using costumes. He wrote:

> The Worshipful Master is no longer simply the Master of a Lodge. The lofty teachings of the Order lift him to the awful seat of Solomon, King of Israel. The Senior Warden is no longer there; it is Hiram, King of Tyre, the friend and bosom companion of King Solomon, the mighty builder.
>
> What should be their dress and insignia? Imagine the heaven-chosen King hearing the confessions of the blackest criminals in his kingdom while seated upon the stool of a camel driver without his kingly robes, sceptre or his attendants!!
>
> The very thought provokes ridicule. . . . The representation should be, as nearly as practicable, a true imitation of the original event, and a faithful reproduction of the costumes and insignia, as well as of the language and demeanor of the original characters. . . . A want of proper care and conformity in regard to clothing and ceremony detracts incalculably from the solemnity and impressiveness of the work in every degree, in every place, and at every time, and no eloquence of the ritualist can supply the lack or entirely atone for the incongruity.[29]

Clark's rhetorical style and word choice indicate that he perceived more to the Masonic ritual than theatricals. He refers to "lofty teachings" and the "solemnity and impressiveness of the work." Clark was not alone in seeing beyond the play acting. Writing in 1916, the internationally acclaimed Universalist preacher and Masonic philosopher Joseph

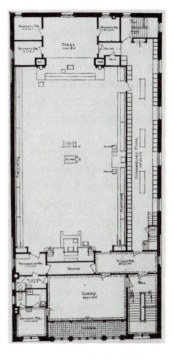

Fig. 3.9. Floor Plan of Kenwood Lodge, Milwaukee, Wisconsin, Leenhouts & Guthrie, ca. 1915. (From G.L.S., "Freemasons as Builders: II The Temple of Kenwood Lodge, Milwaukee, Wis.," *The Builder* 1 [10] [Oct. 1915]: 238. Courtesy of the Chancellor Robert R. Livingston Masonic Library & Museum, New York.)

Fort Newton also recognized the theatrical qualities of Masonry but refused to admit that theater was all that there was.[30] He wrote, "If Masonry is only a dramatic club, whose performances prelude a banquet and a smoker, let us admit it, and not keep up the hoax of having a noble history, a profound philosophy, and a beautiful symbolism."[31] Newton made this suggestion in an article entitled "Taking Masonry Seriously," and he certainly meant it to convey irony. This noted mystic did not believe that Masonry's philosophy and symbolism were a sham. Instead, he believed that there was something beyond the theatrical aspects of the institution. Newton and Clark were not alone in this belief. The material evidence surviving from Freemasonry's heyday makes it clear that enormous amounts of time, effort, and financial resources were expended in outfitting these rooms.

Although recognizing the lodge room as a theater sheds some light on its use, it does not adequately explain the importance of hierarchy and incorporation as manifested in the room's spatial configuration. To further understand the room's formal qualities, we must shift metaphors and view the room not as a theater, but rather as a spiritual space, as a domain that men inhabited in an attempt to deal with forces larger than themselves.

Just as Masonic written records justify the understanding of ritual as theater, Masonic writers also support an interpretation of the lodge room as a religious realm. Although Freemasonry's status as a religious organization was hotly debated during the period under examination, the lodge room was repeatedly identified and treated as a sacred space by the order's members.[32] A Mason from Kansas wrote in 1890, "Freemasonry is not only a brotherhood but a church. . . . It is an essential part of our ceremonial to joyfully recognize our relationship to God, our dependence upon Him, and to express our sense of need. A Masonic temple is a religious temple. The very word 'temple' implies worship."[33]

Similarly, whenever discussion of behavior within the lodge room occurred, the first point of reference was church etiquette. For example, the editor of *The Masonic Chronicle* stated in 1887, "We never could see the propriety of smoking in Lodge Rooms any more than in a church,"[34] and again in 1894 commented, "To pursue the habit [of chewing tobacco] in a lodge-room is scarcely less reprehensible than in a lady's parlor or in a cushioned and carpeted church."[35] *The New England Craftsman* in 1907 noted, "Lodge meetings should be conducted with as much dignity as a church service."[36]

This link between lodge rooms and churches is further substantiated by the fact that at the end of the nineteenth century both forms of ritual space were furnished with the same furniture. The functional tie between the chair of the Masonic worshipful master and the chair of the Christian minister was so close that they assumed the same forms. One manufacturer, in fact, issued two lines of catalog offering the same merchandise. S. C. Small & Company, a furniture firm based in Boston, Massachusetts, which specialized in fraternal furniture, issued two catalogs in the 1880s, one labeled *Church Furniture* and the other labeled *Lodge Furniture*. Both catalogs included a number of identical engravings with identical prices. The only deviation between these images is that in the ecclesiastical catalog the chairs were labeled pulpit chairs, while in the fraternal catalog they were called lodge chairs (fig. 3.10).[37]

In identifying the lodge room as a place of worship, as a sacred space, we come one step closer to fully understanding its significance as a cultural form. Anthropologists, like Clifford Geertz, and sociologists, such as Émile Durkheim and Peter Berger, have shown that religion is a cultural construction, that it is a product of social forces.[38] A fuller comprehension of the forces determining the lodge room's form and directing the design of its furnishings may be reached by comparing the values expressed by these sanctuaries to the religious and social changes taking place in American society at the time.

Fig. 3.10. "No. 4 Lodge Chairs." (From S. C. Small & Co., *Illustrated Catalogue . . . of Lodge Furniture* [Boston: The firm, 1886], 5. Courtesy, The Winterthur Library: Printed Book and Periodical Collection).

The lodge room emphasized hierarchy and corporate identity. These emphases were manifestations of the concerns of the men that designed and created these spaces. American male interest in these two concepts can be explained by examining changes taking place in the workplace and in religion.

During the first half of the nineteenth century, the traditional structure of the workplace had broken down.[39] Artisans found themselves devalued as capitalism redefined them as sources of labor power.[40] Hard work in the complex economies of the late nineteenth and early twentieth centuries was not a guarantee of success. Upward mobility was no longer a matter of time and the development of skills; it had become a matter of chance and social connections.[41] In contrast, the fraternal hierarchy was comprehensible, ascendable, and visible within the lodge room.[42]

At the same time that the American workplace was undergoing change, American religion was also being transformed. In the mid-nineteenth century, American religion underwent what has been termed, by a number of scholars, a process of "feminization."[43] The hallmarks of this transformation have been identified as shifts from the corporate to the individual, from doctrine to faith, from reason to emotion, from ritual to communication, from male authority to female authority, from activity to passivity, and from an emphasis on a stern God to a loving and forgiving Christ.

The spiritualist movement has been identified as the radical edge of this larger religious transformation.[44] It is significant that the spiritualist movement and Masonry are photographic negatives of each other. Spiritualists purposefully avoided dogma or orthodoxy, while the Masons reveled in their mysteries and celebrated their shared knowledge. Spiritualists found that wisdom could be gained when a powerful spirit inhabited the body of a submissive medium. Masons believed that enlightenment was gained through an individual's continued study and personal effort. Spiritualists sought insight through unpredictable revelation. Masons searched for it in the perfect reproduction of a supposedly ancient ritual. While the spiritualists fled the church because it was not transforming quickly enough and instead held their religious events in parlors, within the woman's sphere, men found themselves unhappy in a feminized church and found a place to worship within the masculine realm, in a space shaped and inhabited by men.[45] While the spiritualists sought salvation in the home, the Masons built temples in business districts and found nothing sacrilegious about worshiping at an altar under the same roof as a bank or store.

Understanding the Masonic lodge room as a religious space reveals an explanation for the revivalist decorative schemes used in their elaborate interiors. If this masculine spiritual system was to offer a solution to the Masons' religious yearnings, it could not be just a solace for the present; it must also provide satisfactory explanations for the present, the future, and the past. The universality that adherents claimed for Freemasonry thus had to be temporal as well as spatial. W. C. Atwood, the grand orator of Missouri, expressed this idea in 1908, when he stated, "The principles of Freemasonry are as unchangeable and eternal as God Himself. They are hoary with age; they have endured the crucial tests of generation succeeding generation."[46]

The legends and belief tales of Masonry traced the organization throughout history, stretching back at least to the building of King Solomon's Temple, but in some cases back to Adam himself.[47] Different episodes of the organizational history claimed as ancestors the Egyptians, the ancient Jews, Islamic Arabs, the knights of the crusades, the builders of the medieval cathedrals, the architects of England's architectural renaissance, and America's founding fathers. By citing a particular aspect of this genealogy, the Masons could appropriately decorate their temples in the Egyptian, Gothic, Persian, Norman, Georgian, or American Colonial styles.

In the largest temples, such as those built in New York, Chicago, Philadelphia, and Brooklyn, multiple lodge rooms were located in the same structure and each room was decorated in a different historical style. These buildings—with medieval Europe just down the hall from colonial Virginia and both one flight up from ancient Egypt—materially expressed the organization's ideology of universality and literally surrounded the membership with the message. Masons who may not have been interested in learning about the organization from the printed page could not help but pick up this facet of the ideology from the walls around them.

Further, with the transformations taking place in religion and industry in late-nineteenth-century America, existing conceptions of masculinity had come into question. No longer was the man the spiritual foundation of his family. No longer could the clerk, factory worker, or industrialist carry himself with the traditional pride that came from being a craftsman.[48] The men of this period needed criteria by which they could reassure themselves of their own masculinity.[49] Freemasonry, also known as the "Ancient and Honorable Craft," provided guidelines that had supposedly come down unchanged through eternity. By claiming allegedly ancient Masonic definitions of masculinity as their own, men of this period of flux could pretend that their social frame of reference was not shifting. By ensconcing themselves in rooms that referred to older design traditions, the Masons buttressed their systems of belief.

This Masonic telescoping of history led to curious layerings of patriarchy. For example, in 1898 the lodge in Belmont, Massachusetts, was presented with a chair that had a provenance that supposedly linked it to Henry Price, the first grand master of Masons in Massachusetts in the 1730s and an associate of Joseph Warren and the other revolutionary forefathers. This revolutionary Masonic relic was placed in the lodge room where it served as the master's chair.[50] Thereafter, every time the Belmont lodge of Masons met, the master secured his cultural authority by transforming himself into an ancient religious patriarch while simultaneously occupying the place of one of America's eighteenth-century political forefathers.

In conclusion, while traditional hierarchies were attacked by both liberal theology and the changes wrought by industrial capitalism, the Masonic lodge room, through its use of furnishings and ritual enactment, continued to express order in an understandable manner. As corporate identity fell to the ideologies of free labor and evangelicalism, the furnishing plan of the lodge room continued to emphasize the site where vows of membership were undertaken. The lodge room, then, can be understood as a place in which masculine values that were disappearing in the outside world were preserved. It was a theater in which millions of American men entertained one another by acting out morality plays and a spiritual space where the same men found religious meaning and worshiped what they unconsciously recognized as a disappearing social order.

Notes

I would like to extend my thanks to the Luce Foundation, whose financial assistance, in part, made this essay possible. I would also like to thank Richard Candee, Mark C. Carnes, Edward S. Cooke, Jr., Keith Morgan, and Robert Blair St. George for their comments on earlier drafts of this essay.

1. The best current work on the early roots of Freemasonry is David Stevenson, *The Origins of Freemasonry: Scotland's Century, 1590–1710* (Cambridge: Cambridge University Press, 1988). For the importance of Freemasonry in the United States in the period under discussion, see Lynn Dumenil, *Freemasonry and American Culture, 1880–1930* (Princeton, N.J.: Princeton University Press, 1984). My thoughts throughout this essay have

been informed by Mark C. Carnes, *Secret Ritual and Manhood in Victorian America* (New Haven: Yale University Press, 1989). Although women have been initiated into Masonic lodges in Europe (Margaret C. Jacob, *Living the Enlightenment: Freemasonry and Politics in Eighteenth Century Europe* [New York: Oxford University Press], 1991), Freemasonry in the United States has consistently accepted only men. For a discussion of the relationship of fraternal organizations, and thus of Freemasonry, to women in the period under discussion, see Mary Ann Clawson, *Constructing Brotherhood: Class, Gender and Fraternalism* (Princeton, N.J.: Princeton University Press, 1989), 178–210.

2. W. S. Harwood, "Secret Societies in America," *North American Review* 164 (May 1897): 620–23.

3. Dumenil, *Freemasonry and American Culture*, xi.

4. Harwood, "Secret Societies"; Dumenil, *Freemasonry and American Culture*, xi.

5. Albert Pike, the author of the epigraph above, was the greatest Masonic ritualist of the nineteenth century. Although he spent time as both poet and newspaper editor, his greatest accomplishment was redrafting and expanding the rituals of the Scottish Rite of Freemasonry. The most complete biography of Pike is Walter Brown, "Albert Pike," (Ph.D. diss., University of Texas, 1955).

6. See Carnes, *Secret Ritual and Manhood*, 215n. 3.

7. Although most of the examples in this essay are drawn from the Northeast, the conclusions are more widely applicable, as Masonic culture and architecture varied only slightly throughout the United States in this period.

8. Although not a hard-and-fast distinction, Masonic halls tend to be multiple-use buildings while Masonic temples usually hold only spaces used solely by members of the fraternity.

9. *Henry Price Lodge, A.F.&A.M., Charlestown, Mass. 75th Anniversary* (Charlestown, Mass.: The Lodge, 1933).

10. Quincy Masonic Association, *Quincy Masonic Temple, 1170 Hancock Street* (Quincy, Mass.: The Association, 1927), n.p. The firm of J. Williams Beal, Sons, which was formed following Beal's death in 1919, also designed Masonic temples for Hyannis and Greenfield, Massachusetts. See "Architect Beal Dies in Hanover," *The Boston Herald* (July 8, 1919); "Laying of Cornerstone," *Cape Cod Magazine* 8 (6) (Nov. 1924): 19; and "Greenfield, Mass., to Have New Temple," *New England Craftsman* 18 (10) (July 1923): 295–96.

11. For a discussion of the symbolic significance of the architecture of a Masonic temple, see William D. Moore, "A Gothic House of the Temple," *The Scottish Rite Journal* 100 (10) (Oct. 1992): 42–50.

12. J. W. Richards, "Oration Delivered at the Dedication of the Masonic Temple, at Waterbury, Connecticut," *The Masonic Chronicle* 7 (5) (Feb. 1889): 49.

13. For a sociological discussion of the dialectical relationship between humans and objects, see Peter L. Berger, *The Sacred Canopy: Elements of a Sociological Theory of Religion* (Garden City, N.Y.: Doubleday, 1967), 6–10.

14. The rectangular shape of the lodge room was related to the secondary Masonic symbol of the Oblong Square, which in turn was supposedly derived from any number of Biblical architectural precedents. See the entry for "Oblong" in George Oliver, "A Dictionary of Symbolical Masonry," in Robert Macoy, ed., *General History, Cyclopedia and Dictionary of Freemasonry* (New York: Masonic Publishing Company, 1873), 602–3, and the entry for "Oblong Square" in Kenneth R. H. Mackenzie, *The Royal Masonic Cyclopedia* (New York: J. W. Bouton, 1877), 522–23.

15. William D. Moore, "M. C. Lilley & Company: Manufacturers of Masonic Furniture," *The Scottish Rite Journal* 100 (9) (Sept. 1992): 59–64.

16. "A Model Lodge," *The Masonic Chronicle* 3 (5) (Feb. 1884): 54.

17. My understanding of Masonic ritual is informed by the works of anthropologists Arnold van Gennep and Victor Turner. See especially Arnold van Gennep, *The Rites of Passage*, trans. Monika B. Vizedom and Gabrielle L. Caffee (Chicago: University of Chicago Press, 1960), and Victor Turner, *The Ritual Process: Structure and Anti-*

Structure (Chicago: Aldine Publishing Co., 1969). The Masonic Ritual, which has a tripartite structure on many levels, is a textbook example of the ritual importance of separation, liminality, and incorporation.

18. For a discussion of the importance of high windows in lodge halls, see Dennis R. Brownridge, "Secret Societies and Their Impact on the Architectural Landscape of the West," (Ph.D. diss., University of Oregon, 1976), 43.

19. For example, the lodge rooms of the temple of the Grand Lodge of Massachusetts, built in 1899, are sound proofed with "seaweed quilting in asbestos, in double thickness, and wired to the framing." J. Waldo Denny, *History of Joseph Webb Lodge,* 2d ed. (Boston: L. H. Lane, 1901), 225. This sound proofing may also have been utilized to accentuate sounds, knocks or gavel taps, for example, that were important features of the ritual.

20. "Masonic Temple Marks Centennial of Norman Hall Decoration 1891–1991," *The Pennsylvania Freemason* 38 (2) (May 1991): 3. See also Mark C. Luellen, "The Decorative Designs of George Herzog (1851–1920)," *Nineteenth Century* 12 (3 and 4) (1993): 19–26.

21. James Isaac Buchanan, "Report to Sovereign Grand Commander Henry L. Palmer, August 14, 1898," *Proceedings of the Supreme Council of the Ancient Accepted Scottish Rite for the Northern Masonic Jurisdiction* (1898): 134–40. The fact that John Sartain was a thirty-third degree Mason indicates that he had reached the highest level of the Scottish Rite of Freemasonry. There are three primary divisions of American Freemasonry. "Symbolic," or "Blue Lodge," Freemasonry is composed of the first three degrees and is required of all American Masons. After undergoing the first three degrees, a Mason may choose to participate in either or both the Scottish Rite or the York Rite. The latter is also known as the American Rite. Each of these rites has its own set of degrees and rituals that are conferred upon its members. Throughout much of the nineteenth century, there were other rites in which Masons could choose to participate, but the Masonic establishment ruled these "clandestine" and succeeded in driving them out of existence. There are also a number of related organizations that are open only to Masons. The most well known of these are the Ancient Arabic Order Nobles of the Mystic Shrine, otherwise known as the Shriners, and the Mystic Order Veiled Prophets of the Enchanted Realm, which is called the Grotto.

22. For a discussion of the importance of hierarchy and corporate identity to secret societies in general, see Edward A. Tiryakian, "Toward the Sociology of Esoteric Culture," in Edward A. Tiryakian, ed., *On the Margin of the Visible: Sociology, the Esoteric, and the Occult* (New York: John Wiley & Sons, 1974), 266–67.

23. This understanding is supported by Clawson, *Constructing Brotherhood: Class, Gender and Fraternalism,* 228.

24. H. R. Evans, "Lodge Furnishings and Degrees," *The Builder* 2 (7) (July 1916): 207.

25. Edwin Booth as quoted in Joseph Fort Newton, "Edwin Booth as a Mason," *The Builder* 1 (5) (May 1915): 100.

26. G. L. S., "Freemasons as Builders: II The Temple of Kenwood Lodge, Milwaukee, Wis.," *The Builder* 1 (10) (Oct. 1915): 238–40.

27. "An Effective Masonic Degree Team," *Iowa Grand Lodge Bulletin* 29 (10) (Dec. 1928): 762–64.

28. For a history of one of these firms see Moore, "M. C. Lilley & Company."

29. Arthur W. Clark, *The Masonic Chronicle* 5 (8) (May 1886): 91.

30. Newton was one of the most widely published and influential Masonic authors of his generation, but has received little scholarly attention. The most comprehensive work to date on Newton is Billy Jim Leonard, "Joseph Fort Newton: Minister and Mystic," (Ph.D. diss., Boston University, 1975), which focuses on his Christian writings and largely ignores his Masonic works. Similarly, Newton's own autobiography, *River of Years* (New York: J. B. Lippincott, 1946), skims lightly over his Masonic involvements.

31. Joseph Fort Newton, "Taking Masonry Seriously," *The Builder* 2 (3) (Mar. 1916): 90.

32. For a discussion of the debate over Freemasonry's religious quality, see Dumenil, *Freemasonry and American Culture,* 42–71.

33. Ibid., 31.

34. *The Masonic Chronicle* 7 (3) (Dec. 1887): 29.

35. "For Tobacco-Chewers to Read," *The Masonic Chronicle* 13 (10) (July 1894): 153.

36. *The New England Craftsman* 2 (12) (Sept. 1907): 464.

37. S. C. Small & Co., *Illustrated Catalogue . . . of Lodge Furniture* (Boston: The firm, 1886); S. C. Small & Co., *Illustrated Catalogue . . . of Church Furniture* (Boston: The firm, n.d.). By comparing the chairs in the S. C. Small catalogue images with those in the photograph of the officers of Lynn's Mount Carmel Lodge, it would appear that these men are occupying Small's lodge chair no. 4.

38. See Clifford Geertz, "Religion as a Cultural System," *The Interpretation of Cultures* (New York: Basic Books, 1973); Émile Durkheim, *The Elementary Forms of Religious Life, a Study in Religious Sociology,* trans. Joseph Ward Swain (London: G. Allen & Unwin, 1915); and Peter L. Berger, *The Sacred Canopy.*

39. For a case study of how this process occurred in one community, see Paul E. Johnson, *A Shopkeeper's Millennium: Society and Revivals in Rochester, New York, 1815–1837* (New York: Hill and Wang, 1978).

40. For a theoretical explication of the process by which workers become devalued sources of labor power, see Harry Braverman, *Labor and Monopoly Capital* (New York: Monthly Review Press, 1974).

41. Johnson, *A Shopkeeper's Millennium,* 15–36.

42. For a discussion of how the structure of Freemasonry echoed the traditional structure of the artisan workplace, see Clawson, *Constructing Brotherhood: Class, Gender and Fraternalism,* 145–77.

43. See Ann Douglas, *The Feminization of American Culture* (New York: Alfred A. Knopf, 1977); Barbara Welter, "The Feminization of American Religion: 1800–1860," in *Clio's Consciousness Raised: New Perspectives on the History of Women,* ed. Mary S. Hartman and Lois Banner (New York: Octagon Books, 1976).

44. Ann Braude, *Radical Spirits: Spiritualism and Women's Rights in Nineteenth-Century America* (Boston: Beacon Press, 1989).

45. This does not necessarily mean that Masons stopped attending other religious institutions, only that Freemasonry met men's spiritual needs that were not met by the church. There is evidence, though, that Masonry did take the place of other religious structures within men's lives. Tony Fels, in his article "Religious Assimilation in a Fraternal Organization: Jews and Freemasonry in Gilded Age San Francisco," *American Jewish History* 74 (June 1985): 391, indicates that Masonry was the only religious affiliation of 83.5 percent of the Masonic population of San Francisco in 1890.

46. W. C. Atwood, *New England Craftsman* 3 (5) (Feb. 1908): 179.

47. The best explication of Masonic legends and belief tales appears in Anthony D. Fels, "The Square and Compass: San Francisco's Freemasons and American Religion, 1870–1900," (Ph.D. diss., Stanford University, 1987).

48. For examples of workers' pride in their craft, see David Montgomery, *Workers' Control in America: Studies in the History of Work, Technology, and Labor Struggles* (New York: Cambridge University Press, 1979), 9–15.

49. See Carnes, *Secret Ritual and Manhood,* 94–127.

50. Paul C. Whitney, "The Centennial History of Belmont Lodge, A.F.&A.M., Belmont, Massachusetts," in *Belmont Lodge Centennial Anniversary* (Cambridge, Mass.: Powell Printing Company, 1964), 16.

Chapter 4

Grammar, Codes, and Performance: Linguistic and Sociolinguistic Models in the Study of Vernacular Architecture

Michael Ann Williams and M. Jane Young

For approximately the past twenty-five years, scholars of material culture from a variety of disciplines have tended to rely on models derived from linguistics and sociolinguistics in order to analyze and interpret their data. They derive these models from subareas such as structural linguistics, transformational grammar, elaborated and restricted linguistic codes, and performance theory.[1] Although not explicitly "linguistic," other models for the analysis of material culture include Lévi-Straussian binary oppositions and semiotic theory.[2] One reason for the reliance on such models is that they are particularly productive in uncovering unconscious motivations or deep structures. As one scholar has described such reliance, "We incline to view verbal meaning as the window into the human mind."[3] Also, by suggesting that the "code" of the artifact can be cracked, these approaches give primacy to the artifact itself (actually de-emphasizing reliance on linguistic forms of evidence). Linguistic and sociolinguistic models seemingly render the study of material objects more significant and more profound.

Ironically, this same dependence on approaches derived from linguistics and sociolinguistics shows that the study of material culture remains theoretically dependent on the study of verbal art. In disciplines such as anthropology, folklore, and American studies, which include the analysis of both verbal and visual art, the study of verbal art forms retains analytic primacy. So widely adopted are its explanatory methods that the study of material culture has yet to develop theories or methods truly derived from an understanding of artifactual forms of human expression. For example, in the early days of folklore scholarship, folklore as literature received a great deal of attention, while the study of physical objects was seen as a somewhat limited pursuit.[4] A conceptual division developed in these disciplines—a division marked by an emphasis on either intangible or tangible items, as if scholars in these disciplines had tacitly agreed to pursue the study of either physical objects or spoken texts, but not both. Subsequently, during the 1960s and 1970s (times characterized by the "rediscovery of material culture research"), even though folklorists studying material culture described artifacts as constituting lasting, "truthful," and quantifiable messages about sociocultural patterns,[5] they seemed to feel the need to "validate" their research by drawing on analytical models from verbal arts and linguistics. This pattern became prevalent in vernacular architecture studies as well, and has continued to be used into the present.[6]

Certainly, linguistic and sociolinguistic models have done much to redirect and further the study of vernacular architecture. In Lévi-Straussian terms, they have been perhaps "good to think."[7] However, as the study of vernacular architecture matures, it is time to begin to assess critically the impact our models have had on the development of the field. On the most superficial level, as we have already suggested, these models assert the primacy of the artifact, but at the same time reveal our scholarly insecurity. While espousing alternatives to the theories of stylistic "trickle down" (from high style to vernacular styles), contemporary vernacular architecture scholars seem, in fact, to have embodied these very theories in their own research. By borrowing so heavily on linguistic and sociolinguistic models, they have seemingly enacted a trickle down of scholarly approaches from verbal and literary studies to the study of material culture. Is it not time that we truly turn to our own material for theoretical inspiration?

On a deeper level, we wish to suggest that while interdisciplinary approaches to research are invaluable, simply taking a model from another discipline (in this case, linguistics and/or sociolinguistics) and examining data concerning vernacular architecture through such a lens is not always the most appropriate way to analyze such data. In fact, it often happens that the scholar who employs this approach to vernacular architecture is not a linguist and, therefore, sometimes "borrows" a model that linguists themselves have questioned or perhaps discarded. Further, this borrowing of models frequently leads to a parallel borrowing of terms that, at times, can seem poorly suited to their new application. Often, the resulting scholarship is practically obscured by this inclusion of cumbersome jargon from outside the field.

Structural models provided the earliest and perhaps most influential use of the linguistic analogy applied to material culture. In particular, they suggested a valuable means of understanding variation within form. In vernacular architecture scholarship, the use of structural models demonstrated that, within a building tradition, variation of form has its own inherent logic. Vernacular builders did not simply copy one another or misunderstand high style; instead, they worked from a mental "grammar" of form. The application of Chomskian transformational grammar, as demonstrated by Henry Glassie in his classic *Folk Housing in Middle Virginia,* further provided a means to comprehend how new forms could be generated within a tradition. Just as a person can utter a sentence that is

recognized as grammatical even if it has never been spoken before, new structures can be designed that adhere to a tradition's grammar, even while being novel in form. As vital as these insights have been to vernacular architecture scholarship, however, transformational grammar has been limited in its ability to provide cultural or historical analysis. Even Glassie moved away from a strictly linguistic model to the more free-form Lévi-Straussian type of structural analysis, relying on the concept of binary oppositions to reach a broad form of understanding of the cultural production of artifacts.[8]

It is important to note that during the period when vernacular architecture scholars (especially those in folklore) were beginning to embrace linguistic models, many folklorists studying verbal materials—influenced by the "ethnography-of-speaking" approach—were turning away from models based on transformational grammar because of these models' demonstrated inability to account for language as a social or cultural phenomenon. While a predominantly structural focus may reveal information about the formal elements of language or artifacts, it cannot provide data about their social use. As Dell Hymes has written, language is "organized in terms of a plurality of functions, the different functions themselves warranting different perspectives and organizations."[9] In stressing competence over performance, transformational grammar is also limited in its focus on an idealized speaker, rather than focusing on the actual use of language in real social contexts.

The limitations of transformational grammar are compounded when applied to material culture. The emphasis is on an idealized maker or builder, rather than on actual individuals, which reinforces the stereotype of the anonymous folk artist or builder. The primary focus on unconscious pattern gives little attention to the role of deliberate action or conscious motivation in the production and use of artifacts. Furthermore, the emphasis on production rather than use is even more limited in material culture studies because production and use are fundamentally separate in a way that is not the case in spoken language. In speech, we can at least assume that the producer and user of language are usually one and the same person. This is not necessarily the case with buildings. In the application of transformational grammar to the analysis of vernacular architecture, not only is a vital aspect of the cultural phenomenon of architecture neglected (its use), so too are a sizable number of the people who use buildings and invest them with meaning. While vernacular architecture studies have been touted as "democratizing" history, structural models have tended to construe buildings as being artifacts of the builder. But the question arises, in most cultures, who is presumed to be the builder? Because we generally lack studies of women's contribution to the design and physical construction of vernacular structures, builders are usually assumed to be men.

In understanding the limitations of applying linguistic models to material culture, we must first come to terms with the limitations of these models in comprehending language itself. Second, we must consider how the models have been applied. Finally (and most importantly), we must question the fundamental equation of the production of language with the production of artifacts. Even if we accept the basis of structural analysis, why should we assume that the unconscious is structured in a linguistic rather than in a purely mathematical manner? For example, while folk dance, a primarily nonverbal genre, has been analyzed by some on the basis of linguistic paradigms,[10] one scholar of Balkan dance has shown that, because this tradition focuses on footwork, these dances may be analyzed as a sequence of measures consisting of an even or odd number of weight shifts.[11]

While still using linguistic paradigms, analyses of material culture based on sociolinguistic and performance models overcome some of the limitations of previous linguistic models. In his article "Toward a Performance Theory of Vernacular Architecture," Dell Upton uses Basil Bernstein's notion of elaborated and restricted linguistic codes to expand our understanding of variation of form as a grammar and better links it to social context.[12] Bernstein's theory is also useful in considering the relationship of vernacular and elite traditions. However, the ethnography-of-speaking approach has also demonstrated the two-dimensionality of such sociolinguistic models. The production of speech (or artifacts) is far more complex than the poles between elaborated codes (low degree of syntactical and lexical predictability) and restricted codes (high degree of syntactical and lexical predictability).[13] In vernacular architecture scholarship, we have similarly struggled with the limitations of labeling architecture as either vernacular or elite (or as somewhere in between).

Another failing of the application of structural models is their inability to illuminate explicitly shared meanings and values that are dynamically enacted through time, thus requiring diachronic rather than synchronic models. Performance models have been used to explore the temporal aspects of vernacular architecture, but the emphasis by vernacular architecture scholars such as Bernard L. Herman has tended to be on the physical modification of the structure over time (defined by Herman as "subsequent performances"),[14] hence reinforcing the emphasis on the (usually) male builder. Ideally, performance-oriented material culture studies examine "the ways in which people behave in relationship to . . . objects, the ways in which they mediate, arrange, and manipulate forms in a traditional manner."[15] However, too often studies are labeled "performance-oriented" as a fancy substitute for calling them "contextual." We have too few considerations of the ways in which architecture can be said to be "performed," or whether this is indeed a useful concept to apply to architectural studies.

The main thrust of the ethnography-of-speaking approach is (as its label obviously states) the need for an understanding of spoken language in its ethnographic context. Despite the influence of performance and sociolinguistic models in vernacular architecture scholarship, we have not truly moved toward an ethnography of architecture. Instead, these models have tended to be used to reconstruct context, rather than studying architecture in context. For example, we have surprisingly few vernacular architecture studies that deal with the ethnographic present.[16] Within vernacular architecture scholarship, folklorists are perhaps the best trained to pursue this type of study, but, with a few exceptions, folklorists have supported the concept of vernacular architecture scholarship as predominantly a historical pursuit. Recently, two folklorists have defined vernacular architecture scholarship as "a kind of architectural study with a strong orientation toward historical explanation."[17]

Within historical studies of vernacular architecture, oral history provides one of the best means of reconstructing ethnographic context. However, oral history has only found limited use as a method within vernacular architecture scholarship, and performance and sociolinguistic models have not been applied in oral history–based studies. In fact, the few prominent studies of the 1980s that unite vernacular architecture and oral history, such as George McDaniel's *Hearth and Home* and Charles E. Martin's *Hollybush,* while focusing on real individuals in specific cultural settings, have been particularistic rather than theoretical in nature.[18] Ironically, considering the methodological message of sociolinguistic and performance studies, these models have been applied to vernacular architecture studies in cases in which we know the least, rather than the most, about ethnographic context.

Finally, the adherents of performance models have been no more successful than the structuralists in overcoming the inherent limitations of equating the production of language with the production of artifacts. The lack of fit or discomfort that is often apparent when we try to apply performance theory to material culture is indicative of the fact that, theoretically, language is not al-ways the most appropriate metaphor. The simple fact that production and use can be treated as two separate phenomena in artifactual studies in a way that is not possible in studying language is also an indication of this lack of equivalence. While the concept of performance can be used to encompass both the physical construction (or alteration) and use of a structure, it does not adequately distinguish between the two. Buildings are simply not "performed" in the same sense as verbal art is.

Similar problems are inherent in the application of semiotic theory to material culture, an approach that has become particularly popular in the last decade, due, in part, to a growing concern with context and performance. Described as the study of sign systems and the rules underlying such systems, the semiotic approach is closely related to structuralism, and both approaches could be subsumed within a third area of scholarly concern— the study of communication.[19] In this respect, a sign is a communicative expressive form that "has a multiplicity of functions in the society that produces it."[20] Thus, as with performance theory, as well as functional and symbolic studies, semiotics entails a primary focus on social context. Yet, semiotics focuses on form as well as function, and analyzes messages as well as symbolic meanings within an overall sociocultural framework. While symbolics is the study of what an object represents or "stands for" (frequently an arbitrarily assigned meaning), semiotics is the study of the relation between the object and that which it "points to," or toward which it refers (its significance). This relation extends beyond the bounds of a single event because it embeds the object in an entire communicative network.

Applying semiotic analysis to the creation of material objects is particularly useful because it can provide insight into reciprocal relations between cultural forms and the individual and community that possess that culture. Jan Mukarovský suggests that, from the perspective of semiotics, the work of art is viewed as mediating between the creator and the community capable of the meaningful interpretation of the artifact; thus, the material object stands in a dialectical relationship between its creator and the interactive domains of culture.[21] Petr Bogatyrev, whose study of folk costume has served as an important step toward semiotic analyses of folk material culture, found that the domain of folklore was particularly appropriate for illuminating the multifunctional structures and hierarchical transformations induced by contextual changes and, implicitly, by variation through time.[22] Although most of Bogatyrev's writings in semiotics were published in the 1930s, many of them were not translated into English until the early 1970s. Despite this time lag, his research has particular relevance for scholars today who are taking a dynamic approach to the study of artifacts: a focus on process, which, among much else, involves an awareness of temporal change. Thus, the semiotic approach answers the needs of those who are dissatisfied with the static, synchronic approach of structuralism and the narrowing view of functionalism that sometimes overlooks social context, formal qualities, and the possibility of a multitude of functions in particular relationship to one another. According to Bogatyrev, the addition of the values of semiotics to the functional approach opens new vistas for folklore studies in particular—especially since analyses based on purely formal criteria have proved to be unsatisfactory. He argues, for instance, that a folk costume is simultaneously a material object and a sign, or, more exactly, the bearer of a structure of signs.[23]

Although there is much to be gained from applying semiotic theory to the study of material culture, we find the claim that one can read an artifact as if it were a text to be problematic,[24] particularly in regard to the objections we have already raised about the attempt to establish a one-to-one correspondence between elements of language and aspects of material culture. We do suggest that one should use all available texts—whether written documents or in oral tradition—in attempting to illuminate the meaning of an artifact, but we do not mean to imply the simple equation of material objects with texts; nor do we concur that the activity of apprehending the meaning of an artifact is commensurate with the process of interpreting a folk narrative that has been recorded with complete attention to contextual details. For example, Ricardas Vidutis and Virginia A. P. Lowe use a semiotic model to explore the cultural meaning and function of a German-Catholic cemetery in Indiana; they focus in particular on the concept of the cemetery as a cultural text that contains "information about the social, religious, and aesthetic expectations of the community that maintains it."[25] Their "reading" of the cemetery involves the perspective that it consists of "a variety of signals that compose a delimited and autonomous whole and that carry a culturally significant message."[26] What we find puzzling here is the suggestion that the semiotic approach (reading the cemetery as a linguistic message that should be interpreted in terms of syntax, semantics, and pragmatics) yields different (and better) information than would the attempt to provide as much information as possible about the total ethnographic context of the cemetery.

Although his focus is not on vernacular or folk architecture, Donald Preziosi's *The Semiotics of the Built Environment* is one of the most comprehensive studies of interpreting architecture semiotically to date.[27] According to Preziosi, the built environment, which he designates as an architectonic code, "is essentially a *system of relationships* in which significative entities are defined in terms of their relative positions in a multidimensional network of relationships."[28] Although he suggests that signs in material formations function "in a manner precisely analogous to other semiotic systems such as verbal language or bodily gesturing,"[29] Preziosi also emphasizes that material signs must be regarded as distinctive elements of visual communication: "As a system of signs, a built environment does not exist in a vacuum but is co-occurrent with ensembles of other sign systems in different media. Each sign system offers certain advantages over others under the varying conditions of daily life. A built environment does certain things which verbal language does not do, or only does by weak approximation and circumlocution—and vice-versa."[30]

Similarly, we contend that artifacts, such as vernacular structures, may be said to have a life of their own—an appeal to the senses that is far different from that of words on a page. Some scholars of material culture have even argued that, although objects are often the physical embodiment of ideas held collectively by society, as well as indices of individual motivation, they also provide better historical and cultural evidence than words.[31] Additionally, some "post-processual archaeologists" maintain that "material messages operate over longer timespans than do verbal" and gestural signals;[32] furthermore, there is not a direct correspondence between verbal and nonverbal meaning. Thus, it is "logically improper" to impose "verbal meaning on material behavior."[33] Speaking to another disciplinary perspective, John Kouwenhoven has challenged the over-reliance on verbal data by scholars of American studies by declaring that words are deceptive and misleading due to the inherent limitations of language, such as its inability to convey the complexity of sensory experience. What is needed instead, Kouwenhoven argues, is a sensory awareness of objects as cultural evidence; he regards this sensory awareness as comprised of more reliable sources of data construction than words by themselves can provide.[34]

This sensory approach to material culture, especially vernacular architecture, is beautifully reflected in architect and American studies scholar Rina Swentzell's memory of growing up in Santa Clara Pueblo in the 1940s: "As we are synonymous with and born of the earth, so are we made of the same stuff as our houses. As children, we tasted houses because of their varying textures and tastes. Not only could houses be tasted, they were also blessed, healed and fed periodically. . . . Houses were also given the ultimate respect of dying."[35]

A somewhat similar focus on the sensory and symbolic forms the core of Csikszentmihalyi and Rochberg-Halton's study of the relationships between individuals and domestic objects—"the ties that bind people to the material world around them and the consequences of this relationship."[36] They describe the act of perception that creates "the meaning that releases the symbolic power of things" as "that of seeing them objectively and subjectively at the same time."[37] This position is similar to Miles Richardson's assertion, influenced greatly by sociologist George Herbert Mead, that the "secret capacity to make meaning lies in the artefact," which can, in turn, be described as a "collapsed act."[38] This is a very different approach from that which regards material things as quantifiable objects that are frozen at one point in time and operate according to fixed grammatical rules.

For the reasons suggested above—the primacy it ultimately gives to scholarship on verbal and written forms, the limitations of the models themselves, the misapplication of these models, and problems with the equation of language (or text) and artifact—we believe that models based on language are limited in the degree to which they can serve vernacular architecture scholarship. Still, artifacts should not be studied in isolation. For years, scholars of verbal art have argued that a full appreciation of verbal art requires a wealth of contextual information.[39] We argue that a similar attempt to incorporate all possible contextual information is essential in the analysis of material-culture items—in particular, for the purposes of this paper, vernacular structures. Hence, in rejecting linguistic models, we do not leave consideration of language behind. Rather, we suggest that there is a need to focus on the interrelationship of material and linguistic forms *and* there is a need to develop our theoretical capabilities for interpreting written and oral evidence. Instead of reading buildings as texts, we need to pay attention to our interpretation of textual data, both written and spoken.

Our interest in the subject grew from our concern for focusing not just on form, but also on social use. We were less interested in unconscious motivation than in sociocultural values and deliberate choices; thus, our aim has been to integrate people into the study of vernacular architecture. What better method toward gaining an understanding of the meaning in things—both that which is shared by a community and that which is a result of purely personal choice—can we employ than by talking to the people who built, lived in (or lived nearby), altered, and remember vernacular structures? Of course, personal narratives about buildings follow the pattern of established narrative form and, thus, need to be understood in the context of a particular oral tradition. To this extent, the application of an ethnography-of-speaking approach may be appropriate. Oral narratives may give form to the intangible, experiential aspects of architecture, but they can only be understood in the context of how any members of a particular cultural group express themselves.

The incorporation of oral tradition—i.e., personal narratives that reveal how people feel about and talk about houses as well as the associational values these buildings have for them—not only provides necessary contextual information, but also adds to our sensory awareness of these structures. To return briefly to the "artifact-as-text" argument, we suggest that the spoken word appeals to the senses in a way that is qualitatively different from that provided by the written word. Additionally, we claim that there is no need to turn to structural or linguistic models when one considers expressive behavior (from the most holistic perspective) to involve the dynamic interaction of verbal and visual data, and when one's focus is not only on form but also on social use. This dynamic interaction yields information about ver-

nacular structures that is integrally connected with both the shared and the personal meaning of vernacular structures; it also leads to an emphasis on process rather than on product, reinforcing the idea that change through time is an essential element of cultural communication. Furthermore, the incorporation not only of oral tradition,[40] but also of actual observations of how people design, construct, live in, and change vernacular houses provides us with information about gender roles that has too often been missing in vernacular architecture studies. Especially important in this regard is the active role that women have taken in the creation and alteration of such structures. Some examples from our fieldwork will illuminate these points.

M. Jane Young has been learning the traditional art of pottery making from Mary Lewis-Garcia, a well-known Acoma potter whose studio is the old adobe house in which she lived when she was first married. Mary loves to use this house as her studio because it is somewhat isolated from her large family (who, nevertheless, drop by frequently in their pickup trucks for one reason or another), thus offering her time to concentrate exclusively on her art. The house has no electricity, and Mary's eyesight is troubling her. One day, in a moment of frustration at the dim available light (the door had been kept open, but the cold December wind had forced her to shut it), Mary said, pointing to one long wall that had no window at all, "This summer I'm going to knock a hole in that wall and then we'll have enough light." Concerned about the difficulty of this task, since Mary is about seventy years old, and knowing little about the physical properties of adobe, Young asked, "Won't that be hard to do?" Mary laughed and replied, "Of course not, we Acoma women do it all the time. Adobe is very easy to break through. We change our houses whenever we need to."[41]

Several months later Young was visiting friends (a grandmother, her daughter, her daughter's pregnant daughter) at Taos Pueblo, and, on the spur of the moment, the elderly grandmother said, "Let's take out the wall in the room where you stay [nodding to the pregnant daughter], so there'll be more room when the baby comes." The group of women all moved to one of the back rooms of the house and proceeded to knock out most of the wall in that room so that it expanded into the adjoining room. Young did indeed discover that adobe is a most pliable material when one wants to remove parts of it.[42] Given these examples, it is important to note that, in accordance with historical custom, many Puebloan women today regard themselves (and are so regarded by their relatives and the more conservative members of the various pueblos, at least) as the owners of their houses—thus, they can do with them as they please. Not only do they knock out windows and interior walls, but, where space permits, they also add on rooms to those that already exist (therefore greatly changing the form of the original structure). In addition to providing information concerning the involvement of women as well as men in the design and construction of vernacular structures, these examples illustrate dynamic change through time in accordance with practical necessity and social use.

In earlier work in western North Carolina, Michael Ann Williams used oral narrative to explore the social and symbolic use and meaning of folk houses. She found it was necessary to ascertain not only the truth or falsity of the testimony but also to understand the relationship of the narrative to the physical artifact. Generally, narratives gave form to the experiential aspects of the dwelling in a way that the artifact could not. It was the story rather than the structure that best represented "home." Williams also found that women were generally far more articulate about social and symbolic use than men. Of course, they had a far more intimate experience with domestic interiors than men.[43] However, after later reviewing her fieldwork, Williams realized that the majority of the rural southern Appalachian women interviewed expressed the strong opinion that during most of their lifetimes they far preferred to be outside than inside the house. Their narratives often contained anecdotes about how they managed to spend more time outside. In fieldwork currently being conducted, Williams is focusing especially on rural women's perceptions of inside and outside.

Williams also obtained information on women's roles in designing, altering, and controlling the interior space of houses. Despite assertions that they "worked like a man" in the fields, few women claimed responsibility for physically constructing houses. In a recent interview, however, one woman took responsibility for physically altering her central passage dwelling. Frustrated with her carpenter husband's inability to find time to work on his own house, she took matters into her own hands and did the alterations herself. To her disbelieving husband, she simply noted, "You marry a carpenter, you make a carpenter."[44]

Considerably more evidence was available of women's contribution to the design of houses. This was particularly the case for families who abandoned traditional plans and built larger, popular-style houses in order to take in boarders. During a time when rural men were increasingly selling their labor, some rural women chose to sell their domestic space. Again, in current research, women's control over the design and running of boardinghouses in western North Carolina is being examined.

While giving explicit examples from our own work, we acknowledge that the use of ethnographic observation and oral testimony is limited or impossible in many vernacular architecture studies. Of course, scholars who study the material remains of people who are no longer living find it extremely difficult to reveal the role of individual choice and variation in the construction and use of buildings; certainly, they cannot interview the people who lived in these structures. In such cases, one can, however, use both artifactual and textual evidence to delineate culturally determined patterns and values.[45] In fact, vernacular architecture scholars whose research focuses on the past have often supplemented site maps and other sorts of archaeological evidence with information from documents, including census records, wills, and probate records, where available. For instance, in "Good and Sufficient Language for Building," Catherine Bishir focuses on historical information about the interaction between the client and the craftsman.[46] In this paper Bisher brings sociolinguistic models full circle by applying Upton's vernacular architecture use of Bernstein's sociolinguistic model to written texts—the builder's contract.[47] Coupled with design theory, the model works to make sense of the seemingly paltry evidence found in traditional builders' specifications. Whether Bernstein's theory provides the best method for analyzing such data can be questioned (folklorists might express similar concepts through the use of high context/low context), but Bishir's approach makes sense because she applies linguistic theory to language in a way that is illuminating to vernacular architecture scholars.

Linguistic and sociolinguistic theory is important to vernacular architecture research to the extent that it enhances our understanding of verbal and written data. Beyond that, we need to pursue and give precedence to the interrelationship of architecture and language, focusing our research on questions such as the following: How do people write or talk about vernacular structures? Do contracts express something of the nature of the design process? Do oral narratives give expression to the intangible meanings of the house? How and why do people alter their dwellings over time and what does this tell us about personal preferences, gender roles, and, more generally, cultural patterns? These are only some of the questions that are crucial to an ethnographic approach to vernacular architecture studies—one that combines the study of the building with all available contextual information, including oral tradition and documentary evidence. It is this sort of approach that brings houses alive and invests them with the meaning and sensory impact they had or have for those who interacted with them.

Notes

1. See James Deetz, *Invitation to Archaeology* (Garden City, N.Y.: Natural History Press, 1967), 83–96, for his ground-breaking application of structural linguistics to artifactual analysis. For the use of transformational grammar in the analysis of vernacular architecture, see Henry Glassie, *Folk Housing in Middle Virginia: A Structural Analysis of Historic Artifacts* (Knoxville: University of Tennessee Press, 1975). In Dell Upton's "Toward a Performance Theory of Vernacular Architecture: Early Tidewater Virginia as a Case Study," *Folklore Forum* 12 (1979): 173–96, the author employs Basil Bernstein's notion of elaborated and restricted linguistic codes in his study of vernacular architecture. For other "performance-based" analyses of vernacular architecture, see Bernard L. Herman, "Time and Performance: Folk Houses in Delaware," in *American Material Culture and Folklife: A Prologue and Dialogue*, ed. Simon J. Bronner (Ann Arbor: UMI Research Press, 1985), 155–75, and Mary Corbin Sies, "Toward a Performance Theory of the Suburban Ideal, 1877–1917," in *Perspectives in Vernacular Architecture, IV*, ed. Thomas Carter and Bernard L. Herman (Columbia: University of Missouri Press, 1991), 197–207.

2. Essentially, in *Folk Housing in Middle Virginia*, Henry Glassie uses two different levels of structural analysis: the explicitly linguistic, transformational grammar, based on the theories of Noam Chomsky, and anthropological structuralism, derived from the work of Claude Lévi-Strauss. See Noam Chomsky, *Aspects of the Theory of Syntax* (Cambridge, Mass.: MIT Press, 1970); Claude Lévi-Strauss, *Structural Anthropology*, trans. C. Jacobson and B. G. Schoepf (New York: Basic Books, 1963 [original French ed., 1958]). For uses of semiotic theory in vernacular architecture scholarship, see Diana Agrest and Mario Gandelsonas, "Critical Remarks on Semiology and Archi-

tecture," *Semiotics* 9 (3) (1973): 252–71; Dora Crouch, "Architecture as Symbolic Language," *ETC.: A Review of General Semantics* 28 (1) (1971): 59–66; Jennifer Eastman and Brian Attebery, "Reading Buildings as Texts: A Semiotic Approach to Interpreting Vernacular Architecture," paper given at the annual meeting of the American Folklore Society, Oakland, California, Oct. 1990; Umberto Eco, "A Componential Analysis of the Architectural Sign /Column/," *Semiotica* 5 (2) (1972): 97–117; Ladislav Matejka and Irwin R. Titunik, eds., *Semiotics of Art* (Cambridge, Mass.: MIT Press, 1976); C. F. Munro, "Semiotics, Aesthetics and Architecture," *British Journal of Aesthetics* 27 (2) (1987): 115–28; Donald Preziosi, *The Semiotics of the Built Environment: An Introduction to Architectonic Analysis* (Bloomington: Indiana University Press, 1979).

3. Roland Fletcher, "The Messages of Material Behaviour: A Preliminary Discussion of Non-Verbal Meaning," in *The Meanings of Things: Material Culture and Symbolic Expression,* ed. Ian Hodder (London: Unwin Hyman Ltd., 1989), 33.

4. Simon J. Bronner, "The Hidden Past of Material Culture Studies in American Folkloristics," *New York Folklore* 8 (1982): 1.

5. For an overview of material culture scholarship in the discipline of folklore, see Simon J. Bronner, "The Idea of the Folk Artifact," in *American Material Culture and Folklife,* 3–39. For an exploration of the way in which artifacts reveal messages about sociocultural patterns, see James Deetz, *In Small Things Forgotten: The Archeology of Early American Life* (New York: Doubleday, 1977).

6. Elizabeth Adler, "'My Mother Had One of Those': The Experience of the Pie Safe," in *American Material Culture and Folklife,* 119–28 ; Thomas A. Adler, "Musical Instruments, Tools, and the Experience of Control," in *American Material Culture and Folklife,* 103–11; Glassie, *Folk Housing in Middle Virginia;* Herman, "Time and Performance"; Upton, "Toward a Performance Theory of Vernacular Architecture."

7. Claude Lévi-Strauss, *Totemism,* trans. Rodney Needham (Boston: Beacon Press, 1963 [orig. French ed., 1962]).

8. Glassie, *Folk Housing in Middle Virginia.*

9. Dell Hymes, *Foundations in Sociolinguistics: An Ethnographic Approach* (Philadelphia: University of Pennsylvania Press, 1974), 9.

10. Yoshiko Ikegami, "A Stratificational Analysis of the Hand Gesture in Indian Classic Dance," *Semiotica* 4 (4) (1971): 365–91; Adrienne L. Kaeppler, "Method and Theory in Analyzing Dance Structure with an Analysis of Tongan Dance," *Ethnomusicology* 16 (2) (1972): 173–217.

11. Robert H. Leibman, "Dancing Bears and Purple Transformations: The Structure of Dance in the Balkans," (Ph.D. diss., University of Pennsylvania, 1992).

12. Upton, "Toward a Performance Theory of Vernacular Architecture"; Basil Bernstein, *Class, Codes and Control* (London: Routledge and Kegan Paul, 1971).

13. Hymes, *Foundations in Sociolinguistics: An Ethnographic Approach,* 35–45.

14. Herman, "Time and Performance," 156–57.

15. José E. Limón and M. Jane Young, "Frontiers, Settlements, and Developments in Folklore Studies, 1972–1985," *Annual Review of Anthropology* 15 (1986): 453; Simon Bronner, "'Visible Proofs': Material Culture Study in American Folkloristics," *American Quarterly* 35 (1983): 316–38.

16. See Gerald L. Pocius's review of *Perspectives in Vernacular Architecture, II,* in *Journal of American Folklore* 101 (1988): 87–88. Pocius's own *A Place to Belong: Community Order and Everyday Space in Calvert, Newfoundland* (Athens: University of Georgia Press, 1991) is one of the relatively few exceptions to the lack of vernacular architecture studies that focus on the ethnographic present. See also Joseph Sciorra, "Yard Shrines and Sidewalk Altars of New York's Italian-Americans," in *Perspectives in Vernacular Architecture, III,* ed. Thomas Carter and Bernard L. Herman (Columbia: University of Missouri Press, 1989), 185–98, and Joseph Sciorra, "Puerto Rican

Casitas in New York City," paper presented to the annual meeting of the Vernacular Architecture Forum, Santa Fe, New Mexico, May 1991.

17. Thomas Carter and Bernard L. Herman, "Introduction: Toward a New Architectural History," in *Perspectives in Vernacular Architecture, IV,* ed. Thomas Carter and Bernard L. Herman (Columbia: University of Missouri Press, 1991), 3.

18. George W. McDaniel, *Hearth and Home: Preserving a People's Culture* (Philadelphia: Temple University Press, 1982), and Charles E. Martin, *Hollybush: Folk Building and Social Change in an Appalachian Community* (Knoxville: University of Tennessee Press, 1984).

19. Terence Hawkes, *Structuralism and Semiotics* (Berkeley and Los Angeles: University of California Press, 1977), 124.

20. See Susan Roach, "The Kinship Quilt: An Ethnographic Semiotic Analysis of a Quilting Bee," in *Women's Folklore, Women's Culture,* ed. R. A. Jordan and S. J. Kalčik (Philadelphia: University of Pennsylvania Press, 1985), 55.

21. Jan Mukarovský, "Art as Semiotic Fact," in *Semiotics of Art,* ed. L. Matejka and I. R. Titunik (Cambridge, Mass.: MIT Press, 1976), 3–9.

22. Petr Bogatyrev, "Costume as a Sign: The Functional and Structural Concept in Ethnography," in *Semiotics of Art,* 13–19; Petr Bogatyrev, *The Functions of Folk Costume in Moravian Slovakia* (The Hague: Mouton, 1971 [orig. published in 1937]).

23. Petr Bogatyrev, "Costume as a Sign," 13–19.

24. Eastman and Attebery, "Reading Buildings as Texts: A Semiotic Approach to Interpreting Vernacular Architecture"; Eco, "A Componential Analysis of the Architectural Sign /Column/"; Preziosi, *The Semiotics of the Built Environment;* Christopher Tilley, "Interpreting Material Culture," in *The Meanings of Things,* 185–94; Ricardas Vidutis and Virginia A. P.Lowe, "The Cemetery as a Cultural Text," *Kentucky Folklore Record* 26 (1980): 103–13. Drawing on Bakhtin's theory of language, Robert St. George describes the landscape of early America as comprised of polyphonic, spatial texts. See Robert St. George, "Bawns and Beliefs: Architecture, Commerce, and Conversion in Early New England," *Winterthur Portfolio* 25 (4) (1990): 241–82.

25. Vidutis and Lowe, "The Cemetery as a Cultural Text," 103.

26. Ibid.

27. Preziosi, *The Semiotics of the Built Environment.*

28. Ibid., 2.

29. Ibid., 1.

30. Ibid., 3.

31. Bronner, "The Idea of the Folk Artifact," 14–17.

32. Fletcher, "The Messages of Material Behaviour," 37.

33. Ibid., 38.

34. John A. Kouwenhoven, "American Studies: Words or Things?" in *American Studies in Transition,* ed. Marshall W. Fishwick (Boston: Houghton Mifflin, 1964), 15–35.

35. Rina Swentzell, "Remembering Tewa Pueblo Houses and Spaces," *Native Peoples* 3 (2) (1990): 6–12.

36. Mihaly Csikszentmihalyi and Eugene Rochberg-Halton, *The Meaning of Things: Domestic Symbols and the Self* (Cambridge: Cambridge University Press, 1981), 58.

37. Ibid., 247.

38. Miles Richardson, "The Artefact as Abbreviated Act: A Social Interpretation of Material Culture," in *The Meanings of Things,* 172; George Herbert Mead, *The Philosophy of the Act,* ed. C. W. Morris (Chicago: University of Chicago Press, 1972), 121–22, 368–70.

39. Dell Hymes, "Models of the Interaction of Language and Social Life," in *Directions in Sociolinguistics: The Ethnography of Communication,* ed. John J. Gumperz and Dell Hymes (New York: Holt, Rinehart & Winston, Inc., 1972), 35–71; Richard Bauman, *Verbal Art as Performance* (Prospect Heights, Ill.: Waveland Press, 1977); Richard Bauman, *Story, Performance, And Event: Contextual Studies of Oral Narrative* (Cambridge: Cambridge University Press, 1986).

40. In Rebecca Sample Bernstein and Carolyn Torma, "Exploring the Role of Women in the Creation of Vernacular Architecture," in *Perspectives in Vernacular Architecture, IV,* 64–72, the authors suggest that oral history is vital in reconstructing women's roles in designing and constructing vernacular structures.

41. Tape-recorded interview with Mary Lewis-Garcia, Acoma Pueblo, New Mexico, Dec. 15, 1990.

42. Field notes, Taos Pueblo, New Mexico, March 4, 1991.

43. For the results of this research, see Michael Ann Williams, *Homeplace: The Social Use and Meaning of the Folk Dwelling in Southwestern North Carolina* (Athens: University of Georgia Press, 1991).

44. Tape-recorded interview with Cleva Anderson, Martin's Creek, Cherokee County, North Carolina, July 16, 1990.

45. Deetz, *In Small Things Forgotten;* St. George, "Bawns and Beliefs," 241–82; Robert St. George, *The Wrought Covenant: Source Material for the Study of Craftsmen and Community in Southeastern New England, 1620–1700* (Brockton, Mass.: Brockton Art Center/Fuller Memorial, 1979). In *The Stolen House* (Charlottesville and London: University Press of Virginia, 1991), Bernard L. Herman advocates a method of "folkloristic archaeology" in his combined use of artifactual and written evidence. Although a linguistic metaphor is central to his theoretical framework (he defines material culture as the "discourse of objects"), his analysis rests less on analysis of the artifact as text than on a folkloristic interpretation of written texts as a means to understand the material world and its context.

46. Catherine Bishir, "Good and Sufficient Language for Building," in *Perspectives in Vernacular Architecture, IV,* 44–52.

47. Upton, "Toward a Performance Theory of Vernacular Architecture"; Basil Bernstein, *Class, Codes and Control.*

Part II

Architecture and the
Meaning of Institutions

Chapter 5

Building an Urban Identity:
The Clustered Spires of Frederick, Maryland

Diane Shaw

Up from the meadows rich with corn,
Clear in the cool September morn,
The clustered spires of Frederick stand
Green-walled by the hills of Maryland.

John Greenleaf Whittier,
"Barbara Frietchie" (1863)

During the nineteenth century, the churches of Frederick became symbols of the city. The town's eighteenth-century horizon of low buildings poking above agricultural fields matured into an urban skyline of steeple and spire (fig. 5.1). Although Frederick's urban identity was not solely predicated on its show of churches, recurring allusions to the importance of the city's "clustered spires" demonstrate that church construction played a keen part in the public's understanding of urbanization.[1]

City building emerged as a significant and complex phenomenon in America during the nineteenth century. Between 1800 and 1860, the number of small cities with 2,500 to 10,000 occupants rose from 139 to 1,571.[2] While much has been written on the growth of cities, most case studies focus on the large cities that developed national reputations; as a result, the much more common small cities of state or local importance have been hidden in the shadow of their big-city cousins.[3] By 1850 only 6 percent of Americans lived in cities of over one hundred thousand people; in contrast, three times that percentage resided in small cities of two thousand or more.[4] Nonetheless, it remains

unclear how and in what form small cities took shape in a preponderantly rural country.

Frederick, Maryland, provides a useful case study of how one small city developed its urban form and character: its one-mile-square historic city center is still very much intact, and many primary records, including maps, lithographs, and diaries, further reconstruct the nineteenth-century cityscape. Gazetteers, a type of geographical encyclopedia, typically listed the key features of any urban entry. One noted in 1853 that: "Frederick City . . . is a well built town, with regular, wide streets, and contains a court-house, a substantial building, the county jail, and other public offices; 17 churches, some of them spacious and of fine architecture, several literary and scientific institutions, and about 1,000 dwellings, mostly of brick and stone, and many of them elegant, and 6,028 inhabitants . . . in wealth and elegance it is second only to Baltimore."[5] Frederick enjoyed a strong regional reputation, but it never assumed much importance outside Maryland. It was often noted in travel accounts, but typically as a place to pass through and not as a destination. The townspeople, however, were intensely aware of Frederick's growth and appearance. In addition to his personal journal, one resident also kept a separate construction journal that detailed the physical changes to the city.[6]

Church construction in particular was an integral step in Frederick's architectural transformation into a city. Churches expressed Frederick's inten-

Fig. 5.1. View of Frederick, Maryland. Both sides of Church Street, as well as the church views lining the border, figure prominently in this lithograph of Frederick. ("View of Frederick, Maryland" [Baltimore: E. Sachse & Co.], 1854.)

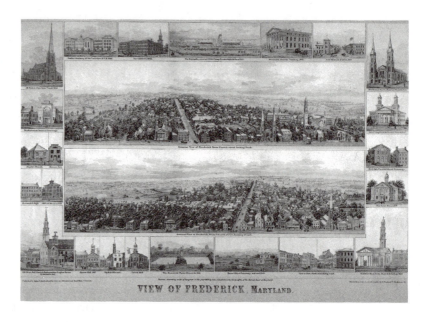

VIEW OF FREDERICK, MARYLAND.

sifying urban refinement in four essential ways. First, the creation of a church district was part of the sorting and classifying of urban space, a practice that characterized the segregated and spatially hierarchical nineteenth-century city. Second, the architectural styles of the new churches showed the congregations' awareness of popular culture in styles and their interest in building monuments that would shine even in cosmopolitan cities. Third, the necessity for high-style edifices forced a re-evaluation of the design process itself, leading the residents to abandon old ways of contracting in exchange for outsiders' new ideas. Fourth, the construction of monuments with towers and steeples created a notable skyline, an urban feature that distinguished the view of Frederick from the surrounding wheat fields and squat villages.

Between 1841 and 1859, the eight congregations in Frederick either rebuilt or substantially remodeled their churches. The costly change of heart—the impulse to build bigger and better churches in prestigious locations—absorbed the congregations. The quadrupling of the population during the period from 1800 to 1860 may have contributed to the changing programmatic needs

of the old churches, but the increasing number of congregants alone did not account for the increasing demand for stylish edifices on specific streets.[7] The congregations' burning ambition to build something monumental, a desire often fanned by ministers' pleas for more space, were not fueled simply by crowded or uncomfortable buildings. The commitment of time and money, the domino-like timing of remodeling, and the resulting ostentatious edifices all indicate that more was at stake than simply pew space. The outcome of the church-building campaigns—a clearly articulated Church Street graced with edifices designed by known architects—redefined both street and neighborhood hierarchies and transformed the colonial, vernacular look of the town into a fashionable city. The accolades at the 1850 consecration of the new Evangelical Reformed Church were applicable to any of the new houses of worship: "It now stands a monument of the zeal and energy of the Pastor and members of the congregations, and an ornament to our city."[8]

Among other building activities, the townspeople viewed church construction as a form of both parochial and urban improvement, since religious life and civic life were closely entwined.[9] The earliest town leaders had been the church pastors. Church networks often channeled work to its membership. Many men, women, and children were involved with church-sponsored activities, not only in the forms of church attendance, Sunday school, and mission work, but also in reading, musical, and sewing groups, and picnics and fairs. Nonparochial, public parades that celebrated the Fourth of July and Washington's birthday typically marched past the Protestant churches, and the public orations often took place in one of the larger church sanctuaries. In all of Frederick County during the 1840s, the total number of residents was matched by an equal number of seats in the county's churches.[10] A townsperson who attended a civic oration, an itinerant preacher's lecture, or even the consecration of a new church was not necessarily a congregant, but rather simply a member of the larger Frederick community. At the consecration of the new Evangelical Reformed Church, one source reported that "the whole city seemed to be wending their way to the new and beautiful sanctuary." Denominational competition mixed with civic pride, for in the next sentence the writer boasted that a larger audience was "probably never assembled in this city."[11] The dual benefit of church and civic improvement helped garner support for the church rebuilding projects that were to come.

The prominence of Frederick's churches in an 1854 city lithograph reflected their cultural preeminence and urban relevance (see fig. 5.1). Urban views tended to emphasize the buildings that gave a city character. The lithograph included border vignettes of the city's landmarks, half of them religious buildings and the remainder primarily civic and educational. The visual message matched the prevailing rhetoric that Frederick was characterized by "good people of this ancient and hospitable, intelligent and religious place."[12] It was no coincidence that the central view showed both sides of the architectural showcase of Church Street, embellished with its fine facades and clustered steeples.[13]

The creation of a prestigious church row, both close to the courthouse square and separate from the main commercial street, occurred in other cities across the country during the nineteenth century. In Baltimore, the "denominations of influence" helped establish "neighborhoods of elegance and respectability."[14] During Chicago's formative years of the 1840s and 1850s, six churches presided over Washington Street, including several that faced the public square, and four more churches provided a parallel development one block over. During the postbellum years in Springfield, Massachusetts, new church-building campaigns established a monumental religious landscape near the court square. Even a cursory review of lithographs of the urbanizing West shows strings or clusters of churches—districts within the overall urban fabric. The concentration of showy churches in a distinct, and often elite, zone was a common stage in many small cities' development of a segmented cityscape.[15]

Frederick residents were building on a century-old townscape. In 1745 an Annapolis land speculator laid out the grid of Fredericktown to serve as a market and administrative center for the fertile Maryland hinterland. The inland settlement flourished, and in 1817 the state officially incorporated the town as a city. Strategic routing of the National Road in 1806 and the Baltimore and Ohio Railroad in 1831 ensured Frederick's access to markets as well as outside ideas.[16] Nonetheless, it was not until mid-century that residents dropped the outdated named of Fredericktown in exchange for Frederick City or, more commonly, Frederick. The concept of a city required more than a legal change of status; it required visible expression of certain urban and urbane elements.

When the townspeople searched for new architectural ideas, they looked to "the city." Baltimore, Washington, and Philadelphia served as sirens of fashion, offering the latest in clothing, furniture,

Fig. 5.2. Methodist Church, 1801. Later rented out as a Masonic Hall, the simple step-gabled facade of the church was a common detail in Frederick. (Detail from "View of Frederick, Maryland" [Baltimore: E. Sachse & Co.], 1854.)

Fig. 5.3. Methodist Church, 1841. This new building was typical of Methodist church designs across the country. (Detail from "View of Frederick, Maryland" [Baltimore: E. Sachse & Co.], 1854.)

and architecture. Frederick residents habitually journeyed to the cities. Among them was the faithful diarist Jacob Engelbrecht, who succinctly set forth his reasons for traveling in an 1832 entry: "I went to Baltimore. . . . Just went to see the Fashions—that's all."[17] The Frederick city council and citizens followed suit. When, in 1828, Frederick needed a new almshouse, the council copied the Baltimore poorhouse. In 1844, the council engaged the engineer at Philadelphia's Fairmount waterworks, Frederick Erdman, for the city's new reservoir. In 1851, an independent cemetery corporation turned to Baltimore for expertise and hired the engineers Thomas P. Chifelle and James Belden to lay out a picturesque rural cemetery.[18] Changing tastes in architecture tempted the residents to look beyond their vernacular community for popular designs, a shift of which the churches

were keenly aware. In the competition among congregations, the final winner was the city of Frederick, bedecked with ornamental architecture.

The church-rebuilding trend began quite modestly. In 1839, the Methodists decided that their 1801 building was "too small and too near the western limits of the town to suit the congregation."[19] The Methodists chose a new site on East Church Street, nearer the center of town (fig. 5.2). Both the peripheral location and the antiquated style of the plain, stepped-gable church prompted the new construction. A nineteenth-century townswoman remembered the old church none too favorably. Susannah Markell shuddered that the wooden lunettes looked like eyebrows and, along with the tilted shutters, gave the whole building a "leering countenance." She added that the "uncovered floor and discolored walls imparted to the interior an air of severe plainness and desolation."[20] A central location resolved the Methodists' self-perceived marginality, and a new edifice remedied their stylistic shortcomings. The new church, completed in 1841, observed the consensually codified design of Methodist construction at the time: the gable-end, brick

Fig. 5.4. Evangelical Reformed Church, 1850, Joseph Wall, Architect. The Greek Revival was a new, American style for a congregation that had just dropped "German" from its name. (Detail from "View of Frederick, Maryland" [Baltimore: E. Sachse & Co.], 1854.)

facade contained two entrances capped by simple round-top windows (fig. 5.3).[21] Within twenty years the congregation remodeled this building into a slightly larger, taller, and thus more imposing structure that nevertheless followed the basic Methodist prescription for facades. As the Methodists' rebuilding and remodeling shows, monumentality, style, and a favorable location were desirable effects and motivating forces. Definitions of monumentality and the proper style, however, were fluid; each congregation's remodeling raised the standards for the rest.

A few years after the Methodists completed their new edifice, the German Reformed congregation determined that its spired church was spatially and symbolically inadequate. In 1845, two prominent citizens of long-established Frederick families formed a building committee led by the Rev. Daniel Zacharias. None of the committee had particular experience in the building trades, but they were receptive to the minister's urging to consider the unfortunate age, size, and style of the existing church.[22] The structurally sound, colonial stone church, built by first-generation German Americans and fortuitously located on Church Street, was converted to a Sunday school and a chapel for German-speaking services.[23] The congregation appropriated a church-owned site across the street, and turned to Baltimore for appropriate architectural leadership. Joseph Wall, the architect of Baltimore's Mount Vernon Methodist Church, designed a monumental Greek Revival edifice with twin towers capped by "Lanterns of Domosthenes." The Greek Revival facade, also reminiscent of Latrobe's 1808 Baltimore Cathedral, the Baltimore Methodist Pew Church, and numerous public buildings in America, crossed denominational as well as institutional lines as it made a bold architectural statement in Frederick (fig. 5.4).

The Greek Revival was a by then conventional and symbolically American style that appealed to the German Reformed congregation's desire for a new, American identity to accompany their rechristening as the Evangelical Reformed Church and their commitment to English-speaking services.[24]

The German-American Evangelical Reformed community warmly received Wall's design. Following the consecration in 1850, one church member boasted that "out of Baltimore it is decidedly the handsomest and most spacious church in the State; and even in the monumental city, I would not know where to look for a prettier and more desirable place of worship." The same account also commended the excellent Church Street site, the "most eligible in location."[25] The newspaper praised the beauty of the new church and urged: "May the example thus set not be forgotten soon, but [be] considered by the rest as worthy of all imitation."[26]

The words were prescient. Church building in Frederick began in earnest as congregations reassessed their own structures. Two weeks after the consecration of the Evangelical Reformed edifice, a local tailor wryly compared it to his Lutheran church: "I counted on Sunday last . . . the pews in the New German Reformed Church of our town—the Church will seat 1058 persons below & above Stairs, including the choir seats—On the same day I counted the Seats in the Lutheran church the old one that will seat 695 down & up Stairs—all right & nothing more."[27]

Jacob Engelbrecht was not the first to find the Lutheran church wanting. Since 1837 the Rev. Simeon Harkey had been clamoring to build a new structure that would better hold his protracted evangelical prayer meetings. At the time Harkey could not generate sufficient enthusiasm for the project, and after years of campaigning he resigned. In 1851 the new Lutheran minister, the Rev. George Diehl, suddenly found a receptive audience to his call for improvements, but the willing congregation nonetheless struggled with building plans. The will was there, but the designs were not.

The struggles suggest that more than programmatic concerns were at stake. The first building committee amply represented the building trades, including a carpenter, brick maker, and plasterer. Despite the committee's construction expertise and the simple directive to employ a "competent person" to make plans for a new church, by 1852 the

Fig. 5.5. Evangelical Lutheran Church, 1855, Niernsee and Neilson, Architects. The height and drama of the facade dwarfed the efforts of the Evangelical Reformed congregation down the street.

undertaking had come to naught. The next year another carpenter, also a church member, submitted his plan to retain the building core but to extend the structure forward to the sidewalk line. The rejected proposal did not describe the future appearance of the remodeled building.[28] Ironically, the congregation ultimately adopted the ground plan of the second proposal, but only after it was advanced by a well-known architectural firm from Baltimore that could be counted on to give the proper expression to the whole. The local craftsmen were now, seemingly, not up to the task of producing fashionably credible plans.

In 1854 the Lutherans abandoned the idea of using local talent for their important venture. A new committee without any building experience traveled to Baltimore for new ideas. This group, composed of a gentleman farmer, a wealthy tanyard owner, and a newspaper publisher, was presumably more sophisticated than the previous committee and would provide the kind of cultivated advice the congregation now sought. When the esteemed delegation returned, it proposed remodeling the edifice in "the Gothic style." There was no need to relocate, as the Lutherans were already strategically located on Church Street. The congregation approved this idea and specified that the committee hire "some architect" to draw up plans.[29] The churchmen hired the prominent Baltimore architectural firm of John Niernsee and James Neilson to extend the church forward and to remodel the interior. Despite some later structural problems, the edifice pleased the congregation; its 150-foot twin towers were higher and the seating capacity larger, if only by 42 seats, than their Evangelical Reformed rival up the street (fig. 5.5).[30]

At the December 1855 consecration of the Lutheran church, the minister asserted "In architectural beauty and adaptation to all the purposes of public worship, [the new church] can scarcely be surpassed."[31] But a challenger was in the wings. Engelbrecht had noted the construction race between the Episcopalians and the Lutherans who were "busy at their towers or Steeples."[32] Just one month after the consecration of the Lutheran church, he recorded the opening of the new All Saints Episcopal Church.

As with the other congregations, location was as important as style to the All Saints parish. The Episcopalians' 1856 church was the third edifice constructed on as many sites. The first Anglican church, completed during the 1750s, presided over the eponymous All Saints Street in the south part of town. During the early nineteenth century, disrepair and the decline of the neighborhood convinced the reorganized Episcopalians to rebuild on Court Street.[33] The Episcopalians enjoyed an elegant but small neoclassical church built by the local McCleery family on the new site in 1814. Highly fashionable and commanding a good site when it was built, the building's prestige had declined by mid-century (fig. 5.6). Noxious hotel stables across the narrow street were an eyesore and a fire hazard. Mixed-

Fig. 5.6. All Saints Episcopal Church, 1814, Henry McCleery, Architect. The outdated style and insignificant location of this church was an embarrassment to the congregation by mid-century. (Historic American Buildings Survey, Library of Congress).

Fig. 5.7. All Saints Episcopal Church, 1856, Richard Upjohn, Architect. Pressures from local church rebuilding campaigns as well as the Ecclesiological movement led the vestry to hire a nationally known architect.

Fig. 5.8. Presbyterian Church, 1828, Peter Mantz, Architect. Constructed by a local builder, this church was out of style within thirty years. (Detail from "View of Frederick, Maryland" [Baltimore: E. Sachse & Co.], 1854.)

use areas such as that along Court Street had long been accepted as the norm, but by the 1850s the Episcopalians felt the situation degraded their church. The Rev. William Pendleton also falsely argued that the church had deteriorated beyond repair; according to one contemporary, he "rowed them up salt river" with tearful pleas for a construction campaign on a new site.[34] Akin to the Lutherans' situation, the clamoring minister resigned unfulfilled, but the new minister persuaded the congregation, now sensitized to the fashionable dictates of segmented urban districts and changing architectural tastes.

The need for a monumental, stylish, and prominently situated church building required a savvy building committee. As in the case of the Lutherans, taste, not construction expertise, was sought. The Episcopalians, now led by the Rev. Charles Seymour, determined that the most useful building committee would be formed of genteel gentlemen: law-

yers, a bank president, and a successful merchant. All but one of these wealthy and influential men lived on the elite courthouse square that was bordered by West Church Street. By selecting a lot on Church Street facing the courthouse, the vestrymen both elevated the stature of the church and ensured the Anglo-American stamp on the public square.

The new minister introduced the idea of using a well-known New York architect whom he had learned of while serving in Brooklyn. Richard Upjohn subsequently designed the brick, Gothic, five-hundred-person-capacity church with a soaring spire. The parish's choice of the Gothic style and of Upjohn reflected pressures from above as well as below (fig. 5.7). Maryland's Bishop Wittingham championed high-church architectural reforms under the rubric of the American Ecclesiological Society. In 1852 the society had placed Upjohn on its list of approved architects, and Upjohn was working on St. Paul's Church in nearby Baltimore during the same period.[35]

Next, the Presbyterians found their situation wanting. A smaller congregation with fewer members and less influential leaders in town affairs, their remodeling efforts paled but were not insignificant. During the 1820s, the congregation had built a new church on West Second Street, moving several blocks closer to the Church Street axis

Fig. 5.9. Presbyterian Church, Remodeled 1858, Charles Haller, Architect. The city's master builder designed the fashionable "Gothick" facade.

Fig. 5.10. Asbury Methodist Church, Remodeled 1851, William Bennett, Architect. African-American congregations also refashioned their churches during this period of intense rebuilding. (From Asbury Methodist Episcopal Church, "104th Anniversary," pamphlet, Frederick, 1922).

and facing the back of its affiliated Frederick Academy on the courthouse square. Now, thirty years later, this church, too, had fallen from grace (fig. 5.8). The two-step gable facade was common in vernacular Frederick, but by 1858 even this highly embellished version with columns *in antis* designed by a Presbyterian-affiliated builder was out of style. Neither moving nor hiring a famous architect, the Presbyterians found a less expensive way to maximize their visibility and keep up with current taste. The congregation selected the most experienced local builder, Charles Haller, who had constructed the stylish new Evangelical Reformed and Episcopalian churches, to bring the church up to contemporary fashionable standards. Haller extended the church ten feet toward the sidewalk and designed a vestry-ordered "Gothick" facade. The extension plan and the stuccoed facade's decorative Lombard arches echoed the Lutheran church, although any steeple was notably missing (fig. 5.9).[36]

The Catholics in Frederick stood culturally and geographically apart from the rest of the city. Their church, convent school, literary academy, and Jesuit novitiate formed a small enclave at the eastern end of Second Street. Yet, even the Catholics,

who had completed an impressive neoclassical church during the 1830s, succumbed in 1854 to the remodeling fever. The local Catholic builder, John Tehan, added a 170-foot steeple to the church whose initial design had been meticulously worked out by the local priest and his Jesuit superiors at Georgetown.[37]

In sharp contrast, African-American churches remained on the periphery, noticeably not part of prestigious Church Street. By mid-century, All Saints Street was clearly of secondary status. The Episcopalians had deserted the street forty years earlier, and it now contained the African-American Asbury Methodist Church, some decrepit housing, a foundry, a railroad line, and an abandoned Baptist church.[38] Only blacks, poor whites, and immigrants lived in the area. African-American congregations did, however, share the mood for remodeling. In 1851 the Asbury Methodist congregation hired a white carpenter to add twenty feet to their one-story, brick, gable-roofed church of 1818 (fig. 5.10). Four years later the same carpenter rebuilt the Bethel African Methodist Episcopal Church on East Third Street. Perhaps its membership tapped into neighboring Shab Row, a neighborhood that included property-owning, free African Americans.[39] Stylistically and geographically, the two-story Bethel church came closer to white architectural experiments, particularly in 1876 when the congregation again remodeled the facade to display a truncated tower and lancet windows.

Low income and low status did not exclude African Americans from participating in the city-wide trend to refashion churches. A similar pattern of rebuilding occurred in Baltimore, where black congregations relocated and remodeled their churches concurrently with white congregations' construction campaigns.[40] Engelbrecht believed that the black assemblies were equally as interested in image as were the white congregations. His remark regarding the Bethel church consecration—"the Darkies did flock into town to see the fashions. . . . It is a handsome edifice"—mirrors his own motivations for visiting Baltimore.[41] Fashion and the city were closely entwined.

The church-building crusades in Frederick illustrate one process by which residents created a recognizably urban cityscape. Urbanization was not simply the quest for style; it was also the process of classifying and sorting city space into social and functional zones. The relocation of churches during the 1840s and 1850s shows the inexorable pull of Church Street as the most desirable and prestigious address. Whereas in 1810 the churches were scattered across town in undifferentiated neighborhoods, by mid-century they were concentrated along a clear axis. The impressive churches on Second and Church Streets enhanced the city's finest homes and public institutions (figs. 5.11 and 5.12).

The architectural style of Frederick's new churches reveals the way residents linked the concepts of urban and urbane. Part of a city's flair came from

Fig. 5.11. Location of White Congregations, ca. 1810. (Kai Gutschow.)

its panoply of the latest fashions. Frederick residents sought a modern and polished appearance for their cityscape; to do so, they built stylish edifices and consciously avoided provincial intimations. The Greek Revival, Italianate, and Gothic Revival facades proclaimed the congregations' awareness and appreciation of national and big-city architectural developments. The churches' freestanding position within their lots ensured that the monumental message would not be lost.

The construction of towers and steeples demonstrates that congregations vied to dominate not just the streetscape but the skyline as well. The "two commanding towers" of the Evangelical Reformed Church doubled the effect of their original church's single spire. The Lutherans' "two-steeple church" outshone the shorter towers of the Evangelical Reformed Church. The clear vista across the courthouse square accentuated the Episcopalians' single soaring steeple. The Catholics embellished their rising steeple with a large, gilded orb. Con-

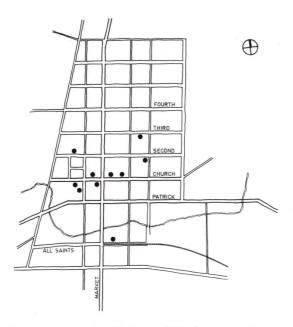

Fig. 5.12. Location of White and Black Congregations, ca. 1856. This map shows the magnetic axis of Church Street. (Kai Gutschow.)

gregations also competed in audible ways: they took great interest in comparing the size, number, and sound of the bells in their steeples. In contrast and reflecting their lowly status, neither the black congregations nor the smaller white congregations contended in the skyline.[42]

While each church steeple may have been a single competitive act of staking out a prominent position, collectively they cooperated in creating a key element of a cityscape—an urban skyline. A city needed tall landmarks to anchor its very identity as an urban place. Tall structures implied a city, a point understood by the townspeople as well as by the poet Whittier and the lithographer Sachse who depicted Frederick.[43] In Whittier's poem "Barbara Frietchie," the "clustered spires" defined the city. In the lithograph, the subject was not the scene *from* the steeples, but *of* the steeples. The point of view is telling; a view from the steeples would have revealed only a low, small

town with few notable buildings; a bird's-eye view of the steeples publicized Frederick's lofty architecture and status.

A skyline not only indicated a city below, but also suggested the type of cultural values that predominated. Although Frederick had other tall buildings, neither the lithograph nor the numerous accounts of Frederick paid much attention to the tower above the combination market house-city hall or the smokestacks of the edge-of-town foundries. As the architectural historian Spiro Kostof insisted, a city's skyline celebrated the "buildings of communal importance" to its citizens.[44] The fact that Frederick's dominant buildings were its churches continued the preindustrial tradition of devoting architectural resources to religious buildings. Moreover, it reflected the underpinning of religion in everyday life, as well as the power of the churches and church leaders to assert their presence in a secular landscape.

The church-building rivalries indicate a changing sensibility toward design, a sensibility that had repercussions on the design process itself. In order to meet the competitive challenge, even the lesser congregations had to extend their architectural horizons. This objective required a forceful minister, a sophisticated building committee, and hearty financial support from the majority of the congregation.[45] Traditionally, the congregations favored their own members when awarding building contracts. The Evangelical Reformed congregation was the first to break out of this pattern by hiring a Baltimore architect. The heightened architectural expectations of the Lutherans led them haltingly to realize that they too must look outside the congregation and the city for an even more inspiring designer. For the Episcopalians, high-church and local building practices impelled the congregation to reach for a nationally famous architect. To achieve the maximum visibility for the minimum cost, the poorer Presbyterians shrewdly hired the builder who had supervised the other church projects. Thus, the building crusades forced a shift in customary hiring and design practices. By looking outside the community and tradition, the residents stepped over the vernacular threshold.

By mid-century Frederick's churches reflected local interpretations of national trends in urban building and design. Frederick's small scale immediately distinguished it from a major metropolis, but its cityscape showed how urban patterns could be adapted to a reduced scale. Districts or zones were demarcated; they were simply fewer, smaller, and closer together. The new architectural styles knew no borders: All Saints church could have stood in any city or town, but no inconsequential town would have held Frederick's variety or enjoyed its urban silhouette. Frederick's churches helped establish the city's own distinct urban iconography: the clustered spires rang out the presence of a city below.

Notes

1. Frederick officially adopted "the clustered spires" as its city seal in 1979; the motif had previously been used in 1945 as the emblem for the city's bicentennial. I thank F. P. Rothenhoefer for bringing this to my attention. I would also like to thank Dell Upton and Kai Gutschow for their insights and comments regarding this manuscript.

2. U.S. Bureau of the Census, *Historical Statistics of the United States: Colonial Times to 1970,* pt. 1 (Washington: Dept. of Commerce, 1975), 12.

3. Several of the most useful small-city studies partially address spatial and architectural relationships, although they focus primarily on the social life and institutions of cities. See, for example, Michael H. Frisch, *Town into City: Springfield, Massachusetts, and the Meaning of Community, 1840–1880* (Cambridge, Mass.: Harvard University Press, 1972); Stuart M. Blumin, *The Urban Threshold: Growth and Change in a Nineteenth-Century American Community* (Chicago: University of Chicago Press, 1976); and Richard C. Wade, *The Urban Frontier: The Rise of Western Cities, 1790–1830* (Cambridge, Mass.: Harvard University Press, 1971). The geographer Michael Conzen addresses small-city form in morphological terms, listing nine physical patterns that can be expected in nineteenth-century American cities. See Michael P. Conzen, "The Morphology of 19th-century Cities in the United States," in *Urbanization in the Americas,* ed. Woodrow Borah et al. (Ottawa: History Division, National Museum of Man, 1980): 119–41.

4. Adna Ferrin Weber, *The Growth of Cities in the Nineteenth Century: A Study in Statistics* [1899] (Ithaca: Cornell University Press, 1963), 39, 40.

5. Fischer erroneously printed that there were seventeen churches. The more likely number is eleven, a number that includes both affiliated church buildings as well as defunct congregations' churches. Richard S. Fischer, *A New and Complete Statistical Gazetteer of the United States of America* (New York: J. H. Colton, 1853), 232.

6. Jacob Engelbrecht, "Building Journal," nineteenth-century ms. in Frederick County Historical Society, Frederick, Md., and Jacob Engelbrecht, *Diary, 1818–1878,* 3 vols., ed. William Quynn (Frederick: Frederick County Historical Society, 1976).

7. There were 2,606 residents in 1798 and 8,054 in 1860. "A Sketch of Frederick County," *The Key,* Feb. 17, 1798, and Engelbrecht, *Diary,* 3: 78 [Oct. 3, 1860].

8. "The New German Reformed Church," *The German Reformed Messenger,* June 8, 1850.

9. The drive to fashion a city that both functioned and looked like a city accelerated during the 1840s and 1850s, as witnessed by the dramatic changes in the urban fabric. Specialized districts became demarcated: commerce

proliferated on the intersecting major through roads of Patrick and Market Streets; manufacturing developed along Carroll Creek and the Baltimore and Ohio Railroad lines; a reservoir and rural cemetery ringed the city edge with parks; and elite residences and institutions extended from the courthouse square along Church Street. New buildings types with stylized facades reiterated the status of the districts: expansive public hotels, the new fire stations, and the Greek Revival female seminary were fashionable pieces of public architecture set in counterpoint to the productive smokestacks of the forges and utilitarian tanning vats.

10. There was a total of 36,405 white and black residents in the county and accommodations for 36,600 persons in the churches. J. D. B. DeBow, *Statistical View of the United States* (Washington: A. O. P. Nicholson, 1854), 248–49.

11. "Consecration of the New German Reformed Church," *German Reformed Messenger,* June 19, 1850.

12. Ibid.

13. It is notable that the lithograph did not overtly celebrate the commercial side of the market town, but chose instead to emphasize religious and civic aspects. No individual businesses were highlighted at all. This is in contrast to many other urban lithographs that celebrated commercial culture. For a New York example, see Hans Bergmann, "Panoramas of New York, 1845–1860," in *Prospects: An Annual of American Cultural Studies,* ed. Jack Salzman (New York: Cambridge University Press, 1985), 129.

14. Sherry H. Olson, *Baltimore: The Building of an American City* (Baltimore: Johns Hopkins University Press, 1980), 126.

15. Daniel Bluestone, *Constructing Chicago* (New Haven: Yale University Press, 1991), 65–68. Frisch, *Town into City,* 145–49. Some examples of church districts depicted in lithographs can be found in Colorado Springs, Colorado (1874), Omaha, Nebraska (1868), Salem, Oregon (1876), and Carson City, Nevada (1876). The lithographs are reproduced in John Reps, *Cities of the American West: A History of Frontier Urban Planning* (Princeton: Princeton University Press, 1979).

16. Frederick's regional importance, though not its interregional contacts, diminished around 1850. When the B&O Railroad reached Frederick in 1831, it was the terminus of the only forty-mile stretch of track in the United States. By 1850, Frederick's elevated status as a railroad terminal had evaporated—8,571 miles of track crisscrossed the country; by 1860 the number had skyrocketed to 29,920 miles. See Weber, *The Growth of Cities,* 25.

17. Engelbrecht, *Diary,* 2: 8 [May 12, 1832].

18. Frederick County Levy Court, *Proceedings 1828–1838,* Maryland Hall of Records, Annapolis. Minutes of the Frederick Common Council, Apr. 20, 1844, Oct. 12, 1844, Feb. 12, 1845. Board Minutes of Mount Olivet Cemetery, Jan. 19, 1853, Apr. 19, 1853, Aug. 1, 1853.

19. Dorothea Harris, "Early History of Calvary Methodist Church," Frederick Calvary Methodist Church "Church Bulletins," no. 28–31, quoting Edward Buckey's nineteenth-century memoirs.

20. Susannah Catherine Thomas Markell, *Short Stories of Life in Frederick in 1830* (n.p: n.p., n.d. [transcript by descendent in Frederick County Historical Society]), 37–39. The option to remodel the existing church was not taken, despite the structure's essentially sound condition. The Masons used the church as a meeting hall before selling it to a Methodist organization in 1859.

21. The style was similar to that of a number of Methodist churches found across the East and Midwest at the time. For Maryland examples, see Robert Neill, *Chestertown, Maryland: An Inventory of Historic Sites* (Chestertown: Town of Chestertown, 1981), 25; Joe Getty, *Uniontown, Maryland: A Walking Tour* (Manchester, Md.: Noodle-Doosey Press, 1983), 32; and Harris, "Calvary Methodist Early History," Church Bulletin no. 29. Other examples farther afield include the 1827 Methodist Church in Portsmouth, New Hampshire, and the 1840 Loutre Island Methodist Church outside St. Louis.

22. Daniel Zacharias, *A Centenary Sermon* (Frederick: Turner & Young, 1847), 41.

23. The church and its 1807 spire are in good condition today, and the church is still used by the Evangelical Reformed congregation as the Trinity Chapel.

24. The English-speaking congregation found it particularly fitting that the old church be used by German-speaking *Einwanderer* (immigrants) from the old country. "Church at Frederick City, Maryland," *German Reformed Messenger,* June 26, 1850.

25. Ibid.

26. "Church at Frederick City, Maryland," *German Reformed Messenger,* June 26,1850.

27. Engelbrecht, *Diary,* 2: 498 [June 27, 1850].

28. Lutheran Church Council Minutes, Apr. 29, 1852, Sept. 19, 1853, Sept. 23, 1853, Wentz Library, Lutheran Theological Seminary, Gettysburg, Pennsylvania.

29. Lutheran Church Council Minutes, Mar. 12, 1854, Apr. 4, 1854, Apr. 20, 1854, June 1, 1854.

30. Lutheran Church Council Minutes, Sept. 4, 1825, Mar. 17, 1845, June 6, 1850. Abdel R. Wentz, *History of the Evangelical Lutheran Church of Frederick, Maryland, 1738–1938* (Harrisburg: Evangelical Press, 1938). Niernsee Papers, Maryland Historical Society, Baltimore.

31. Wentz, *Lutheran Church,* 232.

32. Engelbrecht, *Diary,* 2: 651 [24 May 1855].

33. All Saints Parish, *Vestry Minutes,* 1: 1, 1: 12, 1: 18, Maryland Hall of Records, Annapolis. Ernest Helfenstein, *History of All Saints Parish in Frederick County, Maryland, 1742–1932* (Frederick: Marken & Bielfeld, 1932), 16–17, 38.

34. Engelbrecht, *Diary,* 2: 572 [Feb. 4, 1853]. The church still stands today and is used by the Episcopalians as a church hall.

35. Richard Upjohn letter to the Vestry of All Saints Parish, Jan. 23, 1854, All Saints Parish, *Vestry Minutes,* 2: 19. Phoebe Stanton, *The Gothic Revival and American Church Architecture: An Episode in Taste 1840–1856* (Baltimore: Johns Hopkins University Press, 1968), 185, 298.

36. The Rev. James Hammer recorded his impressions during the 1830s. See James Hammer, "An Early Historical Sketch, 1780–1831," quoted in Mary Keeler and Barbara Batdorf, *The Frederick United Presbyterian Church* (Frederick: Bicentennial Committee, 1980), 33. Freeman Dixon, *Historical Sketch of Frederick Presbyterian Church* (Frederick: n.p., 1905), 6. Engelbrecht, *Diary,* 1: 517 [Nov. 9, 1828], 3: 43 [Nov. 7, 1859]. Engelbrecht, "Building Journal," Sept. 30, 1858. J. F. Minor Simpson, *Monocacy Valley Maryland Presbyterianism: A History* (Frederick: Great Southern Mfg. & Ptg. Co., 1955), 37.

37. Letter from Peter Kenney to John McElroy, Nov. 12, 1832. Georgetown University Archives, Washington, D.C. See also Engelbrecht, *Diary,* 2: 692 [Sept. 20, 1854], 2: 631 [Oct. 7, 1854].

38. The Baptist Church on W. All Saints Street, built in 1773, declined in the nineteenth century. By 1821 the pulpit was vacant, and in 1823 Engelbrecht could only think of four Baptists in town who worshiped in "a very little church." The hipped-roof edifice remained unaltered and unused until after the Civil War, when it became a black congregation's church. Engelbrecht, *Diary,* 1: 55 [Apr. 7, 1821], 1: 245 [Oct. 20, 1823].

39. Nina Hammond Clarke, *History of the 19th-Century Black Churches in Maryland and Washington, D.C.* (New York: Vantage Press, 1983), 195–197, 22–25. Engelbrecht, *Diary,* 2: 508 [Feb. 3, 1851], 2: 651 [May 24, 1855], 2: 659 [Aug. 13, 1855].

40. Olson, *Baltimore,* 126–27.

41. Engelbrecht, *Diary,* 2: 659 [Aug. 13, 1855].

42. "Consecration," *German Reformed Messenger,* June 19, 1850. Engelbrecht, *Diary,* 2: 651 [May 24, 1855], 2: 669 [Jan. 3, 1856].

43. The importance of vertical landmarks and city identity as depicted in artistic and literary urban panoramas are discussed in Bergmann, "Panoramas," *Prospects,* 126.

44. Spiro Kostof, *The City Shaped: Urban Patterns and Meanings Through History* (London: Thames and Hudson, 1991), 282. Another useful discussion of the cultural relevance of skylines is found in Wayne Attoe, "Skylines as Social Indexes," in *Skylines: Understanding and Molding Urban Silhouettes* (New York: John Wiley, 1981), 28–41.

45. The cost of these new edifices was significant; cost totals excluded donations of materials or objects and the proceeds from ladies' church fairs. Approximate costs were as follows: the Evangelical Reformed church, twenty-four thousand dollars; the Lutheran church, twenty-five thousand dollars; the All Saints church, twenty-three thousand dollars; the Presbyterian church, twenty-eight hundred dollars; and the Asbury Methodist church, nine hundred dollars. John Thomas Scharf, *The History of Western Maryland* (Philadelphia: L. H. Everts, 1882), 510, 512, 508, 516. Engelbrecht, *Diary,* 2: 508 [Feb. 3, 1851].

Chapter 6

"A School House Well Arranged": Baltimore Public School Buildings on the Lancasterian Plan, 1829–1839

Peter E. Kurtze

For nearly a century after Baltimore Town was platted in 1730, the growing city lacked a plan for public education. In 1828, the city council passed an ordinance creating a Board of School Commissioners to develop and oversee a system of public schools. Shortly thereafter, city educators began experimenting with a succession of architectural forms in a continuing search for the ideal "school house well arranged." The school commissioners articulated this quest in 1843: "A school house well arranged, having sufficient light, well ventilated and properly heated in cold weather, with good order reigning within its walls, has great influence not only over the social but also the moral sentiments of the scholars: it gives character to the people who have such institutions among them."[1] When the commissioners expressed this concept of the social and moral consequences of efficient school architecture, the public school system was barely fifteen years old; yet, the administrators had already tried and abandoned an entire system of instruction and its associated architectural form. While no structure of the earlier period survives, documentary evidence enables us to trace the early developments in public school architecture that took place in response to changing pedagogical methods.

The first public school in Baltimore opened in September 1829; by December of that year, a total of three schools had opened, serving 269 pupils.[2] These first schools were conducted according to the monitorial system of instruction championed by English educator Joseph Lancaster. A self-styled "patron of education and friend of the poor," Lancaster claimed credit for developing the system in 1798 in response to the educational needs of the urban poor in his native London.[3] In his method, classes of four hundred or more pupils of varying ages were taught by a single principal instructor who was assisted by monitors selected from among the older pupils. Other pedagogical schemes of the day limited the number of pupils per teacher to a far lower figure and could not approach the economy and efficiency that the Lancasterian plan promised. Through his tireless promotion, and often with the help of influential patrons, Lancaster's method spread quickly from Great Britain and Ireland to the Continent and beyond. In Europe, it was applied to the education of both children and adults and was employed to teach the Russian and French armies to read and write.[4] At the same time, the system caught the attention of school administrators charged with setting up new public school programs in rapidly-growing American cities. Lancaster crossed the Atlantic and helped establish three of the nation's first public school programs in New York, Philadelphia, and Washington, D.C. He settled briefly in Baltimore, where he opened his "Lancasterian Institute" to instruct prospective teachers in his methods, before setting sail to carry the good news to South America. The economical method also appealed to educators in smaller cities and towns, such as Albany, New York, Cincinnati, Ohio, and Frederick, Maryland, to cite a few of many examples. It was used in private as well as public schools, and it was applied to children whose parents could afford tuition fees as well as to the children of the poor.

In the Lancasterian curriculum, several hundred pupils occupied a single large room. The master sat at one end of the room with a student called a "monitor of order" or "monitor general" on each side to assist him in observing the proceedings. The pupils sat facing the master at long common desks, each of which held as many as ten pupils. Each desk made up a class; at its head was the class monitor, an older child who was responsible for distributing supplies, hearing recitations, and maintaining order. Recitation formed the basis of the instructional system: the monitors would read lessons or present questions to the class, hear their responses, and offer corrections. Recitations occurred repeatedly at specified intervals during the school day, when the monitors would lead their classes from their desks to form semicircles in the aisles for this purpose (fig. 6.1).

The fundamental architectural requirement of the Lancasterian method was a sizable open room capable of seating a large number of pupils. Many schools were opened in pre-existing buildings that were not designed to suit the program, with disappointing results: the rooms were too small, had poor ventilation or acoustics, or did not afford the master a constant, unobstructed view of his charges. Advocates of the system stressed the importance of constructing school buildings specifically adapted to the monitorial plan.[5]

The ideal Lancasterian school building, described by Joseph Lancaster in one of his numerous promotional booklets,[6] was a gable-roofed structure, rectangular in plan, with a five-to-three ratio of length to width (fig. 6.2). The schoolroom should be located on the ground floor. Flat ceilings were to be avoided, as they tended to act as sounding boards; open rafters were preferred. Alternatively, Lancaster suggested that the ceiling might be placed

Fig. 6.1. Idealized Interior View of Lancasterian School. This illustration shows classes of pupils standing in semicircles in the outer aisle, receiving instruction from monitors. The portrait that appears below the motto "the patron of education and friend of the poor" is presumed to represent Joseph Lancaster. (From [Joseph Lancaster,] *The British System of Education: Being a complete epitome of the improvements and inventions practised by Joseph Lancaster* . . . [Washington: William Cooper, 1812], plate 4.)

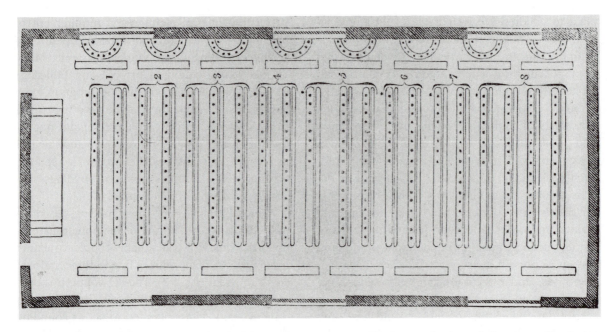

Fig. 6.2. Model Floor Plan of Lancasterian School. The dots represent pupils seated at long desks or standing in semicircles for recitation. The elevated platform for the master's desk appears at the left. (From [Joseph Lancaster,] *The British System of Education: Being a complete epitome of the improvements and inventions practised by Joseph Lancaster* . . . [Washington: William Cooper, 1812], plate 2.)

at the level of the collars rather than at the level of the plate. To reduce the reverberation of sound, the ceiling should not be smoothly plastered, but only "rough cast and lime whited."[7] Walls should range from twelve to eighteen feet in height; as with ceilings, wall finish was affected by acoustical considerations and ideally consisted of plaster applied to brick.[8] The room was to be lighted by horizontally pivoting double casement windows, positioned about six feet above the floor. At the end where the master's desk was located, two entry doors were to be placed, either in the gable wall or in the side walls in a line with the master's desk. Another door in the opposite gable end provided access to the playground and increased air circulation. Ventilation was assisted by windows in the gable ends and ventilators in the roof and at the top of the walls; Lancaster even advocated the erection of a twenty- or thirty-foot mast on the

roof to support a canvas tube, or "windsail," to catch summer breezes. Heating systems had to function with safety and economy. For schoolrooms located on the ground floor, Lancaster suggested a system of underground flues, heated by a stove burning cheap coal.

The most characteristic aspect of the Lancasterian schoolroom was its sloping floor, with the master's desk located on a platform at the lower end, and the pupils' desks rising at an increasing pitch away from it—six inches in the first twenty feet and a one-foot rise to each twenty-foot length thereafter. This arrangement gave the schoolmaster a constant view of every pupil. In rooms not constructed for the purpose, Lancaster granted that part of the effect of the inclined floor could be achieved by further elevating the master's platform and progressively increasing the height of the desks.[9] The floor was preferably paved with brick, for sound-proofing as well as to withstand the daily wear of hundreds of feet as the pupils filed back and forth.

The long pupils' desks had slanted tops, and were arranged in one or two rows facing the master's platform. Desks and benches were firmly fixed to the floor; seats were slanted forward to keep the pupils sitting upright, and corners were rounded to prevent injury as the pupils moved in and out. The width of the aisles was calculated to permit movement associated with the daily routine without wasting space.

The Baltimore school commissioners had neither the budget nor the time necessary to construct new buildings to house the first public schools, so these schools were initially organized in rented quarters. Accommodations included dwelling houses, a church basement, and rooms above a fire-engine house and a "watch house," or police station. These makeshift lodgings soon proved ill-suited for school facilities. Even when the rooms were large enough to serve the purpose, other drawbacks prevailed. A narrow and steep flight of steps led up to the room over the engine house where the first male school was held, and the location of this building in the center of a busy commercial area was inconvenient. The girls in Miss Miles' schoolroom on the second floor of the watch house were disturbed by exposure to the drunken and disorderly persons who were incarcerated downstairs and by the frequent ringing of the alarm bell.[10]

Such problems, the commissioners reasoned, would not beset a schoolhouse constructed for the purpose, sited in a favorable location, and specifically designed to accommodate the Lancasterian system. They determined to construct such a model building as an experiment that would demonstrate the benefits of the monitorial plan both to parents and to a skeptical city council. Its success would encourage citizens to support the public school system; as demand for public education increased, the nominal tuition rate of one dollar per quarter year would render the system self-supporting.[11]

This effort produced Male School No. 3, the first building in Baltimore constructed to house a public school, which was erected in 1830 (fig. 6.3). The commissioners presented a detailed description of the interior of this structure in their annual report; this evidence, in combination with contemporary renderings of its exterior, shows that the building's configuration corresponded in most respects to Lancaster's paradigm.[12] Designed by Baltimore architect William F. Small, Male School No. 3 was rectangular in plan, forty-five feet wide by seventy-five feet deep, and stood one story in height. Its interior suited the requirements of the Lancasterian system: the single large room had a sloping floor, with the master's desk on a platform at the low end. A general monitor sat at either side of the principal's platform. Two rows of twenty common desks, each seating nine pupils, flanked a center aisle; rather than benches, individual seats were provided for greater ease of movement. A slightly raised desk for the class monitor was set perpendicular to each common desk and had a hinged lid for storing supplies. Large windows and roof ventilators admitted light and air; the windows in this building were probably sash, rather than the casements Lancaster recommended. An entrance was located in each side wall at either side of the master's platform and was provided with a small recess or bulkhead; another entrance was centered in the far gable. The commissioners differed with Lancaster on the issue of gable windows, contending "it is better to have no windows at either end."[13] The room was enclosed in a Greek Revival exterior, which the commissioners judged "produces a pleasing effect, by the harmony and sobriety of its colouring, and the just proportion of its parts."[14]

A total of four public school buildings were built to accommodate the Lancasterian system in Baltimore in the early 1830s. The lessons learned through the "experiment" with Male School No. 3 were incorporated into the design of its successors. School No. 4 illustrates the "second genera-

Fig. 6.3. Public School No. 3, Erected 1830. (From a photograph of a watercolor rendering attributed to John H. B. Latrobe in the collection of the Enoch Pratt Free Library, Baltimore, Maryland. Location of original unknown.)

Fig. 6.4. Public School No. 4, Erected 1834. (From an undated photograph in the collection of the Enoch Pratt Free Library, Baltimore, Maryland.)

tion" of Lancasterian schoolhouses in Baltimore (fig. 6.4). These buildings featured a raised basement, which provided accommodations for the female department. This arrangement offered greater economy by allowing a single structure to serve both schools while maintaining strict segregation of the sexes. The commissioners also hoped that what they termed "a rustic basement of considerable height" would help protect the new buildings from such vandalism as had already been wrought upon the chaste exterior of Male School No. 3. They also reconsidered their objection to gable windows and employed four-part casements in at least one of the new buildings.[15] By 1834, Male and Female Schools 1, 2, and 4 had moved into new buildings incorporating these innovations and refinements.[16] Female School No. 3 continued to be held in a remodeled dwelling house.

Lancaster would not tolerate idleness and inattention, which he felt competing pedagogical systems encouraged. His plan was calculated to foster what he once referred to as "the loveliness of order;"[17] with hundreds of pupils in a single room, this was as much a practical necessity as a philo-

sophical goal. Both classroom routine and architectural space were consciously arranged to help control the pupils' behavior.

The class monitors were crucial to the system. While they played a role in the didactic scheme, their primary responsibility was to maintain order. Lancaster explained that "[t]he duty of a monitor . . . [relates] first to order, as it would be of no service to hundreds of children assembled to receive instruction, in the most efficient modes, were it not possible to keep them in order."[18]

The curriculum prescribed specific commands and procedures to control the performance of mundane activities and tasks. For example, Lancaster specified a routine for removing caps, which were doffed on command and kept slung on the pupils' backs. By this means, Lancaster observed, "Every pupil keeps his hat in his own possession, and if he loses it the fault is his own."[19] Another drill kept strict account of slate pencils, so that "if one is lost, broken or mislaid, immediate detection and inquiry follows."[20] Upon dismissal, boys were directed to hold their hands behind them as they went home, as a "preventative to mischief."[21]

The architectural elements of Lancasterian school buildings likewise were designed to foster orderly conduct. The elevated platform and inclined floor, as we have seen, were intended to help the master keep his charges in sight. Desks faced the front of the room, so that, in Lancaster's words, "every pupil will face his master, and thus be conscious of constant superintendance."[22] He went on to observe that "these arrangements not only conduce to order, but, by impressing each child with a conviction, that he is under the master's eye, render him careful to avoid doing any thing in which he would not wish to be seen. The certainty of detection prevents offences. . . ."[23]

Other architectural inducements to order were somewhat subtler. Illustrations of Lancasterian school interiors show semicircles marked out on the floors of the aisles to define recitation areas. Lancaster's recommended window heights, he explained, were calculated to "be just high enough to prevent the pupils easily looking out."[24] The children's comfort was provided for, insofar as it helped avoid disruption; efficient heating systems, for example, helped keep pupils in their seats by eliminating the need for them to get up and go to the stove when they became chilled.[25]

The Lancasterian system was controversial in Baltimore virtually from its inception. While the method found staunch support among the commissioners, the public—and, indeed, some teachers—objected to what they called its "mechanical methods and unprofitable manoeuvres . . . [and] very limited range of instruction."[26] The prescribed curriculum was modified to incorporate elements of alternative programs as early as 1829,[27] and the master of Male School No. 1 began lobbying the commissioners to scrap the monitorial plan in 1836.[28]

The means employed to control large numbers of children contributed to public dissatisfaction with the program. Parents of students selected to serve as monitors felt that those duties interfered with their children's own education;[29] other parents raised charges of inappropriate corporal punishment, which the school administrators perhaps too vehemently denied.[30] These factors ultimately led to the abandonment of the Lancasterian system in Baltimore only ten years after its introduction.

The monitorial plan was replaced in 1839 by the so-called "simultaneous" method of instruction, in which age-graded classes of only one hundred pupils were instructed by adult teachers hired to assist the principal. The advent of a new system of instruction rendered obsolete the early school buildings with their large open rooms, as the new program required separate recitation rooms for smaller groups. In short order, partitions were installed in the open interiors of the existing school buildings to adapt them to the new instructional method. The commissioners passed a resolution in January 1840 to divide the interior of Male School No. 3 "by a Board partition so as [to] afford a convenient room at the East end for the accommodation of the youngest Scholars, by which means the duties of the school can be progressing under the principal & assistant Teachers, at the same Time, without interrupting each other."[31]

Three months later, the commissioners had evaluated the effect of this alteration and pronounced "the experiment . . . well calculated to advance the interests of Public School instruction."[32] In July 1840, they authorized the installation of similar partitions in the rest of the city's school buildings to prepare them for the fall semester.[33]

At the same time that the commissioners were adapting the early schoolhouses to the new curriculum, they began planning for their successors. No new school buildings had been erected in Baltimore for six years, and the commissioners sought to incorporate the latest innovations in the next structure, to be known as School No. 5. Hoping to profit from the experience of other cities, they accepted the offer of one of Baltimore's pre-eminent architects, Robert Cary Long Jr., "to procure information of the best Plan of constructing School Houses while on his visit to Philadelphia."[34] In

March 1840, Long returned a letter with notes and a sketch.[35] This information was referred to the committee that was planning School No. 5. Completed in October 1840, this was the first building constructed to suit the new curriculum. No record of its appearance survives, but the commissioners' description permits a schematic reconstruction of its plan, which marked a radical change from its predecessors. It was a two-story building, measuring sixty-five feet wide by forty-three feet deep, and had two rooms on each floor separated by a central passage. Each room was furnished with a blackboard, rostrum, and forty-eight desks seating two pupils each.[36] The interior layout of School No. 5 became the prototype for primary school buildings of the 1840s. School No. 5 differed from the earlier buildings on the exterior as well, expressing what the school commissioners called the "Quaker" style,[37] perhaps acknowledging its derivation from a Philadelphia model.

These changes were rewarded by sharply increasing enrollment. From a total of 675 pupils in 1838, the enrollment in the primary schools leaped to 1,080 in 1839 and to 1,771 the following year, reflecting the public acceptance of the new system of instruction.

The transition from large, open spaces to smaller classrooms separated by solid walls thus corresponded to a fundamental shift in the system of instruction. Although the commissioners continued to pursue their quest for the ideal "school house well arranged" into the twentieth century, subsequent developments in Baltimore school buildings were evolutionary responses to curriculum refinements or technological innovations. The architectural revolution incited by the abandonment of the Lancasterian plan would not see its counterpart until the 1920s, when national movements for educational reform led to a comprehensive program for the construction of new school buildings in the city.

Notes

1. Annual Report of the Board of School Commissioners to the Mayor and Council of Baltimore, 1843, 65 (hereafter cited as *Commissioners*).

2. Vernon S. Vavrina, "The History of Public Education in the City of Baltimore, 1829–1956," (Ph.D. diss., Catholic University, 1958), 27; Robert L. Alexander, "William F. Small, 'Architect of the City'," *Journal of the Society of Architectural Historians,* 20 (2) (May 1961): 66.

3. Joseph Lancaster, *The Lancasterian System of Education, with improvements, by its founder, Joseph Lancaster, of the Lancasterian Institute, Baltimore* (Baltimore: Author, 1821); *Epitome of some of the chief events in the life of J. Lancaster containing an account of the rise & progress of the Lancasterian system* (New Haven: n.p., 1833).

4. Letter, Benjamin Shaw to Roberts Vaux, Nov. 27, 1818, Vaux Papers, Historical Society of Pennsylvania, Philadelphia.

5. Benjamin Shaw, a member of the board of directors of the Philadelphia Public Schools who had been involved in the propagation of the Lancasterian plan in Europe, counseled his associates, "Unless . . . you build, expressly for the purpose, you will fail in the outset, the superstructure not having a firm foundation, will fall into ruins, and the prospect, commencing with a view of future advantage, will end in disappointment and evil" (Letter, Benjamin Shaw to the Controllers of the Public Schools, Apr. 16, 1818, Vaux Papers).

6. The following description of the ideal Lancasterian school building is derived from *Lancasterian System . . . ,* 1–4.

7. *Lancasterian System . . . ,* 2.

8. Letter, Benjamin Shaw to Roberts Vaux, Aug. 4, 1818, Vaux Papers.

9. *Lancasterian System . . . ,* 5.

10. *Commissioners,* 1832, 4.

11. Ibid., 1829, 60–61; 1830, 68.

12. The following description of Male School No. 3 is derived from *Commissioners,* 1831, 5–6.

13. Ibid., 6.

14. Ibid., 1830, 66.

15. Ibid., 1831, 6.

16. Ibid., 1834, 4.

17. Letter, Joseph Lancaster to Roberts Vaux, Feb. 18, 1819, Vaux Papers.

18. *Lancasterian System . . . ,* 7.

19. Ibid., 27.

20. Ibid., 29.

21. Ibid.

22. Ibid., 1.

23. Ibid.

24. Ibid., 2.

25. Ibid.

26. *Commissioners,* 1838, 38.

27. Ibid., 1829, 67.

28. Ibid., 1836, 3; Minutes, Board of School Commissioners, Sept. 28, 1837 (Baltimore City Archives; hereafter cited as *Minutes*).

29. *Commissioners,* 1831, 14–16.

30. The commissioners wrestled with the issue of corporal punishment throughout the period during which they adhered to the Lancasterian system; denials of the practice, and motions to consider its prohibition, occur repeatedly in their reports and minutes. See, for example, *Minutes,* Mar. 25, 1836.

31. Ibid., Jan. 13, 1840.

32. Ibid., Apr. 20, 1840.

33. Ibid., July 14, 1840.

34. Ibid., Feb. 17, 1840.

35. Ibid., Mar. 23, 1840. The sketches referred to have not survived.

36. Ibid., Nov. 10, 1840.

37. *Commissioners,* 1866, 5.

Chapter 7

Letting in "the World": (Re)interpretive Tensions in the Quaker Meeting House

Susan Garfinkel

In a 1904 history of Philadelphia's Arch Street meeting house of the Society of Friends, author George Vaux relates the following incident: "On one occasion during the Keithian controversy of the early 1690's, Robert Turner, a disciple of [George] Keith, 'with one or more of his followers, entered the [Bank] meeting-house and demolished the ministers' gallery. He was visited by Friends on account of his violent and disorderly action, but gave them no satisfaction, [stating] that he always had a testimony against ministers' galleries, and that he was well satisfied with what he had done.'"[1] Over two hundred years later, Turner's graphic actions—through which personal transgression against authority is played out on the fabric of the meeting house itself—seem to signal for Vaux an ongoing Quaker ambivalence toward collective interpretations of the material world.

The Quaker meeting house is not a sacred space. According to doctrine of the Religious Society of Friends, there is no distinction between sacred and secular spheres—all aspects of life are encompassed by the sacred once a proper understanding is achieved. The source of this proper understanding is the Inner Light, that direct, internal link to God's spirit that is available to each person. There are no inherently sacred objects or spaces. Meeting houses are a convenience—comfortable, regulated spaces for gathered worship, symbolic centers for the Quaker community. "Live in the world but not of it," cautioned founder George Fox.[2]

For Quakerism's followers, theology functions as a discourse about living in the world, based within a community of correct individuals. In prac-

tice, mediation of this theological discourse and the realities of material life proved a complicated undertaking. From the perspective of Truth, each act or behavior is sacred—that is, informed by God's Inner Light. Yet, as Friends continue to live in the larger world, they interact with and take part in a culture grounded in assumptions originating elsewhere. Most ideas about the world come from this somewhere else that is outside theology and must be made to fit the system of belief at hand.

Quakerism, particularly before the mid-nineteenth century, has often been characterized in terms of dichotomies: paired oppositions of meaning such as speaking and silence, plain and worldly, the two plantations.[3] In meetings for worship, the focus on silent and inward reflection is balanced against the needs of the group to communicate. As linked by Friends to the polarities of "Truth" and "the World"—correct understanding of the Inner Light versus the otherness resulting from attention to unenlightened outside culture—this tension highlights the meeting house's role as the space most available for shaping group consensus. As one author notes, the distinction between that which is Quaker and that which is not "is expressed [by Friends] most frequently in spatial terms by such correlatives as 'inward' and 'outward,' 'within' and 'without,' 'internal' and 'external.'"[4]

The meeting house becomes the puzzling site of internal activities that yet contain both internal and external elements. How do we talk about the secular world within a system of "sacred" belief that does not allow it? In my own work on the meeting house, I have found a strong tension between the ideals of Quaker society and the intrusion of outside realities—those nontheological ways of knowing about the world—along with what I can only call a sacred/secular opposition that seems to exist despite itself. This, I would argue, is the presence of the public sphere—"the World" in Quaker terms—within the seemingly sheltered domain of the meeting house walls. This presence is central to my choice of the meeting house as the place to study Quaker attitudes toward the material world. (Re)interpretive tensions refer not so much to my own, outsider's interpretations as to the ongoing and recursive process of (re)interpretation that is inherent to Quakerism and the spaces it inhabits.[5]

Thus, when Edwin Bronner, writing on Quaker landmarks in 1965, again relates the Keithian gallery-smashing story, the significance of the meeting house as site of meaning-laden tensions becomes apparent. He says, "The conflict in the Bank Meeting House reached a climax when the followers of Keith erected a second gallery in the back of the room for worship in the meeting house, and while one Friend spoke to the meeting from one gallery, Keith challenged him from the other. This intolerable situation was halted when rival groups entered the meeting house with axes and demolished both the old and the new galleries."[6] While the episode is from the earliest period of American Quakerism and may seem more reminiscent of the seventeenth-century English radicals who founded the Quaker sect than the staid and prominent businessmen who came to dominate it later, it is exactly this fore-staging that makes the story useful.[7] The gallery-smashing incident is both graphic and instructive, a cruder example of performative tensions that with time were incorporated, not resolved. Did the shape of the meeting house shape Quaker practice? Was it meant to? The presence of raised ministers' galleries (that literally elevated certain members) would seem to be at odds with Quaker goals of egalitarian consensus in worship. As Bronner relates the case, it is not clear whether the eventual motivation of Friends to violence was a matter of factionalism or an overwhelming frustration with the very presence of gal-

leries at all. Either way, dissent is transformed from theological proposition into real and cathartic enactment. By physically demolishing the galleries, dissenting Friends on both sides of the schism signaled the meeting house's position at the center of ongoing debate over the relationship between shared forms and meaningful actions in practice.[8]

The study of Quakerism has suffered from a willingness by scholars to give up at trying to reconcile within a single universe of lived experience—however coherent or fragmentary—both a system of belief and the surviving evidence of the physical world.[9] Here, I examine Quaker meeting houses built and used in the immediate Philadelphia area between 1760 and 1830 as focused sites for heightened and ambiguous interplay between belief and practice, silence and speech, "Truth" and "worldly society," the group and its single members, in a period of religious renegotiation.[10] Developing conventions in the design and use of these structures during the period contribute to their cultural constructedness as settings for religious discourse—as sites of both liminal, open, unrestricted encounters and of controlled and differentiated social relationships. The meeting house functions as both the primary site and primary referent for Quakers to interpret the material world and, through situated action and experience, to enter the (re)interpretive process that is inherent to Quakerism's discursive functioning. Though not a sacred space in theological terms, the Friends' meeting house is still a rarefied cultural site: a physical and psychic container for the discourse that is Quaker theology.[11]

❧

Quaker theology makes no explicit provision for the form of the meeting house—or even for its existence. Like the organization of meetings, the process of disciplinary correction, and other components of Quaker practice, the meeting house emerged within a larger cultural context, evolving in form as an artifact of group consensus over time. While ministry, for example, is recognized in Quaker theology as flowing from God's inspiration, the designation of recognized ministers and their placement on raised facing benches were practical attempts to manage the realities of this ministry during actual meetings for worship. In theology, the Inner Light makes all Friends inherently equal, yet more or less subtle separation of members persisted within the Society: naturalized categories such as gender, race, age, and class were questioned but not eradicated by Friends. Women's ministry led to empowerment, but women's meetings for business—though instituted to allow for the treatment of sensitive, gender-based issues within a protected environment—led to inherent inequalities. While there is no theological basis for separate men's and women's meetings for business, the acceptance and practice of separate meetings came to have an effect on almost every aspect of Quakerism, prime among them meeting house use and design.[12]

Philadelphia's Arch Street meeting house was built in 1803, with a second wing added in 1810 at the repeated urging of women Friends (fig. 7.1).[13] While in session at the Key's Alley meeting house in 1794, the Women's Yearly Meeting recorded in its minutes that "the Situation of this Meeting House, subjecting it to very considerable interruption from the divers Noises in the Streets, and growing inconveniences appearing, and Considerable loss sustain'd, for want of distinctly hearing. This matter is thought necessary to open to the Men's Meeting; and the following friends are appointed to attend on Men friends."[14] Men's Yearly Meeting appointed a committee to the matter that a year later returned a report to the women Friends. The women's minutes state that "it appears that they do not apprehend it expedient at the present time to erect buildings . . . [yet] being sensible of the inconveniences to which Women friends are subjected, much desire their better accommodation and . . . desire the Object may be kept in view by the Yearly Meeting." The women's minutes go on to explain that "this meeting believes it right to inform Men friends; They have never been more sensible of the necessity of providing a more convenient place to meet in, than at this time."[15]

Though the women Friends stressed their needs, men were the final decision makers, and it took

Fig. 7.1. Plan and North Elevation of Arch Street Meeting House (1804-1811), Philadelphia, Pennsylvania. Ink and wash on paper attributed to Owen Biddle, ca. 1803. (Edward Wanton Smith Papers, Quaker Collection, Haverford College, Haverford, Pennsylvania.)

Fig. 7.2. Green Street Meeting House (1814, demolished after 1950), Philadelphia, Pennsylvania. This photograph ca. 1950. (W. W. Dewees Collection, Friends Historical Library of Swarthmore College, Swarthmore, Pennsylvania.)

Fig. 7.3. Interior of Green Street Meeting House (1814, demolished after 1950), Philadelphia. Undated photograph. (J. R. B. Moore Collection, Friends Historical Library of Swarthmore College, Swarthmore, Pennsylvania).

ten years before Philadelphia Women's Yearly Meeting finally convened at the new Arch Street house. Careful attention was given to its planning, however, and once built Arch Street meeting came to serve as the symbolic center for American Quakerism. In their 1968 architectural report on the structure, Lee Nelson and Penelope Hartshorne Batcheler highlight the multi-use concept upon which it was planned and built. Occupying the site of a former Friends' burial ground, Arch Street served as home to men's and women's Yearly, Quarterly, and Monthly meetings. In addition to two large meeting rooms, separate committee rooms and a safe room for the storage of records were provided, and part of the plot of land continued its cemetery function.[16] Though the two main wings were built separately, a drawing by architect Owen Biddle shows a unified facade and fully conceptualized master plan.[17] At Arch Street, the uses and meanings contained within all meeting houses are here appropriately identified and arrayed over a larger, more fully articulated space.

In form, the Arch Street house shows generic conventions typical of meeting houses in the larger Philadelphia Yearly Meeting area. While building materials might differ, Friends' meeting houses shared common features and increasingly common plans as their forms—through alteration or new building—became regularized during this 1760 to 1830 period. In this typical meeting house, the main room is rectangular and lined with rows of long wooden benches in a central area facing front. Several rows of facing benches along the far end turn back toward this central area and provided special, raised seating for ministers, elders, and overseers. Banks of benches aligned with the side walls are also sometimes found in larger houses. Facing benches are most often built on stepped platforms, known as galleries, and sometimes a rear or rear-and-side balcony provides additional seating. The Arch Street house provides separate rooms for men's and women's meetings for business, as did Philadelphia's Twelfth Street meeting house of 1812. In smaller houses there are often two entrance doors symmetrically placed at the front of the building, and frequently there is also a central moveable partition that allowed for worship together but the separation of men and women for business. At Philadelphia's now demolished Pine Street and Green Street meeting houses (built in 1753 and 1814, respectively), partitions served as visible reminders of the need for gender differentiation (figs. 7.2 and 7.3).[18] Throughout the

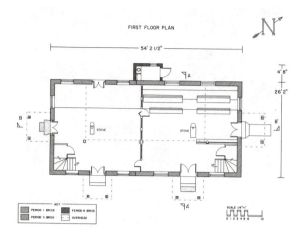

Fig. 7.4. First Floor Plan of Lower Alloways Creek Meeting House (built 1756, addition 1784), Hancock's Bridge, Salem County, New Jersey. (Drawing by Constance Anderton and Theresa Lucas, 1993, Historic American Buildings Survey, Library of Congress.)

Delaware Valley most meeting houses that did not conform to this new generic form were, by the end of the century, significantly remodeled or replaced. In the Lower Alloways Creek Meeting House, the process of this formal articulation is visible in extensive additions made to the structure (fig. 7.4).[19]

Concerned not only with the placement of raised benches or partitions that separate women from men, Friends over the course of the eighteenth century began to worry about more purely physical factors that might affect the quality of their particular style of worship. In 1802 or 1803, as plans for the Arch Street house were being laid, a Friend named Thomas Parker consulted in writing with the noted architect Benjamin Henry Latrobe. Parker's main concern was apparently ease of hearing, as Latrobe's surviving response commences: "You wish to know in what form a room containing about 1,600 persons should be built with a view to the ease of the speaker and the hearer, and in which the situation of the speaker is not fixed." After lengthy discussion on the topic of echo in various spaces, Latrobe concludes that "from what I have said you may infer that I would rec-

ommend a circular, domed, meeting house to your society, as the best adapted to the ease of hearer and speaker, and also as containing the most space within the least quantity of walling." Sensing the radical nature of his suggestion, he closes the letter "with the sincere hope that these remarks may not be altogether useless to you. . . ."[20] Arch Street meeting house is nothing like Latrobe's suggestion. Yet, a Burlington, New Jersey, meeting house of 1680 (now demolished) was octagonal, and the Merion meeting house, built in 1695 and 1713, has a cruciform plan (fig. 7.5).[21]

By 1820, Englishman William Alexander had published *Observations on the Construction and Fitting Up of Meeting Houses &c. for Public Worship,* a book that addressed functional issues within the developed formal expectations. Alexander's approach was to detail what he calls "common defects" in existing meeting buildings ranging from the discomfort to speakers, to poor acoustics and distracting outside noise, to poor conditions of temperature, air flow, lighting, size, and spacing of benches, etc. His purpose was to give advice on buildings, but only as this fell within the realm of predefined acceptability. Under "FORM" he wrote: "An octagon or square is the form most adapted to rooms designed to contain 2000 persons or up-

Fig. 7.5. Burlington Octagonal Meeting House (1680, demolished by mid-eighteenth century), Burlington County, New Jersey. Undated lithograph from an earlier engraving. (Friends Historical Library of Swarthmore College, Swarthmore, Pennsylvania).

wards, but for Meeting Houses in general, an oblong is unquestionably the best; and it is so seldom deviated from, in modern erections, that to mention a square as a defect may be sufficient."[22] By common agreement, then, recognized meeting house features worked to channel potentially chaotic meeting house behavior toward pre-existing, pre-approved modes. The need to continue an already meaningful, fully-encoded form—the rectangular plan—took precedence over architectural innovation.

If architectural continuity and formal clarity became a matter of identity to the Quaker community, the reasons can be found in the situated practices of the meeting house: how and when it was used and by whom. Upon inheriting his Quaker uncle's considerable estate, Richard Lamar Bisset of Madeira visited Philadelphia in 1801. Not a Friend himself, he attended a Quaker meeting for worship with his cousin one Sunday and recorded the experience in his journal. He had a detailed if mixed reaction:

> We arrived at the meeting house—which is very spacious—it was thronged with persons of both sexes—The men divided from the women—the young generally speaking from the old—We all sat with our hats on—It took full half an hour before every person was quite settled in his place—At length everything being quite quiet, an old woman got [up] to address a prayer to the Almighty—immediately every person arose, and the men doffed their hats—The prayer was short but I could not well hear it—Being finished a dead silence reigned for some time—An elderly man then got up and addressed the audience—neither his manner nor the matter of his discourse pleased me. . . . Two or three women at intervals spoke—what I thought quite as great nonsense as the men who had preceded them.
>
> An elderly man (Mr. Savery who is a famous preacher it seems among them) at length got up—he in very plain and unaffected language told them he was happy to see so much atten-

dance of so large a congregation, particularly of the younger friends—and continued, by recommending an attendance of them also upon week days more frequently, assuring them that the time given up to the service of the Almighty would not be thrown away—In a word this man was the only one who appeared to me to understand what he said himself, or could make other people comprehend his discourse—Shortly after this exhortation, the elders shook hands with each other, and this being the signal of the assembly's being dissolved, we all got up and departed[.]

In conclusion Bisset noted, "I [was] extremely fatigued by the heat occasioned by the number of people assembled, and absolutely cured of again wishing to be present at a Quaker meeting."[23] His discomfort and disapproval only highlight the presence of insider categories of behavior and comprehension, categories that he did not subscribe to.

The meeting for worship, as the place where the Inner Light is interpreted through shared experience, is a defining event for the Quaker community. Bisset's description confirms that throughout the sequence of the meeting individual Friends occupy clearly defined roles—roles for which the meeting house is built to provide. Uniform benches may appear undifferentiated, but both members and attenders were segregated by age and by sex. Elders and overseers—those who had been chosen for their experience, wisdom, or status—took places on the raised facing benches at the front of the room. Ministers also occupied the facing benches, for visibility and so that their speaking was most easily heard (fig. 7.6).[24] Youths, and sometimes women, sat in the balcony, removed from activity in this way. Until the early nineteenth century, free blacks or slaves, if present, sat together and in the back or in the balcony. Often they met for worship separately, with white supervision.[25]

We also learn from Bisset that what has come to be known as an unprogrammed meeting had a program after all: an understood agenda and a set of behavioral forms drawn upon by participants according to their status.[26] A prayer preceded the spontaneous sermonizing. Speakers, like William Savery, were most often proven ministers or elders, those whose gift had been previously recorded during monthly meetings for business. Spoken interludes were heard by those assembled in seated straight-ahead silence, and no direct response to the speaking was provided. As recounted by the skeptical Marquis de Chastellux in 1780, at meeting "the brethren, and the sisterhood . . . had all of them a very inattentive and listless air."[27] By shaking hands, elders were designated to end the meeting at just the right moment through some compromise of group readiness and real-time considerations. A set of designated roles was based on experience and religious understanding, but also on worldly relationships: race, gender, seniority, and economic or social class. Access to space defined relationships among the meeting members; it defined some of the spiritual limits or boundaries as well, since access to the performative genres of Quakerism—speaking or shaking hands—elevated certain individuals within the egalitarian mix (fig. 7.7).[28] Along with the form of the meeting house itself, within Quaker discourse a series of patterned behaviors and activities emerged that were marked as peculiarly Quaker, meant to be understood particularly by conversant members of the Society of Friends.[29]

Differentiation in the role and status of individual Friends may have been even more apparent in monthly meetings for business and discipline, the Society's primary mechanism for self-governance. Unlike the meeting for worship, the monthly meeting was open only to members of the Society of Friends. Proceeding on the principles of consensus decision making, Friends considered in variable sequence a number of items of meeting business: marriages, certificates of removal (transferring membership between meetings), financial matters, disciplinary inquiries, and disownment from membership (for violations of the code of discipline). Periods of silent reflection might also occur. A clerk ran the meeting and

Fig. 7.6. "Quakers Meeting." Aquatint by Rowlandson, Pagin and Stadler, published 1809 at R. Ackermann's Repository, London. (Friends Historical Library of Swarthmore College, Swarthmore, Pennsylvania).

worded the minutes based on his understanding of the consensus. Minutes reflected only this final consensus and were not an accounting of all that was said or considered. No theoretical differentiation between members existed. In practice the clerk, but also ministers, elders, and overseers, held interpretational power, as did members prominent in worldly society. High-status men and their wives or close female relatives were more often appointed to committees or to quarterly and yearly meetings.[30] Attenders were not present. Women Friends met separately in a monthly meeting of their own. A written Code of Discipline was compiled and updated from the meetings' deliberations.[31]

Business-meeting consensus could often mask the variety of individual opinions and experiences. In 1780 a group calling itself Free Quakers in support of the American Revolution formed among the ranks of Philadelphia's disowned Friends.[32] Feeling that they were wrongly disowned, the Free Quakers laid a claim to the use of the Society's existing meeting houses for their worship. In 1781 a written request, or "representation," for the use of Friends' property was presented by the Free Quakers to each of the three monthly meetings

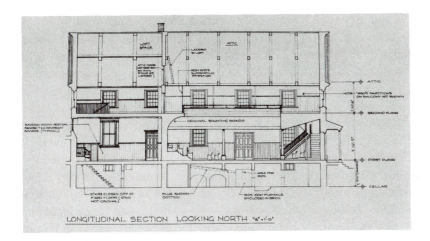

LONGITUDINAL SECTION LOOKING NORTH ⅛"=1'0"

Fig. 7.7. Section Looking North, Twelfth Street Meeting House, Philadelphia, Pennsylvania (built 1812, moved 1971 to Newton, Pennsylvania). (Drawing by John J. Kline, Historic American Building Survey, Library of Congress.)

held in Philadelphia. The outcome of this attempt is detailed in Free Quaker records:

> Timothy Matlack reports . . . That he had called on Henry Drinker who acts as clerk of the Bank Meeting[,] that Henry had informed him a committee had been appointed to consider of the propriety of reading our representation, [and that the] committee had reported to their last Monthly Meeting "That they were of [the] opinion, it was not proper to read" . . . and that the Meeting had concurred in this report; and this, although he acknowledged, that our representation had not been read to the people who thus concurred in the report; and that the Meeting had made no minute of any part of the Preceeding thereon.[33]

Thus shut out—not from an understanding of Quaker discourse, but from its operative sites—the Free Quakers appealed first to the Yearly Meeting and then through legal channels to the state assembly. With governmental support, the Free Quakers built a meeting house of their own in 1784.[34]

At the heart of the Quaker meeting for business is the ability of individuals to competently manipulate their material existence according to shared codes and precepts. This type of meeting most directly ties the space of the meeting house to the spaces beyond, to the larger public sphere. A step closer to "the World" if not to worldliness, here the process of (re)interpretation was not so much about the presence of the Light within as about managing that Light and using it effectively. Disownment—one outcome from the process of disciplinary correction—in this period most often occurred over incorrect behavior in worldly affairs. Yet, despite that outsideness, the issue in question was always brought to the meeting, to be dealt with in the protected meeting house space before it was returned to the outside world. The meeting house served as interpretive resting point through each step of the disciplinary process.[35]

Quaker theology has within it a fundamental crisis of representation. All expressive behaviors, whether spoken, enacted, or built, function as embodiments of this conflict. Since Quaker religious experience is individual and internal, it cannot be directly observed by others. Yet, personal understanding is also, according to Quakerism, most often partial or incomplete. A group gathered together in silent worship is seen as more likely to gauge correctly the leadings of the Inner Light. This means that the individual Friend, with a heightened sense of personal religious experience, is systematically placed in tension with the larger Quaker group. Despite the call for silent and inward reflection, visible and outward expressive behaviors become the only vehicle for demonstrating religious understanding. In meeting and in their daily lives, Friends repeatedly entered a liminal state, as each behavior was (re)interpreted by others for the intentions it revealed. In this suspended moment of betweenness, each action or expression was judged anew.[36]

In practice, the individual understandings of individual Friends were potentially chaotic when brought together. Consensus was necessary to establish shared codes and conventions for consistently reading individual members. Weekly meetings for worship and monthly meetings for business and discipline became the institutionalized methods for monitoring acceptability, for sharing knowledge of interpretive codes. Accepted ways of speaking, and acting, emerged. Sermons spoken at worship and minutes recorded at meetings for business both served to codify the knowledge. So, too, did the meeting house itself, with its benches, balconies, galleries, and partitions. Forms and conventions that arose in Quaker practice share a focus on the ambiguity of such patterned inspiration, theologically distasteful but necessary as it was. Conflict, in the end, was mediated in actual behavior, since it could not be theoretically resolved.

"The meeting house was arranged as it was solely to suit the way it was used, nothing more," writes David M. Butler,[37] a statement that is completely wrong and completely right, both at the same time. Material, cultural practices are always adopted in relation to a particular social, political, and historical context and do not exist outside of them. Modes of expression particular to Friends, and the modes for interpreting those expressions also, were conceptually centered in the Quaker meeting house, which functioned as the place where one learned and continually relearned, through the process of consensus, how to be a Friend. The meeting house contextualized for Friends the many shared modes of community-based expressions—even those that took place outside of it. At the same time, it was completely defined and contextualized by them. The interchanging functions of text and context, shared among the various spoken, written, and other performed or material behaviors of Quaker practice, were ultimately arrayed around the crucial issue of interpreting, processing, and negotiating non-Quaker but still shared cultural modes for living in and finding meaning in the day-to-day physical world.[38]

As a world view and a way of life, Quakerism is a compromise. In a complex world that is not completely Quaker, all manner of societal relationships, world views and discourses are brought into this sheltered arena for reconciliation. While Friends claimed equal access to the Inner Light and a highly egalitarian approach both inside and outside the meeting context, the roles of minister, elder, or clerk, the distinctions between members and attenders, and the separate treatment of male and female concerns all seem to contradict this premise. Formal features of the meeting house served to focus, place, and naturalize these differentiated relationships. The enactment of meetings did the same. Friends used these enactments to absorb, control, or restructure dissent and to incorporate the realities of the public sphere into a shared understanding.

In the meanings specific to the Quaker meeting house, it is possible to identify a long list of opposing modes and roles, including but not limited to:

> nurture/nature
> private/public
> inside/outside
> Inner Light/outward behavior
> Truth/"the World"
> plain/worldly
> silence/speaking
> personal inspiration/communal understanding
> equality/hierarchy
> member/minister
> member/attender
> male/female
> artisan/businessman
> businessman/politician
> country/city

Note that many of these oppositions exist in non-Quaker culture as well. Was the meeting house used successfully by Friends to control and shape their larger world in the period between 1760 and 1830? Are wealth and status, gender, power and politics, style, materials and craftsmanship, the use of space, ideas about the body and the mind, law and property, all successfully deployed? In the meeting house, both theological and societal, Quaker and non-Quaker meanings are closely merged in an enlarged discursive universe of ambiguous, negotiated understanding. Whether on purpose or by default, outside "worldly" discourse has found its way into the meeting house realm. Yet, Quakerism differs from other religious discourse of the period in at least one respect. It was still egalitarian in the sense that the intrusion of these distinctions continued to be problematic and was acknowledged and addressed within the interpretive processes based in the Inner Light.[39]

In mediating various social, political, and doctrinal functions, the meeting house both controlled and was controlled by the discourses of the worldly world. Inside and outside mutually construct each other. Practicing Friends tolerated, and more likely cultivated, an ambiguous space for play at the center of their view of the world. Through their practice, they both celebrated and fought against the need for ongoing (re)interpretation all at once. Are particular styles and forms inherent to particular ideas? If not, then where do they come from and what do they mean? Quaker struggles with this problem—what Stuart Hall has identified as "no necessary correspondence" between an ideology and its particular forms—has continued for three hundred years and mirrors a struggle we begin to identify in our own studies of culture (and material culture) more generally.[40] Forms have meanings, but perhaps meanings do not determine forms.

In practice, the walls of the Quaker meeting house provide boundaries where there are theoretically none. Physical, material boundaries, with their contained demarcation of space, come to function as psychic boundaries for deep discursive ambiguity. Outside and inside, sacred and secular—overlapping discourses converge in the meeting house, where the enactment of conventional behaviors and forms allowed Friends to deal with the multiplicity of meanings in their world, to engage these in a site over which they had control. Through the (re)interpretive process, expressions framed within the meeting house became exemplary, serving as models for the interpretation of customary relationships in everyday life. As the space of contained but rarefied practice, the Quaker meeting house became a testing ground—a site for the enactment of theological ideals in the real, material world.

Notes

This paper is part of an ongoing dissertation project, presently titled "Material Transgressions: The Quaker Meeting House in Philadelphia, 1760–1830." I would like to thank Elizabeth Blackmar and Dell Upton for their helpful comments on presentations of this material.

1. George Vaux, "Early Friends' Meeting Houses and their Relation to the Building at Arch and Fourth Streets," in *The Friends Meeting House, Fourth and Arch Streets* ([Philadelphia], 1904), 16.

2. Fox's famous exhortation from Pardshaw Crag in 1652, as quoted in Richard Bauman, *Let Your Words Be Few: Symbolism of Speaking and Silence Among Seventeenth-Century Quakers* (Cambridge: Cambridge University Press, 1983), 26.

3. See, for example, Bauman, *Let Your Words Be Few*, and Frederick B. Tolles, *Meeting House and Counting House: The Quaker Merchants of Colonial Philadelphia, 1682–1763* (1943; reprint, New York: W. W. Norton & Co., 1963).

4. Maurice A. Creasy, "'Inward' and 'Outward': A Study in Early Quaker Language." Supplement no. 30 to *Journal of the Friends' Historical Society* (London: Friends' Historical Society, 1962), 2. See also William A. Christian Sr., "Inward and Outward Concerns: A Study of John Woolman's Thought," *Quaker History* 67 (2) (Autumn 1978): 88–104. On the basics of Quaker theology, see Howard H. Brinton, *Friends for Three Hundred Years: The History and Beliefs of the Society of Friends Since George Fox Started the Quaker Movement* (New York: Harper & Brothers, 1952); William J. Frost, *The Quaker Family in Colonial America: A Portrait of the Society of Friends* (New York: St. Martin's Press, 1973).

5. See Bauman, *Let Your Words Be Few,* in particular 32–62, 120–36.

6. Edwin B. Bronner, "Quaker Landmarks in Early Philadelphia," in *Historic Philadelphia: From the Founding Until the Early 19th Century,* Transactions of the American Philosophical Society (1953; reprint, Philadelphia: The American Philosophical Society, 1965), 210–11.

7. On the founding of Quakerism, see Hugh Barbour, *The Quakers in Puritan England* (New Haven: Yale University Press, 1964); Arnold Lloyd, *Quaker Social History, 1669–1738* (1950; reprint, Westport, Conn.: Greenwood Press, 1979); Christopher Hill, *The World Turned Upside Down: Radical Ideas During the English Revolution* (New York: Penguin Books, 1972); H. Larry Ingle, "From Mysticism to Radicalism: Recent Historiography on Quaker Beginnings," *Quaker History* 76 (2) (Fall 1987): 79–94.

8. On the Keithian schism and incidents involving the meeting house, see Jon Butler, "'Gospel Order Improved': The Keithian Schism and the Exercise of Quaker Ministerial Authority in Pennsylvania," *William and Mary Quarterly,* 3d Ser., 31 (3) (July 1974): 431–52; Susan Mackiewicz, "Philadelphia Flourishing: The Material World of Philadelphians, 1682–1760," (Ph.D. diss., University of Delaware, 1988), 303–29; J. William Frost, ed., *The Keithian Controversy in Early Pennsylvania* (Norwood, Pa.: Norwood Editions, 1980).

9. See, in particular, Tolles, *Meeting House and Counting House.* It is Tolles who draws attention to the often-repeated order for furniture placed by Philadelphia Quaker John Reynell in a letter to Britain, that calls for "A Handsome plain looking-glass . . . and 2 raised Japan'd Black Corner Cubbards, with 2 doors to each, no Red in 'em, of the best Sort but Plain" (John Reynell Letter Book [1738–41], 6, Historical Society of Pennsylvania). See also *Philadelphia: Three Centuries of American Art* (Philadelphia: Philadelphia Museum of Art, 1976); Raymond V. Shepherd, "James Logan's Stenton: Grand Simplicity in Quaker Philadelphia," (M.A. thesis, University of Delaware, 1968); Sydney V. James, *A People Among People: Quaker Benevolence in Eighteenth Century America* (Cambridge, Mass.: Harvard University Press, 1963); Jack D. Marietta, *The Reformation of American Quakerism, 1748–1753* (Philadelphia: University of Pennsylvania Press, 1984).

10. 1756 is generally given as the year that began a reform movement in Quakerism. The issues of this reform were finally played out in the Hicksite Separation of 1827. See Kenneth L. Carroll, "A Look at the 'Quaker Revival of 1756,'" *Quaker History* 65 (2) (Autumn 1976): 63–80; Richard Bauman, *For the Reputation of Truth: Politics, Religion, and Conflict Among the Pennsylvania Quakers, 1750–1800* (Baltimore: Johns Hopkins University Press, 1971); James, *A People Among People;* Marietta, *Reformation of American Quakerism;* Robert W. Doherty, *The Hicksite Separation: A Sociological Analysis of Religious Schism in Early Nineteenth Century America* (New Brunswick, N.J.: Rutgers University Press, 1967).

11. Michel Foucault, "Of Other Spaces," trans. Jay Miskoweic, *Diacritics* 16, (1) (Spring 1986): 22–27; See also Belden C. Lane, *Landscapes of the Sacred: Geography and Narrative in American Spirituality* (New York: Paulist Press, 1988).

12. On the implications of separate women's meetings for business, see Christine Trevell, "The Women Around James Naylor, Quaker: A Matter of Emphasis," *Religion* 20 (July 1990): 249–73.

13. The design of Arch Street Meeting House has been attributed to Owen Biddle, a Philadelphia Quaker and au-

thor of *Young Carpenter's Assistant; or A System of Architecture Adapted to the Style of Building in the United States* (1805), on the basis of a signed drawing and plot plan now in the collection of the Athenaeum of Philadelphia. This unsigned drawing conforms closely to the meeting house as built, even to the details of the placement of benches. Original balconies at gallery level on three sides of each of the two large meeting rooms are not indicated here. The eastern two thirds of the Arch Street house (at left) were completed first, in 1804, and immediately housed the Philadelphia Women's Yearly Meeting, as well as Philadelphia Monthly Meeting (for the Central District). Upon completion of the western wing in 1811, Men's Yearly Meeting occupied the eastern end while the Women's Yearly Meeting now moved to the newer room. Here too met the men of Philadelphia Monthly Meeting, while the women's business meeting was conducted in the central committee room. Men and women met together in one of the large rooms for worship—an illustration of a contemporary meeting in London (fig. 7.6) provides a rare view of a similar scene. Note by the main entrance a small safe room, built to be fire-proof, for the storage of Friends records.

14. Philadelphia Yearly Meeting of the Religious Society of Friends. Women's minutes, 1794. Friends' Historical Library, Swarthmore College.

15. Philadelphia Yearly Meeting, Women's Minutes, 1795.

16. Lee Nelson and Penelope Hartshorne Batcheler, "An Architectural Study of Arch Street Meeting House, Fourth and Arch Streets, Philadelphia, Pennsylvania" (Philadelphia: Prepared for Philadelphia Yearly Meeting of the Religious Society of Friends, 1968), notes to illustration 5.

17. *Drawing Toward Building: Philadelphia Architectural Graphics, 1732–1896* (Philadelphia: University of Pennsylvania Press for the Pennsylvania Academy of Fine Arts, 1986), 48–50.

18. There is no current or comprehensive work on Quaker meeting houses in America or in the Delaware Valley. See Hubert Lidbetter, *The Friends Meeting House* (York: William Sessions Limited/The Ebor Press, 1961); Horace Mather Lippincott, *Quaker Meeting Houses and a Little Humor* (Jenkintown, Pa.: Old York Road Publishing Company, 1952); John Russell Hayes, *Old Quaker Meeting Houses* (Philadelphia: The Biddle Press, 1911); T. Chalkley Matlack, scrapbooks of Quaker meeting houses, 1928–1933, Historical Society of Pennsylvania; T. Chalkley Matlack, "Brief Historical Sketches Concerning Friends' Meetings of the Past and Present with Specific Reference to Philadelphia Yearly Meeting," typescript, Moorestown, N.J.: 1938; David M. Butler, "Quaker Meeting Houses in America and England: Impressions and Comparisons," *Quaker History* 79 (2) (Fall 1990): 93–104; *Inventory of Church Archives,* Society of Friends in Pennsylvania, Prepared by the Pennsylvania Historical Survey, Division of Community Service Programs, WPA (Philadelphia: Friends Historical Association, 1941). The constraints on available space within developed parts of the city, coupled with the requirements of accommodating a particularly dense Quaker population, led to greater formal variety in meeting houses built within the city of Philadelphia itself (see Twelfth Street Meeting House, fig. 7.7). Green Street Meeting House, however, was built in 1814 according to the region's most typical plan, including multiple symmetrically-placed entrances, a central partition to separate men and women during concurrent meetings for business, facing benches for ministers and elders at front, and gallery-level balconies on three sides. Note the sounding board and the relative invisibility of the open partition structure. Green Street Meeting House was erected to accommodate the growing number of worshipers in the Northern section of the city; Green Street Monthly Meeting established in 1816 would play a significant role in Quaker history as the first meeting to separate itself from Orthodox Friends during the Hicksite separation of 1827.

19. Like other meeting houses, the Lower Alloways Creek Meeting House assumed its complete form through a process of expansion. By 1784 a major addition to the 1756 house included not only a doubling of the size of the structure toward the west, and the erection of the present paneled partition, but the installation of second-floor

balconies on three sides to provide additional seating. Through this two-part construction process, the house came to resemble in configuration the fully articulated form of contemporary meeting houses built of a piece, such as the nearby Salem Meeting House of 1772.

20. Benjamin Henry Latrobe, *The Correspondence and Miscellaneous Papers of Benjamin Henry Latrobe,* 1: 1784–1804, ed. John C. Van Horne and Lee W. Formwalt (New Haven: Yale University Press for the Maryland Historical Society, 1984), 400–407.

21. Lidbetter, *Friends Meeting House,* 50–53. Meeting houses built in the twentieth century show wider variation in form. See Willard B. Moore, "The Preferred and Remembered Image: Cultural Change and Artifactual Adjustment in Quaker Meeting Houses," *Perspectives in Vernacular Architecture, II,* ed. Camille Wells (Columbia: University of Missouri Press, 1986): 120–28. Quaker settlement in west New Jersey and the establishment of Burlington Yearly Meeting both predated the settlement of Philadelphia in 1682, and it was several years before the yearly meetings of the two Quaker colonies were combined. This frame octagonal house was the site of early yearly meetings in Burlington. Versions of this image of Burlington's first meeting house were copied widely and repeatedly during the nineteenth century, both by hand and in printed form. No publication source is given for multiple copies of the present image located in the files of the Friends Historical Library. Written descriptions confirm, however, the general dimensions and octagonal shape of the structure, and the presence of a cupola. Later meeting houses in the Delaware Valley do not echo this form.

22. William Alexander, *Observations on the Construction and Fitting Up of Meeting Houses &c for Public Worship, Illustrated by Plans, Sections, and Descriptions, Including One Lately Erected in the City of York; Embracing in Particular, the Method of Warming and Ventilating* (York: William Alexander, 1820), 8.

23. Richard Lamar Bisset, "Journal of My Voyage to North America," 1801. Entry of Sunday, Apr. 26, Museum Section, Independence National Historic Park.

24. Because of Friends' general sensitivity to images, historical representations of Quakers at worship are few and far between. This contemporary British image shows Friends in worship at the Gracechurch Street Meeting House in London. Members are segregated by sex, with women occupying the left-hand side of the meeting room. The general configuration of the space shown is similar to that at Philadelphia's Arch Street House with the principal difference being in the form of the facing benches and balconies. In each case American examples include more rows of seating in these areas, balconies are often much deeper, and the closed or boxed-in gallery fronts shown here were usually avoided as they led to a greater visual separation of designated speakers than open-front benches or minimal railings. The decorative brackets and high arched windows would also be unusual in an American meeting house.

25. On the place of blacks in Quakerism, see Jean Soderlund, *Quakers and Slavery: A Divided Spirit* (Princeton: Princeton University Press, 1985); Henry J. Cadbury, "Negro Membership in the Society of Friends," *Journal of Negro History* 21 (2) (1936): 151–213. For sources on the role of women, see n. 35 below.

26. In the nineteenth and twentieth centuries, some branches of Quakerism turned to hiring ministers and to including prepared sermons and music in their services. Philadelphia Yearly Meeting continues in the unprogrammed format.

27. Marquis de Chastellux, *Travels in North-American in the Years 1780, 1781 and 1782 by the Marquis de Chastellux, Translated from the French by an English Gentleman,* Vol. 1 (Dublin: Printed for Messrs. Colles, Moncrieffe, White, H. Whitestone, Byrne, Cash, Marchbank, Heery, and Moore, 1787), 286.

28. When the early High Street Meeting House (located at Second and Market Streets at the head of the city's main market) was finally abandoned in 1809, a new house made from some of the same materials was erected farther west at Twelfth Street. Soon after, a new monthly meeting for the Western District was established at this loca-

tion to accommodate the expansion of the city's population. Like the Arch Street Meeting House (fig. 7.1), this large urban structure does not make use of internal partitions—women's business was to be conducted in the large committee room at the rear of the first floor. As this sectional view shows, the bulk of space in the structure is devoted to the central area for worship; perhaps not coincidentally the main facing benches and minister's sounding board reside near the center of the building's mass. From the exterior the deviation from standard meeting house form is hinted at by the unusual but still symmetrical fenestration—only one window separates the two doors on each long side of the house. As rebuilt at Newton Friends' School, Newtown, Pennsylvania, the roof structure above the main worship space has been left exposed to view, to display the great timbers surviving from as early as 1696.

29. On Quaker hierarchy, see Bauman, *For the Reputation of Truth;* Marietta, *Reformation of American Quakerism;* Jean R. Soderlund, "Women's Authority in Pennsylvania and New Jersey Quarterly Meetings, 1680–1780," *William and Mary Quarterly,* 3d Ser., 44 (4) (October 1987): 722–49. I draw here on the concept of sociolinguistic competence. See Bauman, *Let Your Words Be Few;* Dell Hymes, *Foundations in Sociolinguistics: An Ethnographic Approach* (Philadelphia: University of Pennsylvania Press, 1974); Charles L. Briggs, *Competence in Performance: The Creativity and Tradition in Mexicano Verbal Art* (Philadelphia: University of Pennsylvania Press, 1988), especially 1–24.

30. See Soderlund, "Women's Authority" for a comparative analysis of women's familial status and meeting participation.

31. For a thorough contemporary analysis of consensus-based meeting structure, see Michael J. Sheeran, *Beyond Majority Rule: Voteless Decisions in the Religious Society of Friends* (Philadelphia: Philadelphia Yearly Meeting of the Religious Society of Friends, 1983). As in Bauman's title, "For the Reputation of Truth," Friends felt a particular political concern to regulate and record the religious status of members. On the structure of meetings for business, see Lloyd, *Quaker Social History;* Soderlund, "Quaker Organization and Discipline," in *Quakers and Slavery,* 189–94; "Structure of Philadelphia Yearly Meeting," in *Guide to the Records of the Philadelphia Yearly Meeting,* comp. Jack Eckert (Philadelphia: Records Committee of Philadelphia Yearly Meeting, 1989), vii–xii. See also Rayner W. Kelsey, "Early Books of Discipline of Philadelphia Yearly Meeting," *Bulletin of the Friends' Historical Association* 24 (1935): 12–23.

32. The Philadelphia Yearly Meeting took a stand against the proceedings of the revolution on the grounds of pacifism and an obligation of loyalty to the prevailing government; many Quakers were in fact Loyalists for all practical purposes. Many Friends who actively supported the war or its purposes by participating, paying certain taxes, or taking oaths of loyalty were disowned. See Bauman, *For the Reputation of Truth;* James, *A People Among People;* also Sydney V. James, "The Impact of the American Revolution on Quakers' Ideas About Their Sect," *William and Mary Quarterly* 3d ser., 19 (3) (July 1962): 360–82; Arthur J. Mekeel, *The Relation of the Quakers to the American Revolution* (Washington, D.C.: University Press of America, 1979); Richard Alan Ryerson, *The Revolution Is Now Begun: The Radical Committees of Philadelphia, 1765–1776* (Philadelphia: University of Pennsylvania Press, 1978); Eric Foner, *Tom Paine and Revolutionary America* (New York: Oxford University Press, 1976).

33. Rough minutes of the Monthly Meeting of Friends Called by Some the Free Quakers, entry of 3d of 9th Month, 1781. American Philosophical Society.

34. Charles Wetherill, *History of the Religious Society of Friends Called By Some the Free Quakers* (Philadelphia: The Religious Society of Friends Called By Some the Free Quakers, 1894); Charles E. Peterson, "Notes on the Free Quaker Meeting House" (Harrisburg, Pa.: Harbeson, Hougle, Livingston and Larson, Architects to the Commonwealth of Pennsylvania, 1966). The Free Quaker meeting house is located at Fifth and Arch Streets; the inscrip-

tion on the date stone reads: "By General Subscription for the Free Quakers, erected, in the year of our Lord, 1783, of the Empire 8."

35. See Marietta, *Reformation of American Quakerism.* James writes that "the great importance that Friends in the eighteenth century gave to their ecclesiastical Society and its regulation may seem to have been illogical on the part of the people who believed in direct and frequent inspiration as a foundation for all religious life. Indeed, the contradiction implicit in the strict control of each believer by his fellow members of the church and commitment to the doctrine of the Inner Light, provided one of the never-failing dynamic forces in the Quaker church. But to colonial Friends there was no contradiction; the opposing concepts were held together by a theology reinforced by sectarian traditions." *A People Among People,* 2.

36. A liminal state is one of betweenness, as during a ritual that confers a change in cultural status. More recently, the term liminality has been used to describe situations in which the boundaries of social role are temporarily blurred or suspended. See Arnold van Gennep, *Rites of Passage,* trans. Monika B. Vizedom and Gabrielle L. Caffee (Chicago: University of Chicago Press, 1960); Victor Turner, ed., *Celebration: Studies in Festivity and Ritual* (Washington, D.C.: Smithsonian Institution Press, 1982); Mikhail Bakhtin, *Rabelais and His World,* trans. Helene Iswolsky (Cambridge, Mass.: MIT Press, 1968); Peter Stallybrass and Allon White, *The Politics and Poetics of Transgression* (Ithaca: Cornell University Press, 1986).

37. Butler, "Quaker Meeting Houses," 97.

38. On Quakerism in daily life, see Frost, *Quaker Family;* Tolles, *Meeting House and Counting House;* Barry Levy, *Quakers and the American Family: British Quakers in the Delaware Valley, 1650–1765* (New York: Oxford University Press, 1988); Joan M. Jensen, *Loosening the Bonds: Mid-Atlantic Farm Women, 1750–1850* (New Haven: Yale University Press, 1986).

39. The most in-depth discussions of egalitarianism and social status in the meeting house have focused on the role of women. See Soderlund, "Women's Authority"; Jensen, *Loosening the Bonds;* Mary Maples Dunn, "Latest Light on Women of Light," and other essays in *Witnesses for Change: Quaker Women Over Three Centuries,* ed. Elisabeth Potts Brown and Susan Mosher Straud (New Brunswick, N.J.: Rutgers University Press, 1989); Margaret Hope Bacon, *Mothers of Feminism: The Story of Quaker Women in America* (San Francisco: Harper & Row, 1986); Nancy Hewitt, "Feminist Friends: Agrarian Quakers and the Emergence of Women's Rights in America," *Feminist Studies* 12 (1) (Spring 1986): 27–49.

40. Stuart Hall, "The Problem of Ideology: Marxism Without Guarantees," *Journal of Communication Inquiry* 10 (Summer 1986): 28–44.

Part III
Architecture, Ethnicity, and Race

Chapter 8

Mañana, Mañana: Racial Stereotypes and the Anglo Rediscovery of the Southwest's Vernacular Architecture, 1890–1920

Abigail A. Van Slyck

In many ways, the groundwork for the study of the Southwest's vernacular architecture was laid a century ago, when Anglo-American travelers began to reassess the landscapes they encountered in New Mexico, Arizona, and southern California. While adobe structures had prompted early-nineteenth-century visitors to characterize Santa Fe as "a filthy and dull city of mud," by the 1890s these same buildings were the focus of a full-fledged cultural revival supported by the railroad and the fledgling tourist industry.[1]

Although architectural historians have long been aware of this phenomenon, our interpretation of it is now changing in important ways. Initially, David Gebhard and others presented the Spanish Colonial Revival as the *discovery* of the Southwest and sought out historical precedents in order to place revival buildings in objective, stylistic categories.[2] Working along these lines, historians praised designs that revealed a sophisticated understanding of authentic vernacular forms and either implicitly or explicitly interpreted formal accuracy as a thoroughgoing appreciation of southwestern cultures.

The same body of evidence, however, can be seen in a different light. Using Edward Said's study of Orientalism as a guide, scholars in many fields have come to see southwestern revivals less as the *discovery* of the Southwest as an existing cultural landscape and more as the *invention* of the Southwest as a fictive landscape that was constructed by Anglo-American newcomers.[3] Scholars like Chris Wilson are working to reveal the process of selection and adaptation that translated this imaginative construct of the Southwest into built form.[4]

This essay builds on this second method of interpretation. Despite frequent references to Hispanic and Native-American building traditions, it is really about Anglo culture; it touches briefly on the Anglo creation of the image of the Southwest and focuses more specifically on Anglo responses to that image, both by professional architects and by those outside the design fields. Albeit sympathetic to southwestern cultures, this reaction was informed by contemporary theories of social Darwinism. Even the most socially progressive shared a belief in a racial and ethnic hierarchy, with western European culture (and its American offshoots) at its peak, and assumed that the progress of western Europe was the driving force of human history. As a result, the early-twentieth-century revivals of the Southwest's vernacular architecture did not constitute an "unalloyed admiration" of southwestern cultures. Instead, these revivals were predicated on racial stereotypes and an Anglo sense of racial superiority.

The Southwest and Antimodernism

The timing of the Anglo invention of the Southwest is hardly coincidental. The defeat of Geronimo in 1886 and the establishment of regular rail connections made the firsthand experience of mission and pueblo safer, faster, easier, and more economical than it had ever been before. More important, however, were the antimodernist sentiments developing farther east in the face of intense industrial development, massive European immigration, and rapid urbanization. In their otherness, in their apparent simplicity, primitiveness, and closeness to nature, southwestern cultures, their vernacular architectures, and their distinct, natural environments offered an appealing alternative to the modern industrial city.[5]

In this respect, southwestern architectural revivals are not so much a unique regional phenomenon as they are a regional manifestation of national and even international trends. Growing out of the Romantic tradition that emerged in the eighteenth century, southwestern revivals are western versions of English Colonial Revival styles popular in the same years and are subject to interpretations initially developed in conjunction with East Coast developments. Both eastern and western revivals were ultimately rooted in the Arts and Crafts movement of the late nineteenth century, particularly in their veneration of preindustrial traditions, in their respect for handicraft, and in their appreciation of primitive roughness. Both eastern and western revivals appealed initially to a cultured elite. Both eastern and western revivals appeared in settings devoted to leisure before being adopted for a full range of middle-class domestic buildings.[6]

More importantly, in both movements, this Arts and Crafts aesthetic took on particular social meaning in the context of late-nineteenth-century America. In the East, an intensely jingoistic Anglo-Saxon elite feared that massive European immigration endangered the moral and political foundations of the country. By establishing exclusive societies for those who could prove their blood ties to Mayflower passengers and Revolutionary soldiers, this elite used club membership to verify their early occupation of the continent and to support their claim to power. This same group then reiterated that political message in architectural form by building Colonial Revival homes for themselves, for their country clubs, and for their hereditary societies.[7]

The corresponding architectural movement in the Southwest was fueled by a similar desire to demonstrate Anglo-Saxon superiority, but it is not subject to an identical analysis. After all, in the Colonial Revival movement in the East, Anglo-Saxons mimicked buildings like Mount Vernon to underline the finer qualities of the culture of their forefathers and, by extension, used those forms to claim special status for themselves as descendents of earlier builders. In contrast, the Pueblo and Spanish Colonial Revivals appropriated the forms of alien groups, using them as foils against which to measure the assumed superiority of Anglo-Saxon culture.

Los Angeles, ca. 1895

It seems contradictory for supporters of these southwestern revivals to emulate cultures that they viewed as inferior. Nonetheless, Charles F. Lummis and many of his contemporaries negotiated this contradiction successfully. An eastern-born, Harvard-trained journalist and one of the biggest boosters of the region he dubbed "the Southland," Lummis is synonymous with the history of the Anglo rediscovery of this area. Having "tramped across the country" from Ohio to California in 1885, he made frequent and often sustained trips from his home base in Los Angeles throughout the American Southwest (particularly to the Pueblo settlements of New Mexico), as well as to Mexico and South America. Until his death in 1928, Lummis was the organizing force behind many pioneering efforts to protect the natural and cultural resources of the Southwest, including the Landmarks Club (to preserve the Spanish colonial missions of southern California), the Sequoya League (to secure better treatment of Native-American populations), and the Southwest Museum (to promote the study of southwestern archaeology). As the editor of *Out West* magazine until 1905 and as the author of numerous books about the Southwest, Lummis was responsible for bringing a scholarly understanding of Hispanic and Native-American cultures to a popular audience.[8]

Mixing romanticism and scholarship, Lummis's writings point to the complexities that characterized the Anglo reassessment of the Southwest. On the one hand, the understanding of archaeology and history that informed Lummis's writing impressed the scholarly community. When *The Land of Poco Tiempo* appeared in 1893, Frederick W. Hodge of the Bureau of Ethnology in Washington, D.C., called it the best popular work on the Southwest yet published.[9]

The romantic imagery of Lummis's books, however, was still built upon stock images of the Southwest. For instance, the opening passages of *The Land of Poco Tiempo* introduced readers to New Mexico with these words:

> Sun, silence, and adobe—that is New Mexico in three words. If a fourth were to be added, it need be only to clinch the three. It is the Great American Mystery—the National Rip Van Winkle—the United States which is *not* the United States. Here is the land of *poco tiempo*—the home of "Pretty Soon." Why hurry with the hurrying world? The "Pretty Soon" of New Spain is better than the "Now! Now!" of the haggard States. The opiate sun soothes to rest, the adobe is made to lean against, the hush of day-long noon would not be broken. Let us not hasten—*mañana* will do. Better still, *pasado mañana*.[10]

The passage's primary purpose is to present the slower pace of New Mexican life in a positive light. Yet, the specific imagery conjured up—a figure napping outside all day against an adobe wall—is drawn directly from a longer tradition of negative stereotypes. Characterizations of New Mexico as "the national Rip Van Winkle" or (later in the same essay) of Mexicans as "in-bred and isolation-shrunken descendents of the Castilian world" or his choice of the burro as "the sole canonizable type of northern New Spain" call into question Lummis's admiration for the cultures he observed and his sensitivity to their religious beliefs.[11] If an antimodernist outlook inverted old insults into new compliments, it did nothing to dispel the ethnic and racial stereotypes of Mexicans as lazy or Native Americans as backward. Instead, this strain of antimodernism reconfirmed the validity of these stereotypes. Indeed, its rhetorical effectiveness depended on them.

Particularly problematic in Lummis's writing is the continued use of the concept of the primitive, particularly in connection with Pueblo cultures. By labeling contemporary cultural practice as "primitive," Lummis presented these cultures as basically simple, childlike, and essentially unchanging. Likewise, his use of Biblical analogies in stories like "A New Mexico David" at once ennobled his subjects for a Christian audience yet also cast them into a seemingly unretrievable past, a realm made doubly remote by its actual antiquity and by its popularly perceived ahistorical nature.[12]

The hierarchy of value is clear here. Indigenous cultures seemed to contribute to the species by providing an object lesson in the advantages of the simple life. Yet, in defining these cultures as essentially primitive and in presenting them as a collection of easily classifiable, static types, Lummis and his ilk also stripped them of their potential to act. Trapped in amber, these cultures appeared to be isolated outside the stream of evolution. In contrast, Anglo-Saxon culture inhabited a privileged position. Although urbanization and industrialization had led Anglo-Saxon society astray, this setback seemed temporary and reversible. Indeed, for Lummis, the importance of studying indigenous southwestern cultures was directly linked to the antimodernist assumption that the dominant culture could get back on the evolutionary track by relearning forgotten lessons of the simple life exhibited by "primitive" peoples. The implication was that Anglo-Saxons could learn and change, while the indigenous cultures would inevitably stay behind.

The inequality of cultures implied in Lummis's writing had an impact on the way that he and his

Fig. 8.1. Charles Lummis, El Alisal, Los Angeles, 1897–1910. Exterior. (Courtesy of the Southwest Museum, Los Angeles. Photo no. N 37848.)

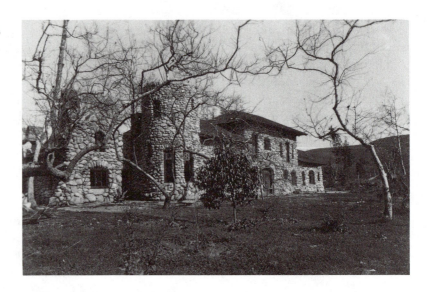

contemporaries incorporated southwestern architectural forms into revival buildings. El Alisal, Lummis's own house in Los Angeles, is a good example (figs. 8.1 and 8.2). Standing on three acres of land in Arroyo Seco, less than four miles from downtown, the house was under construction between 1897 and 1910. With the help of young men of the Isleta Pueblo in New Mexico, Lummis built the house himself by collecting rocks from the property and cementing them in place to form a rugged exterior wall on the southern, entrance facade. The building is L-shaped, with a circular tower at the southwest corner linking the living areas behind the main facade and the dining room/kitchen wing on the west. These wings define a large patio dominated by a sprawling sycamore, one of thirty trees on the site for which the house was named.

In keeping with Lummis's philosophy that "a man's home should be part of himself," El Alisal reflects its owner's interest in and appreciation for several vernacular architectural traditions of the region.[13] Forming walls from rocks collected on the site paralleled the construction methods used in ancient Anasazi cliff dwellings and in New Mexican missions built in the first half of the seventeenth century. The dining room's scalloped gable is a motif borrowed from California's Spanish mis-

sions. The single-pile arrangement of the house, the *zaguan* (or vestibule that links the entrance facade with the patio), the *portales* bordering the patio, and the patio itself are all drawn from Spanish colonial domestic architecture. Even the corner tower may refer to the defensive *torreon* employed by Spanish colonial settlers.

This wealth of visual references to regional architecture reflects the important role that El Alisal played in Lummis's rejection of the polish of Victorian culture and his lifelong struggle to escape what he called "the maw of 'snivelization.'"[14] Yet, to interpret El Alisal only in relation to southwestern traditions is to misunderstand the building's complexity. In its construction, in the social structure of its space, and in its use, the house was embedded in the ideals and cultural practices of late Victorian culture.

The construction of El Alisal was closely linked to the Victorian idea of the single-family house as the most appropriate site for demonstrating individuality. Indeed, there was an element of theater in the construction process. The length of time that Lummis devoted to the house, the way that he continued to work on the house when visitors arrived—sometimes admonishing them to lend a hand—the fact that rough stonework appeared

Fig. 8.2. El Alisal. Museo. (Courtesy of the Southwest Museum, Los Angeles. Photo no. N24267.)

only on the south and west facades, where visitors formed their first impressions of the house—in all of these ways, Lummis staged the construction of the house, controlling the impact his house would make on others. In this respect, the un-Victorian image of rough stone walls was the product of an extremely Victorian desire to create a unique expression of personal identity.

What is more, the theatrical performance emphasized the theme of masculinity. Lummis, for instance, regularly observed to visitors that "any damn fool can write a book. It takes a man to build a house." In a similar vein, he repeatedly referred to the construction process as his "gymnasium," inviting attention to his strength and fitness. Thus, Lummis did not simply reject Victorian culture in its entirety. Instead, he joined his contemporaries in decrying the impact of what was interpreted as excessive feminine influence on Victorian culture and in glorifying manly vigor as a means of regaining authentic culture.[15]

Given Lummis's relationship to Victorian culture—he was critical of it, yet eager to work within it to reform its feminine excesses—it is hardly surprising that the social structure of space at El Alisal reflects Victorian norms.[16] Functionally specialized rooms took on distinctive shapes and paralleled standard Victorian uses. The room that functioned as the parlor was called the *museo,* perhaps a more accurate description of a room type conventionally devoted to display. Despite its single-pile plan, the house was zoned to maintain family privacy, both from visitors on formal calls and from household servants. The *zaguan* functioned much like the hall of the Victorian house, providing ready access to the *museo* at the front of the house, while family activities took place farther from the door (in this case, outside on the patio). The kitchen and laundry were relegated to the back of the house, shielding living spaces from the noise and activity of servants.[17]

The tone and content of the activities that took place at El Alisal are equally telling of Lummis's participation in late Victorian culture. Elaborate salons that Lummis called "Noises" were complex social rituals in which spontaneity was more or less orchestrated. These events typically began with a mock trial, presided over by Lummis himself, "dressed in a tightfitting buckskin coat, covering a soft-bosomed, Spanish drawnwork shirt, which revealed the vivid red Bayeta undershirt beneath" and wielding an old Spanish pistol that he rapped on the table to call the proceedings to order. Newcomers to the groups were arrested and tried for "not knowing what a real, old California

Fig. 8.3. A. C. Schweinfurth,
Hacienda del Pozo de Verona,
Pleasanton, California, 1895-96.
Exterior. (From Barr Ferree,
American Estates and Gardens
[New York, 1906], 213.)

good time was." After the prosecution and defense had presented their cases, the neophytes were formally acquitted and dinner began. The multicourse meal was prepared by Lummis's cook, Elena, and served by Amate, a Spanish folksinger who did double duty as Lummis's gardener. Music was an important part of the meal. Circling the table between courses, Amate played the guitar and sang Mexican and Spanish songs, while everyone present was expected to join in at the chorus. Sometimes "Lummis would put down his fork, pick up the Spanish pistol, and point it at someone around the table. Then that someone would be commanded to sing for his supper."[18]

In these "Noises," we see most clearly that El Alisal was still essentially a Victorian household. Despite the trappings of the Spanish colonial era, this sort of ritualized fun was closely related to contemporary modes of middle-class socializing. Mock seriousness, the threat of violence followed by sociability, even the emphasis on full participation in the evening's entertainment—these could be found throughout the country, from fraternity parties to the annual encampment at Bohemian Grove north of San Francisco.[19]

More important, these events reveal that Lummis's intellectual and emotional appreciation of Hispanic and Native-American cultures did not translate easily or automatically into social practice. Like any other Victorian household, El Alisal's success as a setting for gracious living and memorable hospitality was predicated on the presence of servants, whose inferior position was reinforced by differences of race or ethnicity as well as those of class. Although Lummis adopted Spanish dress, he seemed to take for granted his place at the top of a power hierarchy in which race and ethnicity were both components.

In this context, El Alisal's vernacular elements remained largely superficial. The rough stone walls, the scalloped gable, the corner fireplaces, the Native-American baskets and rugs that decorated the house, even the glass transparencies depicting Native Americans incorporated into the glazing of the front window all functioned essentially as Victorian parlor decorations. Together, they helped convey to visitors a sense of the owner's aesthetic taste, but they were not offered as a serious challenge to the belief in the superiority of Western culture.

Lummis's Impact

By promoting southwestern cultures on many fronts, Lummis helped foster an interest in the region that spread far beyond its immediate geographical boundaries. At times, Lummis's impact

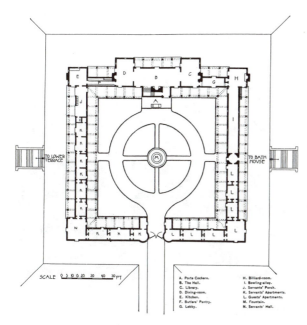

Fig. 8.4. Hacienda del Pozo de Verona. Plan. (From *American Architect and Building News,* May 2, 1896, 46.)

was direct and easily documented, as in 1895 when San Francisco architect A. C. Schweinfurth designed a country house for William Randolph Hearst (figs. 8.3 and 8.4). Located in Pleasanton, California, the house came to be called the Hacienda del Pozo de Verona, after the Italian wellhead installed in its courtyard. Like Lummis's slightly later El Alisal, the Hacienda was inspired by vernacular structures of the Southwest. Indeed, it combined an exterior massing reminiscent of Pueblo forms with a single-pile courtyard plan drawn from Spanish colonial prototypes.[20] Also like El Alisal, the Hacienda functioned essentially like a Victorian house, with functionally specialized rooms carefully arranged to preserve family privacy both from visitors and from household servants who maintained the complex.

The architect articulated his debt to Lummis more fully in his letters to Phoebe Hearst, who appropriated the newly completed house from her son. Hoping to dissuade Mrs. Hearst from hanging French tapestries, which would destroy the stylis-

tic unity of the house, Schweinfurth explained that he intended the house as "a place where a man tired out with the cares and responsibilities of an active metropolitan life could find absolute change . . . where everything would express . . . that he was in the land of *poco tiempo,* and where the feeling of *mañana, mañana* could be cultivated."[21] In quoting the title of Lummis's book and in paraphrasing one of its more memorable passages, the architect revealed both his familiarity with the author's writing and his acceptance of Lummis's cultural stereotypes of unhurrying, lazy New Mexicans. Further, Schweinfurth cited this negative stereotype as the basis for his design decisions. Hispanic and Native-American forms were appropriate in this commission, he suggested, as a means of giving the client a house that would counterweight his "natural" Anglo activity. Schweinfurth's goal was not simply to promote the laziness associated with the region's non-Anglo cultures, but to achieve a balance of Anglo and southwestern cultural stereotypes.

In the end, Mrs. Hearst mixed Native-American baskets and blankets with her substantial collection of European antiques, and installed the lot in this southwestern architectural setting. This mixture may have infuriated her architect, but it reflected her perception of southwestern elements as the latest trend in parlor furnishings. Like European tapestries, they demonstrated the owner's personal taste and buying power, without signaling a fundamental reassessment of late Victorian cultural values.

Santa Fe, ca. 1915

By the second decade of the twentieth century, Lummis's approach to the Southwest's vernacular architecture had been transformed, largely because of developments that Lummis himself had actively encouraged. To begin with, the recognition that an exotic architectural image could attract tourist dollars fueled the revival of Hispanic and Native-American architectural forms in other parts of the

Fig. 8.5. A. Page Brown (A. C. Schweinfurth, designer), California Building, World's Columbian Exposition, Chicago, 1893. Exterior. (The Chicago Public Library, Special Collections Division.)

Southwest. What is more, Lummis's involvement with the preservation and restoration of southern California's vernacular buildings prompted his admirers to look at the cultural resources in their own backyards. Armed with firsthand knowledge of their own regions, decision makers in New Mexico and Arizona abandoned many of the motifs that Lummis had popularized, adopting instead a repertoire of distinctive forms that they hoped would set them apart from California in the minds of prospective tourists and investors.[22]

The most intense focus of activity in this later phase of the southwestern vernacular revivals was certainly Santa Fe.[23] In Santa Fe the movement was spearheaded by the anthropologists and artists associated with the School of American Archaeology and the Museum of New Mexico. As one of the founding board members of the school and as a regent of the museum, Lummis was well known to these scholars.[24] Museum director Edgar Lee Hewett particularly liked and admired Lummis, whom he acknowledged as the "chief spokesman of the Southwest." Their long correspondence reflects the warmth of their affection for one another and reveals that Hewett's attitudes toward historic preservation were anchored in the same

body of Arts and Crafts theory that motivated his friend.[25]

Despite common interests, however, Santa Fe's academically trained anthropologists approached the revival of southwestern forms somewhat differently. For one thing, their professional interest in non-Western cultures resulted in an explicit veneration of Pueblo culture and an implicit devaluation of Hispanic traditions. This Indianism among museum personnel developed steadily, albeit somewhat unevenly, during the last half of the 1910s and is particularly clear in the staff's published discussion of New Mexico's Spanish colonial mission churches. In 1915, for instance, staff archaeologist Sylvanus Morley emphasized the Spanish elements of New Mexico's missions, characterizing the church at Acoma as the oldest European structure in New Mexico, while decrying the "martyrdom" of Spanish *padres* who died there during the Pueblo rebellion of 1680.[26] In contrast, when Hewett wrote about the missions just three years later, he invoked "the hands of Indian workmen" who gave the missions "the character of that remarkable race."[27] This attitude was reiterated by staff artist Carlos Vierra, who argued that New Mexico's missions had more to do with the Indian

Fig. 8.6. Rapp and Rapp, New Mexico Building, Panama-California Exposition, San Diego, California, 1915. Exterior. (Jesse L. Nusbaum, Courtesy Museum of New Mexico. Negative no. 60254.)

culture of the builders than with the Spanish culture of the *padres*.[28] Although couched in historical terms, the erasure of Hispanic contributions to southwestern culture was equally embedded in a contemporary context of intensified anti-Mexican sentiments, fueled in part by Pancho Villa's raids and an influx of poor Mexican immigrants fleeing the revolution.[29]

Equally important, the mantle of scholarly objectivity allowed the museum staff to accomplish more in the way of promoting southwestern revivals than even the energetic Lummis. They not only sought to preserve the historic structures of Santa Fe, but they also used the museum's prestige to push for a new architecture based upon the state's vernacular traditions. Hewett and Morley both served on Santa Fe's first city planning board, the group that carried out the re-Hispanicizing of the city's street names and architectural character. In the same years, the museum's journal, *El Palacio,* often highlighted articles on preservation and restoration, even at the expense of scholarly articles on anthropological topics.[30]

At first glance, the architectural products of this phase do not seem substantially different from their 1890s counterparts. In 1893, for instance,

Schweinfurth (while working in the office of A. Page Brown) had designed the Mission Revival California Building for the World's Columbian Exposition by combining elements drawn from California's best-preserved missions (fig. 8.5).[31] Over twenty years later, the New Mexico building at the 1915 San Diego Exposition was the product of a similar approach. There, architects Ira H. and W. M. Rapp combined the general plan of the mission church at Acoma with a facade balcony borrowed either from the Cochiti pueblo church or from the mission church at San Felipe (fig. 8.6).

To the extent that such fairs attempted to make sense of the modern world by presenting an orderly model of its constituent parts, this eclectic approach was an appropriate one. At the very least, each building served as a mini tour of its state's missions, giving visitors an opportunity to locate the Southwest's Hispanic past on their mental maps of American history. Better yet, these buildings might prompt visitors to make a trip to the real thing.[32]

Yet, in each building, the combination of motifs was motivated by the conviction that the vernacular traditions presented were actually improved by contact with Anglo culture. In the case of the New Mexico building, this assumption was explicitly articulated by the scholars on the museum staff who had collaborated on the building's design. Morley, for instance, explained that "the introduction of a second story balcony between the two towers of the church considerably relieves the monotony of the façade and lightens an otherwise too massive effect" of the original at Acoma.[33] At home in Santa Fe, they based the museum's new Fine Arts Building on their successful exposition building, further "improving" the vernacular originals by using the Laguna church as the model for a new side entrance.[34]

After the fair, the conviction that Anglo scholarship could and should control the revival of southwestern architectural forms prompted the museum staff to take an increasingly prominent role in

Fig. 8.7. Rapp and Rapp, Fine Arts
Building, Museum of New Mexico,
Sante Fe, New Mexico, 1916-17.
St. Francis Hall. (Wesley Bradfield,
Courtesy Museum of New Mexico.
Negative no. 6741.)

Santa Fe's development. Indeed, it was the common ground that united Morley, who continued to favor a revival of Spanish colonial forms, and Vierra, the self-appointed spokesman for the Pueblo revival. Although he worked for the museum as an artist, Vierra supported the scholarly community's claim to leadership in this field, identifying "analysis of the influences which controlled the development of the original" as the quality that distinguished reproduction (which he favored) from mere imitation.[35] Morley disagreed with the particular forms Vierra advocated, but shared his conviction that scholars had a responsibility to lead the way. His own contributions included service on the city planning board, authorship of a 1912 report defining the characteristics of the Santa Fe style, and continuing efforts to promote a popular understanding of these characteristics.[36]

The participation of these anthropologists in the creation of the Santa Fe style complicated the popular understanding of the Southwest's vernacular traditions. The scholarly authority that their work commanded meant that most lay observers accepted their reconstructions as valid replacements for the original buildings. The Fine Arts Building was par-

ticularly influential with locals, who seem to have looked upon it as a repository of approved motifs. Even with the growing popularity of Pueblo forms after 1915, the museum's narrow range of Spanish colonial elements appear repeatedly in the public buildings around the city's plaza.[37]

The museum's involvement in the Santa Fe style also led to more serious misunderstandings, particularly for countless tourists who visited Santa Fe only once. Lillian Gunter, of Gainesville, Texas, was one such visitor, who arrived in 1924 to attend a meeting of the American Library Association. Impressed by the distinctive architectural environment she encountered there, she found it easy to mistake the reconstruction for the genuine article.

More important, Gunter used her impression of Santa Fe to articulate her ideas about the proper form for the small library for the Southwest. In her diary, she recorded a clear vision of the ideal southwestern library as "a blue eyed adobe hut, with a beamed and stick ceiling just like St. Francis hall in the state museum . . . whitewash tempered with a little yellow ochre on the outside, blue doors and window sash, red barn paint for the roof, and inside a neutral color on the walls with all the furniture painted a lovely soft blue."[38] How telling that her model of an ideal southwestern architecture was neither a mission building nor a Native-American pueblo, but a room only eight years old, in a building designed by architects born in Illinois, decorated with murals planned and executed by academically trained artists (fig. 8.7). Convinced by the museum's scholarly reputation, she readily accepted the modern, Anglicized version of southwestern vernacular traditions as the real thing.[39]

At the same time, her reference to a blue-eyed adobe suggests that there was a racial component to her choice, that her ideal was a building inspired by Hispanic traditions, but "corrected" by the contributions of Anglo-Saxons. In fact, Gunter implemented her vision of the blue-eyed adobe in the Negro branch library opened in Gainesville's colored school in that same year.[40] Although Gunter wrote about the "gorgeous" blue-and-orange bookcases without any hint of irony, the situation in Gainesville reveals a complex intertwining of racial and architectural ideas.

❧

What had changed in this thirty-year period? In the 1890s, Lummis had operated on the basis of assumptions he had inherited from the Victorian world. A strong faith in the tenets of bourgeois individualism made him unaware of the degree to which his race and class were responsible for many of the privileges he enjoyed. Confident in what he interpreted as his right to move freely into any cultural setting, he sought to insert himself into the vernacular building process he had encountered in the Southwest. Without recognizing the impact of his presence on the process, he offered to carry on the architectural traditions of a culture he assumed was ill-equipped to adapt to the modern world.

In contrast, the scholars active in Santa Fe a generation later were more aware of the gap that existed between the established cultures of the Southwest and their own group of Anglo newcomers. Rather than repeat Lummis's somewhat naive attempts to bridge the gap, their response was to appropriate vernacular forms. Using the tools of analysis and classification, they conceptually detached these forms from their original contexts and brought them into the realm of professional expertise that the scholars themselves inhabited.

In either case, it is difficult to interpret the Spanish Colonial and Pueblo Revivals as evidence of a thoroughgoing celebration of Hispanic and indigenous cultures. The antimodernist stance that prompted those revivals depended heavily on racial and ethnic stereotypes and used them consistently to establish a privileged position for Anglo-American culture. In fact, racist attitudes lying just below the surface affected both how Anglo Americans perceived southwestern vernacular architectures and how they used these building traditions between 1890 and 1920.

For students of vernacular architecture, this historical episode has particularly chilling implications. After all, at its founding the field of vernacular architecture studies shared both information and cultural attitudes with Colonial Revival movements, both in the Southwest and in the Northeast. Although Lummis's eastern counterparts claimed an objective, scientific basis for their scholarship, they were often sustained by similar nationalistic sentiments and assumptions of cultural superiority. Until we confront the values embedded in the traditions of our field, we run the risk of reiterating the values of the 1890s and imperil an inclusive understanding of cultural landscapes in the 1990s.[41]

Notes

I would like to thank Chris Wilson for sharing with me his expertise on the history of Santa Fe. His comments on an early draft of this paper and our subsequent discussions have helped sharpen my thinking about the issues addressed here. My thanks also go to Paul Ivey for his careful and timely reading of this text.

1. Raymund A. Paredes, "The Mexican Image in American Travel Literature, 1831–1869," *New Mexico Historical Review* 52 (Jan. 1977): 7. For the railroad's role in southwestern revivals, see Virginia Grattan, *Mary Colter: Builder on the Red Earth* (Flagstaff, Ariz.: Northland Press, 1980; reprint, Grand Canyon, Ariz.: Grand Canyon Natural History Association, 1992).

2. David Gebhard, "The Spanish Colonial Revival in Southern California (1895–1930)," *Journal of the Society of Architectural Historians* 26 (May 1967): 131–47.

3. Edward W. Said, *Orientalism* (New York: Vintage Books, 1979). *The Journal of the Southwest* recently devoted an entire issue (32 [4] [Winter 1990]) to "Inventing the Southwest," with contributions by Barbara Babcock, Marta Wiegle, Sylvia Rodríguez, and others.

4. Christopher Wilson, "The Santa Fe, New Mexico Plaza: An Architectural and Cultural History, 1610–1921," (M.A. thesis, University of New Mexico, 1981); Wilson, "New Mexico in the Tradition of Romantic Reaction," in *Pueblo Style and Regional Architecture,* ed. Nicholas C. Markovich, Wolfgang F. E. Preiser, and Fred G. Sturm (New York: Van Nostrand Reinhold, 1990), 175–94; Wilson, *The Myth of Santa Fe: Tourism, Ethnic Identity and the Creation of a Modern Regional Tradition* (Albuquerque: University of New Mexico Press, forthcoming).

5. For a discussion of antimodernism, see T. J. Jackson Lears, *No Place of Grace: Antimodernism and the Transformation of American Culture, 1880–1920* (New York: Pantheon Books, 1981).

6. The relationship of these revivals to the Romantic movement is discussed in Wilson, "New Mexico in the Tradition of Romantic Reaction"; for English Colonial Revivals on the East Coast, see Karal Ann Marling, *George Washington Slept Here: Colonial Revivals and American Culture, 1876–1986* (Cambridge, Mass.: Harvard University Press, 1988); Alan Axelrod, ed., *The Colonial Revival in America* (New York: W. W. Norton, 1985); William Rhoads, *The Colonial Revival,* 2 vols. (New York: Garland Publishing, 1977).

7. Rhoads, *The Colonial Revival,* 1: 434–41, 535.

8. For information on Lummis's multifaceted career, see Patrick T. Houlihan and Betsy E. Houlihan, *Lummis in the Pueblos* (Flagstaff, Ariz.: Northland Press, 1986); Daniela P. Moneta, ed., *Charles F. Lummis: The Centennial Exhibition Commemorating his Tramp Across the Continent* (Los Angeles: Southwest Museum, 1985); Robert E. Fleming, *Charles F. Lummis* (Boise, Idaho: Boise State University, 1981); Kevin Starr, *Americans and the California Dream, 1850–1915* (New York: Oxford University Press, 1973); Edwin R. Bingham, *Charles F. Lummis, Editor of the Southwest* (San Marino, Calif.: Huntington Library, 1955).

9. Bingham, *Charles F. Lummis,* 16–19.

10. Charles F. Lummis, *The Land of Poco Tiempo* (1893; reprint, New York: Charles Scribner's Sons, 1913), 3.

11. Lummis, *Poco Tiempo,* 5, 10.

12. A notable example of Lummis's Biblical comparisons is his *A New Mexico David and Other Stories and Sketches of the Southwest* (New York: Charles Scribner's Sons, 1891).

13. Quoted in Bingham, *Charles F. Lummis,* 22.

14. Charles F. Lummis, Letter to Edgar L. Hewett, Jan. 7, 1927, quoted in Edgar L. Hewett, "Lummis the Inimitable," *Papers of the School of American Research* 35 (1944): 11.

15. Lummis is quoted in Hewett, "Lummis the Inimitable," 3. For Lummis's concern with virility, see Susan Reyner Kenneson, "Through the Looking-Glass: A History of Anglo-American Attitudes Toward the Spanish Americans

and Indians of New Mexico," (Ph.D. diss., Yale University, 1978), 265–66. For a discussion of the general cultural trend, see Lears, *No Place of Grace;* see also Abigail A. Van Slyck, "Gender and Space in American Public Libraries, 1890–1920," *SIROW Working Paper* 27 (1992).

16. The idea of identifying a social structure of space that is independent of a formally consistent plan type was developed in Dell Upton, "Vernacular Domestic Architecture in Eighteenth-Century Virginia," in *Common Places: Readings in American Vernacular Architecture,* ed. Dell Upton and John Michael Vlach (Athens: University of Georgia Press, 1986), 315–35.

17. There was such a clear distinction between public and private rooms at El Alisal that when Lummis deeded the house to the Southwest Museum in 1910, he was able to stipulate that the three museum rooms (presumably, *zaguan, museo,* and dining room) were to be open to the public during certain hours each week, while his family and descendents were to have tenure of the remaining rooms forever. Dudley Gordon, "El Alisal: the House that Lummis Built," *Historical Society of Southern California Quarterly* 35 (Mar. 1953): 26.

18. Ibid., 25–26.

19. At Bohemian Grove, the elite members of the all-male Bohemian Club still begin their annual two-week retreat with an elaborate ritual that culminates in burning the body of Dull Care. The ritualized aspect of the Bohemian Club's activities first manifested itself in the late 1880s and was in full flower by around 1900. John van der Zee, *The Greatest Men's Party on Earth: Inside the Bohemian Grove* (New York: Harcourt Brace Jovanovich, 1974), 28–30.

20. Despite its name (and in contrast to El Alisal), the Hearst house owes less to the forms of the Spanish colonial hacienda than it does to Spanish colonial military outposts. Richard Longstreth, *On the Edge of the World: Four Architects in San Francisco at the Turn of the Century* (New York: Architectural History Foundation, 1983), 283.

21. A. C. Schweinfurth, Letter to Edward H. Clark, Dec. 20, 189[5], Phoebe Apperson Hearst Papers, Bancroft Library, University of California, Berkeley.

22. While this phenomenon is well documented for New Mexico, the Arizona component of the story has been largely ignored. The Arizona work of Henry Trost has been touched on in Lloyd C. Engelbrecht and June-Marie F. Engelbrecht, *Henry C. Trost: Architect of the Southwest* (El Paso: El Paso Public Library Association, 1981). The architects associated with the office of Henry O. Jaastad (including Prentice Duell, Annie G. Rockfellow, and Eleazar D. ["Ed"] Herreras) deserve further investigation.

23. Wilson, "The Santa Fe, New Mexico Plaza"; Wilson, "New Mexico in the Tradition of Romantic Reaction"; Nicholas C. Markovich, "Santa Fe Renaissance: City Planning and Stylistic Preservation, 1912," in *Pueblo Style and Regional Architecture,* ed. Nicholas C. Markovich, Wolfgang F. E. Preiser, and Fred G. Sturm (New York: Van Nostrand Reinhold, 1990), 197–212.

24. Indeed, Lummis's interest in the Museum of New Mexico was interpreted by the curator of the Southwest Museum as "promoting a rival museum" and was one of the causes of his 1915 break with the Los Angeles institution that he had founded. Daniela P. Moneta and Patricia A. Butz, "Lummis in California Life," in Moneta, *Charles F. Lummis,* 59.

25. The tone of the Lummis-Hewett correspondence is clear from the lengthy excerpts that Hewett published in 1944. Hewett, "Lummis the Inimitable," 6–13.

26. Sylvanus Griswold Morley, "Santa Fe Architecture," *Old Santa Fe* 2 (Jan. 1915): 279.

27. Edgar L. Hewett, "On Opening the New Museum," *Art and Archaeology* 7 (Jan.–Feb. 1918): 13.

28. Carlos Vierra, "New Mexico Architecture," *Art and Archaeology* 7 (Jan.–Feb. 1918): 40.

29. For a discussion of the relationship between Indianism and anti-Mexicanism in the early twentieth century, see Sylvia Rodríguez, "Art, Tourism, and Race Relations in Taos: Toward a Sociology of the Art Colony," *Journal of Anthropological Research* 45 (Spring 1989): 77–99. For the historical context of anti-Mexican sentiments in 1910s and 1920s, see Joseph V. Metzgar, "The Ethnic Sensitivity of Spanish New Mexicans: A Survey and Analysis," *New Mexico Historical Review* 49 (Jan. 1974): 49–73.

30. Wilson, "The Santa Fe, New Mexico Plaza," 127–42.

31. Longstreth, *On the Edge of the World,* 265.

32. For an extended discussion of the cultural meaning of the World's Fair phenomenon, see Burton Benedict, *The Anthropology of World's Fairs: San Francisco's Panama Pacific International Exposition of 1915* (London and Berkeley: Lowie Museum of Anthropology, 1983).

33. Morley, "Santa Fe Architecture," 298.

34. The tendency to improve on the original by combining motifs derived from many different buildings is also a dominant theme in English Colonial Revival movements on the East Coast. Bridget A. May, "Progressivism and the Colonial Revival: The Modern Colonial House, 1900–1920," *Winterthur Portfolio* 26 (Summer/Autumn 1991): 107–22; *The American Renaissance, 1876–1917* (Brooklyn: Brooklyn Museum, 1979), 57–61; Marling, *Washington Slept Here,* 156–59.

35. Carlos Vierra, "Our Native Architecture in its Relation to Santa Fe," *Papers of the School of American Archaeology* 39 (1917): 2. Vierra was a Californian who had received his artistic training in New York before moving to New Mexico as a treatment for tuberculosis. Wilson, "The Santa Fe, New Mexico Plaza," 141.

36. The details of the Vierra-Morley debate are well documented in Wilson, "The Santa Fe, New Mexico Plaza," 140–41, and Wilson, *The Myth of Santa Fe.*

37. These include the Federal Building, the La Fonda Hotel, and the Cassell Building (also known as the Onate Theater). Wilson, *The Myth of Santa Fe.*

38. Lillian Gunter Diary, entry of Sept. 7, 1924, Lillian Gunter Papers, Archives Division, Texas State Library.

39. For detailed information on St. Francis Hall and its decorations, see J. K. Shishkin, *An Early History of the Museum of New Mexico Fine Arts Building* (Santa Fe: Museum of New Mexico Press, 1968).

40. Lillian Gunter Diary, entries of Sept. 20, 1924, Oct. 6, 1924, Lillian Gunter Papers, Archives Division, Texas State Library.

41. For a more detailed discussion of the social attitudes of Norman Morrison Isham, Irving Whitall Lyon, and Henry Chapman Mercer, see Dell Upton, "Outside the Academy: A Century of Vernacular Architecture Studies, 1890–1990," in *The Architectural Historian in America,* ed. Elisabeth Blair MacDougall (Washington: National Gallery of Art, 1990), 199–213. In a similar vein, Catherine Bishir has demonstrated the extent to which we service professionals bring a class bias to our study of vernacular architecture. Catherine W. Bishir, "Yuppies, Bubbas, and the Politics of Culture," in *Perspectives in Vernacular Architecture, III,* ed. Thomas Carter and Bernard L. Herman (Columbia: University of Missouri Press, 1989), 8–15.

Chapter 9

Association, Residence, and Shop: An Appropriation of Commercial Blocks in North American Chinatowns

Christopher L. Yip

During the late nineteenth and early twentieth centuries, Chinese-American associations were important parts of the small, clustered Chinatowns of North America, and association buildings became a major element in creating a special identity for the urban Chinatowns of the Pacific Coast. A common facade composition involved translating the traditional Chinese organization of a building's horizontal plan into a vertical composition of the facade (fig. 9.1).[1] Chinatowns usually sat at the edge of central business districts, which explains the presence of a building stock composed of multistory commercial blocks. The existing commercial building stock of most Chinatowns allowed for multiple uses, and the facades of these commercial structures allowed for this sort of recomposition.

There are recurring patterns found in many of the Chinatown association buildings. The buildings appropriated by associations typically covered their lots to the allowable maximum, came right up to the edge of the sidewalks, and rose to a height of two or more stories. The ground floor was commonly devoted to commercial spaces, such as dry goods stores, herbalist shops, and restaurants. The window and display area was maximized to attract customers, turning the ground-floor facade into windows and doors. The middle floors commonly received little decorative treatment, except occasionally for fire-escape balconies. The greatest intensity of decoration was concentrated on the top level of the association rooms. There, one might see a balcony stretching across the width of the facade, possibly decorated with lights on the tops

of the posts and elaborate ironwork in the balustrade. A central door opened onto the top-floor balcony flanked by symmetrically disposed windows on either side. A stone surround with incised and painted characters further could accentuate the importance of the association rooms' facade and the organization within. Often, tiled curving eaves might shelter the association balcony, which could be highlighted by the use of red and green. If a cornice projected above the eaves, it could be shaped to add a final bit of visual vitality.

Chinese-American history and social organization help to explain how the turn-of-the-century, multistoried commercial block was so readily appropriated for use by Chinese-American communities along the Pacific Coast. First, one must examine the demographic structure of the Chinese-American population in the late nineteenth and early twentieth centuries and the forces that shaped it.

The Chinese-American population was overwhelmingly male from 1849 until the 1920s. The first wave of Chinese immigration was composed of male immigrants drawn by the discovery of gold in California in 1848. In general, they were young men who were willing to risk the arduous and dangerous journey to California; many of these "bachelors" had wives and children in south China who were awaiting their triumphant return. By the 1860s the search for employment as laborers replaced gold as the draw, and once again males came alone for the most part, leaving their families back in south China. As a result, the ratio be-

Fig. 9.1. Chinatown, Victoria, British Columbia. On the left is the Chinese Empire Reform Association (now the Lung Kong Kung Shaw) of 1905, and on the right is the Yen Wo Society building of 1912.

tween men and women in the immigrant population was grossly unbalanced. In 1860 and 1900, the ratio of men to women was about the same, nineteen to one.[2] The Chinese represented an extreme example of predominantly male immigration, though it was parallel, to some extent, to the early phases of Italian immigration to San Francisco.[3] The Chinese "bachelor" in the western United States was expected to remit money back to China to support his parents, wife, and children in his native land. As the immigrant aged or died, a son might be sent to the United States to labor abroad for the family, thereby creating a form of chain migration.

The passage of the Exclusion Acts, beginning in 1882, blocked almost all immigration of Chinese into the United States and kept the Chinese-American population predominantly male for decades after the early immigration phase had ended for other immigrant groups.[4] Chinese-American communities, as a result, were structured to serve a predominantly male population.

Discriminatory laws and practices limited employment opportunities to a narrow band of occupations. In 1852 the state of California passed the Foreign Miner's Tax, which was aimed specifically at driving the Chinese out of gold seeking. Later laws and ordinances drove the Chinese out of other occupations, such as fishing, and labor unions, including the AFL, blocked Chinese from unionized jobs in the Far West until the civil rights movement of the mid-1960s. The vast majority of Chinese men found work as manual laborers in agriculture, railroad construction, land reclamation, and mining or found employment in the service trades, particularly laundry and restaurant work.

The merchants, who constituted one of the few classes of Chinese allowed to immigrate into the United States by the Exclusion Acts, formed the elite of the community. The merchants ran businesses that served the male labor force, and they dominated the social and political organizations of the community. This was in stark contrast to traditional China, where scholar-officials (sometimes referred to as the *literati,* a relatively small proportion of the population trained in the Chinese classics) formed the elite.[5] In the Confucian social hierarchy, merchants theoretically were the lowest class. But among the overseas Chinese, the merchant class became the elite group, and the predominantly male laborers replaced the peasants in the traditional social hierarchy.

Legally barred from citizenship through the naturalization process until 1952, Chinese Americans with permanent resident status sought support and protection through the Chinese community associations that they established. These associations helped single males find companionship based upon common ethnic, linguistic, ancestral, and other bonds. As early as 1849, Chinese merchants in San Francisco had formed a *gongsi* (company) to maintain order within the community and to represent Chinatown to the rest of the city.[6] As the Chinese population grew, the *Huiguan* (meeting hall or company) formed; these companies represented people based upon Cantonese subdialect groupings and districts of origin. Other organizations represented villages and clans, since Chinese immigration was based on chain migration from specific locations in south China to specific ones in the United States, repeating the pattern of chain migration to and from south China that had developed centuries earlier in the interactions of China with southeast and east Asia.[7]

Rivalries within large organizations often led to separations into numerous rival organizations, and new organizations based upon the needs of particular groups were continually coming into existence. Large Chinatowns, such as those in San Francisco, Sacramento, Victoria, and Vancouver, had a full array of associations, whereas the smallest communities might have only one or two. To create order among the many, often hostile organizations, many Chinatowns formed an overarching association to which all the others belonged and owed allegiance. In 1882 an umbrella organization, *Jinshan Zhonghua Huiguan,* popularly known as the Chinese Six Companies, was formed in San Francisco and was later incorporated in California.

Associations served a variety of functions, including social, economic, and quasi-governmental ones. Men found jobs through their clan, village, and district-dialect associations and remitted money home to their families through the associations' connections to their native place. Moreover, immigrants sought camaraderie and entertainment at the associations, borrowed money through rotating credit mechanisms of the associations' membership, and used the association as an enforcer of contracts. The associations were also the primary organs engaged in legal battles to defend Chinese-American rights and to mitigate the impact of discrimination. Some associations ran gambling and prostitution activities, while others sponsored temples.

The locations of various Chinatowns help to explain the presence of commercial blocks. The Chinatowns tended to occupy marginal land at the edge of the central business district. Quite often, the growth of the cities during the late nine-

Fig. 9.2. Grant Avenue, Chinatown, San Francisco.

teenth and early twentieth centuries encased these small Chinatowns, leaving little or no room for them to grow. Chinatown growth took the form of increasing density. Other residential districts did not accept Chinese, and expanding central business districts grew at the expense of low-cost housing. As a result, the associations normally were packed into a low rent, working-class zone next to the central business district. In San Francisco, Chinatown formed around the intersection of Clay and Dupont Streets, just two blocks up the slope of Russian Hill from Montgomery Street, which became the core of the city's financial district (fig. 9.2). Similarly, the Los Angeles Chinatown of the late nineteenth and early twentieth centuries occupied a site about two blocks away from the original settlement and sat at the northern edge of the developing central business district. Seattle's first Chinatown—before the Chinese were expulsed in 1886—formed along Main Street between Second and Fourth Streets, only one block from Pioneer Square.[8] A similar pattern existed for the Chinatowns in Canada. Victoria's Chinatown formed along Cormorant Street, just across the Johnson Street ravine from the Jewish quarter at the edge of the original town grid. Chinatown in Vancouver sprang up along False Creek near Gastown.[9]

The building stock in these Chinatowns tended to be composed of commercial structures and residential hotels. The population of single men found rental rooms in low-cost, residential hotels and services along the streets and alleys of the district. The earliest communities were often composed of timber-framed structures. Surviving photographs show early Chinatowns to be dominated by simple, wood-framed, false-front structures, such as those in the Chinatowns of Barkerville, Nanaimo, and Vancouver in Canada, and in San Francisco, Point Alones, and Locke in the United States. In many of these locations, fires in the nineteenth century led to rebuilding inflammable structures in brick; in other communities, increases in building size led to rebuilding in brick. The shift from wood to brick began in San Francisco in the 1850s. Vancouver began the transition in 1900.[10] The building stock of this district within the urban zone between the central business district and the residential districts came to be dominated by multistoried commercial blocks that often housed mixed uses, including residential hotels, shops, restaurants, warehouses, and light manufacturing businesses (fig. 9.3).

In their earliest stage of development, Chinese associations sought any space that was available and affordable, and some ended up being housed in residential hotels, basements, or loft spaces. The associations of greater wealth and power sought locations that expressed their prominence in the community. An association rarely occupied ground-floor street frontages, since such spaces were com-

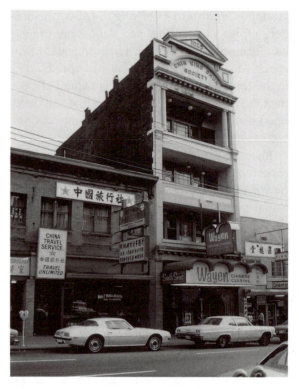

Fig. 9.3. Chin Wing Chum Society Building, 1925, by R. A. M. McKenzie, Chinatown, Vancouver, Canada.

monly reserved for a wholesale or retail business that needed sidewalk exposure and access.

Each multistoried commercial block tended to become a cross section of the Chinese community in microcosm, with businesses, residential space, and associations all under one roof. The commercial street frontages commonly had a large expanse of glass to light the interior that, secondarily, created a visual connection between the shop and the street. In the early years these frontages often opened directly to the street in the manner of the Asian shop house; later shop fronts were built in the style of the typical North American glass front with a recessed entry placed symmetrically in the facade.

A residential hotel occupied the middle floors of multistoried buildings. Buildings with more area per floor often had rather regular floor plans, while small buildings squeezed in as many rooms as they could. This sometimes resulted in contorted floor plans with irregularly placed light wells for the interior rooms. Any remaining space in an association's commercial block was occupied by some combination of warehouses, small factories, temples, and other associations. A gambling establishment might be found in a back room or the basement, and a prostitute's crib might be linked to the passageways of the residential hotel section of the building.

Associations often sought to modify leased or purchased buildings to present a public image that stressed their prominence. The designer or contractor hired by an association attempted to make the common commercial block express the power and importance of the given association housed within. Part of the problem in expressing this prominence lay in the complications of land ownership for the Chinese. During the nineteenth century, the Chinese were reluctant to purchase property in the United States. The gold rush Chinese expected to go home soon, and those laborers who came to work on the railroads and drain the swamps were poor and hardly able to assemble the funds to purchase property. Only a few merchants purchased property; most leased or rented property. The Exclusion Acts that began in 1882, combined with emigration back to China and a high mortality rate, led to a decline in the Chinese-American population. This decline continued until the 1920s and added to a sense of instability and impermanence. The hostility directed at the Chinese, such as the physical expulsion of the Chinese from Seattle in 1886 and massacres of Chinese in Los Angeles and Rock Springs, Wyoming, made residence in the United States seem tenuous indeed. Then, in 1913 the Alien Land Act of California banned Chinese immigrants from owning land as long as they were barred from naturalized citizenship. The ban on naturalized citizenship for Chinese-American residents was not lifted by the federal government until after World War II. Other western states fol-

lowed California in passing alien land laws. As a result, it was not uncommon to find that Chinese Americans owned structures that they had constructed on leased land.

Associations seeking an appropriate visual image faced another problem. What was the most appropriate way to treat the facade of a multi-use commercial block? Traditional Chinese institutional buildings were configured in a way that could not be literally replicated in North American urban settings, since the urban physical settings of China and North America were so different from each other. Typical American building types did not carry any traditional Chinese symbols of prestige or authority and did not necessarily conform to the particular requirements of the associations. As a small minority that was discriminated against, the Chinese and their immigrant institutions had no influence over building codes and practices during the late nineteenth and early twentieth centuries. The associations had to match Eastern and Western images of place to the hybrid collection of uses that they required, and they had to appropriate some American building type. In fact, they were usually limited to adapting the multi-use commercial block to their needs.

The traditional Chinese public building was modeled on the courtyard house: it had a front gate and courts with primary spaces that led back along a central axis. The relative importance of spaces was based upon their placement in relationship to the central axis, the most important space being at the opposite end of the main axis from the entrance. Hierarchy was expressed horizontally in the plan. In the traditional temple or government building complex (*yamen*) in China, one entered a symmetrical courtyard to find the most important structure rising slightly higher and symmetrically placed at the back of the courtyard. Multiple courtyards on the central axis could be used to establish an increasing order of importance from the front of the complex to the most important at the back. This approach to hierarchy led to the design of buildings that emphasized axial symmetry and horizontal sequences of spaces that were organized along the primary and secondary axes of a complex. Hierarchy based on ritual movement horizontally through space was in marked contrast to the vertical architecture of North American downtowns and the tenement districts that surrounded them.

How, then, could the associations appropriate the commercial blocks and tenements, which composed most Chinatowns, to serve the needs and to contain the appropriate symbols desired by these immigrant associations? A number of different strategies were attempted by designers and contractors to meet the desires of the various associations. Given relatively small lots in densely built-up districts, the cost of constructing traditional, horizontal Chinese complexes was out of the question. Each association had to decide how best to express itself architecturally when the opportunity arose, and there was no obvious solution in the beginning. What an association did depended upon its particular stance toward traditional Chinese values, modernity, and North American norms and values, as well as cost and the realities of the local construction industry. Associations varied in the degree to which they wished to remain "Chinese" or become "American" and in how they defined the terms. Relatively few associations adopted Euro-American building forms and decoration.[11]

Most associations sought to express pride in their Chinese heritage and struggled to find a way of translating some of the character of Chinese architecture into the Chinatown setting. The Six Companies association in San Francisco was the most powerful association in North America, and its building of 1908 represented an effort to modify the traditional Chinese scheme to fit a North American downtown lot (fig. 9.4). As the representative of the Chinatown political hierarchy, the association was willing to sacrifice practicality for prestige. The Six Companies, formally known as the Chinese Consolidated Benevolent Association of

Fig. 9.4. Six Companies Building, 1908, Chinatown, San Francisco.

San Francisco, came into existence during the early 1880s. It was formed at the height of the anti-Chinese movement in the United States as an attempt by various associations to provide a unified leadership against the anti-Chinese forces. The formal name was selected by the Chinese envoy in Washington, Zheng Zaoru, but the popular name became the Six Companies, which referred to the six important district associations that composed the core membership at the time of its founding. Its authority was recognized in Chinatowns across the Far West, and branches were established in other Chinatowns, such as Portland's, before 1887.[12] The board of the Six Companies was composed of the presidents of the most powerful Chinese-American associations, and the board functioned as a spokesman for Chinese-American interests to the outside community and as a quasi-government within the Chinese community.

The Six Companies building of 1908 was the most literal attempt to use the compositional elements of traditional Chinese architecture. The multistoried building was set back on its site with a gate on axis in front of the main hall at the center of the ground floor. Lions guarded the gate, and steps established a sense of progression. This scheme reduced the site coverage and did not allow for commercial frontage along the sidewalk. The main hall, used for meetings of the board of directors, occupied the center of the ground floor.

Prestige came at too high a price in terms of site coverage and commercial frontage, and this design was not widely copied by other associations. A more popular design included loggias that covered the facade above the ground floor, a common feature of colonial buildings in the British and Portuguese colonies of Hong Kong and Macao. The loggias bore a relationship to the immigrants' heritage: in south China the balconies and the presence of many windows allowed for ventilation in the hot, humid climate. In Vancouver the replication of loggias across the various floors of a building functioned as a symbolic statement of cultural identity and as decoration (fig. 9.3).

A widely used approach to treating a building facade symbolically translated the traditional hierarchy of the plan into a vertical hierarchy of stacked levels expressed on the facade. Visual movement up the facade and walking up to the top floor substituted for the traditional horizontal movement along an axis. A vertical facade allowed for commercial space along the sidewalk, a residential hotel on the middle floors, and the association rooms at the top. This spatial and facade organization placed the most important spaces at the top, even though most association buildings had no elevators, which meant walking up to reach the association rooms. The symbolic placement of the association at the top of the facade was considered more important than ease of access for the members. Architecturally, a visual hierarchy up the facade of the building and movement from the sidewalk up through the building substituted for the traditional Chinese hierarchy based upon the plan and ritual movement from the entry to the back of an axially organized complex (figs. 9.1, 9.2, 9.3, and 9.5). Unlike efforts to create courtyards and gates on North American urban lots or adoptions of Euro-American forms of spatial and facade organization, this stacked compositional scheme allowed for an expression of the hierarchy of uses inside the building on the facade while accommodating the necessary mix of uses. Stores and restaurants could be located where they would be best able to take advantage of pedestrian traffic, and the association gained in prestige by sacrificing a little convenience. Residential hotels and light industry took up whatever spaces were available, and illicit activities sought out basements and more hidden locations.

Sometimes the exterior of the top floor was graced with elaborate decoration in the stacked hierarchical scheme to visually accentuate its importance. It became common to have a balcony or loggia with overhanging eaves that curved up, and these decorative elements came to be regarded as identifiable signs of Sinocization. Colored tiles on the eaves, coffers, fancy railings, marble-door surrounds with incised calligraphy, and the use of red, green, gold, and yellow were popular, along with the picturesque use of standard American building elements, such as electric lights, to add an increased density of decoration and visual interest. The amount of elaboration was related to the size and wealth of the associations. When there were limited funds, the decorative treatment and materials could be quite simple. Poorer associations and ones located in small communities often had rather spare buildings with little or no decoration. When an association could only lease a portion of the top floor of a large building, its segment of the facade could be treated with a balcony or loggia and some Sinocizing details—either colors or ornaments—such as those found in the International District of Seattle (fig. 9.6).

The associations, which served "bachelor" males in the Chinatowns of North America, declined during the first six decades of the twentieth century. The Exclusion Acts continually made it more difficult for Chinese to immigrate to the United States until immigration was completely

Fig. 9.5. China Alley, Hanford, California.

Fig. 9.6. Victorious Aid Association, Seattle.

ended by the 1924 act.[13] The resident "bachelors" aged, some returned to China to retire, and others died. As the labor pool declined, many small Chinatowns declined and disappeared. Many Chinatowns were affected by the decline of specific industries, such as mining, fishing, railroad construction, farming, and reclamation labor. The nuclear family–structured population that grew as a proportion of the total Chinese-American population after 1920 had less need of the old associations and turned to Euro-American institutions and patterns of life. By the 1960s most Chinese associations were a shadow of their former selves with only small memberships composed of aging single men.

The various schemes for decorating and utilizing buildings by Chinese-American associations were widely employed, and these schemes became one of the important visual symbols of the Chinatowns of the Pacific Coast. These design schemes for buildings constituted an important expression of the Chinese-American experience of the nineteenth and part of the twentieth centuries.

Notes

1. Richard Longstreth, in his typology of commercial building facades, describes the types most commonly adapted by the Chinese-American associations as the two-part commercial block and the two-part and three-part vertical block commonly found in Chinatowns. Richard Longstreth, *The Buildings of Main Street* (Washington, D.C.: The Preservation Press, 1987), 24–53, 82–99.

2. Stanford M. Lyman, *The Asian in the West* (Reno & Las Vegas: Western Studies Center, 1970), 27–32.

3. Dino Cinel, *From Italy to San Francisco: The Immigrant Experience* (Stanford: Stanford University Press, 1982), 2.

4. E. C. Sandmeyer, *The Anti-Chinese Movement in California* (Urbana: University of Illinois Press, 1939), 96–108.

5. Those who successfully passed the state examinations gained status in their communities. Passing the first-level examinations given at local district towns made one a *licentiate* (or "flowering talent"), which was the formal entry into the *literati* class. The second-level examinations ended in triennial examinations in the provincial capital. The successful student won the title of "recommended man," which made him eligible for the third level examination held in Beijing. The successful candidates received appointments to government posts. In this system, all of the government officials, except for princes of the royal family and officers in the military, were credentialed members of the intelligentsia.

6. Him Mark Lai, "Historical Development of the Chinese Consolidated Benevolent Association/Huiguan System," in *Chinese America: History and Perspectives* (1987): 14.

7. As an introduction to this vast topic, see C. P. Fitzgerald, *The Southern Expansion of the Chinese People* (New York: Praeger, 1972), and Lynn Pan, *Sons of the Yellow Emperor* (Boston: Little Brown, 1990).

8. Doug and Art Chin, *Uphill: The Settlement and Diffusion of the Chinese in Seattle* (Seattle: Shorey Publications, 1973), 18.

9. D. C. Lai, *Chinatowns: Towns within Cities in Canada* (Vancouver: University of British Columbia Press, 1988), 184, and Paul Yee, *Saltwater City: An Illustrated History of the Chinese in Vancouver* (Seattle: University of Washington Press, 1988), 31.

10. Yee, *Saltwater City,* 35.

11. The Ning Yung Benevolent Association, a district association representing the immigrants from Taishan, adopted the Italianate Palazzo facade in 1907 for its San Francisco headquarters. Quoins framed the facade, which was articulated by classically derived details. The association rooms occupied the second floor. At the dedication, Jow Doong Tarn, the president of the organization, noted that the rebuilding did not include a temple, which ended part of the old ways and brought the association into greater "harmony" with the rest of the city. See the *San Francisco Morning Call,* Oct. 27, 1907.

12. Him Mark Lai, "Historical Development of the Chinese Consolidated Benevolent Association/Huiguan System," 23–29, 37–39.

13. Shih-shan Henry Tsai, *The Chinese Experience in America* (Bloomington: Indiana University Press, 1986), 56–81.

Chapter 10

"Snug Li'l House with Flue and Oven": Nineteenth-Century Reforms in Plantation Slave Housing

John Michael Vlach

Ella Johnson, a former slave from the Piedmont region of South Carolina, told the interviewer sent to take down her life story, "The houses that the slaves lived in were just little old one-room log cabins." Providing more details, she added, "Usually there were two windows. The floor was wood too, although I know on some plantations the poor old slaves had just the bare ground for a floor."[1] Similar statements collected during the 1930s from other ex-slaves indicate that their quarters, too, were often nothing more than small log structures. Bill Homer, from near Shreveport, Louisiana, reported: "De nigger quarters dere was fifty one-room cabins and dey was ten in a row and dere was five rows. De cabins was built of logs and had dirt floors and a hole where a window should be and a stone fireplace for de cookin' and de heat." In Georgia Robert Shepard experienced comparable conditions, except that on his plantation the cabins had "chimblies made out of sticks and red mud. Dem chimblies was all de time catchin' fire." The slave houses recalled by John Finnely from Alabama could hardly have been more Spartan. "Us have cabins of logs," said Finnely, "with one room and one door and one window hole. . . ." His description closely matches the memory of J. T. Tims from southwestern Mississippi, who recounted that "before the War, we lived in an old log house. It had one window, one door, and one room."[2] Collectively, these testimonies provide harsh words for harsh conditions (figs. 10.1 and 10.2).

There are, however, numerous reports of slave quarters, as well as examples of standing buildings, that appear to convey a different experience. Well constructed in a variety of forms, these houses at first seem to challenge the perception of the slave experience derived solely from the accounts of former slaves. This architectural evidence suggests that the range of housing quality—and what this implies about slave treatment—was much wider than is commonly assumed. The contradictions encountered between the testimonies of former slaves and the surviving record of buildings and documents not only call for more scrutiny but also should cause us to reflect on the mechanisms of social control that were used to enforce the slaveholding regime. While the buildings do suggest that some slaves were provided with a reasonable degree of material comfort and that slavery could appear to be, in some instances, less oppressive than slave testimonies commonly indicate, appearances are deceiving. All slave dwellings are built signs of the complex and often contradictory social relationship that evolved between masters and slaves during the first half of the nineteenth century. By building decent quarters, some planters (particularly those eleven thousand who owned fifty or more slaves) hoped that they might be able to turn their rebellious and resistant field hands into more compliant laborers. These planters clearly understood that housing had the potential to be used as a benign technique of coercion. Consequently, improved slave quarters are, when viewed

Fig. 10.1. Row of Single-Pen Slave Houses at Roseberry Plantation in Dinwiddie County, Virginia, Built ca. 1850 (Photo by Beckstrom, 1936, Historic American Buildings Survey, Library of Congress.)

of this effort to provide upgraded housing for slaves still stands at Bremo, the plantation in Fluvanna County, Virginia, belonging to John Hartwell Cocke. Well known as an early critic of southern agricultural practices, Cocke was also a supporter of attempts to return enslaved blacks to their African homelands.[3] While he was slow to emancipate his own slaves, he did experiment with ways to build better quarters. Cocke extolled the virtues of dwellings constructed with *pisé,* or rammed earth, in an 1821 letter written to *The American Farmer* in which he claimed that after a period of five years these mud-walled buildings had "stood perfectly, affording the warmest shelter in winter and the coolest in summer of any buildings their size I ever knew."[4] Similar evidence of the movement to improve slave dwellings is found among a second generation of planters in the published opinion of

in terms of the slaveholder's agenda, an attempt to disguise the more oppressive aspects of a labor system in which a human being had no more rights than a mule or a hoe blade. As we will see shortly, the reform movement for slave housing was understood in different ways by the slave occupants of the upgraded cabins, and their behavioral responses did not always comply with their owners' wishes.

The history of slave housing is a broad and complex topic ranging over four centuries, diverse region settings, and the production of different commodities. In this essay I will focus primarily on developments in the South occurring between 1830 and 1860, a period when the size of the slave population reached its highest level. In 1860, when over forty-six thousand southern households qualified as plantation estates, there were numerous instances in which planters attempted to improve their properties. As a consequence of these efforts, a variety of domestic house types were used as slave quarters.

By the middle of the nineteenth century, a widespread, although disorganized, movement for plantation improvement was well under way. Evidence

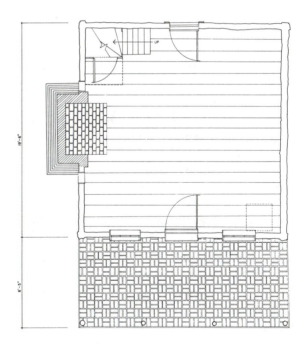

Fig. 10.2. Single-Pen Slave House at the Cavitt Place in Robertson County, Texas, Built ca. 1835. (Drawing by Barbara Pottler, 1980, Historic American Buildings Survey, Library of Congress.)

a Virginia slaveholder, who recommended in 1856 that:

> negro cabins should be built of plank, have large glass windows and good chimneys, and should be elevated at least two feet above ground. . . . The planking is put on up and down, and I use a double course of planking instead of narrow strips, this I find makes a very comfortable cabin for both summer and winter. If the builder chooses to incur a slight additional expense and should dress the outer course and give it a coat of paint, this with a projective eave and some cheap ornamental cornice, makes a very pretty house and obviates the necessity for sticking the negro cabin out of sight of the mansion.[5]

Clearly, slave houses could be built better than common practice may have required.

Throughout the first half of the nineteenth century, planters debated with some regularity the virtues of various types of slave quarters. While many argued that they preferred log cabins because they could be built quickly and cheaply, they were countered by just as many who saw log buildings as the chief source of slave illness. One planter traced common slave health complaints to the spaces or "cracks" between the logs, where he claimed all manner of filth accumulated. "The cracks," he wrote, "should be neatly lined inside and out. If this is not done, the negroes will soon have them filled with rags, old shoes, coon skins, chicken feathers and every other description of trash." Another planter thought the main problem was the "decaying logs," and another theorized about the "*bad air*" he believed was trapped in log buildings that he described as "small, low, tight, and filthy."[6] Some proposed rather modest solutions, such as building better log cabins or providing extant log cabins with plank floors raised at least two feet off the ground. However, the most reform-minded opted for new cabins constructed of wooden frames covered with boards. The substan-

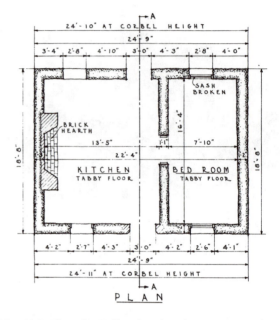

Fig. 10.3. Plan of a Hall-and-Parlor Slave House at the Kingsley Plantation on Fort George Island, Duval County, Florida. This house was built in the 1830s with tabby. (Drawing by H. C. Dozier, W. C. Vaughn, and G. G. Cellar, 1934, Historic American Buildings Survey, Library of Congress.)

tial frame cabins still standing at Tuckahoe plantation in Goochland County, Virginia, represent the sort of buildings that progressive planters generally considered to be the most sensible replacements for their aging "negro cabins."

However, the improvement and, in some instances, the rebuilding of slave dwellings was undertaken for less than altruistic motives, even though one finds that much of the rhetoric in this reform movement was couched in terms of moral obligation.[7] Planters, it appears, were often more concerned with how slave cabins should look than with the comfort of their occupants. Their comments barely disguised their feelings of contempt for their enslaved workers. One planter advised, "The negroes should be required to keep their

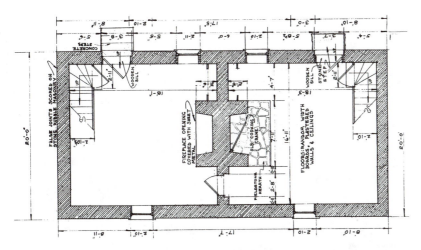

Fig. 10.4. Plan of a Double-Pen Slave Quarter at Hampton, Baltimore County, Maryland, Built ca. 1850. (Drawing by C. C. Boldrick, 1959, Historic American Buildings Survey, Library of Congress.)

houses and yards clean, and in case of neglect, should receive such punishment as will be likely to insure more cleanly habits in the future." While he also recommended that slave cabins be whitewashed because this treatment had a "cleansing and purifying effect, conducive to health," the best argument he could make for whitewash was that "the cost is almost nothing."[8] A Charleston planter went so far as to propose an economic motive for whitewash, arguing that it "*makes the slave prolific . . . and their annual increase* may be estimated as *adding as much to my income* as arises from all other sources."[9]

The range of building types used as slave dwellings extends far beyond the one-room cabins so frequently mentioned in slave narratives and described most often in histories of slavery in the antebellum South.[10] Indeed, scattered throughout the many volumes of ex-slave testimony gathered by the Federal Writers Project are descriptions of two- , three- , and even four-room houses.[11] The variety suggests both flexibility among planters regarding their management of slave conduct and their willingness to experiment with new and potentially improved modes of slave housing.

Slightly larger than cabins of the single-pen type were hall-and-parlor houses, buildings with rectangular floor plans that were divided into two rooms. Examples stood until the 1930s at The Hermitage, slightly upriver from Savannah, Georgia (fig. 10.3).[12] Just as common as single-pen slave cabins were double-pen houses, buildings consisting of two independent dwelling units under one roof. Usually providing shelter for at least two families, subtypes of the double-pen cabin are marked by variations in the placement of fireplaces and chimneys (fig. 10.4).[13] The quarters at The Forks of Cypress, a plantation in Lauderdale County, Alabama, followed the saddlebag variant of this plan in which the chimney is located between the two rooms (fig. 10.5). The other basic configuration, featured

Fig. 10.5. Double-Pen Saddlebag Log House at the Forks of Cypress Plantation near Florence, Lauderdale County, Alabama, Built ca. 1820. (Photo by Alex Bush, 1935, Historic American Buildings Survey, Library of Congress.)

Fig. 10.6. Plan of the Slave House at the Sterling C. Robertson Ranch in Bell County, Texas, Built ca. 1835. (Drawing by Mark E. Adams, 1934, Historic American Buildings Survey, Library of Congress.)

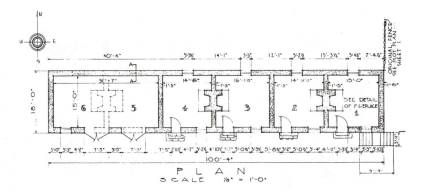

Fig. 10.7. Plan of Dog-Trot Slave Cabin at Thornhill Plantation in Greene County, Alabama, Built ca. 1833. (Drawing by Kent W. McWilliams, 1934-1935, Historic American Buildings Survey, Library of Congress.)

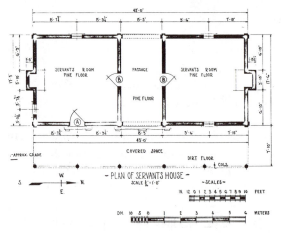

Fig. 10.8. Dog-Trot Log House Used as a Slave Quarter at Belmont Plantation near Belmont, Colbert County, Alabama, Built ca. 1828. (Photo by Alex Bush, 1936, Historic American Buildings Survey, Library of Congress.)

chimneys placed at the gable ends. Some planters even saw the double-pen cabin as the quintessential slave house and created new types of slave buildings by manipulating the double-pen form. At The Grange outside of Millersburg, Kentucky, for example, Edward Stone built a triple-pen house to serve as the quarter for his domestic slaves; it is a double-pen cabin plus an additional room. In central Texas, Sterling C. Robertson commissioned a six-room slave quarter, a structure composed of three double-pen cabins set end to end (fig. 10.6).

In plan, the dog-trot house type consisted of two rooms on either side of an open breezeway.[14]

At Thornhill plantation in Greene County, Alabama, over 150 slaves were housed in cabins of this sort (fig. 10.7). As they had in the double-pen, two different families usually occupied the two halves of the dog-trot cabin while sharing the common space in the middle. When the same house form was built by white yeoman and planters, the doors into the rooms usually opened off the central breezeway. However, if the doors were placed on the front of the two log pens, as they were on the dog-trot quarter at the Belmont plantation in northwestern Alabama, the cabin was readily seen as a structure intended for double rather than single occupancy. Built in this configuration, the dog-trot cabin was

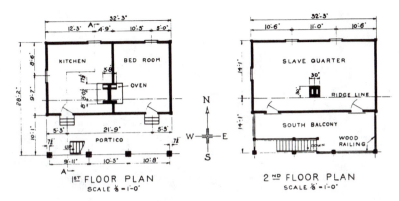

Fig. 10.9. Plans, Elevations, and Section of One of the Slave Houses at Rosemount Plantation in Greene County, Alabama, Built ca. 1835. (Drawing by A. Brandt, 1934, Historic American Buildings Survey, Library of Congress.)

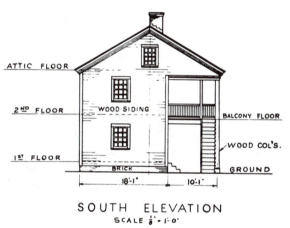

more readily recognized as a slave quarter rather than the home of a free householder (fig. 10.8).

Many one-story slave houses had loft spaces that were used either for storage or as sleeping areas for the children. Occasionally, these spaces were large enough to constitute an extra half story. Standing examples from the Bracketts farm in Louisa County, Virginia, and at Hampton, a plantation just north of Baltimore, Maryland, reveal that these quarters actually functioned as two-story houses. In fact, some slave dwellings were even built to a full two stories in height. The slave houses at Horton Grove in North Carolina contained four separate units set in a two-over-two arrangement. While intended to shelter four different slave families, these buildings were both visually and formally identical to I-houses, the narrow two-story dwellings commonly built by more pros-

perous southern farmers and quite a few planters.[15] The Horton Grove slave houses are exceptional buildings because of their size and substantial construction, but the I-house is not all that rare as a slave dwelling. Other examples can be found at Rosemount plantation in Greene County, Alabama (fig. 10.9), and at "Wickland" in Nelson County, Kentucky.

Most of the designs for nineteenth century slave housing grew out of the fund of Anglo-American architectural customs, which sanctioned the use of square or rectangular units. These units either stood alone as individual dwellings or were arranged in a number of symmetrical configurations.[16] One slave house type not based on this pen system was called a "tenement house." In an

Fig. 10.10. Tenement Plan Slave Quarter at Mansfield Plantation, Georgetown County, South Carolina, Built ca. 1850. (Photo by Charles N. Bayless, 1927, Historic American Buildings Survey, Library of Congress.)

Fig. 10.11. Slave Quarter at the Barbarra Plantation in St. Charles Parish, Louisiana, Built ca. 1825. (Photo by Richard Koch, 1927, Historic American Buildings Survey, Library of Congress.)

1838 description of the house's plan, South Carolina rice planter James Sparkman indicated that it contained three rooms set in an asymmetrical pattern: it had a narrow but deep hall with two sleeping "apartments" off to one side.[17] Later, Frederick Law Olmsted found this same room arrangement being used in the slave housing at several Georgia plantations, generally in a doubled configuration. In his description of one particularly large slave village consisting of about thirty tenement houses, he wrote:

> Each cabin was a framed building, the walls boarded and whitewashed on the outside, lathed and plastered within, the roof shingled; forty-two feet long, twenty-one feet wide, divided into two family tenements, each tenement divided into three-rooms—one, the common household apartment, twenty-one by ten; each of the others (bedrooms), ten by ten. There was a brick fire-place in the middle of the long side of each living room, the chimneys rising in one, in the middle of the roof. Beside these rooms, each tenement has a cock-loft, entered by steps from the household room.[18]

Double-tenement houses matching those described by Olmsted were also used by William Aiken on his Jehossee Island estate in South Carolina, where he built eighty-four such buildings to house his approximately seven hundred slaves.[19] A few tenement houses still stand at Mansfield plantation in Georgetown County, South Carolina (fig. 10.10). While these buildings might from the exterior resemble double-pen cabins, the double-tenement house actually provides eight rooms for two families.

In southern Louisiana highly distinctive slave quarters were derived from local building traditions. Two-room cabins were frequently constructed with deep inset porches, a feature derived from the galleries found on the fronts of Caribbean-influenced Creole houses. Often, these structures were indistinguishable from the houses of Cajun settlers; only the fact that they were set out in straight rows on sugar plantations confirmed that they were occupied by slaves.[20] A slave house from the Barbarra plantation in St. Charles Parish not only followed all the plan requirements of the Creole house—it was two rooms wide and two rooms deep with its chimney located between the two front rooms—but also had other features that immediately revealed its deep French origins. The building's steeply pitched hipped roof with the slight kick at the eaves, its *poteux sur solle* (post on sill) construction, and *bousillage* (mud) plaster were all traceable back to Normandy, the original Cajun homeland (fig. 10.11).[21]

Many of the slave quarters built along the Georgia coast, while they followed the usual single- and double-pen and sometimes the "tenement" models in form, were constructed with a coarse type of oyster shell concrete called *tabby*. Used in the area as early as the early sixteenth century by the Spanish for the construction of mission churches, tabby was reintroduced as a suitable material for plantation structures around 1815 by Thomas Spalding of Darien, Georgia, master of Ashantilly. His example was followed by many of his planter neighbors, who were impressed by his quarters, which proved to be both fire and storm proof. The foot-thick walls may also have provided occupants with well-insulated rooms, keeping them cool during the oppressively hot summers. Constructed with plank forms about two feet in height, the walls of tabby houses are marked by distinctive horizontal bands indicating the seams between the successive two-foot high layers of concrete. Active experimentation with tabby at the Thickets plantation in McIntosh County led to the development of quarters with flat roofs made with tabby bricks that were laid over timber supports and waterproofed with tar.[22]

In addition to the variety of plan forms and construction techniques reviewed here, some slave houses, particularly those set close to a slave-holder's residence, were finished in a variety of decorative styles. Near Ben Venue at an estate in Rappahannock County in northern Virginia, three brick slave cabins stand in a row; each one has parapeted gables stepped at the eaves. These low decorative walls echo the same feature found on the plantation's big house, a gesture of style intended to serve as a visual link between the quarters and the mansion. At Boone Hall, a plantation just north of Charleston, South Carolina, a series of brick slave

Fig. 10.12. Double-Pen Slave Quarter in Gothic Dress at the Plantation Belonging to Robert Gracey near Gallion, Hale County, Alabama, Built ca. 1840. (Photo by Alex Bush, 1935, Historic American Buildings Survey, Library of Congress.)

houses built in the 1840s flank the oak-lined road leading to the main house. That these buildings were meant to decorate the grounds as well as to provide shelter for slaves is indicated by the geometric designs marked on some of their walls with glazed bricks. The brick quarters at Henry McAlpin's Hermitage plantation in Georgia were also designed and arranged to make an ornamental statement. Visitors noted that the slave houses made McAlpin's regency-styled residence seem very grand. Even after the estate was abandoned for several years during the Civil War, a northern journalist noted in 1864: "There are about 70 or 80 Negro houses, all built of brick and white-washed so they look very neat, and rows of live oaks between, making it the handsomest plantation in Georgia."[23]

Official national styles of architecture were, on occasion, also registered on slave houses. George W. Johnson had his slave-quarter kitchen in Scott County, Kentucky, done up in the Greek Revival mode by wrapping engaged pilasters around the exterior of a hipped roofed, double-pen cabin in the imitation of a classic colonnade. Since planter

Robert Gracey of Gallion, Alabama, chose a Gothic design for his own house, he decided that similar embellishments were also appropriate for the buildings in which he housed his domestic slaves. Their double-pen saddlebag houses were covered with vertical board-and-batten siding, featured lancet windows in their gables, and were trimmed with scalloped bargeboards along the eaves (fig. 10.12). In Montgomery, Alabama, the quarters adjacent to the Ball mansion were tricked out in Italianate trim, following the theme of the big house, which was designed as a full-scale Tuscan villa. While the decoration of these quarters was no doubt carried out in order to make the view from the big house more pleasant, the slave occupants of these buildings did benefit as well, since their quarters were more likely to be kept in good repair.

Behind the planters' efforts to provide their slaves with better built, more comfortable, and seemingly more pleasant quarters lay the growing recognition that their slaves were among their most precious economic assets. As early as 1820, a contributor to the *American Farmer* cautioned: "The blacks constitute either absolutely, or instrumentally, the wealth of our southern states. If a planter, as it often happens, is deprived by sickness of the labour of one third, or one half, of his negroes, it becomes a loss of no small magnitude."[24] While the dollar value of slaves varied widely throughout history of the "peculiar institution," the average price of a prime field hand hovered near a thousand dollars during the 1840s and by 1860 was approaching two thousand dollars in some markets.[25] Thus, while crop prices during this same twenty-year period were highly unpredictable and usually in decline, the value of slaves seemed certain to increase steadily.[26] It is not too surprising, then, that from the 1830s onward, planters paid much more attention to the physical welfare of their slaves. Those men who had invested extensively in human property—particularly the rice and sugar planters, who owned hundreds of slaves—not only fixed up their slaves'

dwellings but also built for their slaves dining halls, hospitals, and chapels. Any expense incurred was certain, they thought, to be recouped from either the more dependable, and therefore more efficient, labor of healthy, contented field hands or, if necessary, from the sale of those healthy slaves. In 1857 when Missouri planter Thomas Houston was offered as a gift his choice of either three thousand dollars in cash or a slave family valued at four thousand dollars, he decided to take the money in order to "invest it in negro boys, from 12 to 16 years old." Within a few years, he reasoned, he would be able to more than double the original offer.[27] The favorable market for slave field hands encouraged Henry Clayton, a planter from Barbour County, Alabama, basically to stockpile slaves as a hedge against a potential financial short-fall. His wife, Victoria, explained, "My husband, at the close of each year, having saved up money enough to invest in something to increase our income, was naturally disposed to invest in slaves as being then the most available and profitable property in our section of the country."[28]

Wherever this kind of thinking prevailed among the planter class, slaves were sometimes provided with improved housing. At least old dirt-floored log cabins with gaps in their walls might be replaced with framed houses with wooden floors that were heated with brick fireplaces. Jacob Branch, a former slave at the Double Bayou settlement near Houston, Texas, recalled that his cabin was a "snug li'l house with flue and oven," a definite improvement over the sorts of buildings that even slaveholders would admit were often "knocked up in a very careless, bungling manner—always *too small* and *too low* . . . dirty habitations . . . well-calculated to generate disease."[29]

While eighteenth-century slave cabins were rarely ever more than one- or two-room shelters, by 1860 the repertoire of slave buildings included at least nine different house types. Further variations were created both by manipulations of plans and exteriors. A new picturesque style was supplanting the regimentation that had formerly characterized the so-called "slave street." But while a program of physical improvements to slave housing was being enacted, the possibility that slaves might somehow obtain their freedom by legal means was being deliberately eliminated. Between 1830 and 1860—the period coinciding with the era of noticeable slave housing reforms—all southern states, except for Missouri, made the manumission of slaves illegal and insisted further that any freed blacks must leave.[30] Official avenues for exiting the "peculiar institution" were thus closed off, and the slave status of black southerners was converted into a permanent, inescapable condition. The increasing variety and upgrading found in nineteenth-century slave quarters is, then, the positive face of a cynical strategy employed by planters to encourage slaves to trade their hopes for personal freedom for a list of modest physical comforts.

During the first half of the nineteenth century, a significant number of slaves were given better housing, better rations, improved health care, and greater opportunity for Christian worship. The cost for these advantages was their right to full personhood. Slaves, however, responded by turning their masters' offers of material improvement to their advantage. They defined their quarters as a black cultural domain in which they were able to establish important, if vulnerable, family ties, to create distinctive domestic art forms, and to develop powerful and lasting religious traditions. These were not the creations of an overawed and submissive people. The slaveholders' enticements were transformed into resources that slaves would use to develop further a society of their own. Slave culture was, according to historian Leslie Howard Owens, tied to a special awareness among the slaves that they had a space of their own. He writes that "the Quarters, sometimes partially, sometimes entirely, and often mysteriously, encompassed and breathed its own special vitality into these experiences, frequently assuring that bondage did not snuff out the many-sided existence slaves created for themselves."[31] In refusing to be instruments of their own oppression, slaves turned whatever meager favors that were offered them into resources for attaining their own social goals. That slaves living in "improved" quarters may have sensed a degree of personal empowerment is suggested by the testimony of an unnamed Georgia slave woman owned by a planter who was very much given to progressive management methods. When asked if she belonged to his family, she answered without a second's hesitation, "Yes, I belong to them and they belong to me."[32]

Notes

This essay grows out of a paper that was presented at the Chancellor Porter L. Fortune Jr. Symposium on Southern History held at the University of Mississippi in 1990, entitled "'Not Mansions . . . But Good Enough': Slave Quarters as Bi-cultural Expression," and published in Ted Ownby, ed., *Black and White Cultural Interaction in the Antebellum South* (Jackson: University Press of Mississippi, 1993), 89–114, along with a commentary by historian Brenda Stevenson. While this essay stresses the cultural and political contestation that ensues from the design of slave housing, in the earlier piece I focused more on the symbolic aspects of slave cabins that may have been shared by whites and blacks. In my book, *Back of the Big House: The Architecture of Plantation Slavery* (Chapel Hill: University of North Carolina Press, 1993), I again use some of the same buildings, but mainly to describe generic building types; I then go on to situate those types within the cultural landscape of the plantation along with other structures, such as barns, kitchens, stables, dairies, smokehouses, and other outbuildings.

1. George P. Rawick, *The American Slave: A Composite Autobiography* (Westport, Conn.: Greenwood, 1977), Suppl. Ser., 4: 346.

2. Norman R. Yetman, *Life Under the "Peculiar Institution": Selections from the Slave Narrative Collection* (New York: Holt, Rinehart & Winston, 1970), 168, 265, 124, 304.

3. See the introduction to Randall M. Miller, *"Dear Master": Letters of a Slave Family* (Ithaca, N.Y.: Cornell University Press, 1978).

4. "Remarks on Hedges, Bene Plant, and Pise Buildings," *The American Farmer* 3 (20) (1821): 157.

5. James E. Breeden, ed., *Advice Among Masters: The Ideal of Slave Management in the Old South* (Westport, Conn.: Greenwood, 1980), 130.

6. Ibid., 128, 122, 120.

7. See Albert J. Raboteau, *Slave Religion: The "Invisible Institution" in the Antebellum South* (New York: Oxford University Press, 1978), for a discussion of planter concern for the moral welfare of their slaves, a concern that clearly impinged on their decisions to improve their slaves' living conditions.

8. Breeden, *Advice Among Masters,* 121.

9. Quoted in James Oakes, *The Ruling Race: A History of American Slaveholders* (New York: Knopf, 1982), 73; emphasis is in the original.

10. See, for examples, Kenneth M. Stampp, *The Peculiar Institution: Slavery in the Ante-Bellum South* (New York: Random House, 1956), 292; Eugene D. Genovese, *Roll, Jordan, Roll: The World the Slaves Made* (New York: Random House, 1972), 524; and Mechal Sobel, *The World they Made Together: Black and White Values in Eighteenth-Century Virginia* (Princeton: Princeton University Press, 1987), chap. 9.

11. See, for example, Rawick, *The American Slave,* 4: pt. 1, 55; pt. 2, 182; pt. 3, 253.

12. Henry Glassie, *Pattern in the Material Folk Culture of the Eastern United States* (Philadelphia: University of Pennsylvania Press, 1969), 78, 80–81.

13. Ibid., 102–6.

14. Ibid., 89, 94–98.

15. Fred B. Kniffen, "Folk Housing: Key to Diffusion," in *Common Places: Readings in American Vernacular Architecture,* ed. Dell Upton and John Michael Vlach (Athens: University of Georgia Press, 1986), 7–10.

16. For a more detailed assessment of the architectural acculturation between blacks and whites, see John Michael Vlach, "Afro-American Housing in Virginia's Landscape of Slavery," in *By the Work of Their Hands: Studies in Afro-American Folklife* (Ann Arbor, Mich.: UMI Research Press, 1991), 215–29.

17. J. Harold Easterby Jr., ed., *The South Carolina Rice Planter as Revealed in the Papers of Robert F. W. Allston* (Chicago: University of Chicago Press, 1945), 348.

18. Frederick Law Olmsted, *The Cotton Kingdom: A Traveller's Observations on Cotton and Slavery in the American Slave States,* ed. Arthur M. Schlesinger (New York: Alfred A. Knopf, 1953), 184.

19. Herbert Anthony Keller, ed., *Solon Robinson: Pioneer and Agriculturist* (Indianapolis: Indiana Historical Bureau, 1936), 367.

20. Glassie, *Pattern in the Material Folk Culture,* 118, 120–21.

21. Jay Edwards, "French," in *America's Architectural Roots: Ethnic Groups That Built America,* ed. Dell Upton (Washington, D.C.: Preservation Press, 1986), 64.

22. Julia Floyd Smith, *Slavery and Rice Culture in Low Country Georgia* (Knoxville: University of Tennessee Press, 1985), 120–21

23. Quoted in Ibid., 122. For a description of the mansion house at The Hermitage, see John Linley, *The Georgia Catalog: Historic American Buildings Survey—A Guide to the Architecture of the State* (Athens: University of Georgia Press, 1983), 72–73, 342.

24. Breeden, *Advice Among Masters,* 163–64.

25. Alfred H. Conrad and John R. Meyer, "Economics of Slavery in the Antebellum South," in *Slavery and the Southern Economy,* ed. Harold D. Woodman (Harcourt, Brace & World, 1966), 71.

26. Ulrich B. Phillips, *American Negro Slavery: A Survey of the Supply, Employment and Control of Negro Labor as Determined by the Plantation Regime* (1918; reprint,. Baton Rouge: Louisiana State University Press, 1966), 371.

27. Oakes, *The Ruling Race,* 173.

28. Quoted in Katharine M. Jones, ed., *The Plantation South* (Indianapolis: Bobbs-Merrill, 1957), 272.

29. Jacob Branch's testimony appears in Yetman, *Life Under the Peculiar Institution,* 40; the planter's quote was published originally in the *Southern Cultivator,* 1856 by a Mississippi planter who signed himself "Omo," reprinted in Breeden, *Advice Among Masters,* 127.

30. Eugene D. Genovese, *Roll, Jordan, Roll,* 399.

31. Leslie Howard Owens, *This Species of Property: Slave Life and Culture in the Old South* (New York: Oxford University Press, 1976), p. 224.

32. Quoted in Oakes, *The Ruling Race,* 190.

Part IV
Architecture and Popular Culture

Chapter 11

Cheap and Tasteful Dwellings
in Popular Architecture

Jan Jennings

The dissemination of information about everyday architecture in late-nineteenth- and early-twentieth-century America depended upon trade catalogs, plan books, and architectural periodicals. Of the various kinds of building trades' publications, *Carpentry and Building,* a nationally distributed builder's paper, published from 1879 to 1930 in New York, was unique.[1] Although it has been overlooked as a significant architectural serial, it played a critical role in the establishment of a national vernacular.[2] *Carpentry and Building* provides an inventory of middle-class house designs that reflect domestic architecture values, such as home ownership, private property, and suburban development.[3] The houses portrayed the status of their owners in commerce, the trades, and the professions, and, as such, they generated a new social landscape. The journal also offers insight into architectural practice, especially its emphasis on practicality and replication. As a provider of complete working drawings, *Carpentry and Building* is an excellent reference to study speculative house types. Often, half-tone engravings of photographs document designs that were actually constructed. In this essay, I will focus on the journal's editorial policy that promoted practicality, a decision that led to its interest in design for inexpensive houses.[4]

In the second issue, a correspondent requested designs for "cheap and tasteful dwellings in popular styles of architecture," and *Carpentry and Building* responded: "The architect who succeeds in arranging a comfortable and well-appointed small dwelling will achieve a desirable reputation as well

as confer a real benefit upon those of limited means, yet possessing good taste, who are about to make a home."[5] With that, the journal made its first call for design submissions to meet the correspondent's request and established an expectation about architectural, as well as socioeconomic, desires. These two acts—the correspondent's appeal and the journal's answer—were powerful enough to shift the initial editorial intention of *Carpentry and Building* from a construction-information source to a forum for design ideas.

Carpentry and Building became part of an emerging tradition of diffusing domestic architecture to "the majority of Americans, particularly working people, who could not afford expensive architecture, and who desired a single-family home in the emerging suburbs."[6] Beginning in eighteenth-century England, architects such as Thomas Rawlins accused the architectural profession of ignoring ordinary buildings and the people who lived in them and of neglecting "the practical part of building," which would make their designs "useful and instructive to country builders."[7] American architects who published pattern books of designs claimed that their purpose was to aid people in procuring a comfortable home of their own at a moderate cost. They believed that designing cheap homes was a "special line," "a new system," or "another branch of architecture," because the best and most distinguished architects had relinquished this market, or thought it beneath their consideration, in favor of large buildings.[8] In 1866, D. H. Jacques, in writing *The House: A Manual of Rural Architec-*

ture, promoted the diffusion of domestic architectural knowledge "among the people" and criticized writers such as Downing, Vaux, Wheeler, Cleaveland, and the Backus brothers for casting too narrow a circle in terms of the size and cost of their buildings. Jacques proposed a "wider, if not stronger, influence," a "universal circulation and almost unlimited usefulness," placing "the whole within the reach of every man in America."[9]

The exorbitant costs for architects' commissions had been widely criticized by designers who were interested in providing ordinary domestic architecture, and it became one of the rationales for publishing pattern books and, later, plan books. *Carpentry and Building* furthered the goal of alleviating fees for architectural services. Complete sets of working drawings were contributed by architects without reimbursement to them, and, since the published drawings were intended to be freely reproduced by others, the journal paid no money for copyright protection of architectural designs. In effect, the designs were available with the cost of a subscription. This low overhead obviously contributed to economical production costs and, in turn, was a primary factor in achieving large circulation. As one of the largest periodicals in circulation in the late nineteenth century (a record-setting twenty thousand copies in 1890), *Carpentry and Building* cast a wide net for architects, builders, and potential home owners and provided the "most comprehensive view of the development of the domestic construction industry."[10] The journal became a forum for contributors to display their accomplishments in design and construction; architects obviously supported the journal's intentions regarding replication, and perhaps they also viewed it as a kind of advertising.

Practicality

In its first years, the word "practical" was used frequently to describe the journal's primary objective as a construction-information service. However, the scope broadened quickly as readers' letters helped shape the paper's direction. David Williams, the journal's first publisher, who specialized in technical books, addressed the inaugural issue to the building trades, introducing *Carpentry and Building* as a monthly publication that would be "eminently practical" and "useful." Publishers A. J. Bicknell and W. T. Comstock, who had "extensive acquaintance with the building trades," endorsed the paper and characterized it as a "practical working journal."[11] The journal included sections devoted to particular aspects, such as the departments of "Framing and Construction," "Practical Carpentry," "Plumbing," and "Architecture" and was intended to function as a compendium of information on all building-trades subjects. But unlike its competitor, *Manufacturer and Builder, Carpentry and Building* became not as concerned with building elements, materials, and manufacturing as with the dissemination of designs for low-cost housing throughout the country. Eventually, practicality, as it came to be identified by editorial policy, became the means to make cheap and tasteful houses.

Reviewing *Carpentry and Building's* use of the term practical is an exercise in enigmatic meanings. Sometimes the term is used straightforwardly, as pertaining or relating to practice (consisting or exhibited in practice or action) as distinguished from theory. Up until the late eighteenth and early nineteenth century, the superiority of practical knowledge was well accepted, and theoretical knowledge that was useful to the everyday world was greatly underdeveloped. The 1856 prospectus of *Scientific American* defines practical science as "the promulgation of information relating to the various mechanic and chemic arts, industrial manufactures, agriculture, patents, inventions, engineering, millwork and all the interests which the light of practical science is calculated to advance." But the new science and technology, which included engineering and "architectural science," relied on formal experimentation to identify or to discover principles that underlay knowledge.[12] When theory threatened experience, practicality as an old value was rearticulated. These issues between shop culture and school culture, and between architects and builders, were debated for years.

When *Carpentry and Building* began publication, it solicited designs from practical men who were concerned with practice. It targeted as its initial audience architects and builders who were inclined to action based on a knowledge derived from practice rather than theory. *Carpentry and Building* reported on those who actually did the work of designing, building, supervising, and, in so doing, they made a value judgment that these architects were more useful to society than architectural theorists. In 1887, an Illinois reader, who characterized himself as a "practical builder," found the journal "of more practical use than all the rest put together, not only furnishing all the plans for both cheap and costly houses, but giving the details necessary for their construction without the intervention of an architect."[13] When A. L. Myers, of Lincoln, Nebraska, submitted his drawings for a cottage, he described himself as a "practical man" and credited *Carpentry and Building* as his principal teacher.[14]

In addition to practicality as defined by the scientific community, and obvious parallels about usefulness, *Carpentry and Building* borrowed the term practical from the titles and prefaces of pattern books, where it became an encoded term that embraced a number of attributes. Lewis F. Allen stated that the plans and directions submitted in his book were intended to be of the "most practical kind: plain, substantial, and applicable," and he implied that practical architecture was familiar when he said: "These plans are chiefly original; that is, they are not copied from any in the books, or from any structures with which the writer is familiar. Yet they will doubtless be found to resemble buildings, both in outward appearance and interior arrangement, with which numerous readers may be acquainted."[15] By the 1870s, pattern books defined practical architecture as possessing a specific set of characteristics: the designs were intended for everybody and the buildings were to be erected in all sections of the country; plans should be of convenient arrangement, houses should be compact, and construction costs should be low or moderate; and scale drawings of an entire building were provided, sometimes with specifications and estimates for materials and labor.

Pattern suppliers saw practical planning as the recommended cure for solving problems associated with large, costly, and poorly planned dwellings. "Convenient arrangement" became the accepted canon to explain the relationship between design principles and economical housekeeping. To plan conveniently, a house planner was to consider internal arrangement first, as well as occupants' desires—especially the "housewife's"—rather than form. Convenient planning also called for efficient room arrangement, a concept that was based on step-saving (labor-saving) principles, and the logical arrangement of rooms and their adjacency to the kitchen. Convenient arrangement eventually came to mean reform principles, such as avoiding wasted space (especially large halls, long passages, and extended wings) and removing dust-catching woodwork.

The concept of arranging efficient interior space dovetailed with notions of compactness: if the interior plan was efficient, the exterior form would be compact, as in Laura E. Kingston's first-prize design (fig. 11.1). *Carpentry and Building* supported the notion of compactness, because it was a practical means of delivering low-cost housing, and the journal endorsed convenient arrangement in principle. For example, a 1904 two-family house competition stated that "the conditions require that the building shall be modern in all its appointments and finish, of attractive exterior, and divided in its interior in such a way as to give the most economical and convenient arrangement of rooms for each family."[16] But because *Carpentry and Building* did not ascribe to one-of-a-kind design,

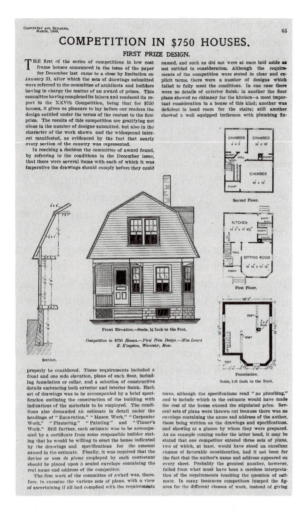

CARPENTRY AND BUILDING, MARCH, 1899. 65

COMPETITION IN $750 HOUSES.

FIRST PRIZE DESIGN.

THE first of the series of competitions in low cost frame houses announced in the issue of the paper for December last came to a close by limitation on January 31, after which the sets of drawings submitted were referred to the committee of architects and builders having in charge the matter of an award of prizes. This committee having completed its labors and rendered its report in the XXVth Competition, being that for $750 houses, it gives us pleasure to lay before our readers the design entitled under the terms of the contest to the first prize. The results of this competition are gratifying not alone in the number of designs submitted, but also in the character of the work shown and the widespread interest manifested, as evidenced by the fact that nearly every section of the country was represented.

In reaching a decision the committee of award found, by referring to the conditions in the December issue, that there were several items with each of which it was imperative the drawings should comply before they could

properly be considered. These requirements included a front and one side elevation, plans of each floor, including foundation or cellar, and a selection of constructive details embracing both exterior and interior finish. Each set of drawings was to be accompanied by a brief specification outlining the construction of the building with indications of the materials to be employed. The conditions also demanded an estimate in detail under the headings of "Excavation," "Mason Work," "Carpenter Work," "Plastering," "Painting" and "Tinner's Work." Still further, each estimate was to be accompanied by a certificate from some responsible builder stating that he would be willing to erect the house indicated by the drawings and specifications for the amount named in the estimate. Finally, the device or nom de plume employed by each contestant should be placed upon a sealed envelope containing the real name and address of the competitor.

The first work of the committee of award was, therefore, to examine the various sets of plans, with a view of ascertaining if all had complied with the requirements

named, and such as did not were at once laid aside as not entitled to consideration. Although the requirements of the competition were stated in clear and explicit terms, there were a number of designs which failed to fully meet the conditions. In one case there were no details of exterior finish; in another the floor plans showed no chimney for the kitchen—a most important consideration in a house of this kind; another was deficient in head room for the stairs; still another showed a well equipped bathroom with plumbing fix-

tures, although the specifications read "no plumbing," and to include which in the estimate would have made the cost of the house exceed the stipulated price. Several sets of plans were thrown out because there was no envelope containing the name and address of the author, these being written on the drawings and specifications, and showing at a glance by whom they were prepared. As an example coming under the latter head, it may be stated that one competitor entered three sets of plans, two of which, at least, would have stood an excellent chance of favorable consideration, had it not been for the fact that the author's name and address appeared on every sheet. Probably the greatest number, however, failed from what must have been a careless interpretation of the requirements touching the question of estimate. In many instances competitors lumped the figures for the different classes of work, instead of giving

CHAMBER | CHAMBER

CHAMBER

Second Floor.

KITCHEN

HALL | SITTING ROOM

PORCH

First Floor.

Front Elevation.—Scale, ⅛ Inch to the Foot.

Competition in $750 Houses.—First Prize Design.—Miss Laura E. Kingston, Worcester, Mass.

Section.

Foundation.

Scale, 1-16 Inch to the Foot.

Fig. 11.1. "Competition in $750 Houses, First Prize Design." (From *Carpentry and Building* [Mar. 1899]: 65. Design by Laura Kingston.)

it paid little attention to an occupant's desires. Eventually, housing-reform literature prescribed design conventions that the journal adopted wholeheartedly.

Including working drawings as a distinguishing characteristic of practical architecture implied that designs were intended to be reproduced without much regard for a specific client or a particular site. In 1879, when the journal acknowledged Bicknell as "the pioneer, in this country, in the

publication of practical architecture books," it recognized pattern books as its predecessor and borrowed the use and meaning of the term "practical" to include the publication of designs with details drawn to working scale that were adaptable to builders.[17] In the journal's first year, Bicknell and Comstock's designs, published more than anyone else's, established a journal standard that included an exterior perspective and elevations, a floor plan, as well as interior and exterior details.[18]

One of the consequences of a practical architecture was the practice of furnishing "alternative designs." In the months following the request for cheap and tasteful dwellings, *Carpentry and Building* published designs for a "Frame House of Moderate Price" by James W. Pirsson of New York City and a "Study in Cheap Frame Houses" furnished by B. O'Rourke of Newark, New Jersey. O'Rourke's solution for producing inexpensive housing was to build a row of dwellings using a single-floor plan but varying slightly the exterior and interior appearance. In addition to O'Rourke's floor plan, the journal published a front and a side elevation for each of his four schemes, which he labeled English, English with tower, Swiss, and French. He also provided three alternative detail drawings of inside finish (fig. 11.2). To achieve exterior variation, O'Rourke kept all the elevations consistent, but manipulated the roof form and smaller architectural elements, such as the porch, gable trim, and interior trim work.[19] O'Rourke's "alternative designs" were a convention established in seventeenth-century furniture and chimneypiece pattern books; in architecture, the plan remained constant while variations in design were offered for elevations.[20] Reliance on the plan meant that the location of openings was constant; deviation in construction costs from one building to the next varied only in terms of materials and finishes. For this reason, alternative designs were often employed to illustrate low-cost, speculative, suburban houses and small stores. In 1869, when Lawrence B. Valk designed three small cottage facades for *The*

Manufacturer and Builder, the journal stated that "perhaps no class of building" would "pay capitalists a better percentage upon investments," especially if laid out in villages located near a railway line at a reasonable distance from the city.[21] Alternative designs remained popular in *Carpentry and Building* because they appealed economically to speculative developers in suburbs. In 1901, when F. R. Comstock designed a row of houses for Leon Morgan, the journal regarded the design as "a more attractive style of architecture" that increased the attractiveness of the street and relieved the monotony of the houses that looked "severely like their neighbors."[22]

It was the changing nature of drawings in the late nineteenth century that encouraged replication as literal copying. Architectural historian Dell Upton observes that "few antebellum designs were copied literally," because "the vernacular process was an additive one in which builders reduced the designs of pattern book writers into distinctive essences."[23] But there was also a practical reason for the lack of literal copying. Many early pattern books did not offer a full set of integrated working drawings for a particular building, so that architects and builders were forced to use the miscellaneous details as "hints and suggestions" and a plan and an elevation as a starting point. The assumption of eighteenth- and nineteenth-century pattern books was that the builder was a craftsman who knew how to construct buildings traditionally; therefore, it was not necessary for everything to be drawn, and the expression "working drawings" rarely appeared.[24] *Carpentry and Building*'s tenure coincided with a time when builders became less reliant on traditional forms of building, when construction practices became more difficult.[25] This, coupled with the idea of publishing full sets of scaled working drawings, changed expectations about the use of drawings and made literal copying much more likely.

Between 1880 and 1884, builders from New York, Nebraska, Arkansas, and Oregon testified

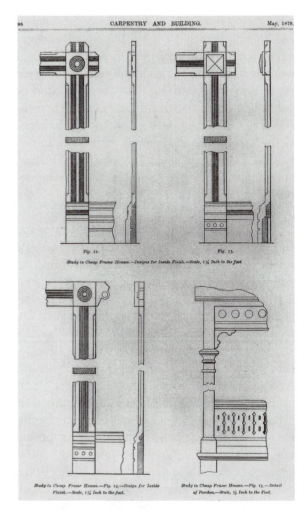

Fig. 11.2. "Architecture: A Study in Cheap Frame Houses." (From *Carpentry and Building* [May 1879]: 96.)

that they had used *Carpentry and Building*'s published drawings to construct houses. One enthusiast, who had constructed two houses from the same plan, considered them the nicest looking cottages for the cost (less than a thousand dollars) in his town. Others wrote that their houses had elicited such a favorable response that they had received other building contracts. By 1884, the journal stated that its published designs had been used for several thousand dwellings.[26] Another sign of the journal's success at diffusion was the reproduction of *Carpentry and Building* designs in English and French journals. However honored the editors might have been, they held these international journals in disdain for not publishing a complete set of drawings, claiming that "the distinction of publishing house designs in such a complete manner as to adapt them without additional drawings to the use of builders belongs exclusively to this journal."[27] Journals like *Carpentry and Building* that published patterns succeeded at diffusing design to a large number of people and sealed the fate of pattern books.[28]

Although borrowing invaded the realm of the elite architect, it was not considered a plagiaristic act to practical architects.[29] Borrowing from one another was an act of sharing, a beneficial trait that would provide good design for those of limited means. Practical architecture was based on cooperation rather than competition, and the journal's relationship with its subscribers reinforced these beliefs. The journal referred to its readers as "friends," "correspondents," "voters," and "submitters," indicating that they were to play an active rather than a passive role in the magazine. From the beginning, readers contributed by writing in, posing questions, answering inquiries from other correspondents, describing their jobs, and voting in the competitions. The journal established regular columns for "Correspondence" and "Questions and Answers." Although discussion and criticism for the published drawings was requested, architectural history or theory did not receive much attention. The tone of the criticism was not harsh, but rather cooperative and helpful. And, most important, the readers submitted their own design work. This single and eminently practical decision to solicit subscribers to supply most of the designs for the journal had long-ranging implications, including the journal's unprecedented high circulation figures, its low cost, and, ultimately, its longevity.

Before *Carpentry and Building,* other journals had published patterns.[30] But in terms of longevity, *Carpentry and Building* was certainly the most

consistent in its intent to promote replication. In 1897, to disseminate the drawings in another form, David Williams issued the first of at least six pattern books in the *Carpentry and Building* series (after 1910, the series became known as *The Building Age* series), which included previously published designs from the journal. Each design included scaled drawings of elevations, floor plans, details, and general specifications, and, in most cases, included a photograph of the completed building. The *Carpentry and Building* series was thematic, organized on the basis of cost, and, in one case, concrete. The shift from offering patterns to operating a plan service was initiated in the June 1916 issue of *The Building Age* with drawings by anonymous architects. But the journal never completely forfeited the idea of publishing patterns, and, beginning in 1922, it resumed the practice by including a blueprint supplement in each issue that featured a complete set of drawings for a house, as well as specifications and estimated costs. These were designed by architects who were identified by name, including the Architect's Small House Service Bureau.

Examining the Language

An explanation of the language and composition of the correspondent's petition, "cheap and tasteful dwellings in popular styles of architecture," reveals *Carpentry and Building*'s motives, as well as the connection the journal had with vernacular architecture. The request appears in the correspondence section of the journal, along with a small notice from the editors that several correspondents had requested designs and plans for moderate-priced, suburban houses. Moreover, the request for cheap and tasteful dwellings clearly struck the right cord with the editors, or, in their words, the request was "a nut the successful cracking of which seems to us quite desirable."[31] As a catalyst of change, the allure of showing affordable houses was potent enough to shift the focus of the journal, but, however beguiling the language of the request, the paradox is that *Carpentry and Building* decided to deliver on only half of the request. It chose to provide cheap and popular houses, but it left style and taste mostly unanswered, because these concepts fell within the purview of style-based architectures, which the journal avoided.

Although we find the term "cheap" to be out of fashion today, it was a commonly used nineteenth-century word in building-trades literature, and, from 1879 to 1904, "cheap" appears in over two dozen *Carpentry and Building* article titles. After the turn of the century, the journal abandoned "cheap" as a description and substitutes words such as inexpensive, moderate-priced, and low-cost. However, the candor of the original term reflects the economic status of the journal's readership, of the builders, and of the building public.[32] In titles, the term cheap was often paired with frame, denoting the use of wood construction as the method for delivering inexpensive houses. Titles such as "Cheap Frame House" link a series of prosaic words, expressions of plainness, a lack of pretentiousness, and honesty regarding expectations of cost, materials, and design.

In the phrase "cheap and tasteful," two disparate adjectives modify what kinds of dwellings to expect and speak to complicated issues involved in design. While cheapness is forthright, tasteful is ambiguous. In nineteenth-century reform literature for the home and farm, tastefulness was akin to generalized ideals or rightness about good design. A house and a farm were tasteful if they embodied modern concepts about economy, health, neatness, comfort, convenience, and beauty. All these ideals were subject to changes in fashion and style; what was currently advocated was modern and, therefore, tasteful. For example, in the 1880s, the "gospel taste" in builders' literature was "honesty of intention," a principle that *Carpentry and Building* interpreted as plain or neat finishes, especially for the interior.[33]

In architectural books, as in the stylebook, tastefulness was linked with the social status of the well-to-do gentleman farmer and the aesthetics of his country house. This "quality of discrimination" was taken up by nineteenth-century architects, who used taste as a way to claim a special status, to distinguish themselves from builders and clients; "architects agreed that builders did not possess taste."[34] However, *Carpentry and Building's* audience did not belong to a privileged group, and the motives of the architects who submitted patterns seemed fairly forthright: they wanted to design rational houses for the masses, and, in the bargain, they wanted to make a good living doing it. So *Carpentry and Building* avoided the term taste altogether and, because of economic reasons, allowed the drawings to interpret taste in their attention to detail in both exterior appearance and interior trim.

The phrase "popular styles" is a misnomer. In popular sources for architecture, such as pattern and plan books, there was little editorial adherence to any stylistic point of view, no aesthetic direction except one that was generally appreciated by ordinary people. There is some evidence that this convention was established in the nineteenth century by architects who avoided the orders of architecture for plain buildings, opting instead to focus on issues of convenience, comfort, and economy.[35] The paper did not engage in trend setting nor did it lag behind what was current, and it rarely used a stylistic term to describe a building. The correspondent who requested drawings for "cheap and tasteful dwellings" asked for submissions to be "characteristic of the modernized Queen Anne, or Gothic, style of architecture." But the editors did not use those style terms, nor any style terms, in their call for design submissions or for any of the competitions. Universal words like "dwelling," "house," "residence," or the more appealing term "home" were used in one-third of the journal's titles for articles. The journal chose neutrally descriptive titles for its pattern books: "low-cost houses," "modern dwellings," "cottage designs," and "suburban homes." The readership seems not to have responded greatly to style either, preferring practicality as an approach. Regarding a first-prize design in a cheap house competition, a New Jersey architect stated: "The house presents a neat, home-like appearance. There is nothing gaudy or flashy about it. It is temperate in its appearance throughout, and in its arrangement, there is much to be commended. There is little or no wasted room. Every inch of space seems to be utilized in the best manner. The general features of the house are such as favor economical construction. The shapes work advantageously. There is very little expensive ornamentation."[36] Convenient arrangement also undermined the necessity of style. According to Louis Gibson, domestic architecture was associated with necessities: "American architecture will be simply carrying out, in an architectural way, the requirements of the American people in their buildings. From their homes the march of progress will be through kitchens, pantries, and dining rooms."[37]

The overwhelming majority of *Carpentry and Building*'s designs can be characterized as aesthetically unspeculative; that is, the architects rarely took any design risks. These architectural moderates designed what they knew, namely, what came from practicing everyday architecture and building construction, and they understood what would appeal to carpenters and builders who would, in turn, offer inexpensive and moderate-cost house designs for the working and management classes.

Many of the houses built from *Carpentry and Building* drawings were sited in small towns and rural areas, but the journal's primary interest was in houses for the suburbs. From 1880 forward, the term "suburban" appears in over one hundred titles, implying that moderate-cost dwellings would be placed in a low-density, single-family landscape out of the city's center.[38] As part of this "tendency toward the suburban home," the journal reported

on national developments regarding "suburban operations," i.e., subdivisions, planned residential communities, and company towns. And the journal reinforced the suburban ideal: "The charm of the suburban home is found in so many delightful features of environment and physical comfort that it is not surprising to find an enormously increasing tendency on the part of businessmen to live outside the congested zones of our cities."[39]

Andrew Jackson Downing and Alexander Jackson Davis have been credited for redirecting American architecture after the late 1830s and for introducing the cottage as the perfect country house (which became the suburban house): "The cottage blends English picturesqueness with republican simplicity."[40] Throughout its history, *Carpentry and Building* frequently used the term "cottage" to describe a house type; cottage was used twice as many times as any other, including "bungalow" or "Colonial." However, when the journal defined its dwelling designs as suburban, their architectural characteristics were not vastly different from those that were not labeled suburban. Suburban houses were often described in terms of their features, such as economy of construction, compact arrangement, and materials. Because the journal was interested in the house as an independent entity, the use of materials ("a suburban cottage of shingled exterior") and experimentation with new materials, such as concrete, terra cotta blocks, and stucco were given primary importance. In truth, the suburban designation referenced an economic condition that had little to do with either architecture or landscape—suburban operations were sites of employment for designers and contractors.

For the most part, *Carpentry and Building* removed landscape considerations from the suburban cottage. The grounds of a house were not greatly considered, because builders had confidence in construction systems that allowed buildings to be adapted to all kinds of site conditions, and, more times than not, sites were leveled to ac-

Fig. 11.3. "Houses in Newark, N.J." (From *Carpentry and Building* [Nov. 1894], plate between 244 and 245.)

commodate the building. When the editors mentioned site at all, it had more to do with conventions of site analysis, such as the avoidance of low and marshy land, orientation to the sun, or accommodating small or corner lots. It was the immediate landscape, the near environment associated with the house, rather than the street or neighborhood that the journal emphasized—a home "somewhat back from the street, surrounded by broad lawns and stately trees." But this established vision rarely matched photographs of the recently constructed *Carpentry and Building* houses: these were raw sites, with young trees, small bushes, freshly laid sidewalks, and newly planted telephone poles (fig. 11.3). Although the pictures reveal order and uniformity in terms of site conditions such as setbacks, sidewalks, and streets, the houses that composed the rows were far from identical in terms of form, size, material, and ornament. It was this variety that expressed the wealth and the individual "taste" of their owners.

In keeping with its dedication to the near environment of the house, *Carpentry and Building*

(more than any journal in its class), demonstrated a healthy interest in the custom design of interior architecture. The architects who submitted work to the journal shared with their style-based peers a belief that a building was holistic and not complete without attention to inside space as well as finish. All the competitions included drawings of original interior elevations, sections, and details, and many of the supplemental plates feature photographs of the exterior and the interior (figs. 11.4 and 11.5). Within this practice lies a contradiction. Replication philosophy implies that architects would specify stock goods in order to save time as well as labor costs. However, the architects who designed for *Carpentry and Building* were artistic, and they designed original woodwork, a practice that was reinforced by the millwork companies.[41] In this case, the journal's goal, and its desire to appeal to the carpenter as craftsman, in addition to the architects' aspiration to make the drawings, all conflicted. But, in the early years, the architects won out, and the carpenter-builder was called on to build all the elements in a cheap house.

Competitions

Although the readership supported the journal's intentions by submitting designs for inexpensive houses, it was the competitions that became the driving force in developing and sustaining cheap housing. *Carpentry and Building*'s first competition, "Designs for Cheap Houses," called for dwellings that were not to exceed a thousand dollars, considerably less than the twelve to fifteen hundred dollars suggested by the correspondent who made the initial solicitation. Thirty entries for the first competition were received. While noting that a few submitters exceeded the price limit, nevertheless the journal awarded four top prizes and, in the ensuing issues, published each of the winning designs.[42]

The four houses share some similarities in achieving moderate cost and tasteful effects (figs. 11.6 and 11.7). In terms of plan, they were rectangular, with a porch-hall figure (two had a cut-out of the plan to accommodate a porch, and two had a projecting porch). All except the first-prize design contained three downstairs rooms composed of a parlor, a kitchen, and a second room whose name and function differed in the different plans. Two of the designs named the second room a sitting room, one a dining room, and another a downstairs bedroom, but nothing about the second rooms' architecture or location confined them to any one specific use. The kitchens were at the backs of the houses with an adjacent small pantry or closet. Upstairs, each house accommodated three bedrooms, but no bathrooms. All four houses followed conventions regarding room adjacency, but the kitchens remained a sizable space that was not yet planned for step-saving. Among the four designs, there was a range regarding square footage (from eleven hundred square feet to fourteen hundred square feet) and first-floor ceiling height (from eight feet, four inches to nine feet, ten inches). Overall, the spaces were fairly compact for the time period; the stairs and entry were combined, but without a reception room. There were three

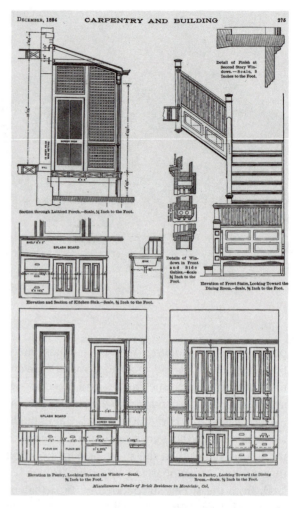

Fig. 11.4. "Brick Residence in Montclair, Col." (From *Carpentry and Building* [Dec. 1894], plate between 272 and 273. Page of interior working drawings by Frank J. Grodavent.)

particular interior elements that contributed to these houses' cheapness, in terms of cost and perception: the lack of a reception room, which was traditional in more expensive housing, quarter-flight stairs, which the building press had already deemed unsafe, and the lack of bathrooms.

All four houses had two stories and were clad in clapboard; shingles were used in three designs, two as decorative panels, and one to distinguish

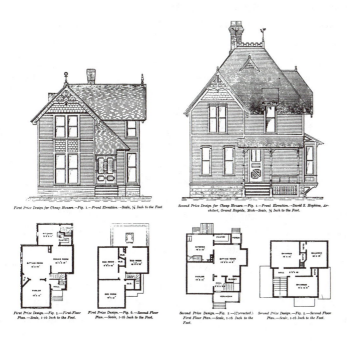

First Prize Design for Cheap Houses.—Fig. 1.—Front Elevation.—Scale, ¼ Inch to the Foot

Second Prize Design for Cheap Houses.—Fig. 1.—Front Elevation.—David S. Hopkins, Architect, Grand Rapids, Mich.—Scale, ¼ Inch to the Foot.

First Prize Design.—Fig. 5.—First-Floor Plan.—Scale, 1-16 Inch to the Foot.

First Prize Design.—Fig. 6.—Second Floor Plan.—Scale, 1-16 Inch to the Foot.

Second Prize Design.—Fig. 2—(Corrected.) First Floor Plan.—Scale, 1-16 Inch to the Foot.

Second Prize Design.—Fig. 5.—Second Floor Plan.—Scale, 1-16 Inch to the Foot.

Fig. 11.5. "Brick Residence in Montclair, Col." (From *Carpentry and Building* [Dec. 1894]: 275. Completed interior.)

Fig. 11.6. "Competition in Designs for Cheap Dwelling Houses." (From *Carpentry and Building* [July 1879]: 124-25; [Aug. 1879]: 144-45; [Sept. 1879]: 166. First and second prize-winning designs.)

one story from another. Although the forms were fairly compact, all showed a cottage sensibility with picturesque massing and effects, achieved with complex roof plans, irregular fenestration, elaborate chimney caps, and stickwork—corner boards, beltings, heavily molded window frames, paneled doors, turned porch posts, vergeboards, gable finish, finials, pendants, brackets, and cresting—to articulate edges and the corners. From July to October 1879, *Carpentry and Building* published each winning competition entry with perspectives, elevations, sections, details, specifications, and cost estimates. Publishing detail drawings for the competition results became one of the journal's mechanisms for communicating aesthetics and for ensuring the replication of inexpensive houses.

In 1880, in response to a request from a Cincinnati subscriber, the journal stated: "We believe in pictures, and are ready to make as many as our columns will hold."[43] Largely due to the popularity of the design competitions, the editorial policy to publish full sets of drawings in scale began in earnest. The journal found that architects were not only eager to enter the competitions, but also that they were willing to draw the details required to make the designs practical for builders to reproduce. In the 1883 competition for a seven-room house, architect Frank J. Grodavent enthusiastically submitted more than the required number of competition drawings. He sent one perspective, a set of floor plans, four exterior elevations, a roof plan, five section drawings, and sixteen detail drawings. *Carpentry and Building* said of his entry: "He has given as much attention to the designing of a comparatively cheap house as is ordinarily bestowed upon mansions costing ten times the sum." In a note accompanying the drawings, Grodavent gave a practical explanation for the extra drawings: "additional elevations are always convenient for the builder in constructing the work."[44]

Carpentry and Building's competitions did not promote just comparative design work among designers who were geographically distant from one another; in several cases, indeed, competitions were based on cooperative efforts toward one product. One such interactive device consisted of a four-phased competition in which designers "piggybacked" on the design of another. An 1881 competition called for drawings of floor plans for an eight-room house. The winning set of floor-plan

Fig. 11.7. "Competition in Designs for Cheap Dwelling Houses." (From *Carpentry and Building* [Sept. 1879]: 162-63; [Oct. 1879]: 182-83. Third and fourth prize-winning designs.)

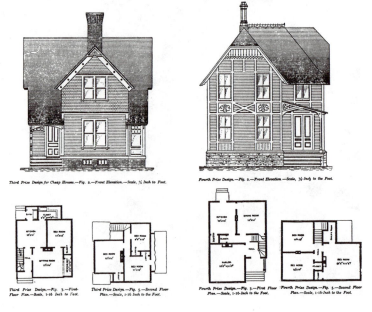

drawings was subsequently used as the basis for a second phase of the competition, the design of elevations and details. In turn, the winning elevation drawings were used as the basis for a third competitive phase, the submission of specifications for materials, and the competition continued into a fourth phase with estimated costs for building the eight-room house. Through the course of four successive competitions, four individual designers from four different states provided the journal with a full set of working drawings, including specifications and estimates.[45]

The journal persisted in its initial promise to publish cheap house designs. The competition designs were most often classified in terms of a generalized building type and an actual price, or a price range, such as "moderate-priced houses." In 1884, *Carpentry and Building* called for submissions of "cheap frame houses" and ran separate contests for an eight-hundred-dollar house and a fifteen-hundred-dollar house; in 1893, a competition was held for a thousand-dollar house; in 1899, there were three competitions for houses costing seven hundred and fifty dollars, a thousand dollars, and fifteen hundred dollars. After the turn of the century, the journal emphasized bungalows as houses of moderate cost, and, in 1909, it sponsored a competition for modern bungalows. Although the competitions often focused on cost, the journal tended to combine price with either materials, such as frame or brick, or number of rooms in a house, as in the tenth competition, "A Cheap Seven Room House." *Carpentry and Building* sponsored several floor-plan competitions, because internal arrangement was another way to deliver convenient arrangement and economy.

The Practical Architects

From 1879 to 1930, all kinds of architects and builders contributed designs to *Carpentry and Building*. Because of the journal's location in New York City, architects dominated in terms of numbers, but the journal's sphere of influence encompassed several regions of the country, developing a widespread interest not only on the East Coast and in the Midwest, but also in the western states.[46] In fact, the journal did very well in the West; there were fifteen architects west of the Mississippi who had a design published more than once. Unlike other journals, *Carpentry and Building* did not establish one primary architect whose designs monopolized its pages; over a thousand contributors had designs published. Most contributors were published only once, and some just a few times; only nine architects had more than fifteen designs published.

The practice of the early contributors reveals that these architects practiced two kinds of architecture simultaneously—design of one-of-a-kind buildings and design for replication. For example, Arthur Bates Jennings, a noted New York City church architect, also submitted house designs and working drawings to be replicated. Like their English and American pattern-book predecessors, these architects believed that style-based design was appropriate for large buildings and that the egalitarian values associated with replication were appropriate for domestic architecture.

Gould and Angell of Providence, Rhode Island, were typical of the architects who practiced the two genres simultaneously. Between 1879 and 1886, they had seventeen designs published in *Carpentry and Building*. Thomas J. Gould first appeared in the journal by himself—he received third prize in the 1879 competition design for "cheap dwelling houses"—and, beginning in 1882, the firm Gould and Angell furnished ten plates in the "Study of Suburban Architecture" series. Each study featured a specific interior space (hall, sitting room, library, dining room, and others). In addition to their designs in *Carpentry and Building*, their one-of-a-kind buildings included the Murray Universalist Church in Attleboro, Massachusetts, that appeared in *The American Architect and Building News;*

Blackstone and Wilson Halls at Brown University; and a Methodist church at Hebronville, Massachusetts. Both Gould and his partner, Frank W. Angell, were members of the American Institute of Architects.[47]

Because he began practice as a style-based architect and through time became an architect of replication, Frank J. Grodavent had the most unusual career of all the *Carpentry and Building* architects I have researched. Grodavent is also distinct in terms of longevity with the journal: twenty-three of his designs were published over a thirty-five-year period, including seven competition designs, nine residential commissions, and seven technical drawings (figs. 11.4 and 11.5). *Carpentry and Building* chronicled Grodavent's migration from Syracuse, New York, where he began practice with Horatio Nelson White, to Leavenworth and Wichita, Kansas, where he partnered with E. T. Carr, and on to Denver, where, as a civilian architect for the U.S. Army, he designed Fort Logan, Colorado. *Carpentry and Building* continued to publish the designs Grodavent submitted in partnership with his brother Herbert as the Grodavent brothers in Denver and as he made subsequent moves to three other western states as an army architect.[48]

Carpentry and Building also served as a publication source for at least thirteen plan book architects, including George F. Barber (DeKalb, Illinois, and Knoxville, Tennessee), E. W. Stillwell (Los Angeles), David S. Hopkins (Grand Rapids, Michigan), who won second place in the 1879 "Design for Cheap Houses" competition, and George W. Payne and Son (Carthage, Illinois).[49] Payne placed in the 1883 estimate competition and in the 1894 floor-plan competitions. George W. Payne and his son Edgar A. were the most published of all the plan book architects, appearing in the journal twenty-five times between 1888 and 1915.[50] The practice intentions of this group who designed exclusively for replication were closely aligned with *Carpentry and Building*'s goals. For example, the title of George W. Payne and Son's first plan book coalesces a design philosophy within the context of practical architecture—*Payne's Modern Homes: A Book of Designs of Cottages and Residences for the Use of Those Who Desire to Build Modern Homes Compact and Convenient in Arrangement and Moderate in Cost*. In keeping with interests which had less to do with style and more with economy, Payne numbered rather than named his designs and gave construction costs for each. The majority of the buildings were under five thousand dollars; most were frame, with clapboard cladding and shingles in the gables. Payne's plan book, published in 1906, featured over two hundred designs that were constructed prior to that date in twenty-two states, but the majority of the houses were built in Illinois. All but four of Payne's designs in *Carpentry and Building* were taken from his book. Field work in the Carthage, Illinois, area, where Payne practiced, revealed that at least thirty-five of the buildings from his 1906 plan book are extant, including the D. H. Miller house, which was published in 1897 by *Carpentry and Building* (fig. 11.8). It currently appears with a side addition; only the chimney and roof cresting are missing (fig. 11.9).

An analysis of architects from *Carpentry and Building* also reveals that there were several family firms. In addition to the Grodavent brothers, and the father and son Paynes, between 1898 and 1907, the journal published nineteen designs from J. A. Oakley and Son of Elizabeth, New Jersey, a firm that represented three generations. Jesse A. Oakley, the senior member of the firm, was first associated with his father in building; later, his son Charles W. joined the company.[51] John P. Kingston's family firm in Worcester, Massachusetts, was even larger; while John was the principal, the firm included his son Charles H. and sometimes his brother George, a builder, as well as John's niece Laura, who, in 1899, was awarded first prize for the Fifteenth Competition in $750 houses (fig. 11.1).[52] John P. Kingston won nine competitions and, between 1893 and 1916, had thirty-two designs published in *Carpentry and Building*. These family firms were prolific designers in terms of the journal alone, but John P. Kingston's obituary suggests the magnitude of these practical architects' contributions to the American building stock—Kingston designed at least five thousand residences in his thirty-six-year practice as an architect.

Reflecting the time period, few of *Carpentry and Building*'s early-twentieth-century architects were

formally educated; many, like Jennings, Gould, Angell, and Grodavent, served apprenticeships with practicing architects. From this sample, those who became architects through the apprentice system seemed to have the most interest in the American Institute of Architects (Gould, Angell, and Grodavent were AIA members; Jennings, Angell, and Grodavent were fellows). A 1909 article featuring the three winners of the bungalow competition revealed that two of the designers supplemented their apprenticeship training with course work from correspondence schools. Some of the architects who submitted designs to *Carpentry and Building* became architects through their association with the construction industry; some, like George W. Payne, had been carpenters; others, like Jesse A. Oakley, had learned the building trade from their fathers.

Carpentry and Building's view toward women architects was fairly supportive, because of a belief that women were pre-eminently suited for architecture due to their practical thinking and for domestic architecture, in particular, because of their experience as housekeepers and homemakers. Several of *Carpentry and Building*'s articles asserted that in terms of house planning, a woman archi-

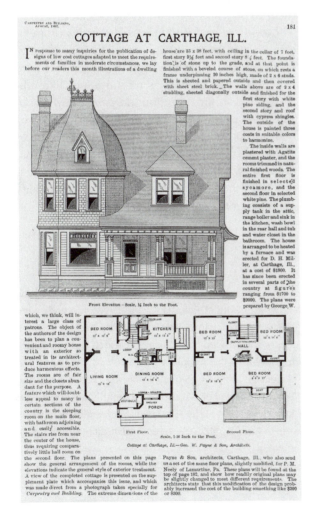

Fig. 11.8. "Cottage at Carthage, Ill." (From *Carpentry and Building* [Aug. 1897], plate between 183 and 184.)

Fig. 11.9. D. H. Miller House, 2334 Cherry, Carthage, Ill.

tect could do better than a man. The idea of women as architects was of some interest to the journal, and, from 1887 to 1917, *Carpentry and Building* devoted eight short columns to the subject. When a woman's drawings were published, they gave little attention, if any, to her gender. For example, when Laura Kingston won the 1899 competition, the journal made no mention of the fact that Kingston was a woman; instead they characterized the submissions, credited her design as standing out among the field, and took the opportunity to reiterate their goal of dissemination: "The results of this competition are gratifying not alone in the number of designs submitted, but also in the character of the work shown and the widespread interest manifested, as evidenced by the fact that nearly every section of the country was represented."[53]

From 1879 to 1910, *Carpentry and Building* reflected the close relationship between architects and builders, and, after 1910, it communicated their dissolution from each other and their solidification into distinctive professional groups.[54] It seems obvious that *Carpentry and Building*'s role

as a journal of replication fostered further alienation of architects from the housing market, but there is no acknowledgment from the editors that they intended to supersede architects altogether, because they relied on architects' designs and drawings to make the journal function. However, through time, it became increasingly clear that as the drawings became more complete, an architect on an ordinary house site was not necessary. The journal elevated the role of builders by increasing their architectural knowledge and by allowing them to play a bigger part in the design process.

Carpentry and Building used designs of architects to stimulate building, especially housing, and it encouraged rapid diffusion of design and construction ideas, as well as reform issues like efficiency and suburbanization. *Carpentry and Building* was a significant journal because it was dedicated solely to a vernacular architecture, an architecture that was intended to be broadcast nationally. We learn from *Carpentry and Building* that both the concept and practice of practicality are another way to define the popular.

Notes

1. The author wishes to thank the Winterthur Museum and Library for the Forman Fellowship, which enabled me to research English and American pattern books. The fieldwork and photographs for the Payne research were undertaken during the summer of 1989 and were made possible by an Iowa State University Research Grant. Proofreading the index of *Carpentry and Building*'s designers was funded by a Design Research Institute Grant from the College of Design, Iowa State University. I am grateful to the people who discussed aspects of the paper with me: Herbert Gottfried, Neville Thompson, Pamela H. Simpson, Sidney Robinson, Paul Groth, and Philip Scranton, and for invaluable aid from researcher Mary Anne Beecher. The author gratefully acknowledges the generosity of the families of the practical architects, including Anna Marie Grodavent, Belzemere Kingsbury Kingston, Neil Kingston Disney, and Mary Johnson, as well as Janet K. McCorison, executive director, Preservation Worcester.

2. Michael A. Tomlan, "Popular and Professional American Architectural Literature in the Late Nineteenth Century," (Ph.D. diss., Cornell University, 1983), 198. Tomlan characterized *Carpentry and Building*'s architectural content as mundane.

3. Published as *Carpentry and Building* (Jan. 1879–Dec. 1909); *Building Age* (Jan. 1910–22); *Building Age and The Builder's Journal* (1922–24); *Building Age and the National Builder* (1924–Sept. 1930). In Its history, *Carpentry and Building* absorbed *The Builder's Exchange*, 1890; *The Builder's Journal*, 1922; *The National Builder*, Nov. 1924; *The Permanent Builder*, 1924. *Carpentry and Building* also published designs for schools, apartments, the-

aters, churches, commercial and business buildings, barns, carriage houses and stables, and automobile garages, but in terms of numbers, houses dominated the designs.

4. Dell Upton's article, "Pattern Books and Professionalism: Aspects of the Transformation of Domestic Architecture in American, 1800–1860," *Winterthur Portfolio* 19 (2–3) (Summer–Autumn 1984), proved an excellent source for my examination. My attempt is to bring Upton's article forward, past 1860, placing *Carpentry and Building* in the next transformation of domestic architecture in America. While we examine many of the same sources, Upton's article looked at the phenomenon of professional expertise in everyday design; I investigate the social and cultural values and the language that described the motives of a "manufactured" vernacular architecture.

5. "Cheap and Tasteful Dwellings in Popular Styles of Architecture," *Carpentry and Building* (Mar. 1879): 57.

6. "Homes for the Millions," *The Manufacturer and Builder* 4 (11) (Nov. 1871): 261. *The Builder and Woodworker* (Oct. 1884): 199, found pattern book publications useful aids for "mechanics, clerks, salaried men, workingmen of every calling, carpenters and builders in cities, towns, and villages."

7. Thomas Rawlins, *Familiar Architecture* (London: Thomas Rawlins, 1768), vi, 1.

8. Late-nineteenth-century pattern book associations that expressed this view were the New York Building Plan Association and the National Architect's Union.

9. D. H. Jacques, *The House: A Manual of Rural Architecture* (New York: George E. and F. W. Woodward, 1866), v.

10. Tomlan, "Popular and Professional American Architectural Literature," 202, states that "in 1890, the *Builder and Wood-Worker,* with a circulation of 8,000, *Carpentry and Building* with a circulation of 20,000, and the Architects' and Builders' Edition of *Scientific American,* with a circulation of 12,000, collectively presented most of the information regarding construction in this country to the building public."

11. Advertisement, "To Our Patrons," *Carpentry and Building* (Jan. 1879), cover.

12. Upton, "Pattern Books and Professionalism," 116–17, states that "the builder's handbooks were the most explicitly concerned with the synthesis of an architectural science." These books combined aspects of customary practice that were common knowledge, along with an explanation of how a builder's skills fit into a system.

13. "Mission of Carpentry and Building," *Carpentry and Building* (Feb. 1887): 35.

14. "A Western Cottage," *Carpentry and Building* (July 1887): 129. The phrase "a practical man" was used to describe designers, architects, or builders—anyone who gained experience through work or was "self-made," such as Sereno Edwards Todd, *Todd's Country Homes and How to Save Money: A Practical Book by a Practical Man* (Hartford, Conn.: Hartford Publishing Co., 1870), cover.

15. Lewis F. Allen, *Rural Architecture: Being a Complete Description of Farm Houses, Cottages, and Out Buildings* (New York: C. M. Saxton, 1852), xiv, xv.

16. "Prize Competitions for 1904," *Carpentry and Building* (Dec. 1903): n.p.

17. "Bicknell and Comstock," *Carpentry and Building* (Jan. 1879): 15.

18. Bicknell's use of the term "constructive," as in *Detail Cottages and Constructive Architecture,* may also have influenced the journal to employ the term "constructive" in a double meaning to reinforce their publication mission. "Constructive" connotes helpfulness and vaguely implies something structural. But *Carpentry and Building* employed the phrase "constructive details" to describe a full set of drawings in a "convenient" scale for reproduction purposes. "Constructive details" appears in the title of all the journal's pattern books.

19. "Architecture: A Study in Cheap Frame Houses," *Carpentry and Building* (May 1879): 92–97.

20. The convention in furniture and chimneypiece plates was to bifurcate a design—say, a chair—vertically in order to illustrate variant treatments on each side.

21. "Cottage and Villa Architecture," *The Manufacturer and Builder* 1 (4) (Apr. 1869): 121.

22. "A Row of Houses in East Orange, N.J.," *Carpentry and Building* (June 1901): 143.

23. Upton, "Pattern Books and Professionalism," 136, 141.

24. Early books that included working drawings were D. H. Arnot, *Gothic Architecture Applied to Modern Residences* (New York: D. Appleton and Co., 1850), n.p.; Richard Upjohn, *Upjohn's Rural Architecture: Designs, Working Drawings and Specifications for a Wooden Church, and Other Rural Structures* (New York: George P. Putnam, 1852), n.p.

25. *Modern Architectural Designs and Details* (New York: William T. Comstock, 1881), n.p. Comstock's pattern book responded to the responsibility of publishing an accurate set of drawings that could be copied by the "practical man" when he included a large number of "complete designs for houses" and chose a more expensive production process (plates that were engraved on stone, rather than the cheaper photo-lithographic process) "in order that every line may be clearly defined and the scale accurately preserved."

26. "A Cheap Set of Plans," *Carpentry and Building* (Feb. 1880): 35; "News and Comments," *Carpentry and Building* (Dec. 1884): 232.

27. *Carpentry and Building* (Dec. 1884): 232.

28. Tomlan, "Popular and Professional American Architectural Literature," 193–95.

29. Upton, "Pattern Books and Professionalism," 117–18, states that the scientific enterprise freed the handbook authors to borrow at will from tradition, as well as from their predecessors and contemporaries, and that "if there was a science of building, there was no way to escape drawing on other people's work." The handbook writers were most concerned with establishing the unity of architectural thought, so they viewed their works as contributions to a common cause. Borrowing architectural designs, however, "invaded the realm of taste."

30. See Mary Woods, "The First American Architectural Journals: The Profession's Voice," *Journal of the Society of Architectural Historians* XLVIII (June 1989): 125, and Tomlan, "Popular and Professional American Architectural Literature," 193, 195. Woods states that *Architectural Review and American Builder's Journal* (1868–70), edited by Samuel Sloan, resembled "a sort of serialized pattern book." In 1873, the *American Builder and Journal of Art,* edited by Charles Lakey, began publishing supplemental sheets of scale drawings of details for architectural elements, such as porches, gables, and ceilings, and in 1879 it began selling its scale drawings.

31. "Cheap and Tasteful Dwellings in Popular Styles of Architecture," *Carpentry and Building* (Mar. 1879): 57.

32. By the 1880s, most pattern and plan books were directing their appeals to "those who intend to build" and the "building public," which included potential home owners, in addition to builders and speculators. A few of the author-architects acknowledged the design help they received from their clientele. In *Hobbs' Architecture* (1873), Isaac H. Hobbs, who designed for *Godey's Ladies Book and Magazine,* thanked the "many ladies throughout the United States who have aided us by their suggestions in preparing many of the ground plans in this volume." From 1897 to 1930, several single and married women are listed as sole owners of houses constructed from *Carpentry and Building* designs.

33. "Domestic Architecture," *The Builder and Wood-Worker* (Jan. 1884): 20.

34. Upton, "Pattern Books and Professionalism," 120–23, states that "despite attempts to define taste, most early nineteenth century writers were vague about its sources." The nineteenth-century stylebook was an attempt to teach taste to clients, with Andrew Jackson Davis reintroducing the connection between social status and taste.

35. In particular, English architects Rawlins (1768), Asher and Raynerd (1806), and American S. B. Reed (1883).

36. "Comments on the Design Receiving First Prize," *Carpentry and Building* (Aug. 1879): 158.

37. Louis H. Gibson, *Convenient Houses with Fifty Plans for the Housekeeper* (New York: Thomas Y. Crowell and Co., 1889), 26–28.

38. Kenneth T. Jackson, *Crabgrass Frontier: The Suburbanization of the United States* (New York: Oxford University Press, 1985), 11, 124–28, states the importance of land developers, cheap lots, and inexpensive construction methods in creating suburbs—things *Carpentry and Building* catered to—and the contribution of balloon-frame construction and the pattern book in creating subdivisions.

39. "A Fine Type of the Modern Suburban Home," *Building Age* (July 1913): 305.

40. John R. Stilgoe, *Borderland: Origins of the American Suburb, 1820–1939* (New Haven: Yale University Press, 1988), 102.

41. Many plan book architects did not provide as many detail drawings of elements, particularly interior ones, as the journal did because they expected that builders would use stock goods.

42. "Architecture: Competition in Designs for Cheap Dwelling Houses," *Carpentry and Building* (July 1879): 124–27. First prize went to F. A. Hale and W. L. Morrison, Rochester, N.Y.; second prize to David S. Hopkins, Grand Rapids, Mich.; third prize to Thomas J. Gould, Providence, R.I.; fourth prize to Clarence W. Smith and Augustus Howe Jr., New York City.

43. "Designs from Our Readers," *Carpentry and Building* (Feb. 1979): 38.

44. "First Prize Design: Eleventh Competition," *Carpentry and Building* (Sept. 1883): 169.

45. The competition was extended to a fifth phase, heating the building, and published in *The Metal Worker*.

46. Boyd C. Pratt, "A Brief History of the Practice of Architecture in New Mexico," *New Mexico Architecture* (Nov.–Dec. 1989): 9, states that in February 1881, the *Las Vegas [N.M.] Morning Gazette* noted three local subscriptions each to *Carpentry and Building, American Architect and Building News,* and *Manufacturer and Builder.*

47. See *The American Architect and Building News* XX (1886): 571, and *Biographical Dictionary of American Architects Deceased* 22, 244–45.

48. For more about Grodavent, see the author's article, "Frank J. Grodavent: Western Architect," *Essays and Monographs in Colorado History* 11 (1990): 1–23.

49. Other plan book architects who had designs published in *Carpentry and Building*: Frank P. Allen, Grand Rapids, Michigan; Architects' Small House Service Bureau; A. J. Bicknell, and Bicknell and Comstock, New York; J. H. Daverman and Son, Grand Rapids, Michigan; C. E. Eastman Co., Des Moines, Iowa; Frederick Thomas Hodgson, Chicago; Home Owners Service Bureau, New York; Alfred Hopkins, New York; James W. Pirsson, New York; Royal Barry Wills, Boston; H. Wittekind, Chicago.

50. From 1888 to 1892, G. W. or George W. was the sole architect; 1897 was the first entry for the firm name, George W. Payne and Son. Edgar A. Payne (1872–1962), a graduate of Carthage College, remained in Carthage after his father's death, specializing in house and school designs. He continued to publish plan books under his name.

51. "Death of Architect J. A. Oakley," *Carpentry and Building* (Feb. 1907): 55. From "Merger of Architectural Firms," *Carpentry and Building* (Feb. 1912): 65, we learn that Oakley and Son merged with Hollingsworth and Bragdon, Cranford, N.J.; the firm's title was retained. For another obituary, see "Jesse A. Oakley," *American Architect and Building News* 91 (Jan. 12, 1907): v.

52. Belzemere Kingsbury Kingston and her son Kirk Kingston, interview with author, Baltimore, Md., Nov. 21, 1991. Belzemere was the daughter-in-law of John Paul Kingston; she typed specifications for the firm in 1922. Her husband Earle, who was "in the business from birth," became an engineer.

53. "Competition in $750 Houses," *Carpentry and Building* (Mar. 1899): 65–68. When Kingston's next design was published, "A Two-Family House Plastered Outside With Cement-Mortar," *Carpentry and Building* (Oct. 1910): 419–23, Laura had dropped her first name, opting for more anonymous initials, L. E. Kingston. However, this time the journal called attention to the design being "planned by a woman, not altogether unknown to the readers of this journal by reason of the recognition which her designs received with several of the house competitions."

54. *Carpentry and Building* was never indexed under architects' or builders' names. The author has compiled an index from 1879 to 1930 of all architects and builders whose designs were published; the index gives their names and locations, their clients' names and locations, as well as other information.

Chapter 12

Cheap, Quick, and Easy, Part II:
Pressed Metal Ceilings, 1880–1930

Pamela H. Simpson

[The popularity of substitute materials at the turn of the century was] fueled by the American desire to find ways of doing things that were "cheap, quick and easy."

Ada Louise Huxtable (1960)

A story published in the magazine *The Metal Worker* in 1915 told the tale of Dan Casey, a small-town contractor. Casey had heard about metal ceilings but did not decide to try them until the plaster fell over the desk in his own office. The metal ceiling he installed was soon the talk of the town:

> News travels rapidly in towns of two thousand, and before nightfall, every villager who could had looked over the job, and held his own opinion as to the merits of metal ceiling versus plaster. Holding one's private opinion in a small town is generally good for much publicity, and the new ceiling was well advertised. There was an artistic effect about it that had never been seen in the village before, and a month later, when a blast of dynamite shot a stubborn pine stump out of the vacant lot alongside . . . [the] grocery, it . . . loosened . . . the plaster and the owner placed with Casey the first real order for a real metal ceiling.[1]

That was the beginning. Next it was the courtroom, then the drugstore, the city hall, the restaurant, the new high school, the barbershop, the dry goods store, and the Bijou Moving Picture Theater. The climax came when the wealthiest man in town,

J. Wetmore Craig, ordered a metal ceiling for his dining room.

The author of this story confessed that some of the characters in it were fictitious, but insisted that Dan Casey was real, and so was the pressed metal ceiling business. Enterprising builders should follow his example and "send out some boys with a catalogue and samples" because "business was ripe" and "the chances for profit were good."[2]

That was 1915 at what was probably the height of the popularity of metal ceilings. But even today thousands of them survive in turn-of-the-century commercial buildings, churches, and even houses throughout America. They are not hard to find. Usually all one has to do is look up. Yet, like other turn-of-the-century new materials, pressed metal ceilings are often ignored simply because they are so ubiquitous, and there is little modern scholarship on them.[3] The object of this paper is to examine the history of this common material and the reasons for its popularity. The investigative method has been to look closely and extensively at period builders' journals, specialist trade magazines, some eighty trade catalogs that the manufacturers used to promote the material, the histories of several of the manufacturers, and individual buildings with documented metal ceilings.

The earliest references to ceilings made of metal came in the 1870s. These were simply corrugated iron meant as a fire-proof separation of floors in buildings such as jails or factories. One such metal ceiling was pictured in the Philadelphia Architectural Iron Company's 1872 catalog.[4] There was a patent granted to a Henry Adler of Pittsburgh in 1875 for a "sheet metal ceiling,"[5] but the earliest successful commercial patents were those issued to Albert Northrop of Pittsburgh in 1884.[6] Northrop's ceilings consisted of small panels of corrugated iron that were laid against furring strips over the ceiling joists. The seams between the panels were covered with molding strips and nailed to the wooden grounds. Northrop suggested that a decorative pattern could be created by varying the direction of the corrugation, and that embossed rosettes could be added to mark the corners. Despite this attempt at ornamentation, the ceilings were criticized for looking "unfinished."[7]

A solution to this problem was suggested in the magazine *Carpentry and Building* in 1886, in an article that reported that a German company had produced a ceiling using small diamond-shaped corrugated panels, enhanced with deeply molded overlapping ribs and embossed center panels with rosettes. The article did not indicate what the center panels were made of, but American manufacturers who began to experiment with similar forms in the 1880s used stamped zinc (fig. 12.1).[8] The sheets of zinc were machine pressed into decorative forms and attached to the corrugated iron base.[9]

The iron with pressed zinc ceilings could be very elaborate. That was the case with those made by the firm of W. R. Kinnear for the Columbus, Ohio, courthouse in 1887, or those for the Council

Fig. 12.1. "Details of Construction of Sheet-Metal Ceiling." (From *Carpentry and Building* [Oct. 1886]: 189.)

Fig. 12.2. "Sheet Metal Ceiling in the Courthouse at Council Bluffs, Iowa." (From *Carpentry and Building* [Mar. 1889]: 63.)

Bluffs, Iowa, courthouse (fig. 12.2) supplied by Bakewell and Mullins, another Ohio firm, in 1889. In both cases the ceilings were praised for being lighter than cast plaster, easier to install, more durable, and cheaper.[10]

A major technological change in the production of metal ceilings occurred in the 1890s, when steel began to replace the corrugated iron and embossed zinc. The steel was stronger than iron and could be produced in larger and thinner panels. The W. R. Kinnear Company was the first to patent the new kind of ceiling in 1888. The key difference was that panels of twenty-eight- to thirty-gauge steel were die pressed as a single unit. Instead of assembling the various bits of zinc ornament and attaching them to an iron base, the ornament was stamped into a single steel panel. The panels were twenty-four inches wide to allow them to be nailed into the furring strips, but their length varied from one to two to four feet. Later, panels as long as seven or eight feet were produced, but the two-by-four-foot panel was the most common. By the end of the century, the stamped steel panels were the standard in the industry.

Technological improvements had reduced the

cost of steel and made it more widely available. Improvements in the drop presses and the consolidation of capital into larger companies meant that the manufacturers could meet the growing demand for metal ceilings and provide them quickly and cheaply. Many companies founded in the 1870s to make sheet-metal roofing, brake-fabricated cornices, and cast-iron storefronts were also making steel ceilings and sidewalls by the 1890s. The Mesker Brothers of St. Louis, for example, were founded in 1879 and were best known for their metal building fronts. They had a booming business in cheap architectural ornament, and metal ceilings were only one product among many that they made. Others, such as the Penn Metal Roofing and Ceiling Company of Philadelphia, had ceilings as one of their major lines.[11] Few companies seemed to have devoted themselves solely to making ceilings. If they made them, they probably also made cornices, exterior sheet-metal cladding, interior stamped sidewalls, storefronts, and metal shingles.

The growth of the metal-ceiling industry is reflected in numerous advertisements that appeared in trade journals. The earliest was Albert Northrop's in 1884, but within five years the advertisements were everywhere. Whole pages of the ads appeared in the builders' journals in the 1910s, and, while there was a decline in the later 1920s, some continued to appear even into the 1930s.[12] Why were metal ceilings so popular? The advantages claimed for them were that they were 1) fire resistant, 2) sanitary in that they did not promote dust, could be easily cleaned, and were "vermin proof," 3) permanent, since they were resistant to moisture and needed little care, 4) cheap compared with other alternatives, and 5) decorative. Let us briefly examine each of these points.

1) Fire resistant. This was a chief selling point in the advertising literature. Pictures and accounts of buildings that caught fire but were saved when a metal ceiling confined the flames to one floor were often repeated in the building magazines.[13] There were claims that insurance premiums were

lower. Reports on official fire tests, such as one conducted by the Association of Metal Ceiling Contractors of Greater New York in 1914, proved that metal ceilings were more fire resistant than wood or plaster ceilings.[14]

2) Sanitary. It was clear that metal ceilings had less dust than plaster and could be easily cleaned. The claim of being "vermin proof," however, was based on the existence of a tight seal between the panels, and that seal depended on proper installation. One Texas contractor pointed out, however, that to be really "vermin proof," the ceiling should not be put up against the unsheathed ceiling joists. Without a wood backing, one lone mouse could "make as much racket as a jackass in a tin stable."[15]

3) Permanence. This, too, was one of the chief selling points. One of the recurring themes in the promotional literature was the advantage of metal ceilings over falling plaster. It was not just Dan Casey who had his office ceiling fall; it seems a lot of other people had theirs fall, too. A writer in the *Metal Worker* in 1895 recorded a visit to a local metal ceiling plant where his conversation with the manager was interrupted by an anxious customer. Just that morning the plaster had fallen in his bedroom only minutes after he had gotten out of bed. He was determined to replace not only that ceiling but also the one in his dining room "as the ceiling there gave promise of demolishing his china."[16] These sentiments were also evident in an 1890 letter from one O. O. Shackleton of Hackensack, who wrote, "The ceilings recently put up in my house . . . are in every respect all that we could wish—neat, beautiful, attractive, clean—and we are not afraid to sit under them."[17] Even as late as 1931, an article in *The Sheet Metal Worker* suggested that contractors use newspaper headlines like "Near Panic as Ceiling Falls at the Medford Prom!" to show the dangers of falling plaster as opposed to the safety of metal ceilings.[18]

4) Cost. All of the literature for metal ceilings promoted them as an economical alternative to plaster or any other ornamental material. In fact,

many advertisements noted that even though the initial price might be more, the low cost of upkeep and the virtual permanence of the material would save money in the long run.

5) Decorative. The metal ceilings were never cheaper than plain wood or plaster. They were cheap only in comparison to other decorative effects. And their decorative effects were their chief selling point. In catalogs and advertisements manufacturers pointed out the "artistic" effects. They divided the designs into stylistic categories such as Greek, Gothic, French Renaissance, Rococo, and Colonial. Some companies even named their products "Art Metal" and "Art Kraft," and many pointed out the "high-class" nature of the buildings with the ceilings.

Today, metal ceilings are most often associated with commercial establishments and churches, partly because these locations are where most have survived. But they were used in a surprising variety of building types, including hospitals, schools, theaters, hotels, restaurants, banks, lodge halls, amusement parks, and residences.

The firms that produced the ceilings were located primarily in Ohio, New York, and Pennsylvania. But there were also important manufacturers in Boston, Massachusetts, Evansville, Indiana, St. Paul and Duluth, Minnesota, Milwaukee, Wisconsin, St. Louis, Missouri, Wheeling, West Virginia, Dubuque, Iowa, and even Nevada, Missouri.

Most of the firms were quite large and advertised that fact in their catalogs with pictures of their plants and boasts of their proximity to railroad lines. Bigger was better in the "age of progress." It meant more selection, lower prices, greater reliability, and quicker delivery.

The story of Longley Lewis Sagendorph and his Penn Metal Company serves as an example of the rise of one of these firms. Sagendorph was born in Hudson, New York, in 1842, grew up in Providence, Rhode Island, and, after fighting in the Civil War, packed up his inheritance in a carpet bag and headed south to start his first fabricating plant in Staunton, Virginia, in 1869. Ten years later he moved the business to Cincinnati to be nearer the center of the iron industry and the rail lines. His Sagendorph Iron Roofing and Corrugating Company grew rapidly as he took out over a hundred patents on a whole series of new products and the machinery and tools to produce them. By the 1890s he had expanded his business to include outlets in Chicago, St. Louis, Birmingham, Jersey City, and Philadelphia. Then he sold the company, moved to Philadelphia, and used his profit to start a new firm called the Penn Metal Ceiling and Roofing Company. He built a new plant and began buying up other factories, eventually expanding to Boston, Camden, and Parkersburg, West Virginia. Sagendorph died in 1909 a very wealthy man and left the business to his two sons.[19]

W. H. Mullins is another example. A young Pittsburgh railroad clerk in 1882, he scraped together enough money to buy a wrecked locomotive, which he disassembled, sold for parts and scrap, and earned a thousand dollars in profit. That was enough to buy into a firm in Canton, Ohio, that became Bakewell & Mullins, one of the earliest manufacturers of metal ceilings. They were best known, however, for their metal statuary: their most famous piece probably was Saint-Gaudins's *Diana* for Madison Square Garden. Mullins borrowed money from his father-in-law to buy out Bakewell and continued to expand his firm and diversify its products into the twentieth century. By the 1940s his company was making automobile parts and kitchen cabinets.[20]

In 1893, William Franklin Norman was employed as a traveling salesman by the Wheeling Corrugating Company of Wheeling, West Virginia. He received $166.67 a month to sell the firm's steel roofing, ceilings, sidewalls, and other products. Since he covered primarily a western territory, Norman settled in Nevada, Missouri. He became convinced there was so much demand for pressed metal that in 1898 he went into business with a local tinner named John Berghauser and founded

Fig. 12.3. Interior of a Philadelphia Restaurant with an Elaborate Pressed Metal Ceiling. Pictured in Penn Metal Ceiling and Roofing Company's 1906 catalog. (Courtesy of the Hagley Museum and Library.)

the W. F. Norman Sheet Metal Manufacturing Company. They started in a small shop making roof crestings and cornices but, in 1901, took over a nearby derelict church building, which they converted into a factory. After a 1909 fire, they built a new, modern plant on the site and further expanded their business. Norman continued as an agent for the Wheeling Company until 1905, but then began to produce his own ceiling line, which he advertised as "Made in the West—They are the Best!"[21]

What these examples show is a pattern of capital investment in new industrialization in the second half of the nineteenth century, a rapid expansion of business, and a lot of pride in that rise to success. What it meant for ordinary people was that the new industrialization made possible by the improved and expanded infrastructure of the railroads and telegraph transformed ordinary life. Mass production, mass distribution, and aggressive advertising meant that products like metal ceilings were readily available—not just in industrial centers, but everywhere.[22]

As reliability and frequency of rail service increased, the wholesaler or jobber, who had been so important in the early nineteenth century, be-

came less so. The manufacturers themselves entered the sales market with direct shipments to customers, and they could do it at a lower cost. In the earlier nineteenth century, the retailer had been largely responsible for advertising, but now the manufacturer took on that investment; the trade catalog emerged as the chief tool for promoting the product.[23] Sometimes the manufacturer had his own agents in cities, but, more likely, he simply gave the catalogs free to any contractor anywhere who wanted one. Thus, Dan Casey in small-town America could open his catalogs, pick out his ceiling, telegraph his order, and collect it from his local freight depot.

The catalogs were often quite elaborate. The goal was to catch the consumers' attention and impress them with the quality of the product. The catalogs usually had very decorative covers, were sometimes a hundred or more pages in length, and were filled with half-tone illustrations of the samples and photographs of buildings where the ceilings had been used (figs. 12.3 and 12.4). The catalog copy boasted of how long the firm had been in business, how reliable it was, and how happy its customers were.

Sometimes the catalogs were advertised directly to the consumer, as in an ad in *House Beautiful,*

Fig. 12.4. Interior of a Church. Pictured in the Penn Metal Ceiling and Roofing Company's 1906 catalog. (Courtesy of the Hagley Museum and Library.)

which offered a "craftsman beam ceiling" in metal.[24] But, even here, the expectation was that the consumer would show the catalog to his contractor and have him do the ordering and installing. The exception to this was the Sears Roebuck ads that began to appear in 1911. The ads claimed that putting up a steel ceiling was so easy anyone could do it. Indeed, the customer really didn't need a contractor, not at least if the ceiling was from Sears.[25]

They were probably wrong. The problems that came with the metal ceilings were largely ones that resulted from faulty installation. The metal ceilings were nailed to furring strips laid on twelve- or twenty-four-inch centers over the ceiling joists. The edges of the panels were usually stamped with a bead that allowed them to overlap or interlock. Where the lap between panels did not conceal the nails, decoratively headed nails could be employed to make them part of the design. Damaged plaster ceilings did not have to be taken down: the furring strips could be applied directly to the old plaster. But problems could occur, especially if an amateur was doing the work. If the old ceiling was uneven and the furring strips were not level, the new ceiling might buckle. Seams could separate. If the measurement of the room was not professionally exact, there might be too much or too little when one got to a corner or an edge. Failure to

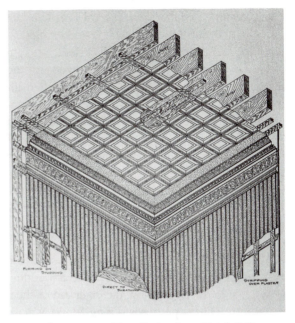

Fig. 12.6. Diagram of Installation for a Metal Ceiling. Penn Metal Company catalog, 1927. (Courtesy of the Hagley Museum and Library.)

caulk and to repaint could let in dirt, moisture, and rust. But properly installed and regularly cared for, the ceilings did last a lifetime; in fact, they lasted several lifetimes (figs. 12.5 and 12.6).[26]

The metal-ceiling business that had begun in the 1880s was booming by 1900. Firms like Willis Manufacturing Company in Galesburg, Ohio, were "making shipments to every state in the Union" and had a large export trade as well. A firm like Berger had agents in New York, Boston, Philadelphia, St. Louis, Minneapolis, and San Francisco. The company was also involved in the export of the ceilings, especially to South America. A 1911 article noted that Berger was supplying ceilings to an Argentinean company, and a 1915 note in *The Metal Worker* reported that several large moving picture theaters in Buenos Aires had recently installed metal ceilings. Research also uncovered several trade catalogs that were produced in New York and Philadelphia but were published in Spanish, probably to meet this market. The 1915

Fig. 12.5. Detail of a Metal Ceiling Installed ca. 1915 in a Store in Lexington, Virginia.

article commented that several local Brazilian factories had begun to stamp their own ceilings using imported American and English steel.[27]

Other countries were also involved in the manufacture of metal ceilings. The Canadian industry is particularly well documented.[28] In Australia, two German immigrants, Ernst and Alfred Wunderlich, began a business in Sydney in 1887 importing zinc from Germany and later steel from England to supply metal roofs and stamped ceilings for buildings all over the country. By the 1890s they had expanded to New Zealand as well. It was a story that paralleled the American experience.[29]

With all its popularity, why did the use of the ceilings decline? The combination of a building slowdown in the Depression, the diversion of sheet metal into military purposes during World War II, and a change in taste in the postwar period when drop-acoustical-tile ceilings became popular helped to spell the end to the widespread use of metal ceilings.[30]

Yet, some companies never stopped making the ceilings, and recent interest in preservation has spurred a mini-boom of popularity. There are at least five companies that still make them.[31] Several, like the W. F. Norman Corp. of Nevada, Missouri, are survivors of the turn-of-the-century period and even use the original dies. The Norman company will reproduce almost any item in its 1902 catalog and is very proud to have furnished the ceilings for Donald Trump's Taj Mahal Casino in Atlantic City. The metal ceilings are still considered fire resistant, clean, durable, and the easiest and quickest way to ornament at the best price.

If this account has thus far established that metal ceilings were popular from the 1880s to the 1930s and that they reflect the mass production, distribution, and advertising revolutions of the period, there is still the question of why they were so popular and what they meant to those who made them and used them.

There is no doubt that the major reason for their popularity was that they successfully met a need. They were a practical, durable, and economical means of achieving a decorative effect. Why, then, are they considered such a "cheap" material today? Even the popular term "tin ceiling" reflects this attitude. The ceilings were never tin, and none of the contemporary literature used that term. At first, they were iron, later steel. There are two possible explanations for the term "tin." One is that it is an inheritance from the nineteenth-century "tinner" or "tin knocker," a craftsmen who worked with tin plate—sheet iron covered with a thin protective layer of tin. Even when other metals were used, this business was still called a "tin shop." It may be that in popular parlance, any thin sheet metal was called "tin," even when it was zinc, copper, or steel.[32]

This may be true, but there is another explanation: the use of the term "tin" for metal ceilings is a reflection of slang that has been used since the nineteenth century to disparage metal building materials. In the mid-nineteenth century, a cheap railroad town with cast-iron fronts was often called a "tin town." In England, a Methodist Chapel was called a "tin chapel." In the twentieth century, we have terms like "Tin Lizzie," and even "tin horn"—usage that suggests cheapness and implies that the object is a base imitation of something else.[33]

In that context, the term "tin ceiling" reflects an attitude that plagued the architectural use of sheet metal for most of its history. For example, in 1876 at the Philadelphia Centennial, the A. O. Kittredge Company of Ohio put up a sheet-metal pavilion to demonstrate the potential of the material. The *American Architect and Building News* attacked it as "the most offensive building on the grounds" and condemned it as a "hollow imitation" that would always be "inferior." They concluded, "If a man has not a natural disgust for shams, it is difficult to argue him into it."[34]

This elitist argument about taste and propriety was at the heart of the debate over the imitative nature of sheet metal. It was a debate that raged in the building press over the use of exterior sheet-metal work, and it was a debate that was inherited by the metal ceiling trade. The manufacturers' sensitivity to this issue is evident in comments like that of Albert Northrop. He wrote in 1890 that his ceilings were "not an imitation of anything," that they "were not a sham" but instead were "real panels, real moldings, real rosettes" not "painted ones" made of "crumbling plaster or inflammable wood" but ones made of "real imperishable iron."[35]

Northrop's claim that the designs were "not imitative of anything," is, however, questionable. The promotional literature makes it very clear that metal ceilings were a substitute for decorative plaster. In an article in *Carpentry and Building* in 1912, one writer cautioned that the metal ceilings should never be painted with a "glossy surface"; instead, they should be a dead, flat white "giving the effect of molded plaster or stucco." In the late 1920s, during the heyday of the Spanish mission style, the ceiling manufacturers even came out with lines that were called "stucco" and "Spanish Texture." In 1931, the minister of the newly remodeled St. Paul's Lutheran Church in Waterloo, Wisconsin, proudly claimed that on the day of the dedication ceremonies, "not one of [the people present] was able to realize that the ceiling was steel."[36]

The architectural elite objected not only to the fact that sheet metal imitated other materials, but also to its mass-produced, mechanical qualities. Frank Lloyd Wright once wrote that it was the "prime makeshift" material of the "American jerry-builder."[37] An Australian critic, Hardy Wilson, wrote of his objection to the "mechanical textureless surface" of the metal ceilings, which "would not have been appreciated at any period earlier than the commercial-Victorian."[38]

To counter the claims that mass production made the ceilings cheap, common, and degraded, proponents argued that mass production was the way of the future, and that metal ceilings were the "modern" solution to building problems. As one

manufacturer wrote, "This is the age of steel and there is scarcely a purpose heretofore served by wood or plaster that cannot now be replaced by steel"—a vastly "superior material."[39] In 1936 a writer in the *Sheet Metal Worker* pointed out that "Steel ceilings and sidewalls were never intended for the pretentious buildings in which expensive decorative treatments are the mode."[40] But, he argued, they were perfect for any "progressive contractor" who would be smart enough to recognize the value of this modern material.

To the thousands of ordinary people who chose them, metal ceilings were a practical and aesthetically attractive material. In 1889 an article in the *Zion Herald* in Whitinsville, Massachusetts, noted that the new Methodist Church ceilings were "an ornament to the Village" and "a joy to all lovers of Zion."[41] In 1915 the editor of the Lexington, Virginia, *Gazette* noted that the new People's Bank ceiling was "handsomely paneled in metal" and that it denoted the "progressive spirit of this enterprising and successful bank."[42] In 1917 the Hirscheimer Brothers of Canton, Ohio, wrote to the Berger Company that the new ceilings in their store made it "one of the most attractive in the city."[43]

Metal ceilings were not a "hollow sham"; they were better than the material they replaced. To choose a ceiling of steel was to choose the best that modern industry and technology could supply. To choose a metal ceiling was also to participate in the spirit of the age of enterprise that had produced them.

A product of new technology, metal ceilings were available because of changes in industrial practices, transportation, and advertising. They were mass produced for the masses. But their popularity was not simply the result of their availability. The masses found them to be a wholly satisfactory, cheap, quick, and easy means to a modern form of ornament.

Notes

An earlier version of this article appeared in *Building Renovation* (Nov.-Dec. 1992): 69–72. Part I of this series was "Cheap, Quick, and Easy: The Early History of Concrete Block," which appeared in *Perspectives in Vernacular Architecture, III,* ed. Thomas Carter and Bernard L. Herman (Columbia: University of Missouri Press, 1989). The author wishes to thank the many people who gave help and support during this project. A Glenn Grant from Washington and Lee University enabled summer travel to collections. A Hagley-Winterthur Research Residency Fellowship in September, 1991, provided key support. Patrick Nolen, Rob Howard, Marsha McHugh, Marian Matyn, and Susan Hengel at Hagley were very helpful. Pat Elliott and Neville Thompson at Winterthur were equally wonderful. Betsy Brittigan at Washington and Lee was very patient and persistent with interlibrary loans. The library staffs at the National Building Museum, the Library of Congress, the Avery Library at Columbia University and the Metropolitan Museum in New York also gave access to key material. In addition, a number of colleagues offered examples, references and review: Catherine Bishir, Richard Candee, Goeff Channon, Mark Edwards, Bryan Green, Herb Gottfried, Betty Hickox, Delos Hughes, Kate Hutchinson, Jan Jennings, Lawrence Kavanagh of the Ontario Heritage Foundation, Travis MacDonald, Ozzie Overby, and W. A. Slagle.

1. "How Casey Came to Sell Ceilings," by the Assistant Manager, *Metal Worker* (Oct. 22, 1915): 528–29

2. Ibid.

3. See Mary Dierickx, "Metal Ceilings in the U.S.," *APT Bulletin* VII (2) (1975): 83–98, and Brian Powell, "Canterbury Shaker Village, Introduction," graduate student paper submitted to Richard Candee, Boston University Preservation Studies Program. Canterbury Village has several well-documented metal ceilings as well as exterior and interior metal wall cladding. See also Ann H. Gillespie, "Decorative Sheet-Metal Building Components in Canada 1870–1930," (M.A. thesis, Carleton College, 1985). Other contemporary and period sources are cited in these notes.

4. Diana Waite, *Architectural Elements: The Technological Revolution* (New York: Bonanza Books, 1976), fig. 7.

5. *The Metal Worker* (Feb. 6, 1875): 2.

6. Dierickx, "Metal Ceilings in the U.S." She was the first to locate this 1884 advertisement in *The American Architect and Building News*. The author confirmed it with some difficulty, since many libraries that have the journal have bound it without the advertisement supplement.

7. "Sheet-Metal Ceiling," *Carpentry and Building* (Oct. 1886): 188.

8. Ibid. This article illustrates a corrugated iron ceiling with decorative rosettes and says it is from a "prominent sheet-metal firm in Germany" and that the illustration is from a book "published in Germany some time since." The article also notes that the original illustrations were in color. A later article in the same journal reported that the iron-with-zinc-ornament ceiling pieces have "been extensively used in Europe" (Mar. 1889, 63). Other writers have claimed a French origin for metal ceilings; I have not been able to confirm this. Period architectural journal articles do make it clear that the metal ceilings were not common in Britain, however, until well after their introduction in the United States, Canada, and Australia. There is a highly suspect claim to an American origin for metal ceilings by Alfred E. Bowers Jr., "The Beginning of Metal Ceilings," *The Sheet Metal Worker* (Jan. 1934): 23–24. Bowers claimed that his father, who was an interior decorator, joined with a plasterer named William Dunn and a wood lather named George Pettit to use "crystallized tin plates" to cover a ceiling in Bowers's house in about 1884. He also claimed that they used real rope and wooden rosettes to cover the seams and joints. Their firm eventually became the Brooklyn Metal Ceiling Co. While the firm was real enough, other aspects of the account are contradicted by the period building literature.

9. Small pieces of ornamental zinc had been used for decoration on exterior cornices and building fronts since the 1870s. They had also been used on interiors in conjunction with plaster to make ornamental centerpieces for ceilings in the 1870s. See "Cornice Work, The Relative Advantages of Stamped Ornaments for Architecural Purposes," *Carpentry and Building* (Feb. 1879): 34.

10. *Carpentry and Building* (Dec. 1887): 244–45, and *Carpentry and Building* (Mar. 1889): 63–64.

11. For more information on the Mesker Company, see Arthur A. Hart, "Sheet Iron Elegance, Mail Order Architecture in Montana," *Montana: The Magazine of Western History* (Autumn 1990): 26–31, and "Design by Mail Order: Mt. Carroll, IL," *National Building Museum Blueprints* 3 (1) (Fall 1984): 10–11. There are good collections of Mesker trade catalogs at the Winterthur Museum and Library, at the Avery Library at Columbia University, and at the Metropolitan Museum. An important archival collection is at the Missouri Historical Society Library in St. Louis. For the Penn Metal Company, see *Seventy-Fifth Penn Metal Year, 1869–1944,* pamphlet at Hagley Museum and Library, Wilmington, Delaware.

12. While the advertisements seemed to disappear in the 1930s from builders' journals like the *National Builder,* a specialist trade magazine like the *Sheet Metal Worker* continued to have regular articles on the metal ceiling trade throughout the 1930s. There was a hint of "boosterism" in the articles, saying that even though times were tough, there was money to be made. The author of several of the articles was the manager of the Steel Ceiling Division of Edwards Manufacturing Co., Cincinnati, Ohio.

13. See "Metallic Relief Ceilings," *The Metal Worker* 15 (3) (July 18, 1891): 36; "Metal Ceilings," *National Builder* (Jan. 1912): 62; or "Here is the Evidence," *Sheet Metal Worker* (Jan. 1935): 15–16, for examples. Metal ceilings were certainly not fire proof, and it was probably the air space between the ceiling and the joists, or the combination of the air space, the old plaster ceiling under the metal one, and the metal that made it fire resistant, but the literature was full of examples and testimonials that claimed that the ceilings would lower insurance premiums and protect the building.

14. *The Record & Guide of New York,* Nov. 14, 1914, newspaper account reproduced in *Mikor Sheet Metal Products,* trade catalog (Milwaukee Corrugating Co., 1915), 246, Avery Collection.

15. "Metal Ceilings for Residences," *The Metal Worker* (Mar. 15, 1912): 383, B. D. Hodges of Hubbard, Texas, a contractor, wrote to the magazine in response to a series of articles on using metal ceilings in homes.

16. "Sheet Metal Ceilings" by Drop Press, *The Metal Worker* (Apr. 20, 1895): 48.

17. Quoted in *All About the Iron Ceilings, Side Walls, etc., Manufactured by A. Northrop & Co.,* trade catalog (Pittsburgh: A. Northrop & Co., 1890), back cover, Avery Collection.

18. The headline was from the *Boston American,* May 16, 1931, and was reproduced in Howard E. Jones, "Steel Ceiling Selling Suggestions," *The Sheet Metal Worker* (Aug. 7, 1931): 470. Another similar point was made in "Even When It Falls Metal Ceiling Is Best," *The Sheet Metal Worker* (June 14, 1929): 381.

19. *Seventy-Fifth Penn Metal Year, 1869–1944.*

20. *The Story, a story of people, the story of Mullins, the story of your job* (Salem, Ohio: Mullins Mfg. Corp., 1947). Seventy-fifth anniversary pamphlet history of the company. Hagley Collection.

21. Neal Quinto, "A Case for the Historic Preservation of the W. F. Norman Corporation in Nevada, Missouri," typescript supplied by the Norman Corp., copy in the Missouri Department of Natural Resources, Division of Historic Preservation Office, copy supplied by Steven Mitchell.

22. See Alfred D. Chandler Jr., *The Visible Hand: The Managerial Revolution in American Business* (Cambridge, Mass.: Harvard University Press, 1977), for a succinct statement of the nature of the change. I am indebted to Professor Geoffrey Channon of the University of Bath for pointing this out to me.

23. Trade catalogs were important for many manufacturers, especially in the hardware and building trades. See "How Catalogues Should Look and What They Should Contain," *The Canadian Manufacturer* 134 (1) (June 1914): 39–40.

24. *House Beautiful* (Apr. 1913): iv, "A Craftsman Style Beam Ceiling in Sheet Steel. Why put up an inflammable wood ceiling when an incombustible one of equal appearance can be obtained? Stamped steel ceilings in Tudor, Jacobean designs—different from the usual and superior to stucco in appearance and durability." Northrop, Coburn and Dodge Co., New York.

25. *The National Builder* (Sept. 1911): 70–71.

26. Much of the trade literature suggests that all that was necessary to put up a metal ceiling were ordinary carpentry skills. Local building contractors did order directly from the manufacturers and install the ceilings, but local tin shops also continued to be suppliers of the ceilings throughout the 1880–1930 period. The tin shops would order the ceilings from the manufacturer, or have them stockpiled, and sometimes specialized in installing them for the contractors. One "tin man," who has been in the business since 1941, scoffed at the idea of an ordinary home owner putting up his own metal ceiling. He pointed out that even when local building contractors ordered the ceilings from the manufacturers they asked his shop to install them. Interview with W. A. Slagle, Klugel Architectural Metal Works, Emporia, Virginia, Oct. 10, 1991.

27. *The National Builder* (May 1911): 56, and *The Metal Worker* (June 11, 1915): 846.

28. See Margaret Carter and Julian S. Smith, *The Metallic Roofing Co. Showroom, A Look at Preservation* (Nov. 1987–Jan. 1988), Ontario Heritage Foundation. In examining the order books for 1897 to 1902, they found that the company was shipping metal ornament and ceilings to a number of foreign countries, including Japan and South Africa. Also see Gillespie, "Decorative Sheet-Metal Building Components," and Gillespie, "Ceilings of Metal," *Canadian Heritage* (May–June 1983): 8–10, 48.

29. Terence Lane and Jessie Serle, *Australians at Home: A Documentary History of Australian Domestic Interiors from 1788–1914* (Melbourne and New York: Oxford University Press, 1990), 376–77; Miria Worthington, "Pressed Metal Ceilings in Western Australia," *Heritage Australia* (Autumn 1986): 31–32; and *Forty Years of Wunderlich Industry, 1887–1927* (Sydney: Wunderlich, 1927).

30. One of the criticisms of steel ceilings was that they carried sound. Various solutions had been suggested, such as weaving building paper between the furring strips, but the modern acoustical tile obviously offered a better sound insulation. For a discussion of the acoustical problems, see "Metal Ceilings for Residences," *The Metal Worker* (Mar. 8, 1912): 342–43.

31. They are Shanker Steel, Secaucus, New Jersey (founded 1912); W. F. Norman Corp., Nevada, Missouri; Old Jefferson Tile Co., Jefferson, Texas; A. A. Abingdon Affiliates, Brooklyn, New York; and Chelsea Decorative Metal Co., Houston, Texas. A number of how-to-put-up-a-metal-ceiling articles appeared in the 1970s and 1980s, reflecting a new preservation interest in the material. See David Bell, "Patterns Overhead," *Americana* (July–Aug. 1979): 52–59; Barbara Schiller, "Metal Ceilings," *The Old-House Journal* (Mar. 1979): 1, 29–33; and John Kosmer, "Tin Ceiling, An Installation Guide," *Victorian Homes* (Winter 1988): 56–61, for examples.

32. W. A. Slagle, owner of the Klugel Architectural Metal Works in Emporia, Virginia, says that "most people who walk into the shop and want any sort of metal work, ask for 'tin'" and that the shops themselves were called "tin shops" and the workers were called "tinners" well into the twentieth century, even when most of the work was done in steel. Slagle interview.

33. *Oxford English Dictionary*, 2d ed. (Oxford: Clarendon Press, 1989), XVIII: 115–17, see especially entry "d." The manufacturers' literature and the building periodicals never used the term "tin" for the ceilings, but it may have been a slang usage even then, as it is today.

34. "Sheet-Metal Architecture," *The American Architect and Building News* (July 22, 1876): 234–35.

35. *All about the Iron Ceilings . . . ,* trade catalog, A. Northrop & Co., 1890, Avery Collection.

36. "An Object Lesson in Getting Business, Why Sheet Metal Was Used So Generously in Remodeling St. Paul's Lutheran Church at Waterloo," *The Sheet Metal Worker* (Dec. 25, 1931): 738–39. Another wonderful example of the objection to sheet metal's imitative properties was expressed by the Grand Rapids Carved Moulding Company, which advertised its wood mouldings as "not pressed, mashed or burned. They are cut in solid wood, not pressed metal. They are the real thing!" *Carpentry and Building* (Dec. 1899): xvii.

37. Frank Lloyd Wright, "In the Cause of Architecture, VIII. Sheet Metal and A Modern Instance," *Architectural Record* (Oct. 1928): 334–42.

38. Lane and Serle, *Australians At Home,* 377. This criticism reflects the arts and crafts movement's machine-hating view.

39. E. E. Souther Iron Co., St. Louis, trade catalog no. 18, n.d. (The text notes that they are in their forty-second year of business.) Metropolitan Museum Collection.

40. *The Sheet Metal Worker* (Jan. 1936): 18.

41. *All About the Iron Ceilings . . . ,* A. Northrop & Co., trade catalog, 1890, Avery Collection.

42. Lexington, Virginia, *Gazette,* Feb. 17, 1915.

43. *The National Builder* (July 1917): 105.

Chapter 13

The Eichler Home: Intention and Experience in Postwar Suburbia

Annmarie Adams

Live your New Way of Life surrounded by every convenience imaginable! The carefully developed Eichler floor plans create more usable living space, inside and out, than is offered in any other home! Step-saving, work-saving space-arrangement . . . construction and material innovations . . . and the latest built-in appliances . . . add time to your day and years to your life. You'll live better in the Wonderful World of Eichler.

> "Enter the Wonderful World
> of Eichler" (ca. 1960)

But is her house in reality a comfortable concentration camp? Have not women who live in the image of the feminine mystique trapped themselves within the narrow walls of their homes?

> Betty Friedan,
> *The Feminine Mystique* (1963)

The seemingly contradictory views of the postwar middle-class home offered by Betty Friedan and the publicists of Eichler Homes, Inc., to Americans in the early 1960s shared a common presumption: both assumed the prescriptive power of architecture in the lives of middle-class women. Like most observers of the postwar cultural landscape, both Eichler, a developer, and Friedan, a social reformer, saw women as passive figures moving in "man-made" space, realizing social ideals prescribed by their physical surroundings.[1]

There is no doubt that the mass movement of young American families to the suburbs in the 1950s

and early 1960s had devastating implications for women's status in middle-class culture. The suburbs isolated them from political, social, and financial power and segregated them from opportunities for employment, education, and cooperative parenting. As Friedan pointed out, as a result of their physical isolation in the suburbs, many postwar housewives became desperate and depressed.

But the postwar home also acted in another capacity. Suburbia was an arena in which women fought back. Isolated in their houses, women expressed their own ideas about making space, often originating in dissatisfaction, and contested male power in architectural terms.[2] The postwar house, neither paradise nor prison, was a significant zone of contention between builders and the middle-class family.[3] As a case study of how one family followed and countered what some promoters and critics of domestic architecture *supposed* them to experience, this study is an attempt to explore the dynamic relationship between a family and the domestic space they occupied. It analyzes a single house from the "inside"— that is, as it was actually experienced—and relates that information to the world "outside," as it was intended by its builders. In this way, it is an attempt to locate the intersection of real and ideal lives in the postwar cultural landscape. The promotional literature of Eichler Homes, Inc., and the photographs and memories of a female child in the 1960s are the perimeters of this study; between them stands the primary source for the project—the house itself.

They were a typical postwar couple. Both Joan and Frank Clarkson had been in the armed forces during the war, marrying in 1946.[4] While Frank finished his business degree at the University of California, the Clarksons lived in a rented apartment in Berkeley. Joan worked as a secretary until the birth of their first child, John, in 1951. With the arrival of their daughter Gail three years later, they moved into a small house in Albany, a medium-sized suburban town just north of Berkeley. Frank secured a position with the Bank of America in San Francisco after graduation, qualifying for a mortgage under the Veterans' Administration mortgage guarantee program.[5] Like most other American families that took advantage of the VA program's generous financing, the Clarkson family chose a home in the suburbs.

The Clarkson family purchased their house in Terra Linda, California, in 1961; Joan Clarkson was then expecting their fourth child, Willy, and the family needed another bedroom.[6] She had read about the developments of Eichler Homes in *Sunset Magazine,* where they had been described as ideal environments for raising children. Indeed, the company, founded in 1947, had been awarded the *Parents'* Magazine National Merit Award for the "best home for families with children" nearly every year between 1951 and 1959.[7] That record, together with the reputation of Marin County's schools as among the best in the Bay Area, had helped to convince Joan—and through her, Frank—to move to Terra Linda.

In contrast to their Albany house, the Clarksons' new home was part of a totally planned, newly shaped landscape.[8] Thirty minutes' drive from San Francisco, the new suburb was planned for forty-five hundred houses, three shopping areas, schools, recreation areas, and churches. There were few businesses and no other cultural institutions. Terra Linda was typical of postwar American suburbs in its peripheral location, low density, stylistic conformity, and racial and economic homogeneity (fig. 13.1).[9]

The Clarksons ordered Plan No. 131 on Lot No. 88 in Terra Linda Valley Unit 4, agreeing to pay

Fig. 13.1. Cover of Brochure Published by Eichler Homes. This cover shows locations of seven Eichler communities in the San Francisco Bay area.

$27,500.[10] They still live in this house today, and it has remained relatively unchanged over the past thirty years (figs. 13.2 and 13.3). It is a typical Eichler home: a ranch house with a flat roof, visible structure, and plenty of glass. Defined by prefabricated wood frame structures on heated concrete slabs, the plans of Eichler houses are fairly open.[11] The major living spaces in the house are distinguished by their spatial continuity, rather than functioning as discreet volumes, as in a traditional nineteenth-century house. These major rooms open toward the backyard, leaving the facade of the house blank save for a few windows intended for ventilation. Up and down the block, and throughout Terra Linda, are houses just like the Clarksons'. They differ slightly in size and some details, but bear a distinct resemblance to one another and are immediately recognizable as "Eichlers."[12]

They are named for the founder of the second best-known "merchant-building company" in America, Joseph L. Eichler (1900–74), who constructed thousands of prefabricated, suburban, middle-class houses in California during the postwar era. Eichler's houses were a well-known house type in the San Francisco Bay area, distinguished by their "modern" appearance—the stark, undecorated structure and

Fig. 13.2. Plan of the Clarkson
House, Terra Linda, California.
(Measured by the author and
Mark Brack, 1992, drawing by
Jennifer Beardsley).

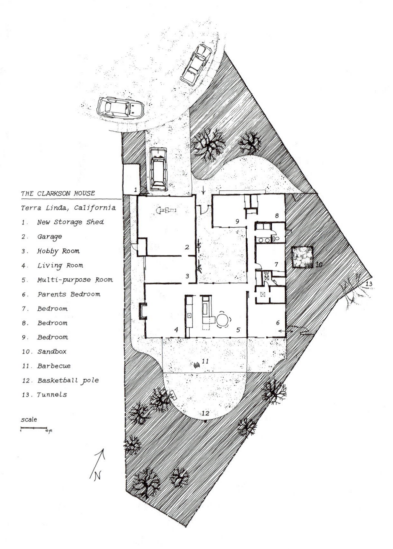

THE CLARKSON HOUSE

Terra Linda, California

1. New Storage Shed
2. Garage
3. Hobby Room
4. Living Room
5. Multi-purpose Room
6. Parents Bedroom
7. Bedroom
8. Bedroom
9. Bedroom
10. Sandbox
11. Barbecue
12. Basketball pole
13. Tunnels

scale

N

relatively blank facade. In terms of a recognizable product, they were the equivalent—at a much higher price—of William Levitt's houses in the Levittowns on the East Coast.[13]

The Eichler name and the predictable architecture that it represented were marketed as positive features to potential home buyers. So, too, was the revolutionary manner in which the company enticed prospective customers with attractions that reached far beyond the home itself. An Eichler house often included a full set of appliances and well-known, brand-name materials and fixtures; the lawn, landscaping, patio, and fences were also often part of the initial arrangement with the builder.[14] The Clarkson contract included kitchen cabinets, garage doors, plate-glass mirrors, door chimes, and all the plumbing fixtures. Building materials and details were specified by the family after it had inspected a model home in Terra Linda.[15] The company's one-stop architectural shopping, like the marketing techniques developed much earlier by mail-order companies such as Sears, Roebuck and Company and Montgomery Ward, proved to be an extremely successful approach.[16] Five hundred houses were constructed in Terra Linda in one year; they sold immediately.[17]

Unlike most other builders of the time, Eichler hired well-known architects to design models from which his houses were constructed.[18] That decision reflected both a desire and a quite pressing need for professional design expertise. The combination of a growing demand for larger houses and the increasing prevalence of smaller building lots convinced builders like Eichler to look to architects for more efficient and sophisticated solutions to the perceived space problem.[19] "I'd never used architects before because I didn't think design was necessary to sell houses," admitted one builder in 1954. "But today the market is so competitive that builders need good design to sell."[20] Eichler himself likened the reliance of builders upon architects to the need of a dress manufacturer for professional fashion designers.[21] Anshen and Allen, the architects of the Clarkson house, began designing merchant-builder houses in 1949 after having supposedly convinced Eichler of the "possibilities of good design" by showing him Anshen's work on his own house.[22]

The association of Eichler homes with the world of custom-built, architect-designed houses added to the "designer" appeal of the buildings. Indeed, the houses were characterized by a unique combination of common, ordinary elements—economical materials, prefabricated elements, and neighborhood conformity—and high-style features—blank facade, visible structure, window walls, flat roof. The rapid acceptance of the blank facade was surprising, even to its designers. Anshen claims that the first builder for whom they designed a house with a blank front was "leery" of the idea; it was one of five designs tested as model houses. According to the architect, this model was so popular that the other, presumably more traditional models were impossible to sell.[23]

The merchant-builder house into which the Clarkson family moved in 1961 featured much more, however, than up-to-date styling. At every level of its construction—from the interior detailing to site planning—it suggested or assumed a standard of relations between suburb and city, between neighbors, and between the members of each family. That deliberate construction of social relations began at the level of the neighborhood site plan. The seemingly close relationship of the house to the outdoors, in its use of large areas of glazing, was belied by the actual separation of yard

Fig. 13.3. View of the Clarkson House from the Street.

from yard in Terra Linda. The Clarkson house is located in a cul-de-sac of five identical houses; the yards are separated by high fences that were included in the contract with the builder. "The fence protects us," claimed one customer when questioned about the large areas of glazing in Eichler homes. "We don't feel like goldfish at all."[24]

The house itself also acted as an impenetrable wall, reinforcing the larger gesture of withdrawal and isolation expressed in both the peripheral location of Terra Linda and in its site planning. The front of the Clarkson house, as already noted, is nearly blank; the large, two-car garage encompasses most of the building's width. Even the front door, a solid wooden door, does not lead into the house, but rather into an open atrium space. The "real" entry to the house, from the atrium to the multipurpose room, is a sliding glass door. In this way, explained the architect, "The entrance court attained privacy from many casual visitors."[25] In contrast to the street-facing orientation of traditional American houses, family life was directed to the back of the lot in the Eichler home. In an effort to "protect" mothers and children, Eichler had actually surrounded the family with architecture. The opacity of the front and sides of the house, the enclosed courtyard, and the high fences around the yard ensured that family life was focused within the property lines of the suburban home.

The central interior space in the Clarkson house, the huge multipurpose room, reflected this new concern. Eichler houses were typically promoted as appearing much larger than they were. "In a small house," explained the architect, "the economics of the selling price indicate that rooms cannot be as large as might be desirable, and therefore, in order to provide at least one space which gives at least a visual sense of large size, the architect finds it desirable to 'throw together visually' as much space as possible."[26]

This "capturing" of additional space in the design of the house was also attempted at the larger scale of the suburb. The distant views of the Marin

hills through the large windows of the Clarkson house served to "extend" the apparent boundaries of the lot. The constructed views in contemporary houses, claimed a journalist, made prospective buyers feel they had "space to breathe in—enough space to walk around in without being crowded." The window wall in the rear of the house and the careful siting of the building extended the room, and the family's sense of territoriality, into the distant landscape.[27]

The open plan of the multipurpose room at the center of the house also expressed the new emphasis placed on motherhood in the design of houses during the baby boom era.[28] From this combination kitchen, dining, and playroom—the "living-center of an Eichler Home" as the company's own publicity described it—mothers like Joan Clarkson could survey all the major spaces in the house.[29] She could, while preparing dinner, "keep visual control of children's activities over the house."[30] In this way, the kitchen was intended not only as a place to prepare meals but also as a virtual command post for a person whose full-time job was watching. "The architects arranged glass walls and doorways in front or side yards so a mother could keep an eye on the children," the magazines reported, adding almost as an afterthought that she might "even share in the pleasure of outdoor living herself."[31] Furthermore, the kitchen, "placed squarely in the center of

Fig. 13.4. Postcard Published by Eichler Homes, Inc., Showing the Uninterrupted View of the Multipurpose Room and Backyard from the Kitchen.

the floor plan . . . commands all situations—visually, psychologically, and operationally."[32] The Eichler company included in its promotional materials a colored postcard picturing the house interior as seen from the kitchen, emphasizing the breadth of this zone controlled by the mother (fig. 13.4).[33]

Maternal power was also closely linked, in the eyes of the designers, with domestic technology.[34] As most of the appliances were included in the arrangement with the builder, female control was, in a real sense, built into the architecture of the house. The Eichler kitchen came equipped with a Waste King dishwasher and garbage disposal unit and a Thermador range and oven.[35] Corporate publicity emphasized the labor-saving materials found throughout the house, such as Philippine mahogany wall paneling—"beautiful, durable, easy to clean," and Armstrong flooring, which required "little or no waxing."[36] Other details were designed specifically to accommodate small children. The kitchen faucet in an Eichler, for example, could be controlled with one hand, in case a mother had an infant in her arms. The radiant-heated concrete floor was described as being not only clean and durable, but also as "perfect for children's bare feet."[37]

In its reliance on domestic technology as a means of enhancing female power in the home, the Eichler house was, in a way, the realization of a strain of domestic design ideology that looked back to Catharine Beecher in the mid-nineteenth century and had affected kitchen design throughout the twentieth century. Since the construction of the "progressive" house, sixty years earlier, designers had consistently emphasized kitchen technology as a key to lightening women's labor and elevating their status.[38] This was billed in the prewar house as a means to professionalize women's position as homemakers, in order to give their work a social value measurable in the same terms by which all labor was measured.

The Eichler kitchen, however, aspired not to revalue household labor, but simply to make it more pleasant and less disruptive to the other duties of domestic life. Undecorated surfaces, sharp edges, and the open plan made the house a showcase for good housekeeping. Another postcard produced by the company, as well as many photographs in its brochures, featured women in the kitchen, talking to men and children who were eating or playing (fig. 13.5). The "world's most efficient, most beautiful kitchen" allowed women to complete household tasks while participating fully in family life.[39]

The central position of the kitchen in the Eichler home was also directly connected to patterns of child care developed long after Beecher's era. Dr. Benjamin Spock, in his best-selling *Common Sense*

Fig. 13.5. Postcard Published by Eichler Homes, Inc., Showing the Openness of the Kitchen.

Fig. 13.6. Photograph from Promotional Material Published by Eichler Homes, Inc. This photo suggests how a social gathering could occupy several rooms of a house.

Book of Baby and Child Care of 1946, had convinced parents to adopt a more instinctual approach to mothering.[40] Spock told mothers that their behavior carried enormous consequences for children and placed particular emphasis on the closeness of mother and child. "If relationships are good," claimed the doctor, "[children] don't have to be forced to eat, forced to use the toilet."[41] Spock's approach to mothering, whereby the mother was a constant and close companion, demanded an architecture in which she could observe every gesture of the child, hear every whimper, and respond instantly. The Eichler plan, with its kitchen as an observation station and large expanses of glazing between indoor and outdoor spaces, was intended to facilitate this instinctual mode of mothering.[42] Instinctual mothering would have been impossible, that is, in a house in which cooking and playing occurred in separate spaces.

The ideal space for Spock-style mothering was the atrium in the Eichler house. This space was intended by the architects of the house to act as a form of filter, like the entry vestibule in a traditional American house, where salesmen or other unwanted visitors could be encountered before they reached the inner sanctum of the family home. It was also intended as a dining area and, according to the company brochures, as the perfect play space for kids, who could benefit from the open air while mothers watched from inside, assured of their children's safety.

Eichler promotional material suggests that the overall plan was further intended to accommodate the woman of the house in her anticipated role as the hostess of cocktail parties for her husband's business associates. In the 1950s corporations began to scrutinize closely the wives of job applicants to ensure that they were pleasant, satisfied with their marriages, and willing to accept their husbands' transfers. Cocktail and dinner parties in the family home for the husband's associates at work became a routine part of middle-class life. The Eichler plan allowed and even encouraged the responsible housewife to prepare drinks and food in the kitchen, while entertaining guests at the same time. Company brochures showed how large social gatherings could spread from the multipurpose room into the atrium or the backyard, taking advantage of the open plan of the house (fig. 13.6).

The details of the house also were designed to facilitate women's ability to serve as both mother and hostess. The built-in dining table, for example, was hinged and could swing into the kitchen or into the multipurpose room. Projected into the latter area, the table was perfect for adult formal dining. As part of the kitchen, it was more suitable for children's meals. The dining table encapsulated the overall design principles implicit in Eichler's collaboration with Anshen and Allen: adaptability within a larger framework of implicit, controlling social expectations.

Thus far we have looked at the Eichler home in terms of how it was *supposed* to function, noting the position of women in the house as one of relative (but limited) power as surveyor of nearly all the family's activities. We have noted the turning of the house away from the street, the enclosed atrium, the high fences, and the absence of any shared spaces with neighbors as an effort to "capture" space and to preserve the appearance of openness within carefully closed and segregated spaces. But did real families live in the ideal ways pictured in publicity brochures and postcards? How did actual life in an Eichler compare with the life prescribed by the physical arrangement of spaces in the house?

The memories and family photographs of the Clarkson family and the present condition of their house indicate that they followed, to some extent, the expectations built into postwar suburban architecture. Mr. Clarkson earned the family living in the distant city, while Mrs. Clarkson remained in the home and suburb and was responsible for child care. But Joan Clarkson and her children did not simply follow blindly the architectural instructions spelled out by their house. They assumed active roles in the "construction" of their own spaces, contesting many of the relationships presumed by the house. In this way, the Clarkson home was a carefully negotiated compromise between ideal and real, a compromise mostly realized through the rearrangement of furniture and the appropriation of spaces intended for other uses. Because it exists in behavior rather than in built fact, the landscape inhabited by women and children is completely invisible in the traditional sources of architectural history.

Nearly every aspect of the ideal use of the house as represented by "The Wonderful World of Eichler" was subject to some modification by the Clarksons. To begin, the strict territorial boundaries constructed to separate families in Terra Linda—the high fences, the enclosed atria, and the general turning of Eichler houses away from the street—were ignored or overcome in the real lives of the inhabitants, particularly the children.

The family's major "misuse" of Eichler's site plan was in the Clarkson children's use of the street as a play space. Every evening, a kickball game was organized among the twenty-four kids who lived in the five houses of the cul-de-sac. Although each lot had a relatively large backyard, intended for carefully supervised playing, the older children of Terra Linda preferred the relatively "neutral" space of the street, outside the area easily supervised by mothers cleaning up in the kitchen after dinner. Perhaps the mothers of Terra Linda did not want to supervise more than necessary; although American child rearing has always placed a premium on the child's independence, mothers also may have valued time spent alone.[43]

Other active play zones were also located beyond the gaze of Joan Clarkson: in the side yard and the garage. The side yard was the preferred play space of the Clarkson children (fig. 13.7). The oldest kids, John and Gail, had special garden plots in the side yard. It was also the home of the family dog, Casey, for whom the children were supposedly responsible. The side yard's exclusiveness as a "kids' space" was guaranteed by the fact that a special door led out to it from the combination bathroom and laundry room. Probably intended by Eichler and his architects as a minor side entry to the house, this door was easily appropriated by the children because it led from their own bathroom inside the house.

The Clarkson children also tried to "demolish" the barriers between the backyards on their cul-de-sac by digging carefully planned tunnels under the high fences that separated their world from those of their friends. Gail Clarkson and her childhood friend Lori passed messages through their subterranean tunnel.

Also outside of Mrs. Clarkson's line of vision was the garage, which was the setting for special games. Although the two-car garage was obviously intended for the family automobiles, it became the relatively permanent setting for both hopscotch and Ping-Pong when the children were young, en-

Fig. 13.7. Photograph of the Side Yard of the Clarkson House Looking Toward the Backyard.

abling them to play "outside" the house in rainy weather. Once the chalk lines for hopscotch were drawn on the concrete floor of the garage, remembers Gail, the space was hers. This reapportionment of space was a conscious choice on the part of the family; they preferred to park their two cars on the driveway and street in order to gain this ad-hoc "games room" for the kids. In a more traditional builder's house, the basement may well have served this purpose.[44]

While brochure descriptions and photos, as we have seen, billed the enclosed courtyard as the perfect space for child care, real children preferred to play in less visible areas. As a result, many residents in Terra Linda transformed their underused atria into other kinds of spaces. Immediate neighbors of the Clarksons kept reptiles in their courtyard; most atria became elaborate gardens. The Clarksons stored bicycles and other bulky items in their outdoor room.

Admittedly, the Clarkson children sometimes played in the atrium; they especially liked to sleep under the stars on camp cots in the courtyard. Again, it is interesting to note that the children preferred to use this space when mothers were noticeably absent from their "command post" in the multipurpose room.

The continuous supervision of children by mothers implied in Eichler's architecture depended on vast areas of glazing around the atrium and facing the backyard. This afforded, as already noted, uninterrupted views from the kitchen.[45] What the publicists of Eichler homes seldom mentioned was the consequent high visibility of parents' activities to children. Just as the Clarkson children chose to play in spaces that lay outside their mother's guard, so too did the Clarkson parents block their own visibility by simply drawing the curtains, transforming their windows into walls. Nearly every extant photograph of the family, outside and inside, shows the windows of their house completely curtained. In this way, the Eichler house could function as a traditional American suburban house with opaque walls. Whenever the parents were in the master bedroom, remembers a Clarkson child, the curtains were drawn (fig. 13.8).[46]

Men were afforded little space of their own in the Eichler home. In other suburban, postwar houses, however, the basement and backyard were often associated with the husband and father, accommodating his technology—the workshop and the barbecue. The Eichler home, though, had no basement, and the backyard barbecue was in full view of the command-post kitchen, which was controlled by the woman. Furthermore, the backyard area immediately adjacent to the Clarkson house was paved, appearing as an extension of the indoor flooring. Ceiling beams, too, extended out from the indoor area and blurred the distinction between inside and outside, transforming "dad's kitchen" into a simple extension of the regular cooking space.[47]

The children's bedrooms in the Eichler home, on the other hand, were fully enclosed, private spaces, pierced only by small windows for ventilation, rather than the large sliding-glass doors of the parents' room. These cramped, boxy rooms—they averaged about ten-by-ten feet—acted as the antithesis, in both spatial and psychological terms, of the open, multipurpose room shared by the entire family. While the multipurpose room provided an arena for family togetherness, more traditional American values concerning independence and individuality were the special preserve of the bedroom wing, or "quiet zone," of the Eichler home.[48]

Fig. 13.8. Photograph of the Clarkson Children behind Their Home. Most family photographs of the house show curtained windows.

Bedrooms were where children nurtured their own individuality by spending time alone—playing, reading, or simply thinking.[49] The typical child's bedroom of the 1960s expressed, in its arrangement and decoration, the personality of its tiny inhabitant.[50] Wall color or wallpaper pattern was based, first and foremost, on gender; books and toys were displayed in bedrooms; older children often exhibited posters of music or television stars, showing their awareness of and association with popular culture.

The lack of storage space was another distinguishing feature of Eichler's architecture. Although two standard hall closets were provided and the bedrooms each included a clothes closet, there was negligible "back stage" space in the house. The laundry room, for example, was located just off the main circulation corridor. The slab construction system, of course, meant that there was no basement or crawl space to use for storage beneath the main floor of the house. The challenge of storing the typical accoutrements of middle-class life—bicycles, sports equipment, camping gear, off-season clothing—led to many small-scale, but significant, changes in the Clarkson house. Frank Clarkson constructed a storage shed beside the garage almost immediately after the family moved in. This extra space was intended to accommodate large equipment; with the appropriation of the garage as a play space for children, there was little room remaining for lawn mowers and other tools. Inside the house, Mrs. Clarkson extended the kitchen cupboards up to the ceiling, eliminating cupboard tops that only attracted dust while increasing kitchen storage space.

More significant still in the family's redesign of the architecture was the "addition" of a free-standing dining table to the Clarksons' multipurpose room (fig. 13.9). The presence of this second table completely defied the flexible, "multipurpose" nature of the space as intended by Eichler and recalled the separate dining room of the traditional American house. The table presumed the need for

Fig. 13.9. Photograph of the
Clarkson Multipurpose Room
Looking Toward the Kitchen. This
photo shows the juxtaposition of
the two tables.

different kinds of rooms for formal and informal
eating, just as traditional houses had. The Clarksons'
extra table thus transformed the huge, undifferentiated multipurpose space into two distinct rooms:
a kitchen and a dining room. Although the tables
were actually only five or six feet apart, the difference in their meanings acted as a thick wall between the two parts of the room. Despite their apparent preparedness for guests, the Clarksons never
once hosted a cocktail party for Frank's business associates. "My mother was never into cooking or
parties," remembers Gail. "If we had people over
it was usually family."[51]

Due to the isolation of individual houses in postwar suburbs, most housewives, including Joan
Clarkson, did not form close friendships with the
other mothers in the immediate vicinity; observers
of the postwar cultural landscape have concluded
from this that suburban women led extremely lonely
existences, confined, as Friedan noted, within the
"narrow walls of their homes." By 5:30 P.M. on most
days, reported one journalist, many women were
glad to see their husbands, so desperate were they
for adult conversation.[52]

Again, reality and experience reveal completely
different stories. Mrs. Clarkson and most postwar
housewives led busy "public" lives in Terra Linda,

participating in significant relationships outside the
family. Every afternoon Joan Clarkson took her children to the public pool, like hundreds of other
mothers in California suburbs. At the recreation
center in Terra Linda, women watched swimming
lessons and admired back flips, but they also
formed lasting friendships with other women with
whom they interacted on a daily basis in a public
place.

Joan Clarkson was also involved in charitable
organizations. The members of the Summer Hills
Club to which she belonged met regularly in various Terra Linda houses in order to plan their annual fund-raising events. At the pool, in the living
rooms, and in countless other spaces, the supposedly private sphere of women in the suburbs was
invisibly extended and ranged widely.[53] Telephones
and cars, as well as the employment of "cleaning ladies," enabled postwar women to break down the
"confining walls" of their physical environments.

American suburban housewives, claimed Friedan,
"learned to 'adjust' to their biological role. They [be-
came] dependent, passive, childlike; they [gave] up
their adult frame of reference to live at the lower
human level of food and things."[54] Friedan attributed this adjustment to women's isolation, and she
described the situation in specifically architectural

terms: the house was a concentration camp. She assumed, like many others, that women were mute victims of their social and physical situations. The Women's Liberation Movement of the 1960s also used the metaphor of imprisonment or containment in its battle for equal rights, precisely the same language used by architects and developers to promote postwar houses.[55]

The architectural evidence suggests, however, that the "adjustment" of the postwar housewife may also have occurred in the opposite direction of that indicated by Friedan. Although Mrs. Clarkson obviously conformed to the standards prescribed by the built environment, she also "adjusted" or redesigned the meanings and the uses of the spaces in her house, setting in motion a completely different standard of relations between neighbors and between members of the family than that established for her.

While this study of the Clarkson house is a very limited sample, it nonetheless demonstrates that there is a major gap between actual use and descriptive or prescriptive literature on houses. If historians continue to project women's lives into the ideal spaces prescribed by architects and builders, they will propagate an inadequate history, dominated by the designers of the postwar cultural landscape. It is only by investigating domestic space from the interior—and comparing that information to ideals established on the exterior—that we can begin to understand how houses actually worked and represented women's true experiences of the built environment.

Notes

1. The author would like to acknowledge the assistance of Jennifer Beardsley, Mark Brack, Chandos Brown, Elizabeth Cromley, Peter Gossage, Paul Groth, Janet Hutchison, Rick Kerrigan, Margaretta Lovell, Eric Sandweiss, Eleanor McD. Thompson, Dell Upton, Abigail Van Slyck, and an anonymous reviewer, and to thank the family in the case study, especially daughter Gail, whose photographs were the initial inspiration for the project.

2. For reviews of the literature on women in architecture, see Sally McMurry, "Women in the American Vernacular Landscape," *Material Culture* 20 (Spring 1988): 33–49; Carolyn Merchant, "Gender and Environmental History," *Journal of American History* 76 (4) (Mar. 1990): 1117–21; Gerda R. Wekerle, "Women in the Urban Environment," *Signs,* 5 (3) (suppl.) (Spring 1980): S188–S214. Toward a feminist analysis of architectural space, see Judy Attfield and Pat Kirkham, eds., *A View From the Interior: Feminism, Women, and Design* (London: Women's Press, 1989); Jos Boys, "Is There a Feminist Analysis of Architecture?" *Built Environment* 10 (1) (Nov. 1, 1984): 25–34; Cheryl Buckley, "Made in Patriarchy: Toward a Feminist Analysis of Women and Design," *Design Issues* 3 (2) (Fall 1986): 3–14; Matrix, *Making Space: Women and the Man-Made Environment* (London: Pluto, 1984); Daphne Spain, *Gendered Spaces* (Chapel Hill: University of North Carolina Press, 1992); Leslie Kanes Weisman, *Discrimination by Design: A Feminist Critique of the Man-Made Environment* (Urbana: University of Illinois Press, 1992).

3. The relationship between middle-class families and their housing, particularly during the progressive era, has been explored by many scholars. See, for example, Elizabeth Collins Cromley, *Alone Together: A History of New York's Early Apartments* (Ithaca: Cornell University Press, 1990); Sally McMurry, *Families and Farmhouses in Nineteenth-century America: Vernacular Design and Social Change* (New York: Oxford University Press, 1988); Albert Eide Parr, "Heating, Lighting, Plumbing, and Human Relations," *Landscape* 19 (1) (Winter 1970): 28–29; Robert C. Twombley, "Saving the Family: Middle Class Attraction to Wright's Prairie House, 1901–1909," *American Quarterly* 27 (1) (Mar. 1975): 57–72; Gwendolyn Wright, *Moralism and the Model Home: Domestic Architecture and Cultural Conflict in Chicago, 1873–1913* (Chicago: University of Chicago Press, 1980).

4. In the interest of privacy, I have changed the name of the family described in this study. All other details given are factual.

5. This plan allowed veterans to borrow the entire appraised value of a house without a down payment. While not entirely prescriptive, the VA loan program offered strong incentive for home buyers to buy in suburban neighborhoods. See Kenneth T. Jackson, *Crabgrass Frontier: The Suburbanization of the United States* (Oxford: Oxford University Press, 1985), 233.

6. Betsy Clarkson, the third child, had been born in 1959.

7. Eichler won many other national awards, including the *Life* Magazine Award of Merit, 1953; National Association of Home Builders of U.S., 1954; *Living* Magazine Award, 1955; AIA-House and Home, 1956; *Sunset* Magazine, 1956; and the AIA-NAHB Award of Honor, 1959.

8. Terra Linda was reportedly the first planned community in America to have all contemporary houses. See "Terra Linda: California's Newest Planned Town," *House and Home* 6 (3) (Sept. 1954): 155.

9. These five characteristics of postwar suburbs are cited in Jackson, *Crabgrass Frontier,* 238–41.

10. Contract between the purchasers and Eichler Homes, Inc., and a letter from Mr. and Mrs. Clarkson to Joseph L. Eichler, July 2, 1961, in possession of the family.

11. Because the heating pipes in many Eichler houses burst and could not be repaired, new occupant-added, rooftop heating systems are an additional signature Eichler feature. See Dale Mead, "Leaky Floor Heat-Pipes Plague Old Eichler Tract," *San Jose Mercury,* Sept. 23, 1971.

12. Even the changes made to the houses by residents are remarkably consistent. For example, a typical street in an Eichler community will now comprise houses with pitched roofs of varying angles, second-floor additions, or two-story additions. See note 11.

13. The term is taken from Ned Eichler, *The Merchant Builders* (Cambridge, Mass.: MIT Press, 1982), which includes valuable information on his father's firm in the broader context of the American home-building industry; also see Marc A. Weiss, *The Rise of the Community Builders: The American Real Estate Industry and Urban Land Planning* (New York: Columbia University Press, 1987); for a comparison of approaches between Eichler and Levitt, see Ned Eichler, *The Merchant Builders,* 116–18. Further biographical information on Eichler is offered in his obituaries in the *San Francisco Chronicle,* July 27, 1974, and the *San Francisco Examiner,* July 26, 1974.

14. The basic package varied from project to project; a typical cost breakdown is included in "Subdivision of the Year," *Architectural Forum* 93 (6) (Dec. 1950): 87.

15. The understanding that their new home would be identical to the model home they had inspected, with the exception of an agreed-upon expansion, was articulated in a letter from the Clarksons, dated July 2, 1961, to Joseph L. Eichler, in which the family complained to him about the materials used in their fireplace and noted a rumor of substandard workmanship in the unit. The letter is in the possession of the Clarkson family.

16. On merchant building as an outgrowth of the 1910s and 1920s, see Weiss, *The Rise of the Community Builders.*

17. "Terra Linda," 155.

18. Ned Eichler, *The Merchant Builders,* 86–87.

19. Whereas in 1951, three-bedroom houses were considered ample, by 1954 the purchasers of most new homes wanted four bedrooms. See "Four Bedrooms Solve Space Squeeze," *House and Home* 5 (6) (June 1954): 116.

20. Ibid., 116.

21. "Subdivision of the Year," 80.

22. Robert Anshen, "Design—Today's Contemporary House," *AIA Journal,* (Sept. 1960): 44–48; "Subdivision of the Year," 80.

23. See Anshen, "Design—Today's Contemporary House," 47.

24. Eichler's use of high fences was in contrast to other postwar merchant builders; fences were forbidden in

Levittown because they were thought to appear cluttered and to detract from the landscape design. See "Subdivision of the Year," 81.

25. Anshen, "Design—Today's Contemporary House," 47.

26. Ibid., 48.

27. "Terra Linda," 157; Lynn Spigel has explained the ambiguity between indoor and outdoor space in postwar suburban houses as the simultaneous urge to separate from and integrate into society. See Lynn Spigel, "The Suburban Home Companion: Television and the Neighborhood Ideal in Postwar America," in *Sexuality & Space,* ed. Beatriz Colomina (Princeton: Princeton Architectural Press, 1992), 186–87.

28. The birth rate in 1960 was 3.52 children per woman, compared to 2.10 in 1940. Mary P. Ryan, *Womanhood in America: From Colonial Times to the Present,* 3d ed. (New York: Franklin Watts, 1983), 268; on the design of kitchens prior to World War II, see Ellen Lupton and J. Abbott Miller, *The Bathroom, The Kitchen and the Aesthetics of Waste: A Process of Elimination* (Cambridge: MIT List Visual Arts Center, 1992).

29. "Enter the Wonderful World of Eichler," n.p.

30. "Courtyards for a Builder's House," *Architectural Record: Record Houses of 1960* (May 1960): 114.

31. "Four Bedrooms," 123.

32. "The Hub of the House," *House Beautiful* 94 (9) (Sept. 1952): 97.

33. This view was also featured in many magazine articles on Eichler homes. See *Record Houses of 1960,* 115. The concept of the "fitted kitchen" was marketed in postwar Britain as a particularly American feature. See "The American Dream," in Sally MacDonald and Julia Porter, *Putting on the Style: Setting Up Home in the 1950s* (London: Geffrye Museum, 1990), n.p. On the association of domestic interiors with women, see Bonnie Lloyd, "Woman's Place, Man's Place," *Landscape* 20 (1) (Oct. 1975): 10–13.

34. A closer analysis of the relationship of maternal power and domestic technology in earlier houses is offered in my "Architecture in the Family Way: Health Reform, Feminism, and the Middle-class House in England, 1870–1900," (Ph.D. diss., University of California at Berkeley, 1992).

35. "An Eichler Home Invites Comparison," publicity brochure, n.d., n.p.

36. Ibid.

37. Ibid.

38. On the rationalization of housework in the early twentieth century, see Bettina Berch, "Scientific Management in the Home: The Empress's New Clothes," *Journal of American Culture* 3 (3) (Fall 1980): 440–45, and Christine E. Bose, Philip L. Bereano, and Mary Malloy, "Household Technology and the Social Construction of Housework," *Technology and Culture* 25 (1) (Jan. 1984): 53–82. On technological change throughout the century, see Ruth Schwartz Cowan, "The 'Industrial Revolution' in the Home: Household Technology and Social Change in the Twentieth Century," *Technology and Culture* 17 (1) (Jan. 1976): 1–23, and *More Work For Mother: The Ironies of Household Technology from the Open Hearth to the Microwave* (New York: Basic Books, 1983); Joann Vanek, "Household Technology and Social Status: Rising Living Standards and Status and Residence Differences in Housework," *Technology and Culture* 19 (3) (July 1978): 361–75, and "Time Spent in House Work," *Scientific American* (Nov. 1974): 116–20.

39. "Enter the Wonderful World of Eichler," n.p.

40. Christina Hardyment, *Dream Babies: Child Care From Locke to Spock* (London: Jonathan Cape, 1983), 223; the relationship of Spock's ideas to the plans of ranch houses is discussed in Clifford Edward Clark Jr., *The American Family Home, 1800–1960* (Chapel Hill: University of North Carolina Press, 1986), 206–7.

41. Steven Mintz and Susan Kellogg, *Domestic Revolutions: A Social History of American Family Life* (New York: Free Press, 1988), 188. See also Nancy Pottishman Weiss, "Mother, the Invention of Necessity: Dr. Benjamin Spock's

Baby and Child Care," in *Growing Up in America: Children in Historical Perspective,* ed. N. Ray Hiner and Joseph M. Hawes (Urbana: University of Illinois Press, 1985), 283–303.

42. The multipurpose room was also called the "don't say no" space. See Gwendolyn Wright, *Building the Dream: A Social History of Housing in America* (New York: Pantheon, 1981), 255.

43. The potential security offered by the enclosed spaces in the house and yard obviously left an impression on the Clarkson children, despite their attempted defiance of it. Gail Clarkson and her husband, now expecting their second child, are considering moving into the house when her parents vacate it later this year simply because she "can send [their son] in the backyard with his little cousins and keep him completely in sight." Personal letter from Gail Clarkson, June 11, 1992, in my possession.

44. On the appropriation of the garage as multipurpose family space in the postwar period, see J. B. Jackson, "The Domestication of the Garage," in *The Necessity For Ruins and Other Topics* (Amherst: University of Massachusetts Press, 1980), 108–11.

45. As the mild California climate did not require double glazing, the window wall was actually cheaper per square foot than a conventional wall. See "Subdivision of the Year," 80.

46. Telephone interview with Gail Clarkson, Apr. 28, 1991.

47. The general absence of men's space in the Eichler home may be a mark of the occupants' more progressive ideals than those of the inhabitants of traditional suburban houses. Ned Eichler has noted that his father's clients considered themselves "avant-garde." See Ned Eichler, *The Merchant Builders,* 82. On the dissent of men from the breadwinner ethic of the time, see Barbara Ehrenreich, *The Hearts of Men: American Dreams and the Flight from Commitment* (New York: Anchor, 1983).

48. Wright, *Building the Dream,* 254.

49. Elaine Tyler May, in *Homeward Bound: American Families in the Cold War Era* (New York: Basic Books, 1988), argues that the reliance on domestic "containment" or enclosure was directly connected to the political climate of the cold war era.

50. The concepts of self-expression and individuality were equally important characteristics of bedroom design in the late-nineteenth- and early-twentieth-century house. The postwar bedroom for children, however, differed in that it was used extensively during waking hours for play and also that it contrasted so dramatically by its degree of enclosure with the family spaces in the house. On earlier bedrooms, see Elizabeth Collins Cromley, "A History of American Beds and Bedrooms," *Perspectives in Vernacular Architecture, IV,* ed. Thomas Carter and Bernard L. Herman (Columbia: University of Missouri Press, 1991), 177–86.

51. Telephone interview with Gail Clarkson, Apr. 28, 1991.

52. "Midwest Suburbia," *Look,* May 16, 1967, 79.

53. Spigel has suggested that the television, too, mediated the postwar family's occupation of public and private space. See Spigel, "The Suburban Home Companion," 185–217. Also, there is considerable debate among historians about the historical significance of women's activities outside the home in the postwar period. Some scholars see women's memberships in clubs and charities as foreshadowing the feminism of the 1960s, while others claim it only served to codify women's subservient status in the family. For diverse views on the issue, see William Henry Chafe, *The American Woman: Her Changing Social, Economic, and Political Roles, 1920–1970* (Oxford: Oxford University Press, 1972), 219–25; Eugene Kaledin, *Mothers and More: American Women in the 1950s* (Boston: Twayne, 1984); Susan M. Hartmann, *The Home Front and Beyond: American Women in the 1940s* (Boston: Twayne, 1982).

54. Friedan, *The Feminine Mystique,* 296.

55. Sara Evans, *Personal Politics: The Roots of Women's Liberation in the Civil Rights Movement and the New Left* (New York: Vintage, 1979), 15.

Chapter 14

Rural Adaptations of Suburban Bungalows, Sussex County, Delaware

Susan Mulchahey Chase

Scholarship on the bungalow as an architectural form has relied heavily on two sources of information.[1] First, scholars have made extensive use of popular literature of the late nineteenth and early twentieth centuries. Such prescriptive literature, most especially the substantial body of writing devoted to the design of houses, cottages, and bungalows, is frequently taken as normative. In fact, the actual behavior of builders and home owners may, and often does, differ from what the literature would lead one to expect. Second, scholars have based conclusions about many twentieth-century architectural forms on the examination of urban and suburban models. While the bungalow is popularly thought of as a suburban house form, the American version of the style originated as a summer vacation cabin built in a rustic, wooded setting and, as the following discussion demonstrates, was eventually erected in agricultural landscapes as well.[2]

To depend largely on popular literature and suburban models may easily lead one into false conclusions about the interior arrangement of space within a bungalow when such conclusions are based upon the dwelling's exterior appearance. Recent field studies in rural Sussex County, Delaware, offer a persuasive argument in favor of caution. One may be tempted to believe that if a dwelling exterior conforms to the pattern of a particular architectural form—in this case the bungalow—that the interior will, as a matter of course, also conform to the style's usual arrangement of interior space. The rural bungalows provide unambiguous examples of interiors that do not follow the expected pattern.

During the opening months of 1990, an extensive program of fieldwork was conducted in rural Sussex County to evaluate a 1985 survey that had identified 539 cultural resources dating from 1945 and before. The 1990 evaluation effort assessed the possible eligibility of sites for nomination to the National Register of Historic Places. Of the survey total, 436 sites survived, and, of these, fourteen were dwellings identified as examples of "early-twentieth-century domestic architecture." Three of the houses were square-type dwellings (popularly known as "four-squares"), three were Colonial Revival–style houses, and eight were examples of the bungalow type.[3]

Three of these bungalows were examined intensively, and they articulate a particular rural interpretation of the bungalow type. They are a significant departure both from the suburban ideal that is usually associated with the bungalow and from the traditions that prevailed on the rural landscape where they were constructed. Each of the three dwellings possesses the major exterior characteristics of the bungalow. Each has a long gable roof, full front porch, and deep, overhanging eaves. The interiors, however, set the houses apart from the suburban bungalows that they resemble on the exterior. While Wilmington's suburban builders produced structures that had fireplaces and built-in furniture, the rural bungalows have few of these expected features. They follow far more closely the long tradition of one or two largely unadorned rooms common among many rural Sussex dwellings. While presenting an external appearance that conforms to the suburban pattern, the rural bungalows adhere to an older pattern in interior planning and details.

Various interpretations of the bungalow form are found throughout the world. The form is marked by wide diversity, varying with the country, climate, and society in which it is built, yet always carrying the bungalow name.[4] Publications and surviving structures from the first three decades of the twentieth century identify the primary exterior characteristics of the suburban American bungalow. Most striking initially is the low-pitched roof, projecting in deep, overhanging eaves and supported by substantial, though simple, brackets. The ground-hugging outline of the one- or one-and-a-half-story house is graced by a broad porch that ranges across the front and is anchored solidly at the corners by heavy pillars. The fenestration and door placement varies among structures, although there is regular use of bay windows to add light to the interior and interest to the design.

Capitalizing on the image of a safe, snug home, many interior plans had fireplaces with rustic hearths and such built-in furniture as cupboards, buffets, bookcases, and window seats. A sample of house plans published between 1910 and 1924 indicates that the average bungalow had five or six rooms, including a living room, a dining room, a kitchen, and two or three bedrooms plus bath. Of these typical dwellings, 80 percent had fireplaces, 41 percent had at least one bay window, and 93 percent had some sort of built-in furniture.[5]

The public for whom the early-twentieth-century bungalow was intended was comprised largely of those individuals who earned enough to own their own homes but who needed to husband their resources. Paint manufacturer Sherwin-Williams recognized this inclination toward frugality when it published *Cottage-Bungalow* in 1910. The pamphlet was filled with decorating advice and offers of assistance from the company's Decorative Department. Clearly identifying the bungalow clientele, the pamphleteer acknowledged that "busy with other interests, few people have the opportunity to investigate the full possibilities of practical and artistic home decoration, while only those of large means can afford to employ . . . expert decorators and designers." The assistance of the Decorative Department was, the writer continued, "by no means intended only for expensive homes."[6]

Bungalow designs were flexible and varied. Contemporaries seemed to prize this "limitless adaptability [as] one of [the style's] chief beauties . . . the desires of the owner and the demands of the situation being the only guides to planning such a house. The result . . . is a large amount of individuality among the houses of the bungalow type."[7] As one bungalow builder stressed, the interior could be modified "to suit individual tastes without changing the outside appearance."[8]

Magazines as well as design books featured the bungalow in articles and floor plans. As early as 1908, for example, *House Beautiful* carried advertisements for booklets of bungalow plans available by mail. One California architect claimed that his plans were "practical in any part of the country" and could be made "suitable for building . . . in cold as well as warm climates."[9] In 1919, the *Ladies' Home Journal* initiated a house-plan service that offered readers the opportunity to purchase for one dollar the working drawings, details, and elevations necessary to create a complete set of blueprints.[10] In addition, plans and construction materials were available from a number of companies manufacturing ready-made houses. Perhaps best known among the producers of prefabricated homes was Chicago's Sears, Roebuck and Company. The combination of mass media and mass production helped plant on the rural landscape the bungalow, a house form most often linked to the suburban periphery of cities.

The simple, adaptable design and relatively low construction cost made the bungalow attractive to city dwellers eager to move to the new developments springing up around American cities. Between 1880 and 1920, Wilmington's population grew from forty-two thousand to a hundred and ten thousand, dropping slightly to a hundred and seven thousand in 1930.[11] As the urban population grew, trolley companies extended service into the countryside surrounding the city. Developers began to subdivide land along the trolley lines, creating residential communities distant from the city and yet linked to it by ties of employment made possible by public transportation. In offering suburban building lots to Wilmingtonians, the real-estate development companies promised fresh air, pure water, and the benefits of home ownership. Developers sought to create a suburban landscape, an environment so strikingly different from the city that families moving from a crowded city landscape of crowded, narrow streets lined by narrow row houses would immediately recognize the relief that suburban subdivisions offered. The new suburbs were clearly distinguished from the city by their architecture, and the bungalow was a popular favorite in this new suburban setting.

Builders in the Wilmington vicinity erected a variety of bungalows in the new suburbs. The impulse to adopt the style was encouraged by a series of floor plans published in Wilmington's *Sunday Morning Star,* beginning in January 1910.[12] In the following months, the newspaper published several sets of plans whose exterior characteristics and interior features paralleled designs published nationally. Of the eleven bungalow floor plans displayed on the real estate pages of the *Sunday Morning Star* in 1910, ten had fireplaces, five included bay windows, and two offered built-in buffets. The bungalows that survive in Wilmington's suburbs conform to these patterns, incorporating both exterior and interior features expected of the style.

Throughout the period, newspaper advertisements for new suburban developments around Wilmington linked the suburbs and the bungalow. In 1909, the developers of Gordon Heights described their subdivision as "The Best Place for a Suburban Home"[13] and offered "Desirable Residence and Bungalow Sites."[14] The Ashley Syndicate advised that "bungalow hill," a section of Ashley,

was "an ideal place to build,"[15] and E. B. MacNair stood ready to assist in the building process. "We have at Hillcrest and Gordon Heights," he proclaimed, "30 plots of land on which we want bungalows built."[16] To encourage such construction, he offered to sell an Aladdin bungalow for a hundred dollars. Developers of other suburban tracts made similar suggestions. A. K. Taylor, the man behind "Brack-Ex—The Wonderful Suburb," used the sketch of a bungalow and asked "How About A Bungalow Like This at Brack-Ex?"[17] Repeatedly during the 1920s and 1930s, real-estate advertisements connected the bungalow with suburban home sites that were only a single, five-cent trolley fare from work in the city.[18]

Although Sussex County is remote from Wilmington, lying some ninety miles south of the city, its residents nonetheless had access to styles and changes in Wilmington, including architectural developments like the inexpensive, easily built bungalow. As Wilmington's *Sunday Morning Star* declared in 1905, "Since the establishment of rural mail service even the remotest sections [of Sussex] have been in touch with current events through the medium of the daily papers."[19] The ready availability both of plans in newspapers and magazines and of prefabricated building materials enabled residents to bring the bungalow, a new dwelling form, to their rural setting.

When they did so, however, they adapted the bungalow into a particular Sussex County version of the form, joining predictable exterior features with unexpected interior characteristics. While their outward details suggest the Sussex County bungalows as examples of the form so closely associated with the suburbs, their arrangement of space inside deviates substantially from the suburban bungalow form. Compared to the forty-eight traditional farm dwellings identified in the 1990 fieldwork, it is readily apparent that relatively few farm families adopted the new form that the twentieth century offered, but those that did, did so in a particular and noteworthy way.

The landscape on which this interpretation of

a suburban house form began to appear in the early years of the twentieth century could hardly be considered suburban. In 1900, the Bureau of the Census classified 47 percent of Delaware's population as urban, that is, as living in settlements of twenty-five hundred people or more. In the same enumeration, only 3 percent of Sussex County's population was counted as urban. The suburbs that had developed on the periphery of the state's largest city, Wilmington, by 1930 resulted in over half (52 percent) of the state's population being classed as urban, compared to 4 percent of the population of Sussex.[20]

Houses on Sussex farms followed a long tradition in residential architecture. For perhaps a century, the typical rural dwelling (fig. 14.1) was a more or less symmetrical two- or two-and-a-half-story, three- or five-bay, single-pile structure of frame construction. Often clad in shingles produced from locally harvested cedar, it had a one-story kitchen wing extending from the rear of the structure and either a single, centrally located interior chimney or a pair of interior chimneys, one in each gable end. The rooms of a typical farmhouse followed a traditional pattern, established as early as the eighteenth century, of two rooms placed side by side.[21] Such houses were sited some fifty to a hundred and fifty feet from the road in farmyards encircled by the various barns, sheds, and other outbuildings that made up the farm complex. It was in this landscape, shaped by the agricultural pursuits of its residents and by long-established architectural traditions in house styles, that the bungalow appeared.

The rural builders of bungalows treated the country road as if it were a city street. While neighboring farmhouses, following long-established tradition, are built away from the road, the bungalows adhere to a suburban pattern in size, orientation, and utilization of space. They sit as if on small lots along the road, often with sidewalks leading to the front doors and hedges marking the yards.

The McCabe house (fig. 14.2) was built around 1910 and moved to its current site before 1924 when the present owners' parents bought the property with the building in place. While the farm on which the house is located had only forty-six acres, less than the average seventy-seven acres for Sussex at the time, it was typical in the crops cultivated: corn, beans, chickens, and strawberries.[22] Sited like a suburban dwelling—it is only twenty feet back from the county road—the bungalow represents

Fig. 14.1. J. Layton Farmstead, Selbyville Vicinity, Delaware.

Fig. 14.2. McCabe Bungalow Exterior, Roxana Vicinity, Delaware.

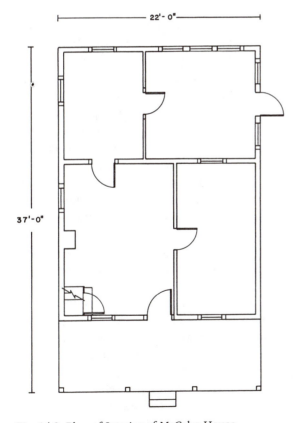

Fig. 14.3. Plan of Interior of McCabe House.

an incisive version of the style. Its sweeping gable roof ends in wide, overhanging eaves that shelter a broad porch across the entire front. The interior (fig. 14.3), however, departs markedly from the one that one might expect to accompany the bungalow exterior. With neither fireplace nor built-in furniture, it is instead singularly plain and built in a traditional plan of two rooms plus a rear lean-to. This contrast of spare interior with stylish exterior forms the pattern for the rural bungalows of Sussex County.

Documentary evidence suggests that the Rickards-Hudson bungalow (fig. 14.4) was built between 1928 and 1930. At the death of Samuel D. Rickards in 1928, his eighty-acre farm was divided equally among his three children, Samuel, John, and Dora. Samuel, a bachelor, apparently received the portion of land containing the farm dwelling; his brother lived in Philadelphia, and Dora was married and shared a home with her husband. Shortly after he took possession, tax records indicate that Samuel made improvements to his property. He may have renovated an older house to look like a bungalow; the present owner reports that the bungalow incorporates an earlier building. The current house has a twelve-foot-by-fifteen-foot wing that dates from the early nineteenth century, and it is possible that Samuel Rickards built the bungalow as an addition to the smaller, older dwelling. Samuel was single at the time of his father's death

Fig. 14.4. Rickards-Hudson Bungalow, Dagsboro Vicinity, Delaware.

Fig. 14.5. Plan of Rickards-Hudson
House.

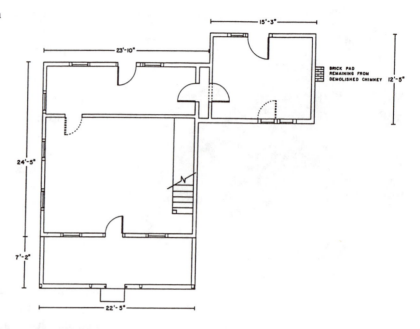

Fig. 14.6. Miller-Hudson Bungalow, Williamsville
Vicinity, Delaware.

in 1928, but by 1930 he was married, and his efforts to improve the house may have been in
preparation for the arrival of his bride. Samuel and
his wife, Lizzie, farmed the entire eighty acres, cul-
tivating crops typical of the period. They raised
chickens and strawberries; the crops were substantial enough to warrant chicken houses and a
strawberry pickers' house on the property.[23]

The Rickards-Hudson house is not built close to
the road like a suburban bungalow. Instead, it is
oriented like neighboring farmhouses, set back
fifty feet in the midst of a yard that once held a
complex of outbuildings—a barn, chicken houses,
a smokehouse, and a strawberry pickers' house,
none of which survive. The interior (fig. 14.5) follows the pattern of rural bungalows in its plain
design. It is based on a traditional single-room
plan with a lean-to kitchen at the back; it totally
lacks the interior features, such as fireplace or
built-in furniture, common to suburban bungalows.

The Miller-Hudson house (fig. 14.6) was built in
1928 by Levin and Margaret Miller on a five-and-
three-quarter-acre lot adjacent to their hundred-
and-thirteen-acre farm.[24] The bungalow served as
the main dwelling for the farm, which produced
chickens, corn, tomatoes, and strawberries for distant markets as well as butter and eggs for the local general store. The farm's success in these endeavors provided the Millers with the means to
buy a bungalow plan, the Westly (fig. 14.7), from
Sears, Roebuck and Company. Using timber cut on

Fig. 14.7. The Westly Model Bungalow from Sears, Roebuck and Company, Showing the First-Floor Plan. (From *Houses By Mail, A Guide to Houses by Sears, Roebuck and Company* [National Trust for Historic Preservation], 123.)

their own land and milled locally, the Millers built a suburban-style dwelling with sidewalk and hedge on their rural lot. Departing slightly from the Sears exterior, on the dormer balcony the Millers used balusters brought from Philadelphia by Charles Hudson, their son-in-law. They adhered to local tradition in their use of exterior shingle, long produced in Sussex from local cypress, although Levin Miller's daughter suggested the color scheme: "I got that idea [for dark brown shingles and white trim] from up around Philadelphia."

Sears house plans were noted for their flexibility and versatility, and, after the Millers purchased the plans, they modified them by adding four feet to the length of the house, removing the fireplace, adding a porch to the rear, and relocating the bathroom from the second floor to the first. The most significant change, however, was to the front entry. Originally, the floor plan called for a front entry hall with a staircase at the rear of the hall. The Millers shifted the staircase to the opposite interior wall and moved it closer to the front door. In so doing, they eliminated the wall that would have separated the entry hall from the living room, creating a traditional two-room plan at the front of the house. Thus, while retaining the exterior appearance of the Westly, the interior of the Sears design (fig. 14.7) was heavily modified so that the plan of the Miller-Hudson house (fig. 14.8) is much closer to a traditional plan. The divergence from the usual bungalow room arrangement and furnishing in favor of a traditional interior form fits the pattern of Sussex County's rural bungalows.

Substantial changes in Sussex County agriculture at the turn of the century exerted a key influence on the rural landscape, both in terms of crops cultivated and in terms of economic well-being. The production of fruits, vegetables, and poultry made possible by improvements in farming complemented by improvements in rail service made the new crops a lucrative source of income. Sussex farms able to take advantage of agricultural progress could produce greater quantities of such crops with the assurance that their output would reach market in good time. As a result, they and their families enjoyed a level of prosperity that allowed them to make changes to their homes.

Physical access to distant places increased with improved highway and rail transportation. Publications insured regular, frequent exposure to urban changes, both in Wilmington and in the nation. Inhabitants of Sussex County were aware of Wilmington's growing number of suburban developments, many of which included the bungalow as a new housing style. The bungalow's thrifty, easy-to-build design made it attractive to both rural and urban dwellers, who were encouraged by the simultaneous proliferation of bungalow advertisements, floor plans, and decorating ideas published in the popular literature.

The contrast between exterior and interior in these three Sussex bungalows is a powerful ex-

Fig. 14.8. Floor Plan of the Miller-Hudson House.

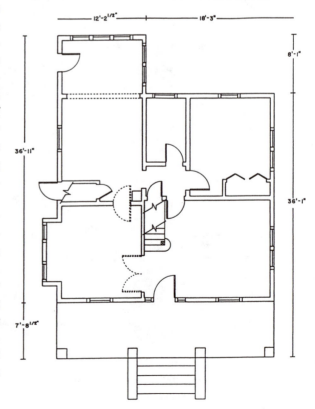

ample of the reluctance of people to depart from tradition, a reluctance that Henry Glassie recognized in his discussion of Delaware Valley folk building of the eighteenth century. He concluded that "people are most conservative about the spaces they must utilize and in which they must exist." While one may change the exterior features of a structure, he writes, one does "not change the arrangement of the rooms or their proportions."[25] This speaks directly to the circumstances of the rural bungalows. The exteriors are fashioned to conform to twentieth-century design trends. Exterior designs common to the developing suburbs appear full blown on the agricultural landscape. But within the entry door lies a more traditional arrangement of one or two unadorned rooms, not the segmented interior of the bungalow with its complement of built-in furnishings. While presenting a contemporary appearance to the world, the bungalow owners revert to a familiar, older form of organization for the interior space in which they live.

It is the juxtaposition of modern exterior with traditional interior in all three of these houses that strongly suggests ambivalence on the part of the owners about accepting all aspects of the new style. Their willingness to adopt a modern appearance but reluctance to transform the interior space is an example of the not uncommon effort to mediate popular ideas and traditional values. The bungalows provide important testimony of an attempt to bridge the gulf between the safety and comfort of the familiar and the conventional and the risk and anxiety of innovation and change.

While the scholarship that focuses on the bungalow as an architectural form provides information to complement the data gathered in the field, most writers give only limited notice to the interiors of the dwellings. Clay Lancaster, for example, proposes the architect-designed bungalow as the ideal and dismisses the suburban dwelling, whose more modest style is generally associated with the "bungalow" label.[26] Such unflattering comparisons between the suburban versions and the "sophisti-

cated example" provided by high-style houses rely heavily on bungalow design books and catalogs for prefabricated houses for information about the numbers and types of rooms and their details; woefully little use is made of actual dwellings as sources.

In *The Comfortable House: North American Suburban Architecture, 1890–1930,* Alan Gowans limits discussion to exterior characteristics, based on the essential features of the "original" bungalow form from India.[27] While creating a checklist of the hallmarks by which one may identify a bungalow, such scholarship does not add measurably to one's knowledge of how interior space was arranged.

Examining the organization of space within urban bungalows, Frances Downing and Ulrich Flemming provide a method for assessing the interiors of houses.[28] Their discussion and analysis, however, appear to be relevant only to an urban or suburban setting. Their argument that functional requirements "determine the nature and size of the spaces in a plan" as well as relationships between spaces or between interior and exterior does not hold in the case of the rural bungalows. The interior of the Sussex County houses met the functional needs of the occupants but lacked the segmented spaces found in similar urban dwellings. Downing and Flemming's contention that long, narrow urban lots imposed certain context requirements and limitations on construction of bungalow buildings also applies to the rural bungalows. Despite the generous size of most rural building plots, the Sussex bungalow owners constructed houses that had the same appearance as like urban dwellings restricted by the dimensions of city lots.

Existing scholarship offers excellent background information regarding the context out of which bungalows emerged as a separate, identifiable architectural form and provides the vocabulary with which to consider the bungalow as a document of the society in which it was built. The evidence of the rural bungalows of Sussex County, however, suggests that one must go beyond external appearance in drawing conclusions about the interiors of structures. Field studies of actual buildings make clear that exteriors embodying the essential characteristics set out in plan books and popular literature as the hallmarks of bungalows may shelter interiors that do not adhere to plan book patterns. In addition, while the exterior and interior of urban and suburban bungalows may complement one another in worthy examples of the style, the incongruence between the exterior appearance of the rural bungalows and their interior details confirms that the bungalow is a less predictable architectural form than has previously been imagined.

Notes

1. The author would like to thank Bernard L. Herman, Gabrielle M. Lanier, and Margaret H. Watson for the assistance they provided by reading and commenting upon earlier versions of this paper.

2. See, for example, William T. Comstock, *Bungalows, Camps and Mountain Houses* (New York: William T. Comstock, 1908).

3. Susan A. Mulchahey, Rebecca J. Siders, Gabrielle M. Lanier, Nancy K. Zeigler, and Bernard L. Herman, *National Register of Historic Places Eligibility Evaluation: Baltimore Hundred, Sussex County, Delaware* (Newark: Center for Historic Architecture and Engineering, College of Urban Affairs and Public Policy, University of Delaware, 1990).

4. Anthony D. King, *The Bungalow: The Production of a Global Culture* (London: Routledge and Kegan Paul, 1984), 2.

5. *Shrewesbury's House Plans* (Chicago: The Shrewesbury Publishing Company, 1924), 6, 8, 9, 11, 14, 17, 20, 21, 24, 25, 28, 29; Katherine Cole Stevenson and H. Ward Jandl, *Houses by Mail—A Guide to Houses from Sears, Roebuck and Company* (Washington: The Preservation Press, 1986), 71, 72, 76, 86, 114, 120, 122–27; Jud Yoho, *The Craftsman Bungalow Book* (Seattle: The Craftsman Bungalow Company, 1913), 19, 24, 25, 31, 47, 50, 55, 56. See also a Wilmington newspaper, *Sunday Morning Star,* for plans published during 1910. Always on page 14, floor plans for bungalows appeared in issues published on Jan. 9, Jan. 23, Feb. 20, Feb. 27, May 8, July 10, Nov. 6, Nov. 20, Nov. 27, Dec. 18, and Dec. 25 that year.

6. *Cottage-Bungalow* (Cleveland: Sherwin-Williams Company, 1910), n.p. See also *Walls and how to decorate them: The Alabastine Book* (Grand Rapids: The Alabastine Company, 1911), n.p.

7. *The Book of Little Houses* (New York: The Macmillan Company, 1914), 42.

8. Yoho, *The Craftsman Bungalow Book,* introduction, n.p.

9. Clay Lancaster, *The American Bungalow, 1880–1930* (New York: Abbeville Press, 1985), 148.

10. Alan Gowans, *The Comfortable House: North American Suburban Architecture, 1890–1930* (Cambridge: The MIT Press, 1986), 67.

11. U.S. Bureau of Census, *Decennial Population Census of the United States* (Washington: U.S. Bureau of Census, 1880–1930).

12. *Sunday Morning Star.* See n. 5 above.

13. *Sunday Morning Star,* May 30, 1909.

14. *Sunday Morning Star,* May 23, 1909.

15. *Sunday Morning Star,* May 21, 1911.

16. *Sunday Morning Star,* September 14, 1913.

17. *Sunday Morning Star,* July 5, 1914.

18. *Sunday Morning Star,* July 7, 1916; June 3, 1917; May 26, 1918; Mar. 27, 1921; Apr. 12, 1931.

19. *Sunday Morning Star,* Feb. 12, 1905.

20. U.S. Bureau of Census.

21. Bernard L. Herman, *Architecture and Rural Life in Central Delaware, 1700–1900* (Knoxville: University of Tennessee Press, 1987), 19–21.

22. Interview with owner, Virgil McCabe, May 15, 1990.

23. Interview with owner, Mabel Hudson, Mar. 1990.

24. Interview with owner, Helen Miller Hudson, Levin and Margaret Miller's daughter, Mar. 9, 1990.

25. Henry Glassie, "Eighteenth-Century Cultural Process in Delaware Valley Folk Building," in *Common Places: Readings in American Vernacular Architecture,* ed. Dell Upton and John Michael Vlach (Athens: University of Georgia Press, 1986), 407.

26. Lancaster, *The American Bungalow,* 142, 155. See also King, *The Bungalow,* who depends throughout on published pattern books.

27. Gowans, *The Comfortable House,* 76–77.

28. Frances Downing and Ulrich Flemming, "The Bungalows of Buffalo," *Environment and Planning B* 8 (1981): 269–93.

Part V
Architecture in Rural and Urban Geographies

Chapter 15

Building in Stone in Southwestern Pennsylvania: Patterns and Process

Karen Koegler

Despite the pressures of urbanization and industrialization, almost three hundred vernacular stone houses have survived in four Pennsylvania counties south of Pittsburgh. Built from the last quarter of the eighteenth century through the first half of the nineteenth century, these houses offer subtle witness to patterns and processes of settlement in that region.

Southwestern Pennsylvania possesses an unusual concentration of stone houses.[1] Judge John Moore, a prominent citizen of Westmoreland County, built one of these houses late in the eighteenth century. A county historian, writing a hundred years later, understood this house to be the measure of the man: "A comfortable stone dwelling, still in pretty good condition, marked the place of his residence, and indicated a man in advance of the rude civilization of that day."[2] After standing for two centuries on the outskirts of Greensburg, Westmoreland's county seat, Judge Moore's house was demolished in 1990. This research is the first systematic attempt to analyze these stone houses and what they reveal about the "rude civilization" of southwestern Pennsylvania.[3]

Study Area and Sources

Reconstruction of past landscapes often begins with the selection of a key landscape element. The distribution of the element is then used to delimit regions of broader social processes. Southwestern Pennsylvania constitutes a distinctive subregion in which there was an early trans-Appalachian fusion from seaboard cultural hearths.[4] Though southwestern Pennsylvania has been viewed as receiving influences from elsewhere, a newer conception resituates the region as a generator of cultural influences in its own right. In this conception, southwestern Pennsylvania is viewed as a landscape transformation zone,[5] weaving a new settlement fabric from diverse strands of migration proceeding from the Philadelphia and Susquehanna counties in Pennsylvania as well as incorporating influences from Maryland and Virginia.

Like moss-covered boulders embedded in the wooded hillsides of southwestern Pennsylvania, surviving stone houses stand in the landscape as markers of a dynamic, interactive past. The challenge lies in how to interpret the development of southwestern Pennsylvania's regional identity through these markers. A historic landscape is not simply the sum of its objects—it harbors subjective meanings beyond its probate inventories and taxable animals. Conversely, though it has been fashionable to decry "the sterility of classification" in material culture studies,[6] good interpretation hinges on collection and classification. As researchers attempt to recapture the *genre de vie* of historic settlement and, in particular, the cultural consciousness of those who have gone before, nothing is more grounded in life-as-lived than the dwelling.

In this research, evidence about the stone houses was sifted through different sieves: 1) the surviving population of houses field surveyed in 1989 and 1990; 2) the built environment of the late eighteenth century examined through the 1798 U.S. Di-

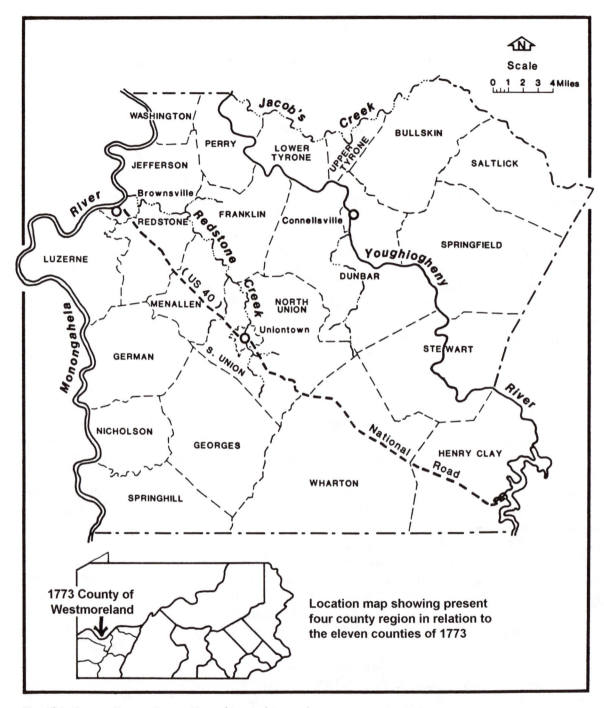

Fig. 15.1. Current Fayette County Townships and Pennsylvania Counties in 1773.

rect Tax; 3) the distribution of the stonemason trade at mid-century traced through the 1850 U.S. Census. In addition, ethnographic sources, like newspaper advertisements, congressional records, and travel diaries contemporary to the houses' construction, supplemented the statistical and location data. Flaws compromise each of these sources: census materials are broad but not deep; personal narratives are deep but not broad. Patterns were sifted from the evidence using this "triangulation" of sources—not progressively finer-meshed sieves, but sieves with differently shaped meshes to capture different facets of the past. This synthetic approach comes closer to imparting the settlers' milieu than other single-minded research approaches. Such an approach recognizes that southwestern Pennsylvania was both a geographical region and a perceived space.

For the purposes of this study, southwestern Pennsylvania has been defined as four of the five counties that make up the Monongahela River drainage basin in the state: Fayette, Westmoreland, Greene, and Washington.[7] These counties share a common historic lineage in that they were erected from the larger pre-Revolutionary county of Westmoreland (fig. 15.1). The ethnic diversity characteristic of southeastern Pennsylvania was also present west of the mountains. Settlers with Celtic surnames dominated in all four counties in 1790, equaling or exceeding their percentage in the state as a whole. Migration from Virginia and Maryland gave an English stamp to Washington and Greene Counties. More Germans settled in Fayette and Westmoreland Counties than in Washington or Greene, but even their proportion in those counties—estimated at between 10 and 15 percent—was less than half their statewide presence.[8] Cartographic analysis presented in this paper is confined to Fayette County, but conclusions about the stone houses are drawn from the four-county region.

The Place of Stone Construction, 1798

In examining a residual landscape of stone houses in southwestern Pennsylvania, it is important to acknowledge their rarity during their period of construction. Fortunately, documentation survives that provides an original view of the built environment of late-eighteenth-century Pennsylvania: the U.S. Direct Tax Lists for 1798.[9] The mother county of Westmoreland was a mere twenty-five years old when the new federal bureaucracy reached into the trans-Appalachian wilderness to assess the value of the cabins in the clearings. The Direct Tax is a unique record. Sporadically collected and never repeated, this "Glass Tax" lists owners, occupants, acreage, outbuildings, valuations, and, in the case of the finer homes, building material, dimensions, and windowpanes.[10]

Table 15.1. Construction Materials of Finer Houses, 1798

County	Total	Stone	%Stone	Log	Frame	Brick	Other/Unknown
Fayette	656	49	7.5	513	73	13	8
Greene	172	11	6.4	139	20	0	2
Washington	703	26	3.7	607	50	7	13
Westmoreland	384	16	4.2	344	19	3	2

SOURCE: Compiled by author from the *U.S. Direct Tax of 1798: Lists for the State of Pennsylvania*, Microcopy 372, National Archives.

Fig. 15.2. William Guthrie House, Derry Township, Westmoreland County, Pennsylvania, 1789. Rear elevation has irregularly spaced fenestration. Front facade is five-bay.

Fig. 15.3. Banocy Road House, Derry Township, Westmoreland County, Pennsylvania. Gable end with 1797 date stone.

What proportion of dwelling houses in turn-of-the-century Pennsylvania were constructed of stone? Because building materials were specified only for houses whose value was perceived to be greater than a hundred dollars, the percentage can be calculated only for the "finer homes" in these early settlements (table 15.1). Pennsylvania's sylvan hills provided the building material of choice: log. In a landscape dominated by log dwelling houses, stone houses apparently represented little more than 5 percent of the finer homes. The proportion of stone houses was probably even smaller because the vast majority of dwelling houses in southwestern Pennsylvania in the late eighteenth century were appraised by local assessors as being worth *less* than a hundred dollars, and building materials for these "lesser" houses were *not* specified.

Derry Township in Westmoreland County illustrates the dilemma of these hidden houses. Twenty-nine houses are listed in Particular List A in 1798 as being worth more than a hundred dollars. The majority of these "finer homes" were constructed of "square logs." Only one house, that belonging to William Guthrie, was built of stone (fig. 15.2). This substantial 32-foot-by-40-foot, five-bay house was appraised at $750, the highest valu-

Fig. 15.4. Rear Facade of Andrew Rabb House, German Township, Fayette County, 1773.

ation for the township and the county's highest with the exception of a house in the county seat. When one turns to Particular List B, however, an additional 247 dwelling houses are listed for Derry Township, but building materials are not specified for these humbler abodes, most described by the assessor as six- or eight-dollar "cabins." Guthrie's house represents 3.4 percent of the finer homes taxed in Derry Township, then, but .36 percent of all houses in the township.

Guthrie's stone house was rare, but not singular. Less than a mile from Guthrie's house stand a pair of two-bay stone houses, one of which bears a 1797 date stone in its gable (fig. 15.3), indicating that smaller stone houses or those under construction are hidden in Particular List B. Two additional Derry stone houses noted by the assessor in Particular List B hint at a transformation in the settlement landscape at the close of the eighteenth century: John Bartlett was assessed for "1 new stone house and kitchen not covered" and John Sloan had "1 stone house 32'x30' the wall not quite raised."[11] One senses the arrival of the assessor, James Parr, at these farmsteads just as the owners were consolidating their tenure and replacing log buildings.

Similarly, in Redstone Township in Fayette County, thirteen stone houses appeared on Particular List A (table 15.2) and six were noted on the B list, some with the same owners. Among the owners of these stone houses were Basil Brown, the founder of Brownsville; Peter Colley, whose lucrative tavern predated the National Road and anticipated its routing; Basil Brashear, whose stone tavern in Brownsville sheltered Lafayette; and Andrew Rabb, a prominent miller who rented the Redstone farmstead while residing in a larger stone house in German Township (fig. 15.4). Basil Brown's finer stone house on Particular List A mea-

Table 15.2. 1798 Tax Assessments for Fayette County's Finer Houses by Township

Township	Total	Stone	Brick	Log	Frame	Avg. Stone	Avg. All
Bullskin	*67	3	1	61	1	$300	$190
Franklin	43	7	-	35	1	270	197
Georges	61	1	-	60	-	175	131
German	33	**4	-	29	-	500	186
Luzerne	69	7	1	49	12	300	165
Menallen	18	2	-	15	-	475	157
Redstone	70	13	2	28	27	463	295
Salt Lick	10	-	-	10	-	-	146
Springhill	46	1	2	32	11	600	193
Tyrone	17	1	2	13	1	200	177
Union	***195	5	5	161	17	334	314
Washington	21	5	-	14	2	325	172
Wharton	6	-	-	6	-	-	173
Totals	656	49	13	513	73		

SOURCE: Compiled by author from Particular List A, vol. 697, *U.S. Direct Tax of 1798*.

NOTES:

  * Materials were not specified for one house in Bullskin Township.

  ** One of the four stone houses in German Township was unfinished and had no valuation; only three valuations were averaged.

  *** Includes seven houses that had combinations of materials, frame and brick or frame and log.

sured thirty-six feet by twenty-six feet, while his stone house noted on list B measured twenty feet by twenty feet, again demonstrating that smaller or unfinished stone houses were underreported on list B.

Distribution of Stone Houses, 1798

If stone houses represented such a small proportion of the housing stock in turn-of-the-century southwestern Pennsylvania, can any conclusions be drawn from the distribution of the hundred or so stone houses enumerated in the 1798 Glass Tax lists? The pattern of distribution in Fayette County, where almost half the finer eighteenth-century

stone houses were located, illustrates siting decisions common to the four-county region (fig. 15.5).

Half-mountainous and buffered by Washington and Westmoreland Counties from Native-American incursions, the county cradled relatively compact settlements and included many of the earliest sites in the four-county region. Stone houses were clustered in older townships—those embracing the county seat and bracketing the Monongahela River—where land values and assessments were highest (fig. 15.1). These more densely populated townships were landscapes in flux at the turn of the century, with the smallest acreages and highest tenancy rates in the county.[12] Mountain townships in the eastern half of the county, like Salt Lick and Wharton, contained few houses per-

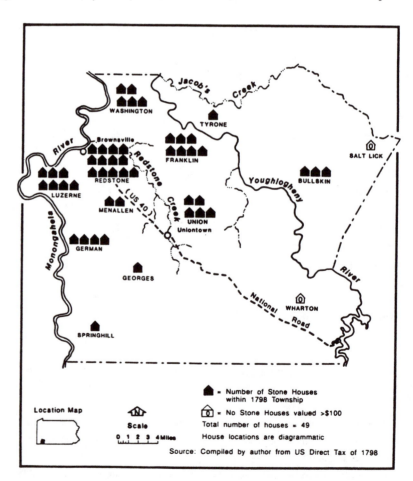

Fig. 15.5. Distribution of Stone Houses, Fayette County, 1798.

ceived to be worth more than a hundred dollars and no stone houses. By contrast, the Monongahela River townships in the northwestern quadrant of the county—Franklin, Washington, Luzerne, and Redstone—contained the greatest share of the forty-nine houses listed in the 1798 Direct Tax records (fig. 15.1 and table 2). As indicated above, the largest concentration of stone houses in any township in the four-county region occurred in Redstone Township, where the percentage, 18.6 percent, represents the strongest showing of stone as a building material in the finer housing stock of the time period. Further, this pattern of locations, sketched by the tax assessors at the turn of the century, functions as a template for where stone houses were built in successive decades.

Site and Situation of Surviving Stone Houses

Distribution of almost three hundred surviving stone houses in southwestern Pennsylvania's counties reveals that the pattern set in the late 1700s was augmented by more stone construction in succeeding decades. In Fayette County, for example (fig. 15.6), the heaviest concentration occurs in the northwestern Monongahela River townships, while the empty eastern townships that straddle the Chestnut Ridge are punctuated only by the regularly spaced inns along the National Road. Most of the surviving stone houses trace the route of the National Road, or its nascent roadbed, the Nemacolin Trail (fig. 15.7), as it traverses the county from the southeast to the

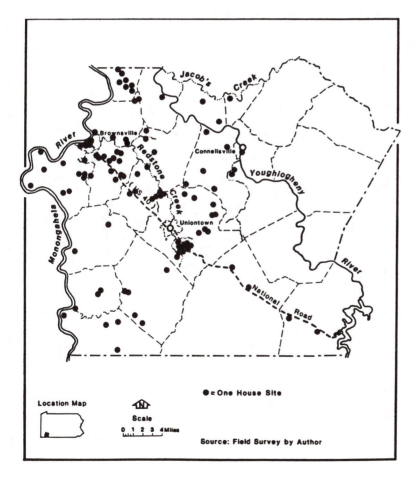

Fig. 15.6. Distribution of Stone Houses, Fayette County, 1989.

northwest. A second line of stone houses, crossing the first from northeast to southwest in the shadow of the Chestnut Ridge to form a rough X, echoes another Native-American route, the Catawba Trail.

Proximity to the primary migration routes that channeled people into and through this region— particularly those carved by the axes, hooves, and wagon wheels of Forbes's and Braddock's military expeditions over paths etched by Native Americans—would appear to "explain" location at a gross level of resolution. Indeed, the significance of the National Road in the creation of a stone house region cannot be overstated. The catalytic effect of the road is apparent in the distribution of Fayette County's surviving stone houses (fig. 15.6). Similarly, in Washington and Greene Counties, al-

most half of the houses are located within three miles of the road, and about half of those houses could be described as "on the road." The road and its commercial activities stimulated the acquisition of capital among some residents. The road brought artisans who could build stone houses in contact with the residents who desired their skills. The road was a membrane between the countryside and the migrants through which notions of style and identity passed.

The network of ancillary roads that developed— many of which were based on old Native-American trails—was more closely tied to the location of smaller watercourses like Redstone Creek and prospects for good milling sites. There is a strong correlation between mill sites and stone houses. In

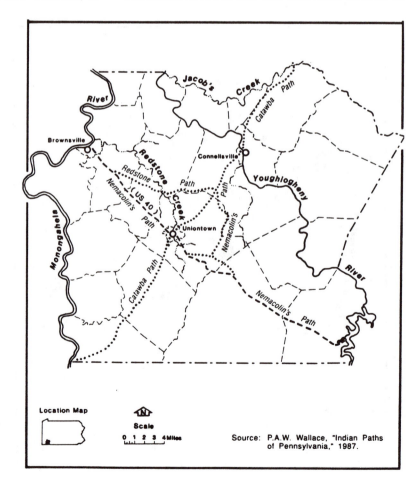

Fig. 15.7. Native American Trails, Fayette County.

Fig. 15.8. Taylor House, Centerville, Washington County, 1797 (Left Section) and 1843.

ment story was coupled with a rear elevation in which the basement was underground. Less commonly, the houses were built with the front or gable end into the slope.

Hillside siting incorporates the water table, as the majority of the houses also overlook creeks, streams, or springs. In some cases, the springs flow through the basement. Fifteen percent of the surviving stone houses retain their stone springhouses (fig. 15.8), but there is little sense that a stone farmstead landscape existed in southwestern Pennsylvania. Only two stone barns associated with stone houses remain in the four-county region, and the few stone walls observed date from this century.

early legislative records, citizens petitioned that roads be built to connect their farms to local mills.[13] At the inaugural court meeting of newly organized Fayette County in 1783, for example, the first order of business was to divide the county into nine townships; then the justices proposed that a road be built from Uniontown to Andrew Rabb's mill on Brown Run.[14] This road to Rabb's estate, which he called High German Mill Seat (fig. 15.4), was the first road in German Township.

A constellation of associated factors illuminates the builders' original decisions in regard to the lay of the land. As noted above, most surviving stone houses are located on old roads or overlook them. The front facades are commonly aligned to southern exposures. The minority of houses aligned to other compass directions occupy roadside sites where the roadbed and its associated commercial considerations determined their orientation.

With few exceptions, the surviving stone houses of southwestern Pennsylvania have hillside sites where they appear to be almost organically one with their surroundings (fig. 15.8).[15] The ubiquitous hillside siting resulted in buildings where the story height differs markedly from front to rear. In the most common arrangement, a two-and-a-half-story front facade with a visible or walk-out base-

Masonry Character and House Form

The choice of stone as a building material was not governed by distance to the resource. Coal-measure sandstones could be obtained in all counties in massive beds at several horizons and in an abundance of float rock.[16] In Fayette County, for example, several different sandstones—gray when fresh, weathering to brown, then black with soot—were utilized. Coal-measure sandstones possess different properties related to their deposition. The Waynesburg sandstone, for example, found in all four counties, can vary from flaggy to massive in deposition and from coarse to fine in grain. At its finest, it possesses the characteristics that masons seek: it "works well, both in lifting from the bed and in dressing to shape" and though "soft when freshly quarried . . . the surface hardens in time and preserves tool marks indefinitely."[17] Thus, even though almost all of the extant houses in the four counties were built of sandstone, the stonework varies both from each mason's touch and the variety of sandstone. Some of the variation in stonework from house to house can be traced to the presence of small quarries on individual farmsteads. That is, though sandstone was commercially quarried in all four counties, in most places houses were built from farm quarries worked only for a single house and barn foundation.

The dry-laid masonry does exhibit some common denominators. More labored attention to dressing and coursing the stone was lavished on the front facade. The rear wall was less dressed than the front facade, but more finished than the gable ends, which were usually laid up as random rubble. Like dovetailed joints on a wooden blanket chest, large stone quoins at the corners served structural and decorative purposes; these stones were dressed to be roughly rectangular and were often of a slightly different texture and color than the body of the house. Houses with ashlar stone walls were more common at the beginning and the end of the stone construction era. Voussoirs and finely-cut keystones appeared more often before the turn of the century and were replaced by the coursed lintel or simple stone slab after 1800. Whether ashlar or rubble, front walls often mimic a Flemish bond pattern. Date stones were found on one of every four houses—proclaiming ownership seems to have been part of the Pennsylvanian experience.[18]

The form that the stone house took in southwestern Pennsylvania was drawn from an architectural code of convergence rather than divergence.[19] The vernacular house incorporating Georgian influences—the "double pile, central passage plan set in a cubical mass with a repetitive ordered facade"[20]—was built throughout the period, from the late 1700s through the 1850s. The three most common morphologies for massing and floor plan were the two-room-deep, five-bay center-passage plan, the three-bay side-passage plan set in a cubical mass, and the I-house with both three- and five-bay iterations.[21] Proportions were almost formulaic: the relationship of the sides in the four-over-four houses was three to two or four to three; the attenuated profile of the I-houses was expressed as almost two to one; and the dimensions of the side-passage houses measured within three feet of one another. It could be said that the region's elite had accepted a single housing model[22] that could be built in a small, four-room version (the I-house), a four-room version that provided more square footage (the double-pile, side-passage, or "two-thirds Georgian"), and the large eight-room version (the four over four). Though more large houses appear toward the end of the period, all forms were built throughout the region and time period—even the four-bay facade, which is often perceived to be an incomplete evolution to Georgian symmetry.

Additional commonalities included two-and-a-half-story height, stone ells on about a fifth of the houses, paired gable-end chimneys, irregular fenestration on rear facades, paired attic windows in the gable ends, gable doors to the basement, walk-out or visible basement stories, and date stones on a quarter of the houses. While the products were not identical, they were remarkably similar throughout the time period and throughout the region. It is clear that western Pennsylvanians shared mental images about how stone houses should look and be constructed.

Stone House Makers: Owners and Masons

To live in a stone house in southwestern Pennsylvania in the late eighteenth and early nineteenth centuries was a rare thing. What did this choice say about the occupants? When we examine the mental context of vernacular building, we find traditions from Europe merged with ideals about design in the New World. These mental pictures are then tempered by the available raw materials, the social setting, the cost and availability of artisans, and the owners' economic situation. Some previous studies have stressed the persistence of ethnicity in the built environment,[23] but the stone house landscape of southwestern Pennsylvania does not support such a conclusion. Neither owners nor masons can be neatly pigeonholed by European origins. While many stone house owners were German, a high proportion of surnames were Gaelic. While the Irish have been associated with the stonemason's trade, some masons working in southwestern Pennsylvania were German. While some owners built their own homes, some commissioned building crews. Consequently, the commonalities of the vernacular stone houses suggest the existence of a historic region of fusion in southwestern Pennsylvania—an American core where the European moorings of the colonists were finally severed. Further, the rarity of stone houses suggests that they form an index of elite settlement, particularly those houses built during the period of first effective settlement.[24]

Examination of owners' histories indicates that about 40 percent of the stone house owners in the region were of German descent. Only a few other individuals—French, Dutch, and Swiss—had Continental origins. Irish names are also prominent, but disaggregating the Irish from the Ulster Irish and the

Scotch is thorny. All three Gaelic groups probably make up about 30 percent of the stone house owners. Lastly, owners of English descent, including some Quakers, make up about 20 percent of the total.

Some information about stone house builders can be garnered from the distribution of masons at mid-century, with the important caveat that most of these stonemasons, aged in their twenties and thirties, are the sons of the men who worked on the stone houses.[25] By mid-century, most stonemasons with British, Irish, or German surnames were born in Pennsylvania. Foreign-born masons, usually Irish, resided in the river cities of Fayette County or in shanties associated with railroad construction in Westmoreland County.

In Fayette County, stonemasons cluster in the northwestern quadrant of the county (fig. 15.9),

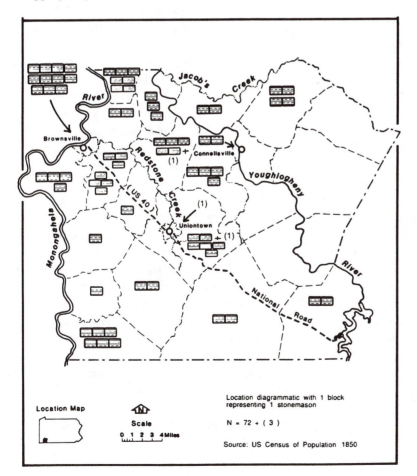

Fig. 15.9. Fayette County, Distribution of Stonemasons, 1850. (Figures in parentheses refer to masons believed to be stonemasons but described as "masons" in the census.)

mirroring the pattern of the stone houses in 1798 and the surviving houses' distribution. Adjacent cities Brownsville and Bridgeport on the Monongahela River had thirteen stonemasons resident in 1850, and townships bordered by Redstone Creek and the Youghiogheny River also had a higher ratio of stonemasons relative to their male populations than in the county as a whole.

From the travel writers of the 1700s to the dissemination of *Albion's Seed* in 1989,[26] an equation persists: a stone house denoted a solid citizen. The built environment was perceived as a sort of evolutionary ladder with log structures on the bottom rung. Into this perception of a hierarchy of building materials, travel writers introduced notions of the type and character of settlers using each mode. Dr. Benjamin Rush expressed this concept of successive waves of settler-builders in 1786. The "first settler"—"generally a man who has outlived his credit or fortune in the cultivated parts of the State"—built a log cabin. He was succeeded by the second settler, who enlarged the cabin with a hewn log addition, built a log barn, planted an orchard, and fenced his property. Despite these improvements, his house and farm "bear many marks of a weak tone of mind." The third settler, "a man of property and good character," was often the son of a prosperous farmer from one of Pennsylvania's "ancient counties." He erected a barn, preferably of stone, built a spring house, and mended his fences. His "commodious dwelling house," generally of stone, could be bequeathed to his son.[27]

Sharing this image, Uria Brown, a Quaker blacksmith from Chester County, Pennsylvania, decreed that Uniontown, Fayette County's county seat, "had too many wooden houses for the credit of the place" when he traveled through southwestern Pennsylvania in the early 1800s. Geologist David Thomas, traveling at the same time as Brown, admired the "laudable activity" of proprietors who had built "good houses of durable materials."[28]

The idea of a hierarchy in house construction became so ingrained nationally that an 1842 ac-

count of the succession of fences in Maine concluded that "all these are so many regularly advancing steps in the settlement and improvement of a district like the log hut, the frame house, the brick dwelling, and the stone mansion."[29] The generics swell grandly with the ascension in building materials: huts become houses, then dwellings, then mansions. Indeed, newspaper advertisements for southwestern Pennsylvania properties usually described stone dwellings as mansions.

The succession of construction materials even occurred on individual properties. Col. John Irwin, an early settler and mill owner in Westmoreland County, built his stone house, Brush Hill, in 1792–93 after two previous homes on his property were leveled. A log building was burned by Native Americans; the frame house was lost in a lightning fire. Colonel Irwin is reputed to have said: "I'll build a house that neither the Indians nor the Devil can destroy."[30]

Perceptions of the prestige of stone house ownership are borne out by the 1798 tax assessments. Stone houses were consistently the highest assessments throughout the four-county region; not only were stone houses, on average, more highly valued *in every township* in 1798, but also individual stone houses usually received the highest assessment in each township (table 2).

The rarity of stone construction in the 1798 tax lists can be ascribed to two parallel yet contradictory developments on the western frontier of Pennsylvania: urbanized areas like Pittsburgh and Washington were already "beyond" stone construction, because brick and frame technologies were available and fashionable; yet farmers in most of the region did not yet possess the wherewithal to build with the permanence of the "third settler." Poised on the cusp of the nineteenth century, the Glass Tax entries reflect both the beginning and the end of stone construction among Pennsylvania's vernacular builders. This mode of construction was simultaneously going out of style and just coming into fashion for the next four decades. The elites of the late 1700s had already shaped their landscapes and built their mansion houses to impart their hegemony in southwestern Pennsylvania.

Michael Rugh Jr. was one such archetypal individual. Born to German immigrants in Berks County, east of the mountains, Rugh migrated to Westmoreland County in 1772.[31] After acquiring wealth through mills and stills, he constructed his stone house (fig. 15.10) around 1798 following his family's capture by Native Americans and over a decade spent in Canada in captivity. The third Rugh dwelling house on the site after two log houses, it was often referred to as "the Philadelphia Mansion" by locals because Rugh reportedly returned to the Philadelphia area for the building plans. Less than two miles away stands another stone house built five decades after Rugh's house.[32] What mindset can we impute to the individual who chooses a stone house half a century after the first effective settlement of the region? Can it be said that he, too, desired a Philadelphia mansion?

These two individuals represent the extremes of the vernacular stone house era in western Pennsylvania. Rugh was one of "the power brokers" of the first effective settlement of the region. A list of stone house owners in the 1700s and the first few years of the 1800s reads like a veritable "who was who" on the frontier: the millers and ironmasters,

Fig. 15.10. Michael Rugh House, Murrysville, Westmoreland County, ca. 1800.

the judges and legislators, the movers and shakers. The stone houses built by these settlers were nodal in the development of communities and must have sent powerful symbolic synapses through the hills of southwestern Pennsylvania.[33]

A second boom in stone house construction, from 1810 to 1819, coincides with the building of the National Road. Whether offspring of the first wave or direct migrants from southeastern counties like Lancaster and Cumberland, these settlers, "the consolidators," still held some notions about the stone house as a symbol of permanence in the landscape, even though brick was also readily available and fashionable. Their shelter needs coincided with the influx of new laborers and masons into the region.

Finally, "the late-bloomers," those prosperous individuals who erected stone houses or additions in the 1830s and 1840s (fig. 15.8), chose a building material that no longer held progressive connotations, but perhaps held regional resonance for them. They no longer needed to look "back East" for models; they could just look around them at the homes of the power brokers.

Conclusion

Stone houses impart some sense of the cultural image held by that Pennsylvania society. To amplify the questions of who commissioned and who built, we must also ask why stone was chosen as a building material. A similar synergy of variables revealed by Coffey's research on Ontario's mid-century housing stock characterizes southwestern Pennsylvania's stone house building era.[34] First, though German surnames are disproportionately associated with stone house ownership relative to their overall proportion in southwestern Pennsylvania, as the building material was ubiquitous throughout the region, some portion of each ethnic group was able to build stone houses. Second, settlers with more capital were able to make the transition from log housing earlier: in the late 1700s, such settlers included local politicos, fledgling industrialists, and millers; during all decades of the era, some German farmers and millers were among the well-endowed. Third, as suggested by Coffey's contrast in social and spatial organization between the Lowland and Highland Scots, most stone houses were built in the areas of southwestern Pennsylvania with maximum interaction among ethnic and occupational groups—near the county seats and along major riverine and overland routeways—and are absent in the peripheral areas of western Washington County, most of Greene County, and the mountainous half of Fayette County. Areas of maximum contact contained heterogeneous populations with a variety of skills and, equally important, opportunities for the exchange of ideas. Fourth, the periodic tides of new masons streaming in to build the National Road, the Pennsylvania Canal, and, at mid-century, the Pennsylvania Railroad appear to have stimulated the waves of stone house construction in the region. Finally, just as Coffey found that ethnicity of ownership did not correlate to ethnicity of stonemasons and bricklayers, the majority of stonemasons in southwestern Pennsylvania at mid-century represented the British Isles and Irish nativity in particular.

All of the above suggests that the construction of a stone house resulted from a complex interplay of factors, including the presence of the raw material, the availability of labor, the timing of owners' settlement, the capital available to owners, the presence of culture groups with affinity for the

material, the level of development within the subregion, and intangibles like the aesthetic values of the individual and his culture group. In a sense, this interplay reinforces the idea that houses are built by individuals, not groups or regions. The individual may be operating within group norms and regional identity—the meaning of the house is socially constructed, after all—but the statement in stone is unusual in and of itself.

The distinctive stone house region that emerges from these mappings of southwestern Pennsylvania, then, is not distinguished by number of houses, but by the meaning such houses held. The choice of masonry represents neither the progression of material culture in southwestern Pennsylvania—transitional between log and brick technologies—nor the affinity of an ethnic group for a particular construction material. Instead, the individual settler was making a statement about his elevated place in the settlement hierarchy. Building something beyond what was necessary and building something that reinvented traditions of southeastern Pennsylvania could only enhance the display.

Beyond satisfying the functional need for shelter, vernacular houses operate on a symbolic level in the landscape: "They serve the obvious purpose of communicating position and authority to one's neighbors, or, conversely, the degree to which one is in harmony with them."[35] The beauty of the stone house was that it enabled the occupant to live in harmony with the basic form of his neighbors' homes, while differentiating himself through the choice of stone construction.

Notes

1. Richard Pillsbury, "The Construction Materials of the Rural Folk Housing of the Pennsylvania Culture Region," *Pioneer America* 8 (1976): 98–106. Pillsbury's examination of modes of construction in the Pennsylvania region represents a singular attempt to consider frame, brick, stone, and stucco in this area. He maps stone housing as "dominant" in southeastern Pennsylvania and "significant" in southwestern Pennsylvania. For an excellent examination of different construction materials in a region, see Brian J. Coffey, "The Irish, English, and Scots in Ontario," in *To Build in a New Land: Ethnic Landscapes of North America,* ed. Allen G. Noble (Baltimore: Johns Hopkins University Press, 1992), 44–59, which is distinguished by the completeness of its data source and the potential applicability of its conclusions. See also John C. Hudson, "Frontier Housing in North Dakota," *North*

Dakota History 42 (1975): 4–15; Peter O. Wacker, "Relations Between Cultural Origins, Relative Wealth, and the Size, Form, and Materials of Construction of Rural Dwellings in New Jersey During the Eighteenth Century," in *Geographie Historique du Village et de la Maison Rurale* (Paris: Centre National de la Recherche Scientifique, 1974), 201–30; Stanley W. Trimble, "Ante-bellum Domestic Architecture in Middle Tennessee," *Geoscience & Man* 25 (1988): 97–117.

2. J. N. Boucher, *History of Westmoreland County, Pennsylvania* (New York: 1906), 1: 322.

3. The conclusions in this paper are drawn from the author's dissertation, "Building in Stone in Southwestern Pennsylvania," (Ph.D. diss., University of Kentucky, 1992). This research was generously supported by an American Fellowship from the American Association of University Women. Primary sources for this paper include field surveys by the author in 1989 and 1990; the *U.S. Direct Tax of 1798: Tax Lists for the State of Pennsylvania,* microcopy 372; and the *U.S. Census of Population, 1850,* microcopy 432.

4. Kniffen and Glassie's often-reproduced map illustrates this commingling in southwestern Pennsylvania. Newton's identification of a back-country hearth he dubbed the Upland South and Mitchell's description of southwestern Pennsylvania as a tertiary area of settlement (1780–1820) also hints at this fusion. Discerning the relationship between southwestern Pennsylvania and the hearth area of Middle Atlantic regionalism has been problematical because the location of the core has not been settled: both Philadelphia and the Susquehanna watershed claim such a role, but the relict landscape does not support the exclusivity of either claimant. Fred B. Kniffen and Henry Glassie, "Building in Wood in the Eastern United States: a Time-Place Perspective," *Geographical Review* 56 (1966): 40–66; Milton Newton, "Cultural Preadaptation and the Upland South," *Geoscience and Man* 5 (1974): 143–54; Robert D. Mitchell, "The Formation of Early American Culture Regions: An Interpretation," *European Settlement and Development in North America,* ed. J. R. Gibson (Toronto: University of Toronto Press, 1978), 66–90. For an expanded treatment of the southwestern Pennsylvania *region* as delimited by stone construction, see the author's "Identity in a Frontier Region: Building in Stone in Southwestern Pennsylvania" (forthcoming).

5. Richard Pillsbury, "The Pennsylvania Culture Region: A Reappraisal," *North American Culture* 3 (2) (1987): 37–54.

6. Denis Cosgrove, "Towards a Radical Cultural Geography: Problems of Theory," *Antipode* 15 (1983): 1–11.

7. Allegheny County has been omitted from the survey because Pittsburgh's urbanization precludes the usefulness of the two dozen surviving stone houses there as representative of historic patterns. In addition, the archival evidence indicates that Pittsburgh evolved from a log town to a brick town with minimal use of stone construction.

8. Assaying the relative proportions of ethnic groups in Pennsylvania's counties in 1790 through surname classification has become more sophisticated since the Bucks' pioneering effort. See Solon J. and Elizabeth Hawthorn Buck, *The Planting of Civilization in Western Pennsylvania* (Pittsburgh: University of Pittsburgh Press, 1939), 152–55. See R. Eugene Harper's succinct discussion of proportions and methodologies in *The Transformation of Western Pennsylvania, 1770–1800* (Pittsburgh: University of Pittsburgh Press, 1992), 5–7, 214–15, and the map in the *Atlas of Pennsylvania,* ed. D. J. Cuff et al. (Philadelphia: University of Temple Press, 1989), 88. Statewide figures for 1790 can be roughly generalized as 40 percent Celtic, 40 percent German, and 20 percent English.

9. The source for all of the following material related to the 1798 tax lists is the *U.S. Direct Tax of 1798: Tax Lists for the State of Pennsylvania,* microcopy 372. Washington, D.C.: The National Archives, 1982, rolls 22, 23, 24, vol. 690–717.

10. This distinction between Particular List A and Particular List B is important. Some studies have used figures and percentages generated from list A to characterize the dimensions and building materials of a region's housing stock, resulting in a skewed image of the built environment of the late eighteenth century. For example, S. T. Swank's linkage of building material and ethnicity in southeastern Pennsylvania townships is completely falla-

cious because statements like "According to the 1798 tax schedules, Lower Salford Township contained 75 dwellings. The predominant building material was stone (47 percent) . . ." are based only on data for the finer homes. (Swank, "The Architectural Landscape," in *The Arts of the Pennsylvania Germans,* ed. by Swank et al. [New Wilmington, Del.: W. W. Norton for the Winterthur Museum, 1983], 20–34). Michael J. Chiarappa, "The Social Context of Eighteenth Century West New Jersey Brick Artisanry," in *Perspectives in Vernacular Architecture, IV,* ed. Thomas Carter and Bernard L. Herman (Columbia: University of Missouri Press, 1991), 215n. 45, and Gabrielle Lanier, "Samuel Wilson's Working World: Builders and Buildings in Chester County, Pennsylvania, 1780–1827," in *Perspectives, IV,* 212n. 5, also fail to make this distinction.

11. *U.S. Direct Tax of 1798: Tax Lists for the State of Pennsylvania,* microcopy 372, roll 22: Westmoreland County, vol. 691.

12. R. Eugene Harper, *The Transformation of Western Pennsylvania, 1770–1800* (Pittsburgh: University of Pittsburgh Press, 1992), 17–39. Harper's 1969 dissertation, the classic reference on southwestern Pennsylvania's political, economic, and social structure at the end of the eighteenth century, is finally more accessible.

13. Boucher, *History of Westmoreland County,* 1: 231.

14. Franklin Ellis, *History of Fayette County, Pennsylvania* (Philadelphia, 1882), 502.

15. Hillside farms have been associated with the Ulster Irish. See Estyn E. Evans, "The Scotch-Irish in the New World: An Atlantic Heritage," *Journal of the Royal Society of Antiquities of Ireland* 95 (1965): 42, 44, and Henry Glassie, "Irish," in *America's Architectural Roots,* ed. Dell Upton (Washington, D.C.: Preservation Press, 1986), 74–49. This association is commonly explained as cultural preference or adaptation resulting from German pre-emption of the best lands, leaving what Estyn Evans calls "the broken country" to the latecomers. Yet, hillside siting is also identified as Germanic. See Edward Chapell, "Germans and Swiss," in *America's Architectural Roots,* 68–73. On southwestern Pennsylvania's eroded plateau, some members of all groups built stone houses sited at half-slope at similar elevations overlooking creeks and roads.

16. Ralph Stone, *Building Stones of Pennsylvania* (Harrisburg: Pennsylvania Geological Survey, 1932).

17. Ibid., 167.

18. Date stones include dates, owners' initials or surnames, and decorative motifs. Since the wife's name or initials often appear beside those of the husband, these marks represent the only female subtext in what is essentially an androcentric study of shared covenants between male owners and male masons about how a stone house should look and what its ownership meant. The use of male pronouns throughout this paper is intentional. This study does not deny the female voice in the choices made or the meanings projected, but recovering these undocumented influences for this time period is difficult. Even masons' identities remain in the shadows: a singular date stone in Fayette County couples initials with what appears to be a mason's mark; a singular date stone in Greene County lists the full names of owners and masons (see n. 25).

19. This paragraph condenses material in chap. 5 of the author's dissertation.

20. Dell Upton, "Early Vernacular Architecture of Southeastern Virginia," (Ph.D. diss., Brown University, 1980), 292.

21. Representative floor plans from the Dorsey, Roberts, Johnston, and Stewart stone houses can be found in Charles M. Stotz, *Early Architecture of Western Pennsylvania* (Pittsburgh: University of Pittsburgh Press, 1936), which is to be reissued.

22. Pillsbury, "The Pennsylvania Culture Region," 44, came to a similar conclusion.

23. Stone housing regions have been linked with specific ethnic groups in North America—for example, Germans in the hill country of Texas, Ulster Irish in the Kentucky Bluegrass, and the Huguenots and Dutch settlers of Ulster County, New York. In these instances, hundreds of extant houses mark the historic settlement of ethnically discrete groups. By contrast, Hudson's study of frontier housing in North Dakota and Coffey's examination of Ontario's housing stock in the mid-1800s suggest that the choice of building material is more complex than

congruence between resource availability and ethnicity. Neither Chapell in his chapter on "German and Swiss" nor Glassie in his chapter on "Irish" building in *America's Architectural Roots* mentions a particular affinity of these groups for stone or consider stone as diagnostic of their folk housing tradition. See Terry G. Jordan, "German Houses in Texas," *Landscape* 14 (1964): 24–26; G. Leiding, "Germans in Texas," in *To Build in a New Land: Ethnic Landscapes of North America,* ed. Allen G. Noble (Baltimore: Johns Hopkins University Press, 1992), 362–78; Carolyn Murray-Wooley and Karl Raitz, *Rock Fences of the Bluegrass* (Lexington: University of Kentucky Press, 1992), 201n. 9; M. Hurewitz, "Built to Last: New York State's Extraordinary Stone Houses are Monuments to Dutch and Huguenot Craftsmanship," *Historic Preservation* 38 (1987): 49–53.

24. "First effective settlement" was coined by Wilbur Zelinsky, *The Cultural Geography of the United States* (Englewood Cliffs, N.J.: Prentice-Hall, 1973), 13, to describe the disproportionate influence on the cultural geography of a region by the people who create the earliest viable settlement. If landscapes can be said to be authored, the hands of these folks pressed down most firmly on the page.

25. Older stonemasons also appear in the records. A notable example is the appearance of sixty-two-year-old William Donahoo on the 1850 list for Franklin Township in Greene County. Donahoo is one of two builders whose names appear in the date stone of the Sayer stone house, extant in Franklin Township. The date stone, *the only one of its kind* found in field survey, definitively links owners, masons, and structure and reads: "1822 Ephraim and Mary Sayer Built by Perry A Bayard and W Donahoo." From the census, we know that the Maryland-born stonemason built this house when he was thirty-four years old.

26. See chap. 4 in Koegler, "Building in Stone in Southwestern Pennsylvania," which is based on an earlier seminar paper, for examples of the bias for masonry construction. Travel writers often provided "house counts" by materials for the small towns of southwestern Pennsylvania, signaling their approval for masonry construction as indicative that a town had truly come into its own. In a modern overstatement of this credo in *Albion's Seed,* the stone buildings of the English Quakers and the German Pietists in southeastern Pennsylvania are seen as emblematic of their concern for permanence: "Settlers in other culture regions threw together temporary wooden buildings with the utmost economy of time and materials. On Pennsylvania farms, even the smallest outbuildings were built for the ages with heavy stone walls and strong slate roofs" (David Fischer, *Albion's Seed: Four British Folkways in America* [New York: Oxford University Press, 1989], 559).

27. Benjamin Rush [1786] in *Pen Pictures of Early Western Pennsylvania,* ed. John W. Harpster (Pittsburgh: University of Pittsburgh Press, 1938), 195–98.

28. Uria Brown, "Journal" [1816] in *Pen Pictures,* 262; David Thomas, *Travels through the Western Country in the summer of 1816* (Darien, Conn.: Hafner Publishing Co., 1970 [facsimile of 1819 ed.]), 48.

29. J. S. Buckingham [1842] in Wilbur Zelinsky, "Walls and Fences," *Changing Rural Landscapes,* ed. E. Z. and M. J. Zube (Amherst: University of Massachusetts Press, 1977), 55–56.

30. Helene Smith and George Swetnam, *A Guidebook to Historic Western Pennsylvania* (Pittsburgh: University of Pittsburgh Press, 1991), 361.

31. Michael Rugh Jr. house survey form. Pennsylvania History and Museums Commission. Harrisburg, Pennsylvania.

32. This house, allegedly built by Samuel Hilty for David Wallace (Smith and Swetnam, *A Guidebook to Historic Western Pennsylvania,* 365), was one of the few where the owners refused photographs or any contact.

33. Stone houses were pivotal buildings and landscape reference points in the developing frontier's interactions. Indeed, it would not be unreasonable to apply Giddens's awkward term "power containers" to these structures. See Cole Harris, "Power, Modernity and Historical Geography," *Annals of the Association of American Geographers* 81 (1991): 671–83. The nodal quality of mill sites has already been noted. Stone houses converted to or built as taverns also served as focal points in their communities. They were centers for the diffusion of people,

products, and ideas into the surrounding hinterlands and, conversely, acted centripetally to draw settlers together for social and political functions like voting, tax assessment adjustments, and newspaper circulation. Some stone houses, like Jacob Bowman's fort-store-post office in Brownsville, were nuclei around which settlement accreted. Stone house owners also figured prominently in the development of southwestern Pennsylvania's settlement network. As town platters and county seat locators, they laid out the towns of Amity, Derry, Greenfield, Jefferson, Fayette City, Connellsville, and Brownsville, among others.

34. Coffey, "The Irish, English, and Scots in Ontario."
35. Upton, "Early Vernacular Architecture," 151.

Chapter 16

Private Dwellings, Public Ways, and the Landscape of Early Rural Capitalism in Virginia's Shenandoah Valley

Warren R. Hofstra

Travelers in eighteenth-century Virginia knew well "the distinction between Private and Public entertainment," as Johann David Schoepf put it in 1783. Strangers to the land, they were often pleasantly surprised at the warm reception they received in private houses. According to Thomas Anburey, "The hospitality of the country was such, that travellers always stopt at a plantation when they wanted to refresh themselves and their horses, where they always met with the most courteous treatment, and were supplied with every thing gratuitously." These same travelers, however, jealously guarded their own privacy in public accommodations. Isaac Weld, for instance, complained often of "a prying set of Americans, to gratify whose curiosity it is always necessary to devote a certain portion of time after alighting at a tavern." In these contradictory experiences, recounted time and time again in their writings, eighteenth-century travelers traversed the boundaries of public and private space that shaped the landscape they took such care to describe.[1]

This examination of that landscape begins with a question: why did one particular landscape element, the I-house, become so pervasive and universal a cultural symbol in precisely that area of colonial America in which cultural diversity was greatest? The answer lies where the people who created this landscape drew the boundaries between public and private—the public space of the road or market and the private space of the home and household economy. More specifically, this study focuses on the Shenandoah Valley—and a

particular community that developed along the banks of the Opequon Creek in the northern or lower portion of that valley—as part of a culture area that reached south from central Pennsylvania into much of the eighteenth-century southern backcountry. Beginning in the 1730s, large numbers of new immigrants came into this region from the north of Ireland, the Rhine Valley, England, and the English colonies. They carried with them vernacular building traditions varying considerably from one another and often from those already long established in Virginia. In spite of a heritage of ethnic pluralism, the I-house became the most common form of domestic architecture in this hearth area from Pennsylvania to the Shenandoah. From there, it spread throughout the rural communities and small towns of nineteenth-century midland America.[2]

The sources of the form and appearance of this architectural type have been examined extensively. Most investigators conclude that this two-story, single-pile, three- or five-bay dwelling as it had evolved by the late eighteenth century was an adaptation of earlier vernacular forms to Georgian design principles that stressed balance, symmetry, the ordered arrangement of architectural elements, and the rational allocation of public and private space (fig. 16.1). Although it represented an international popular culture, the I-house and its pervasiveness cannot be accounted for solely according to the social and geographical diffusion of Georgian standards.[3] The emergence of the Georgian I-house coincided with basic economic

Fig. 16.1. David Glass House. Although Glass died in 1774 or early 1775, evidence in his inventory suggests that he built and lived in at least a portion of what became this structure. The house was demolished in the 1970s.

changes in eighteenth-century life, commonly called the "transition to capitalism" by economic historians. Shifting orientations in production from household independence to market demands produced a dramatic transformation of the landscape. The development, proliferation, and meaning of the I-house must be viewed from the perspective of its context in the landscape of an emerging rural capitalism.[4]

The course of this transformation in the Shenandoah Valley can be plotted in three phases. The first phase of household production began in the 1730s with the establishment of multiethnic, dispersed, rural, kinship communities like that at Opequon. With the trans-Atlantic rise in grain prices after 1750, the second phase began: these autonomous communities became woven into complex, regional settlement systems in which dense road networks linked individual farmsteads to commodity markets at mills and towns. Increasingly during this second phase, and particularly after 1780, farm production and the social fabric of rural communities became subject to market forces emanating from urban centers. Throughout the late eighteenth and early nineteenth centuries, markets were civic functions carefully regulated by govern-

ing bodies in the public interest. Thus, urban marketplaces, public thoroughfares, mills, and farms represented the extension of public commercial space across the landscape. During the third phase, which can be dated approximately to the second quarter of the nineteenth century in the Shenandoah Valley, the public nature of the market diminished in scope—both economically and geographically—in the face of private trading in a liberal economy driven more by self-interest than by public interest.

The organization of space and the arrangement of architectural elements within the I-house was determined by the I-house's physical orientation to the public arena of the marketplace during the second phase in the transition to capitalism. Between 1780 and 1830, older, asymmetrical house forms gave way to the symmetry of the I-house as a response to the same impulse to order and regulate that structured the form and function of the market. Within the structure, central passages served as extensions of public space that reached from house to market by a network of public thoroughfares. Moreover, the pervasiveness of the I-house among various ethnic groups was a product of the solvent influence of commercial interest. An understanding of the I-house, then, must begin with an examination of the settlement systems and road networks in which it was embedded.

I

European settlement of the Shenandoah Valley began in the 1730s not as a manifestation of the westward push of tidewater Virginia's tobacco economy, but as a response to specific land-policy initiatives of the colonial government that appealed directly to the interests of new European immigrants streaming through Pennsylvania.[5] Most of these men and women were fleeing dependent relations in Europe fostered by institutions of tenancy and problems of chronic debt. For these people the most meaningful social distinction was not one of class, but one between dependence and independence. Independence meant acquiring a competence in sufficient agricultural assets—land, stock, tools, and buildings—to sustain the yearly subsistence of the family and to insure the long-term continuity of the family unit.[6]

Accordingly, the Virginia policy for western lands allowed for the private ownership of land in fee simple with exclusive rights to profit by labor on the land or devise land by deed or will. Since it imposed no requirements to establish towns or even clustered settlements, this land policy encouraged population dispersal as individuals searched for good land.

Virginia's land policy proved very effective. By 1734 as many as 150 settlers had taken up tracts in the lower Shenandoah Valley alone, and ten years later, when the new county of Frederick first polled its tithables (taxable adults), the resident population had reached approximately five thousand.[7] The Germans, Scotch-Irish, and other immigrants this policy attracted brought with them traditional, diversified agricultural systems based on grains and livestock. Estate inventories reveal that, in the process of farm building, settlers cultivated wheat, corn, rye, barley, oats, buckwheat, flax, hemp, and hay, but very little tobacco. They also raised cattle, pigs, sheep, geese, and horses. Diversity, however, did not mean self-sufficiency. The exchange of labor and agricultural surpluses was essential to the success of emerging rural communities and the ability of individual families to achieve a competence.[8]

Other elements of a landscape shaped by the drive for independence and a competence began to appear during these first two decades of settlement. Robert Brooke, the first surveyor to work in the region, documented at least two mills by 1734 and mentioned an additional five mill runs. The Brooke surveys also referred to three wagon roads and an equal number of paths.[9]

Farmsteads, mills, and roads proliferated as landscape elements during the course of the eighteenth century. By the early 1760s, the population of

Frederick County numbered more than eleven thousand, and, by the first federal census in 1790, nearly twenty thousand people lived in the county, now reduced to one-sixth its original size by division to form new counties. In the five years between 1743 and 1748, orders for roads from the Frederick County Court mentioned at least seventeen mills, and by 1800 the county possessed more than four hundred mills, most established after 1783. Road orders also called for marking off at least thirty-two roads by 1748 in the portion of the lower Shenandoah Valley that would remain Frederick County and mentioned other key features of the emerging landscape, such as ordinaries, ferries, churches, and a courthouse. All of these elements would increase in proportion to population by 1800.[10]

What had emerged during the first phase in the transition to capitalism was, then, a decentralized settlement system characterizing a people whose objective in taking up and developing the land lay in building a competence through household production and local exchange. Virginia land policy had accommodated the desires of these people by awarding extensive powers of land ownership and permitting dispersal in the search for prime seats for farms, mills, ferries, and other locations crucial to production and exchange in a household economy. What allowed this system to work for its inhabitants was a network of roads.

This road network assumed a vernacular character. The shape of the network grew organically in response to cultural decisions made not according to any predetermined order superimposed by colonial officials, but according to the immediate needs of occupants as adjusted to the natural terrain. Early roads at the Opequon community, for instance, consistently followed upland ridges, and the emerging road network connected any one farmstead to virtually every other farm or mill in the community.[11]

The administrative procedures for constructing and maintaining roads were all intensely local.

Laying out a road began with a petition from the people who needed it. In 1738, for instance, forty-five settlers, mostly German and Scotch-Irish, complained to the court of Orange County that they "lay under great illconveniency for want of a Road" from Jost Hite's mill on the Opequon Creek to a ferry on the Shenandoah River. On the merit of such appeals, courts designated one of the petitioners to "view, mark, and lay off" the route. The viewer's report in turn justified the appointment of a road overseer authorized to order out all tithables within two or three miles of the road to labor on its construction and afterwards on its maintenance.[12]

Because roads were laid out, built, and maintained to serve collective needs for communication and exchange within local communities, road systems, like other elements of vernacular landscapes, varied greatly from region to region. Travelers understood this all too well. "There are either too many or too few roads," the marquis de Chastellux complained in 1782. "People always think they have given sufficient directions to travelers, who seldom fail to go astray." On one occasion near Leesburg, Virginia, Johann David Schoepf found himself "not without having gone wrong at times; for the universal answer one gets, on asking the way, is: Keep in the main road, or, Straight on;—everybody knowing the roads in the parish and thinking that even strangers must find it easy to keep in the straight path which commonly is very crooked."[13]

The petition and subsequent court order for a road from Hite's mill was the earliest in the lower Shenandoah Valley. Hite himself had been instrumental in securing valley settlers for the colonial government and had fixed his own settlement where the Philadelphia wagon road crossed the Opequon Creek (fig. 16.2). Around him, the Opequon community took shape. Thirty-two tracts of land taken up in the 1730s and 1740s supported a landowning population of twenty-three families. At least five were German, and fourteen were Scotch-Irish. Estate inventories probated between

Fig. 16.2. Jost Hite House. This house was also called Hite's Fort.

1749 and 1768 documented a diverse grain-livestock economy and a variety of trades, including woodworking, coopering, shoemaking, distilling, brewing, and weaving. Hite's was the earliest mill on the creek, but archaeological evidence exists for an additional seven during the eighteenth century. The Opequon settlement provides a good example of a decentralized, mixed-farm community in the early phases of the transition to capitalism. Typically, settler families dispersed on individual tracts of land, located farmsteads with respect to terrain rather than social needs, and engaged in varied economic pursuits individually to secure a competence and collectively to achieve a high degree of community self-sufficiency.[14]

County road orders reflected the needs of Opequon settlers to reach practically every neighboring farmstead or mill. The Philadelphia wagon road and Hite's road provided external contacts, but more significant were the internal contacts created by the emerging road system—at least seven routes established by order of the court before 1748 connected key locations at ferries, mills, and ordinaries. This road system represented a truly vernacular component of the cultural landscape carefully adjusted to the demands of a decentralized household economy in a settlement community formed to sustain collectively the competence of each individual member family.[15]

II

New influences, however, began to reshape the road system at Opequon and other rural communities in Frederick County during the last half of the eighteenth century. With the encouragement of the justices of the peace, the county clerk announced in 1744 that he had surveyed twenty-six half-acre town lots on land he owned along the Philadelphia wagon road, six miles north of Opequon. He set aside four lots for public use. This fledgling county town, to be called Winchester, grew slowly at first, but by the 1750s the key elements of a courthouse, jail, church, and a few stores were in place. A 1752 charter from the Virginia House of Burgesses granted the townspeople rights to hold two fairs annually "for the sale and vending all manner of cattle, victuals, provisions, goods, wares, and merchandizes, whatsoever." The legislation, however, provided for no regular public market.[16] Provisioning troops during the Seven Years' War gave the town a needed boost, but it remained poorly integrated into the autonomous household economies of surrounding rural communities.

The second phase of the transition to capitalism would change this. By the late 1760s, grain prices in the Atlantic economy had risen high enough to offset transportation costs from inland areas as far west as the Shenandoah Valley. Farmers responded by producing flour for market, but only so far as the market did not curtail economic independence. Winchester benefited little from these developments initially, because most flour departed the valley from merchant mills in a decentralized pattern of exchange firmly established earlier in the formation of rural communities.

The regional importance of the town began to increase rapidly during the 1780s, however, as local merchants organized an import trade in retail goods demanded by rural residents, who were now enjoying greater consumer power. A 1779 charter of incorporation granted townspeople the authority to enact ordinances for self-government through a mayor, board of aldermen, and common council.[17] It also conferred rights "to hold and keep within the said town . . . two market days in every week of the year" under the direction of a clerk of the market, "who shall have assize of bread, wine, beer, wood, and other things." Travelers Harry Toulmin and the duc de La Rochefoucauld-Liancourt found a "well stocked market" in the 1790s with more than sixty items for sale.[18]

At this stage in the transition to capitalism, the town still functioned as a commercial community in which public order depended on the authority of town officials, like Winchester's market clerk, to manage trading in the common interest. Town ordinances set prices of important commodities like meat or bread and restricted most business to the public market, where the clerk controlled the hours of trading, insured the quality of goods, and enforced honest weights and measures. In 1794, for instance, Winchester's common council declared that any person "marketing at any other place in this Borough, on the [market] days aforesaid, than the Market-house . . . shall forfeit and pay one dollar each for every such offence." Additional ordinances prohibited practices such as forestalling, engrossing, and regrating, which represented free trading outside the marketplace.[19] In fact, the term "private enterprise" would have been a contradiction in terms in this system because all enterprise or trade was by definition public and subject to regulation for the public good. Self-interest represented a threat to public interest because local economies were still regarded as zero-sum equations in which one individual's acquisitiveness diminished the common wealth and endangered the welfare of others.[20]

During the final stage in the transition to capitalism, economies came to be regarded as capable of growth, and individual entrepreneurship was recognized as a means of actually increasing available wealth. The objective of public order and a regulated market, however, was to render livelihoods secure by limiting competition, not by maximizing opportunity. No one grew wealthy under this system, but all could prosper. Free of speculative booms and busts, livelihoods and competencies remained secure in a process historian Jack P. Greene has called "improvement." As Greene has argued:

> Individuals came to the new societies of colonial British America not merely in quest of personal independence but also with the complementary hope of transforming those new societies into *improved* societies that could both guarantee the independence or, for the fortunate few, affluence they expected to achieve and enable them to enjoy the fruits of that independence or affluence to the fullest possible extent. . . . Settlers sought to improve their situation by securing the necessary capital and labor to develop their lands and fortunes; towns that would provide them with local markets in which they could exchange the produce of their lands for finished goods; bounties that would encourage them to experiment with new crops; and roads, bridges, and ferries that would provide them with better access to wider markets and link them more closely to economic and administrative centers.[21]

Insofar as market regulations rendered safe the returns of trade, so roads linked the competencies—for which farm families labored so hard—with the centers of authority securing their improvements. Certainly, the street grids that ordered eighteenth-century urban space contrasted vividly with the curvilinear space defined by country roads, but those roads were also ordered with great precision by natural terrain and community consensus (fig. 16.3). Like grids, country road networks were neither random nor arbitrary. Furthermore, these roads joined the farmer to the ordered world of the public market. Improvement then became synonymous with a settlement system composed of town and country unified by roads in a common conception of public order.

Thus would Winchester exert a growing influence over the regional road system. Early nineteenth-century internal-improvement maps indicated at least fourteen long-distance routes emanating from the town (fig. 16.4). The old wagon road, soon to become a turnpike, located the town on a central axis from Pennsylvania to the Carolinas. Four routes led east over separate gaps in the Blue Ridge to ports in tidewater Virginia. Another three headed west to Appalachian settlements and Ohio River towns. Four of the radial routes from Win-

Fig. 16.3. Map of Winchester, 1777, by Andreas Wiederholdt. Roads leading to the town conformed to the natural terrain and generally followed ridges. (Van Pelt Library, University of Pennsylvania, Philadelphia.)

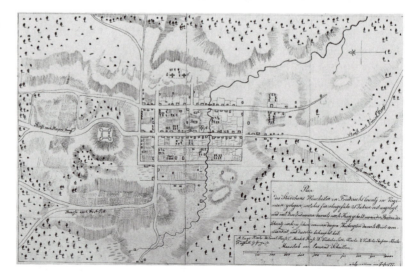

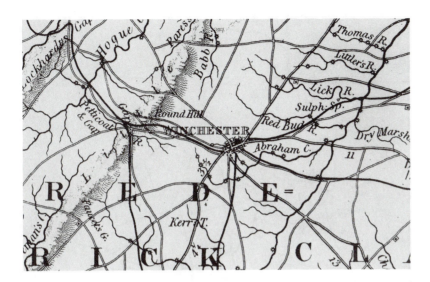

Fig. 16.4. Detail from Herman Böÿe, "A Map of the State of Virginia," 1825. (Virginia State Library, Richmond.)

chester passed through the Opequon community. The older, dense network of roads serving a dispersed rural economy there was progressively integrated into a radial system of routes under the centralizing influences of ordered marketplaces in an improved society (fig. 16.5).[22]

III

The most striking aspect of the road system as it stretched the ordered, commercial space of the town across the rural landscape was revealed in the spatial relations of houses, farmsteads, and roadways. On a journey through the Shenandoah Valley from Staunton to Winchester, La Rochefoucauld-Liancourt, for instance, noted particularly that "the habitations do not stand at a great distance from the road."[23] What was not characteristic of the landscape of the late-eighteenth- and early-nineteenth-century Shenandoah Valley, then, were houses or farmsteads secluded at the ends of long, private lanes. First, these lanes all led somewhere. Developed to serve settlers in household economies, roads linked farms to mills, or mills to ferries, or simply roads to other roads. Second, roads were

not private. Passersby could be expected at farmhouses at any time. Farmers, carters, travelers on their way to grind grain, saw timber, buy supplies, market produce, attend court, or simply visit a neighbor would pass from farmstead to farmstead along the way (fig. 16.6).[24]

At Opequon, rural houses were sited in a consistent pattern with roads passing squarely in front of houses and often between houses and barns. Today, the remains of the David Glass house lie in a pasture near the Opequon Creek far from any road (fig. 16.1). Glass belonged to the first generation of Opequon settlers and to a family that included a father, at least two brothers, and a brother-in-law who also owned land nearby along the creek. Glass's house grew in segments with the addition of single units, but the result was an I-house. Essential to understanding this expression of order and symmetry is not only the additive process of its growth correlating with the basic economic and geographic transformations of eighteenth-century life, but also its relation to the local road network. The house originally stood at the intersection of a very early route that linked settlements along the Opequon Creek and a road connecting across the creek to one of the primary radial routes

Fig. 16.5. Road Network at
Opequon during Its Most
Developed Stage in the Late
Eighteenth and Nineteenth
Centuries. (Drafted by James
Wilson, James Madison
University, Harrisonburg,
Virginia.)

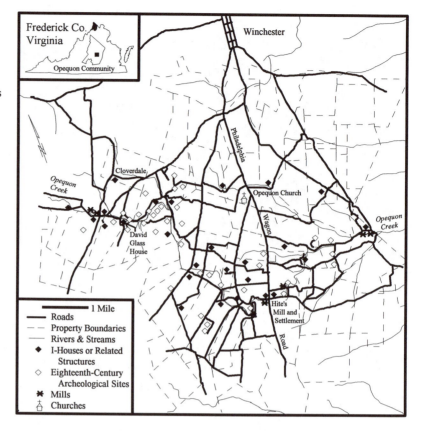

Fig. 16.6. Layout of William
Buckles Farmstead, Shenandoah
Valley, Jefferson County, Now
West Virginia. This side-passage
structure demonstrates the
relationship between house,
road, and farmstead common in
the nineteenth-century
Shenandoah Valley. (From *James
E. Taylor Sketchbook,* Western
Reserve Historical Society,
Cleveland, Ohio.)

Fig. 16.7. Cloverdale.

leading to Winchester. Near another intersection of now-abandoned roads stood a similar structure, Cloverdale (fig. 16.7). It also grew additively during the eighteenth or early nineteenth century, and, although isolated today, it too once stood squarely fronting a road leading to Winchester and another connecting to the Opequon settlements.

The essential relation determining house siting was not direction, view, aspect, or slope, then, but orientation to the road. Farmsteads, furthermore, were laid out in relation to the road, not according to the perpendicularity or linearity of roof lines. Rural families regularly selected road intersections as sites for their houses, barns, and yards. Because farmsteads were often located centrally within farm tracts, these roads traversed private properties instead of conforming to property boundaries.[25]

The single most important inference to be drawn from this pattern of roads, tracts, houses, and farmsteads is that the men and women of early-nineteenth-century rural America did not seek rural seclusion; on the contrary, they wanted to link their fortunes as directly as possible to market and commercial centers. They sought to join their private pursuits of labor on the land with the regulated public order of the market precisely because that order meant security in the possession of their competencies.

The I-house was certainly an expression of success in an agrarian world, but the balance, order, and symmetry of the design was also a product of the same drive that compelled townspeople to order the marketplace.[26] Reversing patterns characteristic of earlier and later vernacular dwellings, I-houses were conceptualized from the outside in. Asymmetrical structures, such as the Rhenish *Flurkuchenhaus,* or *Ernhaus* (fig. 16.2), and single-unit, two-bay dwellings that probably characterized early Scotch-Irish building in the Shenandoah Valley either gave way to new, symmetrical structures or were modified according to Georgian principles.[27] The arrangement of architectural elements was based, therefore, not on the interior needs of the house's inhabitants, but on the need for an outward expression of order. Sited on roads, these structures were intended to be viewed from the road. Eight- to ten-foot-wide central passages not only matched the average width of a roadway but literally and symbolically extended the road into the house. Little wonder that travelers found an open welcome here.

In this sense, I-houses represented a form of public architecture. They communicated the same relationship between house and road—between private and public—that urban dwellings expressed toward the public arena of the street. "Town, where we become citizens and can be seen," as John B. Jackson has pointed out, "begins directly outside our door, where the road stands for public life."[28] Moreover, many public structures were themselves I-houses. In Winchester, for instance, the county courthouse, clerk's office, jail, and a Presbyterian church all presented the same balanced order of elements to the public as I-houses did in the surrounding countryside.

That in plan and appearance the I-house mediated the private space of the family and the public space of an ordered commercial world explains its pervasiveness amid the ethnic diversity of the American settlement frontier. In the processes of community formation and economic development at Opequon, German, Scotch-Irish, English, and other settlers maintained separate identities in pat-

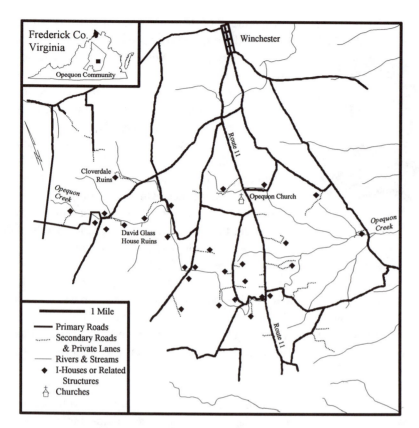

Fig. 16.8. Road Network at Opequon by Mid-Twentieth Century. (Drafted by James Wilson.)

terns of marriage, kinship, land conveyance, and religious affiliation, but members of all groups traded regularly and freely with one another. As Winchester grew and took on market functions, commerce progressively linked ethnic communities into a continuous town-and-country settlement system. Not surprisingly, the I-house provided a powerful statement of the common position of everyone in that system.[29]

IV

The early-nineteenth-century American landscape of towns and farms dominated by the I-house and knit together by roads had taken shape during the middle phase of the transition to capitalism. By the second quarter of the nineteenth century, however, this landscape was already passing. As early

as the 1780s, the notion of the town as a commercial community that protected the exclusive privileges of its trading members was under attack. At the vanguard of this movement, which would lead to the final stages in the transition to capitalism, were the principles of economic liberalism articulated by Adam Smith. Self-interest, regulated by the "invisible hand" of competition, would soon replace corporate or civic interest as the organizing principle of the marketplace. By 1800 no major American municipality enforced a comprehensive system of price regulation, trade monopolies, and public markets. During the next three decades, private shops replaced public markets as centers of trade.[30]

Winchester maintained market regulations throughout the first half of the nineteenth century, but efforts by butchers to evade restrictions on trade and the licensing of merchants to sell meat in shops undermined the public function of the market. As one townsman put it in 1831: "Public spirited citizens . . . have a proper sense of what they owe to the public as well as to themselves, and . . . see and feel that while they are contributing to the public benefit they are essentially promoting their own interest."[31]

As this municipal revolution reduced the authority of the town as an ordering agent in both economic life and the landscape, the public significance of the road diminished. Maps of late-nineteenth-century America clearly indicated the progressive abandonment of roads, and in the twentieth century, county and state road departments recast road networks in the interest of the automobile and long-distance travel.[32] Civil engineers armed with books of uniform specifications replaced the local road overseer and community consensus in the construction and maintenance of roads.

Towns, meanwhile, took on new functions. In the Shenandoah Valley, the decline of grain farming by the end of the nineteenth century meant that mills dispersed on streams no longer served vital economic functions. Roller technology and steam or electric power forced mills to increase in size, decrease in numbers, and relocate in towns. As large-scale apple and peach orchards replaced grain farms, Winchester captured the processing, packing, and storage industries and exerted an ever-stronger centralizing force on the rural landscape. The routes radiating from Winchester were incorporated into the state road system, and the smaller connector routes so important in the decentralized economy of the early Shenandoah Valley reverted to private use (fig. 16.8).

The outcome of these developments was a private landscape of secluded houses at the end of long lanes leading to hard-surface highways. The countryside became for many a retreat from a competitive and often chaotic world of commerce. As industrial metropolises replaced older corporate communities, rural Americans often preferred to be cut off from urban life. Although the I-house would survive, it served more and more as a core for the decorative devices of various nineteenth-century revival styles that appealed to desires for individualized self-expression, not a uniform public order. By the twentieth century, the I-house would primarily serve the needs of the rural poor—people isolated from the mainstream of economic development. The public landscape of commercial communities, regulated markets, public thoroughfares, and I-houses had passed with its particular stage in the transition to capitalism.

Notes

1. Johann David Schoepf, *Travels in the Confederation, 1783–1784,* vol. 2, trans. and ed. Alfred J. Morrison (1911; reprint, New York: Bergman Publishers, 1968), 35; Thomas Anburey, *Travels through the Interior Parts of America,* vol. 2 (1789; reprint, Boston: Houghton Mifflin, 1923), 198; Isaac Weld, *Travels through the States of North America,* vol. 2 (1807; reprint, New York: Johnson Reprint, 1968), 134–35. For similar sentiments, see François Jean, marquis de Chastellux, *Travels in North America in the Years 1780, 1781 and 1782,* vol. 2, trans. Howard C. Rice Jr. (1786; reprint, Chapel Hill: University of North Carolina Press for the Institute of Early American History and Culture, 1963), 441; John Davis, *Travels of Four Years and a Half in the United States of America during 1798, 1799, 1800, 1801, and 1802* (New York: Henry Holt, 1909), 373.

2. As Edward A. Chappell has commented, "The overwhelming dominance of the I-house in the Valley is striking when compared to the diversity of vernacular house forms that were built in nineteenth-century Piedmont and Tidewater Virginia." See "Acculturation in the Shenandoah Valley: Rhenish Houses of the Massanutten Settlement," *Proceedings of the American Philosophical Society* 124 (1980): 56. The I-house received its name when

first documented in the I-states of Indiana, Illinois, and Iowa, where it dominates the rural landscape. See Fred B. Kniffen, "Folk Housing: Key to Diffusion," *Annals of the Association of American Geographers* 55 (1965): 553.

3. The term I-house is problematic. As employed here it refers not to an immutable house type, but rather to a way of thinking about the arrangement of formal elements—especially of the facade—and their relation to internal and external space. Emphasis, therefore, lies more on the origins of this way of thinking in the late eighteenth century than on its most coherent expression in the next century. For discussions of the origin and diffusion of the I-house, see Henry Glassie, "Eighteenth-Century Cultural Process in Delaware Valley Folk Building," *Winterthur Portfolio* 7 (1972): 29–57; Glassie, *Folk Housing in Middle Virginia: A Structural Analysis of Historic Artifacts* (Knoxville: University of Tennessee Press, 1975), 91–113, 156–66; Glassie, *Pattern in the Material Folk Culture of the Eastern United States* (Philadelphia: University of Pennsylvania Press, 1968), 65–77, 107–12, 124–25, 150–57; Kniffen, "Folk Housing," 549–77; Richard Pillsbury, "Patterns in the Folk and Vernacular House Forms of the Pennsylvania Culture Region," *Pioneer America* 9 (1977): 13–31; Dell Upton, "New Views of the Virginia Landscape," *Virginia Magazine of History and Biography* 96 (1988): 441–42; Upton, "The Power of Things: Recent Studies in American Vernacular Architecture," *American Quarterly* 35 (1983): 270–74; Upton, "Vernacular Domestic Architecture in Eighteenth-Century Virginia," *Winterthur Portfolio* 17 (1982): 95–119. Bernard L. Herman's analysis of vernacular architecture in rural Delaware is most helpful. See Herman, *Architecture and Rural Life in Central Delaware, 1700–1900* (Knoxville: University of Tennessee Press, 1987), 14–41, 109–10, 149–56, 167–68, 191, 231–33.

4. The literature on the "transition to capitalism" is sizable, but the best review article is Allan Kulikoff's "The Transition to Capitalism in Rural America," *William and Mary Quarterly* 3d ser., 46 (1989): 120–44. For additional material, see Christopher Clark, "The Household Economy, Market Exchange and the Rise of Capitalism in the Connecticut Valley, 1800–1860," *Journal of Social History* 13 (1979): 169–89; James A. Henretta, "Families and Farms: *Mentalité* in Pre-Industrial America," *William and Mary Quarterly* 3d ser., 35 (1978): 3–32; Gregory H. Nobles, "Capitalism in the Countryside: The Transformation of Rural Society in the United States," *Radical History Review* 41 (1988): 163–77; Michael Merrill, "Cash Is Good to Eat: Self-Sufficiency and Exchange in the Rural Economy of the United States," *Radical History Review* 3 (1977): 42–69; Bettye Hobbs Pruitt, "Self-Sufficiency and the Agricultural Economy of Eighteenth-Century Massachusetts," *William and Mary Quarterly* 3d ser., 41 (1984): 333–64; Winifred B. Rothenberg, "The Emergence of a Capital Market in Rural Massachusetts, 1730–1838," *Journal of Economic History* 45 (1985): 781–808; Rothenberg, "The Emergence of Farm Labor Markets and the Transformation of the Rural Economy: Massachusetts, 1750–1855," *Journal of Economic History* 48 (1988): 537–66; Rothenberg, "The Market and Massachusetts Farmers, 1750–1858," *Journal of Economic History* 41 (1981): 283–314.

5. Warren R. Hofstra, "Land Policy and Settlement in the Northern Shenandoah Valley," *Appalachian Frontiers: Settlement, Society, & Development in the Preindustrial Era,* ed. Robert D. Mitchell (Lexington: University Press of Kentucky, 1990), 105–26; Frank W. Porter, "Expanding the Domain: William Gooch and the Northern Neck Boundary Dispute," *Maryland Historian* 5 (1974): 1–13; Manning C. Voorhis, "The Land Grant Policy of Colonial Virginia, 1607–1774," (Ph.D. diss., University of Virginia, 1940), 108–65.

6. For discussions of independence and dependence in eighteenth-century social structure, see Jack P. Greene, "Independence, Improvement, and Authority: Toward a Framework for Understanding the Histories of the Southern Backcountry during the Era of the American Revolution," *An Uncivil War: The Southern Backcountry during the American Revolution,* ed. Ronald Hoffman, Thad W. Tate, and Peter J. Albert (Charlottesville: University Press of Virginia for the United States Capitol Historical Society, 1985), 3–36; Greene, *Pursuits of Happiness: The Social Development of Early Modern British Colonies and the Formation of American Culture* (Chapel Hill: Uni-

versity of North Carolina Press, 1988), 15–16, 98, 195–97; Henretta, "Families and Farms," 18–19. On the matter of competency, see Daniel Vickers, "Competency and Competition: Economic Culture in Early America," *William and Mary Quarterly* 3d ser., 47 (1990): 3–29.

7. William Couper, *History of the Shenandoah Valley,* vol. 1 (New York: Lewis Historical Publishing Co., 1952), 220, 239–40; Robert D. Mitchell, *Commercialism and Frontier: Perspectives on the Early Shenandoah Valley* (Charlottesville: University Press of Virginia, 1977), 29, 30. In one expression of the process of settlement organization, Frederick County was established in 1738, but the first court did not meet until 1743.

8. Orange County Will Book 1, Orange County Courthouse, Orange, Va.; Frederick County Will Book 1 (hereafter cited as FWB), Frederick County Courthouse, Winchester, Va.; Mitchell, *Commercialism and Frontier,* 133–60.

9. Robert Brooke Survey Book, 1732–1734, Virginia Historical Society, Richmond, Va.

10. U.S. Census Office, First Census, 1790, *Return of the Whole Number of Persons within the Several Districts of the United States* (Philadelphia, 1793), 48; Raymond C. Young, "The Effects of the French and Indian War on Civilian Life in the Frontier Counties of Virginia, 1754–1763," (Ph.D. diss., Vanderbilt University, 1969), 436; Mitchell, *Commercialism and Frontier,* 144, 175; Frederick County Order Books 1–3 (hereafter cited as FOB), Frederick County Courthouse, Winchester, Va.

11. Clarence R. Geier and Warren R. Hofstra, "An Archaeological Survey of and Management Plan for Cultural Resources in the Vicinity of the Upper Opequon Creek," report, Virginia Department of Historic Resources, Richmond, Va., 1991, 48–64.

12. Nathaniel Mason Pawlett, *Historic Roads of Virginia: A Brief History of the Roads of Virginia, 1607–1840* (Charlottesville: Virginia Highway & Transportation Research Council, 1977), 3–10; Petition to Orange County Court, 1738, as quoted in William J. Hinke and Charles E. Kemper, eds., "Moravian Diaries of Travels through Virginia," *Virginia Magazine of History and Biography* 12 (1905): 142.

13. Chastellux, *Travels in North America,* 2: 405; Schoepf, *Travels in the Confederation,* 2: 41.

14. Geier and Hofstra, "Archaeological Survey," 39–93; FWB 1–3.

15. FOB 1–3. The area was first mapped extensively during the American Civil War, but the road system portrayed by military cartographers in the 1860s had matured before the end of the eighteenth century. See G. L. Gillespie, "Map of the Upper Potomac from McCoy's Ferry to Conrad's Ferry and Adjacent Portions of Maryland and Virginia," *The Official Military Atlas of the Civil War,* ed. George B. Davis, Leslie J. Perry, and Joseph W. Kirkley (Gettysburg, Pa.: National Historical Society, 1978), plate 69, 1; Jed Hotchkiss, "Map of the Shenandoah Valley," Handley Library Archives, Winchester, Va.

16. William W. Hening, ed., *The Statutes at Large: Being a Collection of All the Laws of Virginia, 1619–1792,* vols. 5 and 6 (Richmond, Va., 1809–1823), 78–80, 269–70; FOB 1, 264.

17. Carville V. Earle and Ronald Hoffman, "Staple Crops and Urban Development in the Eighteenth-Century South," *Perspectives in American History,* 10, ed. Donald Fleming and Bernard Bailyn (Cambridge, Mass.: Harvard University Press, 1976), 68–78. For a discussion of the limits placed on market engagement by eighteenth-century rural Americans, see Alan Taylor, *Liberty Men and Great Proprietors: The Revolutionary Settlement on the Maine Frontier, 1760–1820* (Chapel Hill: University of North Carolina Press for the Institute of Early American History and Culture, 1990), 7–9.

18. Hening, *Statutes,* 10: 172–76; François, duc de La Rochefoucauld-Liancourt, *Travels through the United States of North America . . . in the Years 1795, 1796 and 1797,* 2d ed., vol. 2, trans. H. Neuman (London: R. Phillips, 1800), 208; Harry Toulmin, *The Western Country in 1793: Reports on Kentucky and Virginia,* ed. Marion Tinling and Godfrey Davies (San Marino, Calif.: Huntington Library, 1948), 45–47.

19. *Bowens Virginia Centinel & Gazette: or, the Winchester Political Repository,* May 5, 1794, 3. See also "An Act Re-

ducing into One and Amending the Several Acts for the Regulation of the Market . . . ," Winchester City Council Ordinance Book (hereafter cited as WCCOB), 1819–1852, 35–48, Clerk of Council, Winchester, Va.; Pat Ashby, "The 1821 Market House," *Winchester-Frederick County Historical Society Journal* 5 (1990): 59–75.

20. Jon C. Teaford, *The Municipal Revolution in America: Origins of Modern Urban Government, 1650–1825* (Chicago: University of Chicago Press, 1975), 3–46, 91–110.

21. Greene, "Independence, Improvement, and Authority," 15–16.

22. Herman Böÿe, "A Map of the State of Virginia: Constructed in conformity to Law from the late Surveys authorized by the Legislature and other original and authentic Documents," 1825, 1859, Virginia State Library, Richmond, Va.; Claudius Crozet, "A Map of the Internal Improvements of Virginia," 1838, Virginia State Library, Richmond, Va.; John Wood, "Frederick County, 1820," Alderman Library, University of Virginia, Charlottesville, Va. See also E. M. Sanchez-Saavedra, *A Description of the Country: Virginia's Cartographers and Their Maps, 1607–1881* (Richmond, Va.: Virginia State Library, 1975), 55–86.

23. Rochefoucauld-Liancourt, *Travels through the United States,* 2: 184.

24. For similar conclusions, see Margaret Purser, "All Roads Lead to Winnemucca: Local Road Systems and Community Material Culture in Nineteenth-century Nevada," *Perspectives in Vernacular Architecture, III,* ed. Thomas Carter and Bernard L. Herman (Columbia: University of Missouri Press, 1989), 120–34.

25. Geier and Hofstra, "Archaeological Survey," 39–93.

26. The association of the I-house with agricultural success provides a common explanation for its popularity in late-eighteenth- and nineteenth-century rural America, see Chappell, "Acculturation in the Shenandoah Valley," 56; Kniffen, "Folk Housing," 555.

27. Chappell, "Acculturation in the Shenandoah Valley," 55–89; Chappell, "Germans and Swiss," *America's Architectural Roots: Ethnic Groups that Built America,* ed. Dell Upton (Washington D.C.: Preservation Press, 1986), 68–74; Warren R. Hofstra, "Adaptation or Survival? Folk Housing at Opequon Settlement, Virginia," *Ulster Folklife* 37 (1991): 36–61; K. Edward Lay, "European Antecedents of Seventeenth and Eighteenth Century Germanic and Scots-Irish Architecture in America," *Pennsylvania Folklife* 32 (1982): 2–43; William Woys Weaver, "The Pennsylvania German House: European Antecedents and New World Forms," *Winterthur Portfolio* 21 (1986): 243–64.

28. John B. Jackson, *Discovering the Vernacular Landscape* (New Haven: Yale University Press, 1984), 27.

29. Warren R. Hofstra, "Land, Ethnicity, and Community at Opequon Settlement, Virginia, 1730–1800," *Virginia Magazine of History and Biography* 98 (1990): 423–48.

30. Teaford, *Municipal Revolution,* 91–110.

31. WCCOB, 1819–1852, 86–87; WCCOB, 1852–1870, 207; *Winchester Republican,* Mar. 31, 1831, 2.

32. Commonwealth of Virginia, Department of Highways, "Map of Frederick County Showing Primary and Secondary Highways," (Richmond, Va., 1932); *Frederick County, Virginia* (Philadelphia, Pa.: D. J. Lake, 1885); U.S. Geological Survey, "West Virginia-Virginia: Winchester," (1894). Virginia established the Department of Highways and Transportation in 1906. See Pawlett, *Historic Roads of Virginia,* 39.

Chapter 17

The Architectural and Social Topography of Early-Nineteenth-Century Portsmouth, New Hampshire

Bernard L. Herman

On any given workday, dawn caught the workers, shopkeepers, artisans, and traders of early-nineteenth-century Portsmouth, New Hampshire, making their way from home to employment. For some, like Nathaniel Souther, who lived at the corner of Pleasant Street and Cottars Lane, the "journey to work" led from an upstairs sleeping chamber to a downstairs bakehouse and shop. For other Cottars Lane residents, like ropemaker Samuel Shereve, the path to work traversed the length of the seaport city; still others, like Shereve's neighbor, shoemaker Samuel Rand, made their respective ways to shops located in the new brick buildings erected in the city's commercial center following devastating fires in 1802, 1809, and 1813. Souther, Shereve, and Rand were three of eighteen Cottars Lane residents listed in the city's first street directory published in 1821. The eighteen occupied ten residences ranged along the lane and its intersection with Pleasant Street just above South Bridge (figs. 17.1 and 17.2). The streets to employment took some of Portsmouth's working folk to shops and stores at fixed addresses; for others, such as unskilled laborers and truckmen working the seaport's busy wharves, the site of employment varied from day to day.[1]

Nestled at the foot of Pleasant Street, Cottars Lane is a starting point enabling us to ask questions about Portsmouth's urban landscape and vernacular architecture in the early 1800s. What was the social, occupational, and architectural topography of Cottars Lane and Portsmouth's South End—defined for our purposes as the city area south of State Street, east of Pleasant Street and South Mill Pond, and west of the Piscataqua waterfront? Who were Portsmouth's laboring citizens, and what was the texture and import of their individual paths to work? How did the buildings of the South End reflect the social dynamics of what has been termed "the walking city?" What do the styles and construction dates of houses, shops, and stores tell us about pattern and process in the changing urban landscape? How do the buildings of Portsmouth compare with the architectural stock of other early American port cities, not only in matters of style and appearance, but also—and just as importantly—in terms of ordinary society and the symbolic meanings of everyday life?

As we begin, it will help to set forth a few ideas to bear in mind as we begin to retrace Samuel Rand's walk to work over the Portsmouth streets of 1821.[2] First, there is the notion of objects—in this case architecture—as texts. The use of objects as texts, a central tenet in vernacular architecture and material culture studies, recognizes the communicative nature of artifacts. Houses are obviously shelter, but they are also statements about the nature of basic social relationships. In some instances, the architectural symbolism of wealth, taste, and authority is intentional and obvious. In most vernacular buildings, however, the textual content of architecture functions beneath the level of articulated observation. The experience of architectural discourse—the setting in which our building texts were "read"—could take the form of parades and special events or Samuel Rand's daily walk to work.

Fig. 17.1. View of Cottars Lane and the Lower End of Pleasant Street from South Mill Pond. The Cottars Lane houses, including the Barnard-Lord house in the foreground, are visible to the right; the backs of the Pleasant Street mansions range behind the pondside work structures in the center of the photograph.

Second, I would like to introduce the idea of movement. Our Cottars Lane citizens walked to work and back again often twice in a day. In addition to work, Portsmouth citizens went to market, church, funerals, auctions, social gatherings, and public events. Portsmouth, like all early American cities, was a city in motion, and it embodied traits of the "walking city" and "processional land-scapes." The notion of the "walking city" refers to an urban landscape "where houses, shops, and storehouses were clustered within a two-mile 'walking' radius of the wharves." The interpretation of the walking city is far from uniform. Some readers of the urban landscape argue that cluster-ing produced a sense of social mutuality between all classes due to their close proximity to one an-other; others emphasize the compactness of the cityscape as a determining factor in social and ar-chitectural segmentation. In our brief look at Ports-mouth, the architectural texture of the walking city and the experience of physical movement through the city's streets and lanes are the essential ele-ments for our understanding of the built land-scape.[3]

To read the text of Portsmouth as the walking city, we need to recognize the nature of move-ment in an economically and socially layered environment. Here, the idea of the "processional landscape" will serve us well. The concept of the "processional landscape" as developed by Dell Upton was first applied to the eighteenth-century plantation landscapes of Virginia.[4] The basic prin-ciples are that architecture represents a category of social experience, that the perception of the land-scape changes with movement, and that, in addi-tion to being hierarchical in nature, landscapes may also represent a series of fragmented experi-ences. At the center of the southern plantation countryside stood the great planters' houses and their articulated networks of buildings and social relationships, ranging from the plantation plan to church and courthouse. Portsmouth as a proces-sional landscape has at its social and symbolic center the houses of the mercantile elite with their architecturally articulated connections to the seats of commerce—the wharves and waterside stores, and associational culture—the library, meeting house, and fraternal clubs.[5]

Third, the textual and processional qualities of the South End's architectural topography repre-sented the broader organization of domestic life. These values may have gone unarticulated in spo-ken or written language, but their substance in brick and wood was there for all to see. We tend to perceive and interpret the urban landscape from the street, but houses, shops, and stores were permeable spaces with interior hierarchies of their own. The rooms of even a modest house, like Samuel Rand's, were fitted with trim and given different designations that described both function and social value. As we move up the architectural scale to elaborate eighteenth-century merchants' houses, the interior housescape becomes more dramatically distinctive.[6]

With these ideas in mind, we can return our attention to the streets of Portsmouth. The Ports-mouth streetscapes of the 1820s were represented by three categories: thoroughfares, cross streets, and side streets or lanes. Thoroughfares connected the urban core to the suburbs and rural backcountry. The thoroughfares of the South End and its environs were Water, Pleasant, and State (formerly Buck) Streets. Each of these thoroughfares possessed a distinctive character in terms of building types, population patterns, and position in the social and economic landscape.

Water Street, which split from South Road just above the bridge across South Mill Pond, wound its way parallel to the waterfront north to its termination at State Street. Water Street was the principal street that provided access to the major con-

Fig. 17.2. Plat of Cottars Lane with a List of Residents, ca. 1820. Based on Hale's map of 1813, this detail shows the footprints of Cottars Lane houses and the names and occupations of residents. (Drawn by Gabrielle M. Lanier.)

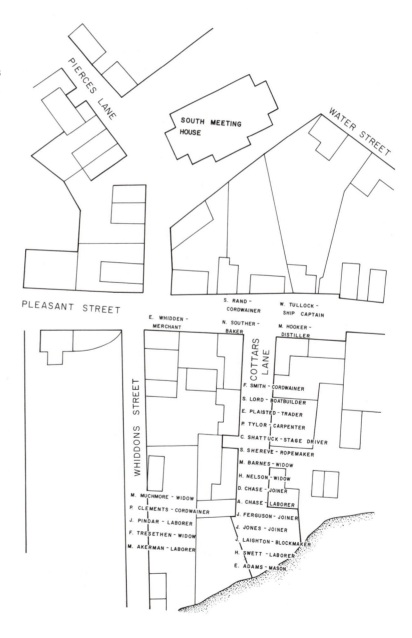

PIERCES LANE

SOUTH MEETING HOUSE

WATER STREET

PLEASANT STREET

WHIDDONS STREET

COTTARS LANE

S. RAND - CORDWAINER
W. TULLOCK - SHIP CAPTAIN
E. WHIDDEN - MERCHANT
N. SOUTHER - BAKER
M. HOOKER - DISTILLER
F. SMITH - CORDWAINER
S. LORD - BOATBUILDER
E. PLAISTED - TRADER
P. TYLOR - CARPENTER
C. SHATTUCK - STAGE DRIVER
S. SHEREVE - ROPEMAKER
M. BARNES - WIDOW
H. NELSON - WIDOW
D. CHASE - JOINER
A. CHASE - LABORER
J. FERGUSON - JOINER
J. JONES - JOINER
J. LAIGHTON - BLOCKMAKER
H. SWETT - LABORER
E. ADAMS - MASON

M. MUCHMORE - WIDOW
P. CLEMENTS - CORDWAINER
J. PINDAR - LABORER
F. TRESETHEN - WIDOW
M. AKERMAN - LABORER

centration of Portsmouth's public and private wharves. While the 1821 directory lists Water as home to fifty-two individuals, there were an additional twenty-four who noted Water as the location of their shops, stores, and wharves. Pleasant Street, roughly parallel to Water, was a wider, straighter avenue that defined the western edge of the South End. The building stock of Pleasant was considerably different from that of Water. The northwestern reach of the street was lined with large, freestanding, fashionable houses occupied by prosperous merchants, traders, and ship masters; the southeastern end was home to artisans and less well-to-do traders. Pleasant was also the street characterized by the greatest percentage of owner-occupied housing, and it exhibited the most dramatic gap between the average value of owner-occupied and tenanted dwellings. The majority of these houses faced eastward, looking across Pleasant toward the neighborhood of mariners, artisans, poorer widows, and laborers who inhabited the smaller frame houses linking Pleasant to Water. Finally, State Street ran east to west and defined the southern border of Portsmouth's rebuilt commercial core. The westward extension of State Street was one of the two major thoroughfares connecting the heart of the city to its rapidly developing western suburbs. Whereas Water Street can be characterized as a mixed-use, working waterfront thoroughfare and Pleasant Street as a mercantile residential avenue, State Street presented the aspect of a modern, crowded, commercial district lined with two- and three-story structures designed to contain ground-floor businesses and upper-story residences.[7] State's commercial character rendered it one of the most heavily tenanted streets in or near the South End—a situation that is made more dramatic by the fact that commuters like Rand doubled the daytime population.

Ranking below the thoroughfares in our hierarchy of streets were the cross streets. Cross streets did not lead in and out of the city, but simply connected the major avenues. The cross streets of Portsmouth's South End included Pitt and Gate, which connected Pleasant and Water, and Washington, which linked State to the lower end of Pleasant. Cross streets were more uniformly residential, and buildings occupied a much narrower range of value and, as a group, tended to be more consistent in appearance and population. The overall pattern was punctuated by corners anchored with more valuable houses that were more likely to be owner-occupied by the middling ranks of the mercantile and trading class. The few separately listed businesses occupied one ground-floor room in houses inhabited by the business owners.

The third category of streets can be categorized as side streets and lanes, which subdivided the cityscape into a number of irregularly shaped blocks. Side streets included the bunched network of lanes defining the neighborhoods to the immediate north and south of Puddle Dock, as well as the narrow streets descending from Water to Mechanic Street and the evenly ranked lanes extending behind the Pleasant Street mansions to South Mill Pond. Some side streets, like Cottars Lane, were home to an emerging middle class of city residents engaged in craft work; others, such as Puddle Lane, were primarily tenanted with multiple households composed largely of mariners, dock workers, and widows.[8] The side streets of the South End were predominantly residential, with the exception of small workshops clustered along the north side of Puddle Dock and Gravesend Street. The value difference between owner-occupied and tenanted houses was considerably less on the side streets than on the cross streets and thoroughfares. Side streets were occupied by artisans (many employed in ship and boatbuilding trades) and a large number of mariners, truckmen, and laborers. The majority of Portsmouth's widows lived down the city's lanes and side streets. Some widows were able to maintain themselves on inherited allowances, but others had to supplement their income by keeping small shops, by working as milliners or seamstresses, or by renting out rooms and providing board in their houses.

In the hierarchy of streets, the houses of Cottars Lane span a short but intensive period of land speculation and development. At the turn of the nineteenth century, all the lands behind the houses fronting Pleasant Street were still open. By 1810 all the property on both sides of Cottars Lane had been subdivided; by 1815 all the houses lining the lane had been erected and their interiors were at least partially finished. The architectural development of Cottars Lane exhibits two qualities identified in other American seaport cities in the decades following the Revolution. First, the subdivision of land by speculators (often merchants) occurred independently of later building activity. Second, the actual construction of houses often took place through limited partnerships involving investor-artisans. These artisan-developers found that by pooling both their financial resources and their personal connections to a larger laboring population, they were able both to realize monetary profit and to clamber onto the lower rungs of the real estate speculation ladder. Their larger goal, of course, was a successful ascent into the ranks of the urban mercantile class.[9]

The hallmarks of the Portsmouth development process were a brief period of land acquisition and subdivision, often characterized by a rapid sequence of property sales and mortgages. Once acquired by the builders, the construction of houses followed with little delay. Sometimes the new dwellings served as the homes of the builders or the tradesmen employed for the buildings' construction. More often, the new houses were sold as rapidly as possible and the proceeds were plowed into new ventures. After the sale of the lot and dwelling, the property usually enjoyed an extended period of residential stability. For some of the Cottars Lane properties, stability manifested itself in the presence of long-term owner-occupants; for others, stability expressed itself in the equally long-term ownership of houses as rental units. The history of the Chase and Plaisted houses at the foot of Cottars Lane illustrates this process. Langley Boardman, a self-styled cabinetmaker with extensive mercantile interests—including Atlantic shipping and land speculation throughout Portsmouth—acquired the entire south side of the street in the early 1800s and immediately began to subdivide it and sell building lots.[10] In 1804 Boardman sold the lot abutting South Mill Pond at the end of the street to house wright John Locke. That same year Locke transferred the still undeveloped lot to Samuel and Joshua Rand. The Rands, who identified themselves as shoemakers, lost no time in commissioning a double-dwelling house. In 1806 Joshua Rand advertised in the city newspaper that he had moved from his shop located in the center of town to his new house in Cottars Lane, "where his customers and friends are invited to call and purchase BOOTS & SHOES of the newest fashions."[11] Whether Samuel Rand occupied the other half of the building is unclear. In 1817 Samuel Rand sold his half of the building to Dudley Chase, who listed himself as a joiner in the 1821 street directory; in 1818 Joshua Rand conveyed his residence to Elisha Plaisted, a dealer in wood and lime. Meanwhile, Samuel Rand continued to live in the neighborhood, occupying an older style, center-chimney house on Pleasant Street at its intersection with Cottars Lane. Joshua Rand moved to nearby Atkinson Street.[12]

While the specifics of property transfers and lot histories do not offer us much in the way of narrative excitement, they do enable us to distinguish between fundamental aspects of urban architectural history: architecture as property and architecture as experience. Archeological research and excavations along Deer Street in the northern part of the city, for example, relate the history of property ownership to property use and kinship. A brief example from the Hart and Cutts families illustrates this point. In the early eighteenth century, blacksmith Samuel Hart moved into the Deer Street community, where his son Samuel married Bridgett Cutts, his neighbor's granddaughter. By the late 1700s, the house of Samuel and Bridgett Cutts Hart had descended to their son Richard, who rented the dwelling to his brother Daniel. Meanwhile, neighboring properties were being occupied by various siblings, cousins, and other relatives. By the 1790s a half dozen of Samuel and Bridgett's descendents and their families were residing on Deer Street as neighbors and kin. Thus, through inheritance and continued marriage ties, the Deer Street neighborhood continued a "kin dominated residential pattern that lasted for over one hundred years."[13] Archeologists also found that the documentary record, combined with artifacts retrieved from numerous Deer Street features, revealed "strong kinship and inheritance bonds between households."[14] For example, shards of a painted porcelain tea bowl excavated from a Hart family site matched a set owned by another branch of the family. Archeologists examining the property history and the artifacts concluded that the tea set had been divided between Daniel Hart's heirs after his death in 1792. One tea bowl ended up broken at the bottom of the family privy; another tea bowl descended through a different branch of the family until, generations later, it was deposited in a museum collection. While ownership histories separated the Deer Street lots from one another on

the basis of who historically had possessed and developed the land (individual action), customary relationships between neighbors established the lots as integral elements in an urban community (collective or public interaction). The lesson for looking at Cottars Lane, and indeed the historic domestic environments of all early American cities, is the disjunction and potential conflict resident between land ownership and use.

How did Cottars Lane fit into the economic and class landscape of Portsmouth? Nine of the Cottars Lane houses were owner occupied—an unusually high rate for an artisans and minor merchants' enclave—and at least two had been built as double houses.[15] The median house value stood at $400, but the average value for a house in Portsmouth was considerably higher at just under $625. The presence of a handful of valuable urban mansions with high values is counterbalanced by the just over four-fifths of all the housing in the city that fell below the $625 average (figs. 17.3 and 17.4). In a city where 38 percent of the taxable population owned houses and a mere 10 percent held more than one dwelling and where nearly half of all houses assessed at $1,000 or less were rented,

Fig. 17.3. Portsmouth Housing Values, ca. 1820, Showing Percentage of Dwellings by Assessed Value.

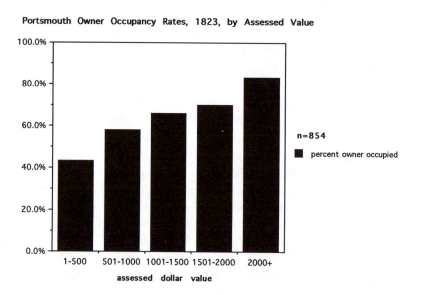

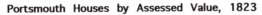

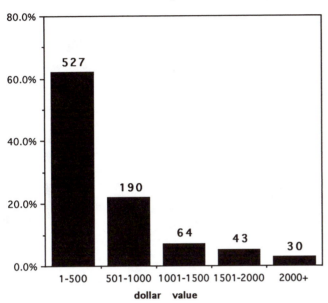

Fig. 17.4. Portsmouth Housing Values, ca. 1820, Showing Percentage of Owner-Occupied Dwellings by Assessed Value.

Cottars Lane represented a newly developed commuter artisan suburb.

In form and finish, the Cottars Lane houses combined urban and rural features.[16] The Rands' dwellings built as double houses were designed as side-passage plan dwellings with a front parlor and back dining room and kitchen (fig. 17.5). The upstairs rooms appear to have been limited in use as family chambers and apartments for lodgers. Across the street, Nathaniel Frost and Henry Beck erected comparable houses (fig. 17.6). The three other dwellings erected on Cottars Lane, however, drew on a tradition of freestanding single dwellings. The Laighton house at the foot of the lane was erected as a two-story, center-passage plan dwelling with a cellar kitchen (fig. 17.7). The Barnard-Lord house, located behind the Rands' buildings, also made use of a cellar kitchen, but the plan of the main floor varied with its use of a lobby entry containing the stair (fig. 17.8). Behind the entry, the builders were able to define a small, unheated ground-floor chamber. Of particular note in the Barnard-Lord house is the architectural evidence for the house having been partially unfinished for the first ten to twenty years of its existence. Differences in molding profiles and trim suggest that the house was built and initially sold with the finishes of the best room left to the discretion and pocketbook of the purchaser. Like the Barnard-Lord and Laighton houses, the Fernald-Tyler house contained a well-defined kitchen placed in a position secondary to the principal ground-floor rooms. The front rooms of the Fernald-Tyler house were identical in plan to those on the principal floor of the Barnard-Lord dwelling. Instead of a vertical relationship between service and the main rooms, though, the Fernald-Tyler residence incorporated the kitchen into the house through an original lean-to ell.

In all the Cottars Lane houses, we find that a comparable amount of area in terms of actual square footage was occupied by the principal rooms of the house regardless of plan and orientation to the street. The real differences between these houses as built lay in the definition and allocation of service space—specifically the kitchen. In the Chase-

Fig. 17.5. Plan of Rand Houses,
Cottars Lane, First Floor. (Drawn
by Gabrielle M. Lanier and Nancy
Van Dolsen.)

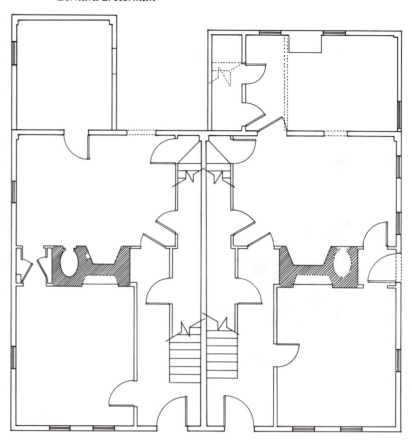

Plaisted and Frost-Beck houses, cooking shared the same space as the dining room; in the Laighton and Barnard-Lord houses, food preparation was placed in cellars; in the Fernald-Tyler dwelling, the kitchen was placed in a lean-to behind the dining room. Thus, the Cottars Lane dwellings suggest two areas of inquiry. First, how do we account for diversity of house forms within what appear to be standardized notions of house size? Second, how do we explain the variations in kitchen placement? The answer to these questions relies in part on the rise of standardization in the preparation of construction timber and in what we might think of as the "sizing" of architecture. Following the fire of 1813, which destroyed the city center, for example, builders advertised houses and building frames in the city newspaper in ways such as these: "A TWO story building 34 feet by 18—stories 9 and 8 in the clear, new sills and flooring, well calculated for a dwelling house, store, or stable," and "A TWO Story Dwelling, partly finished, 38 feet by

18."[17] Also, other houses of similar date and plan are found in nearly identical dimensions throughout the city. Standardization in the building trades, however, does not explain the conflicted notions of service placement within the house. Here, the more likely explanation derives from the ambiguous urban quality of Portsmouth's cityscapes. Undoubtedly a city by eighteenth-century American standards, much of Portsmouth continued to exhibit the village or town-like quality of lots that contain freestanding houses. Thus, on Cottars Lane we see the equivalent of row houses facing full fronted center-passage, single-pile dwellings. Predictably, we also see the urban economy of space associated with cellar kitchens and combination dining room-kitchens side by side with a lean-to cooking room. This sort of ambivalent urban vernacular architecture was far more common in eighteenth- and early-nineteenth-century American cities including even Philadelphia and Baltimore than the row houses associated with those centers in popular images.

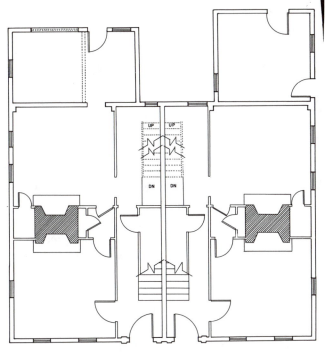

Fig. 17.6. (Above) Plan of Frost and Beck Houses, Cottars Lane, First Floor. (Drawn by Gabrielle M. Lanier and Nancy Van Dolsen.)

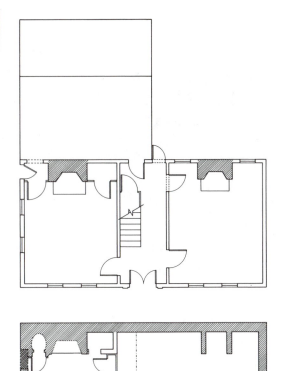

Fig. 17.7. (Right) Plan of Laighton House, Cottars Lane, First Floor and Basement with Kitchen. (Drawn by Gabrielle M. Lanier and Nancy Van Dolsen.)

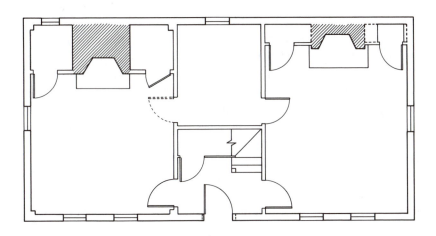

Fig. 17.8. Plan of Barnard-Lord House, Cottars Lane, First Floor. (Drawn by Gabrielle M. Lanier and Nancy Van Dolsen.)

Fig. 17.9. View of the Langdon Mansion on Pleasant Street. (Courtesy, Strawbery Banke Museum Library.)

Returning to the Cottars Lane commuters themselves and the question of human movement in the urban landscape, we now see that the course to work brought the inhabitants of the little community into varying levels of contact with an economically diverse, socially complex architectural environment. Samuel Rand's path to work took him from the doorway of his modest house situated opposite distiller Michael Hooker's mansion and northward up Pleasant Street past the increasingly grand merchants' seats that lined the way to the city center (fig. 17.9). Depending on the actual location of his shoemakers' shop on State Street, Rand may have continued all the way to State or turned east and walked down Pitt through the older, more modest neighborhood north of Puddle Dock. At Washington or Atkinson, Rand would have turned north on the final leg of his morning trek and proceeded past the post-fire buildings to his rented shop in one of the newer storefront tenements built by speculators. Each turning in Rand's course reinforced his place and the place of those whose houses he passed in the evolving urban landscape.

Samuel Rand's way to work and back took him into three different and architecturally distinct environments—his own modest house, the mansions of Pleasant Street, and the State Street commercial district. In looking at these three very distinct environments, we will turn our attention to two aspects of the urban built world shared by Portsmouth with other cities: first, the architectural representation of social hierarchy and segmentation and, second, the process of standardization.[18] Finally, we will return to Rand's own dwelling and take a brief look at the types of housing associated with artisans, minor merchants, and others. Undoubtedly, Rand also encountered in his walks through the city the houses of transient residents and the urban poor, but, due to the current lack of information about the lives and precarious lifestyles of Portsmouth's least affluent residents, they fall outside the scope of this essay. Still, they continuously imposed themselves and their material circumstance on the consciousness of the city's population just as similar individuals did in every other eastern seaboard urban port.[19]

As he turned up Pleasant Street in the morning or returned home at twilight, Samuel Rand passed by the impressive Georgian and Federal houses of several of Portsmouth's mercantile elite. The Wendell, Haven, Wentworth, and Langdon mansions had all been commissioned by Portsmouth's most affluent citizens from the mid-eighteenth century through the early nineteenth. Built with broad stair passages flanked by two rooms on either side and finished with stylish stairs and paneling, these buildings symbolized the social and economic distance between Rand, the shoemaker, and his merchant neighbors. Moreover, where Rand's house possessed a narrow walk that led to a cramped back garden and privy, the mercantile gentry's dwellings possessed deep rear yards furnished with formal gardens, woodhouses, stables, and tenements that were occupied by widows, artisans, laborers, and mariners. The great houses of Pleasant Street presided over the urban landscape in the same manner that their owners' ships dominated the trade that flowed in and out of the city.

The Pleasant Street mansions represented neither the only enclave of elite housing nor the most valuable, highly-assessed mansions in the city. Early colonial-period merchant dwellings, like the MacPhaedris-Warner and Jaffrey houses, were typically sited close to the wharves. The pattern of the close proximity of home place and work place, however, was one that had already become old fashioned by the 1770s. Among the elite houses that continued this pattern was the William Gardner mansion on Mechanic Street, built on rising ground across the street from the wharves and storehouses. In the last quarter of the eighteenth century, Portsmouth's wealthiest citizens were increasingly likely to group themselves in suburban settings, such as the west end of the city along Middle, Islington, and Congress Streets. Here, the most pretentious and stylish Portsmouth houses occupied the crucial points where urban thoroughfares entered and exited the city.[20]

The new mansions of the post-Revolutionary era stood well away from the seat of commerce and were situated along the land routes that connected Portsmouth to its backcountry instead of close to the waterfront that linked the city to trans-Atlantic trade and culture. When people entered the city from the water, their passage went from the seat of economic power inland to the neighborhoods of social authority.[21] After entering the city from the backcountry, folks passed the suburban mansions on their way to the city's business and shipping district. Thus, in a landscape characterized by movement and hierarchy, the "new" suburban mansions occupied the central thoroughfares at the thresholds in and out of the city. If we think of architectural meaning as achieved through strategic location, then the disposition of Portsmouth's nineteenth-century elite neighborhoods actively and symbolically engaged both economic and social imagination to claim the city.

The urban mansions passed by Samuel Rand in 1821 symbolized a cityscape in the process of transformation. The mansions of early-nineteenth-century Portsmouth, both old and new, relate to distinct communities. Their imposing scale, rigid symmetry,

stair-passage plans, and fashionable trim exerted an architectural authority over the urban landscape. In the case of the Pleasant Street houses, architectural authority also defined a social community of cosmopolitan individuals bound together by shared tastes in architecture, literature, and the arts as well as common and competitive interests in the world of trade and urban development. Poor by comparison to merchant families like the Wendells and Havens, Rand still belonged to a comfortably well-off middle class of artisans, shopkeepers, and less affluent traders who owned their houses and operated their own businesses. Rand's house, valued at four hundred dollars, fell in the lower middling range of house values in terms of the total number of dwellings in the city; the best houses, such as the Samuel Larkin and James Sheafe mansions, were worth ten times more. The social effect of the material world of a middle-class Portsmouth artisan like Rand would have been equivalent to that of a "common" Virginia farmer, who, as Dell Upton has pointed out, "was part of the intended audience of the processional landscape, and it served to affirm his *lack* of standing in it."[22]

In the trans-Atlantic world of trade, Portsmouth ship captains and businessmen came in regular contact with other individuals in distant ports who defined a type of "Atlantic culture."[23] As Henry Glassie has demonstrated, the colonial builders of neoclassical or Georgian architecture drew on two lines of architectural thought: the customary meanings encoded in "traditional" house forms and finishes and the social distinctions implicit in academic architectural principles.[24] Merchant housing defined and represented participation in two material and social contexts. On one hand, mansions, like the Gardner house, dominated the local landscape and stood as monuments to individual attainment and power; on the other, these same houses stood on equal footing with similar houses in other cities.[25] The Georgian-style houses of Portsmouth's social elite represent this second community, which we can identify as a broadly defined mercantile society connected not by place but by economic and cultural interests. However, at the same time that the domestic architecture of the urban elite was becoming increasingly regional in character, the lesser buildings of the cityscape were being developed along standardized lines. This seeming paradox is resolved if we look at how dwellings function as social markers. By the late eighteenth century, a truly international urban Atlantic culture was becoming increasingly concentrated in a handful of major trading cities like London, Liverpool, Bristol, New York, Philadelphia, and Boston. As other colonial ports slipped into secondary status or backwater oblivion, they became increasingly provincial in nature. The realm for competitive displays in architecture was no longer so much trans-Atlantic as local. Simultaneously, there was increased desire to develop urban real estate efficiently and profitably. The architectural options that best met speculators' goals were forms of double houses or modified indigenous dwelling types redesigned for urban settings. These are the houses of Cottars Lane.

Samuel Rand's cordwainers' business was situated in one of the ground-floor shops along the brick rows of State Street. Rand's journey to work symbolizes the growing physical separation between work and home that was occurring in early-nineteenth-century urban America. The architecture of the building in which he rented shop space illustrates the growing standardization of Portsmouth's urban environment in a manner that was broadly consistent with other American port cities. The opportunity for remaking Portsmouth's urban appearance was made possible through land clearance, which was facilitated by a series of devastating fires culminating in the catastrophe of 1813.

The burned district, which had once been "the most populous and compact part of town," provided the ground and opportunity for completing the rebuilding of the new commercial center occasioned by the fire of 1802. Response to the loss of housing and commercial areas occurred in several ways. First, the demand for accommodations com-

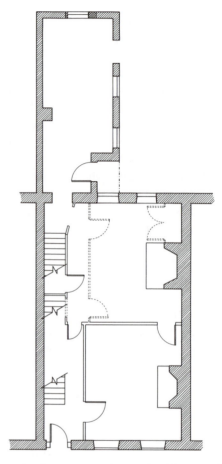

Fig. 17.10. Sheafe Street, Townhouse Plan. The ground floor of this Sheafe Street dwelling consisted of a divided side-passage arrangement with a ground-floor front parlor and back dining room. A service stair ascended from the back passage and a low, one-story shed-roof kitchen extended from the rear of the dwelling. Dashed lines indicate missing, but known, features. (Drawn by Gabrielle M. Lanier.)

pelled people to relocate into other parts of town and forced a temporary rise in multiple households contained in individual buildings. Second, house carpenters quickly banged together roughly finished building frames that could be purchased and moved onto gutted lots. Third, land speculators began to form partnerships for the purpose of acquiring now empty lots and erecting speculative housing.

One such partnership, composed of joiner Jonathan Folsom, cabinetmaker Langley Boardman, and merchant John Abbott, purchased land along the north side of Sheafe Street, where a "house, barn, and other buildings" had stood before the fire.[26] Together they built a row of four three-story brick houses (fig. 17.10). Each dwelling contained an entry and stair passage that opened onto a front parlor and also led to a rear "keeping" or dining room and one-story kitchen wing. Built on nearly identical plans and fitted with similarly executed interior finishes, the four houses were quickly sold to different buyers. In plan, value, and class the Sheafe Street row was part of a national, rather than a regional, image of urban living. Comparable rows composed of houses with similar architectural features and histories of ownership had been erected between 1785 and 1800 on Crown Street in Philadelphia's Southwark and Northern Liberties, along the developing streets of Alexandria, Virginia, and in the new squares of Savannah, Georgia. We also find that the new merchants personified by Boardman and his partners were individuals who accrued capital first through the manipulation of land and secondly through trade.[27] Their vision of the urban landscape was epitomized in the regular brick fronts of the Sheafe Street houses and in the magnificence of their own mansions situated on the city's western thoroughfares. To better understand the significance of the Sheafe Street houses, we will return to Samuel Rand's house at the head of Cottars Lane.

Rand's house was a two-story frame building situated with its gable end to the street and fronting a shallow dooryard and "passage" or pathway that led to the rear of the fenced lot that backed onto South Meeting House Square. The plan and situation of the house represented a type of Portsmouth townhouse that first appeared in the mid-eighteenth century and continued to be built with variations in chimney placement in the decades following the American Revolution. In plan, Rand's house conformed to a center-chimney, lobby entry type found throughout the city. One room deep, the house was organized with its best room, or parlor, overlooking the street. Behind the parlor stood the entry and then the back parlor or dining room. A kitchen wing extended from the rear gable elevation. Shoemaker Jonathan Mendum's Mason Street house, surveyed in 1823, illustrates the plan of one of these dwellings as they were modified in the early 1800s (fig. 17.11). Built with two chimneys placed along the back wall of the house and with a functional progression from formal front parlor back through either the entry or unheated bedroom behind the stairs, keeping or dining room, and kitchen to the separate privy situated in the back corner of the lot, the Mendum house is part of the same formal tradition represented by the Barnard-Lord house on Cottars Lane. Houses following this plan and situated either facing or gable end to the street survive throughout the South End and in other New England seaports, such as Salem and Marblehead.[28]

Why, though, did these gable-fronted houses of Portsmouth gain preference over the sorts of row houses associated with the architecturally redeveloped city center? When we compare the individual plans of the terrace of houses built on Sheafe Street with the number and types of spaces found in the Rand or Mendum houses, we find that they are roughly equivalent. Both possess a lobby entry or passage with a stair to the upper floors, both have two principal downstairs rooms (front parlor and back dining room), and both have evidence of a service wing. The same functional and formal equivalence extended to the new houses of Cottars Lane, where a variety of plan types were used to generate the same sorts of household spaces. In terms of the conservation of urban land, however, the Sheafe Street dwellings and comparable ranges of buildings on State Street were much more efficient than infill houses on other Portsmouth streets. Still, where the economics of land and architecture permitted, folks were more likely to follow the precedent of custom. Despite the presence of compa-

Fig. 17.11. Jonathan Mendum
House Plat. Drawn and recorded
in the Rockingham County deed
books in the early 1800s, the
Mendum plat illustrates the same
basic plan as the Barnard-Lord
house on Cottars Lane. The
service room of the house
abutted the gable end farthest
from the street.

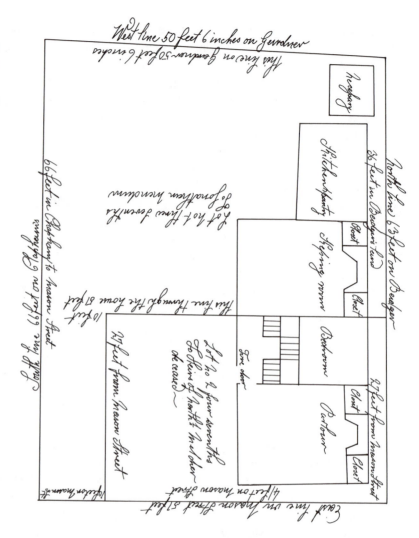

rable household spaces, row houses could not replicate the flow of traditional household traffic or the forms of social interaction associated with older plans. Unlike Baltimore, Philadelphia, New York, London, Hull, or Bristol, Portsmouth did not reach the critical point where land values and an aesthetic vision of a well-ordered city encouraged the creation of solid architectural blocks and the construction of row houses. Without the pressure of rising property values and the intensified use of urban land, there was little incentive to forsake custom.

The image of the neat and regular urban row was an attractive one for developers. Rows made the maximum use of street frontage and provided a standardized product that could be extended the length of a city block. The idea of the row seems to have been attempted with varying degrees of success throughout the length of the eastern seaboard. Early nineteenth-century rows, such as the Union Street block, were built in Salem. The Middle Street row in Newburyport, Massachusetts, was altered within a few years after its construction to incorporate the original open passages from the street to the backyard as finished entries into the houses. In New Castle, Delaware, Cloud's row was erected near the town hall and market house around 1800, but the idea of terraced housing did not become generally popular in the town for another twenty years. Similarly, in Savannah the general acceptance of terrace housing into the domestic urban landscape would not occur until the mid-1800s. In Portsmouth, however, the Sheafe Street row and the double houses of Cottars Lane stand as examples of urban landscape development and housing that defined a threshold that was never crossed.

Samuel Rand's multiple paths through Portsmouth's architectural landscape, like those of his Cottars Lane neighbors, took him past widows' houses, merchants' dwellings, and the shops and stores of the city's commercial core. His daily passage, his house, and the houses of his neighbors affirmed his place in Portsmouth's urban society as surely as networks of debt, partnership, and wealth. Movement through the city was also movement through a changing landscape and changing social relationships characterized by the architectural expression of standardized, segmented, processional landscapes. It was also movement through an urban landscape where customary considerations of house form and function were tested and ultimately retained into the mid-1800s. The separation of home on Cottars Lane from work on State Street, the architectural hierarchy of Pleasant Street, the regular brick rows of State and Sheafe Streets, the crowded households of South End widows that made up the experience of Samuel Rand's walking city, however, were common not just to Portsmouth, but to other American and British port cities of the eighteenth and early nineteenth centuries.

Notes

This essay could not have been written without the help and friendship of Richard Candee. Richard graciously provided great masses of detail about the property histories of the sites discussed here as well as offering a helping hand in the field. His own work is the starting point for anyone interested in the architecture and history of the Portsmouth and Piscataqua River region. I am additionally indebted to David L. Ames, Edward Chappell, Brock Jobe, Gabrielle Lanier, Johanna McBrien, Holly Mitchell, Rebecca Siders, Gerald and Barbara Ward, and the research staff of Strawbery Banke Museum and the Portsmouth Atheneum.

1. The idea of the "walking city" was first advanced in the work of Sam Bass Warner. See *The Private City: Philadelphia in Three Periods of Its Growth* (Philadelphia: University of Pennsylvania Press, 1968; 2d ed., 1987), 11, 13. The "journey to work" appears as the central theme in Theodore Hershberg, Harold E. Cox, Dale B. Light Jr., and Richard R. Greenfield, "The 'Journey-to-Work': An Empirical Investigation of Work, Residence and Transportation, Philadelphia, 1850–1880," Theodore Hershberg, ed., *Philadelphia: Work, Space, Family, and Group Experience in the Nineteenth Century* (New York: Oxford University Press, 1981), 128–73.

2. For background information on property histories and architectural expression throughout Portsmouth, see James Leo Garvin, "Academic Architecture and the Building Trades in the Piscatqua Region of New Hampshire and Maine, 1715–1815," (Ph.D. diss., Boston University, 1983); C. S. Gurney, *Portsmouth Historic and Picturesque* (1902; reprint, Hampton, N.H.: Peter E. Randall for Strawbery Banke Publications, 1981); John Mead Howells, *The Architectural Heritage of the Piscataqua* (Baltimore: Architectural Book Company, 1937).

3. Warner, *The Private City* (1968 ed.), 16–19.

4. Dell Upton, "White and Black Landscapes in Eighteenth-Century Virginia," in *Material Life in America 1600–1860*, ed. Robert Blair St. George (Boston: Northeastern University Press, 1988), 357–69.

5. For other aspects of the processional landscape, see Robert Darnton, "A Bourgeois Puts His World in Order:

The City as a Text," *The Great Cat Massacre: And Other Episodes in French Cultural History* (New York: Vintage Books, 1984), 107–43; Susan G. Davis, *Parades and Power: Street Theatre in Nineteenth-Century Philadelphia* (Philadelphia: Temple University Press, 1986). In his analysis of the processional city, Darnton notes, "In Montpelier, as in India, *homo hierarchicus* thrived through the segmentation of society rather than from its polarization. Instead of dividing into classes, the social order rippled past the onlooker in graduated degrees of *dignités*." The onlooker "noticed invisible demarcations," and "Exclusion and inclusion belonged to the same process of boundary drawing, a process that took place in men's minds as well as in the streets" 123–24. Discussions of urban processional landscapes emphasize the procession itself and focus on the event as civic affirmation or symbolic inversion. While such studies focus on the structure of the event (actual in Davis's work; a literary metaphor in Darnton's), they seldom touch upon the environmental theater of the event. Processions generally are seen as moving past a certain point, as if the historian, like any onlooker, is locked statically into place. The landscape, like the parade or procession, is a dramatic entity with points of emphasis and heightened meaning—but when the parade is over, the processional landscape and all its attendant significances remain.

6. By the early nineteenth century, however, the visual divisions of the house became increasingly subtle as the functional specificity of rooms became more ingrained in the architectural language.

7. The new brick buildings of State Street were occupied in a variety of ways. In some, the ground floor was rented to a commercial tenant, while the upper floors or even the upper rooms were let to one or more tenants. In other instances, the buildings might have single occupants, either owners or tenants, who lived with their families above their shops. Still others were used solely for commercial purposes with the upper floors set aside for storage.

8. There is little consensus and much debate over the qualities that characterize an emergent, early-nineteenth-century American urban middle class. See Stuart M. Blumin, *The Emergence of the Middle Class: Social Experience in the American City, 1760–1900* (Cambridge: Cambridge University Press, 1989).

9. For the basics of urban real estate development, see Thomas Doerflinger, *A Vigorous Spirit of Enterprise: Merchants and Economic Development in Revolutionary Philadelphia* (New York: W. W. Norton, 1987), 178–79, and Elizabeth Blackmar, *Manhattan for Rent, 1785–1850* (Ithaca: Cornell University Press, 1989). Sylvia Porter and Sarah Pearson offer an English perspective in *Whitehaven, 1660–1800* (London: Her Majesty's Stationery Office for the Royal Commission on the Historical Monuments of England, 1991). The process of social emulation and its relationship to urban house design can be found in Blumin, *The Emergence of the Middle Class,* and Peter Borsay, *The English Urban Renaissance: Culture and Society in the Provincial Town, 1660–1770* (Oxford: Clarendon Press, 1989), 42–79, 225–56.

10. The property histories of all the Cottars Lane lots are summarized in Richard M. Candee's *"An-Old-Town-By-the-Sea": Urban Landscapes and Vernacular Building in Portsmouth, New Hampshire, 1660–1990* (Portsmouth: Vernacular Architecture Forum, 1992), 68–73. Langley Boardman's career has been explored in depth by Johanna McBrien. See "The Furniture Industry of Portsmouth, New Hampshire, 1798–1840," in *Portsmouth Furniture: Masterworks of the New Hampshire Seacoast* (Hanover: University Press of New England, forthcoming), and "The Architecture of Portsmouth, New Hampshire, in the Early Republic," (manuscript, 1991).

11. *New Hampshire Gazette,* May 6, 1806. An ad in the *New Hampshire Gazette,* May 1, 1804, noted that Joshua Rand "Has taken the chamber lately occupied by Mr. Josiah Blake, (Buck-street)."

12. *New Hampshire Gazette,* May 6, 1806.

13. Martha Elaine Pinello, "Archaeological Formation Processes and Household Boundaries at Four Domestic Lots in the North End of Portsmouth, New Hampshire, 1730–1830," (M.A. thesis, University of Massachusetts, Boston, 1989), 60–63, 132. See also Aileen Button Agnew, *The Historic Archaeology of Deer Street, Portsmouth, New Hampshire,* (Yarmouth, Maine: Maine Center for Archaeological Studies, 1989), and Kathleen Wheeler, *Prelimi-*

nary Findings from the Phase I Archaeological Survey of 113 Bow Street, Portsmouth, New Hampshire (Brentwood, N.H.: Kathleen Wheeler for the 113 Bow Street Trust, 1990). For other examples of the descent and management of property among women, see Holly Bentley Mitchell, "'Power of Thirds': The Material Lives of Widows, Portsmouth, New Hampshire, 1816–1826," (M.A. thesis, University of Delaware, 1991).

14. Pinello, "Archaeological Formation Processes," 151. The ensuing discussion of the Hart family tea service appears on 66–68.

15. The statistical information on housing values is derived from the Portsmouth city tax assessment for 1823 located in the Portsmouth Public Library. The Cottars Lane and adjacent Pleasant Street dwellings ranged in value from two hundred to fifteen hundred dollars with an average value of just over five hundred dollars. The assessor valued the Chase and Plaisted houses at four hundred dollars each. Also rated at four hundred dollars was the Laighton dwelling across the street. Sampson Lord's house, situated on the lot behind the Rands' former property, stood at three hundred dollars. Farther up the block, the Fernald house had been erected as a single-family residence. By the 1823 assessment, though, the building had been subdivided into two three-hundred-dollar units occupied by a carpenter and shoemaker and their respective households. The two houses at the corners of Cottars Lane and Pleasant Street received the highest valuations. On the west, looking across Pleasant to the home of Samuel Rand, stood Nathaniel Souther's house and the attached bakery, valued together at seven hundred dollars; on the opposite corner loomed the three-story mansion built by William Marshall but used in the 1820s as rental housing for sea captains and minor traders. The most valuable residence, at fifteen hundred dollars, stood around the corner on Pleasant Street and was occupied by Michael Hooker, a successful distiller and merchant; the least valuable house, at two hundred dollars, belonged to stage driver Chester Shattuck.

16. For a summary of Cottars Lane houses and their history of ownership, see Richard M. Candee, *Building Portsmouth: The Neighborhoods and Architecture of New Hampshire's Oldest City* (Portsmouth: Portsmouth Advocates, 1992), 68–73.

17. *New Hampshire Gazette* LIX (12) (Feb. 15, 1814), and LIX (16) (Mar. 22, 1814).

18. Yi-Fu Tuan, *Segmented Worlds and Self: Group Life and Individual Consciousness* (Minneapolis: University of Minnesota Press, 1982), 3–32 and 52–85.

19. Historians have developed increasingly sophisticated ways of discovering and describing the textures and import of ordinary urban lives and material culture. See Billy G. Smith, *The "Lower Sort": Philadelphia's Laboring People, 1750–1800* (Ithaca: Cornell University Press, 1990); Karie Diethorn, "Domestic Servants in Philadelphia, 1780–1830," (research paper for Independence National Historical Park, Philadelphia, 1986); S. J. Wright, "Sojourners and Lodgers in a Provincial Town: The Evidence from Eighteenth-Century Ludlow," *Urban History Yearbook* 17 (Leicester: Leicester University Press, 1990), 14–35; Elizabeth Blackmar, *Manhattan For Rent, 1785–1850* (Ithaca: Cornell University Press, 1989), 44–71.

20. The old mercantile city possessed a backcountry of lesser urban dwellings that gradually merged into the countryside; the new mercantile city used that old backcountry as a buffer between the great houses and the wharves.

21. The passage from waterfront to the western suburbs was neatly summarized by Thomas Aldrich in 1883: "As you leave the riverfront behind you, and pass 'up town,' the streets grow wider, and the architecture becomes more ambitious—streets fringed with beautiful old trees and lined with commodious private dwellings, mostly square white houses, with spacious halls running through the centre" (Thomas Bailey Aldrich, *An Old Town by the Sea* [Boston: Houghton Mifflin, 1893], 22).

22. For those citizens without real property and who typically rented rooms in houses such as Lydia Amazeen's divided house, the gulf between their lot and that of Samuel Rand was dramatic; between themselves and the successful trading class, the gulf was likely incomprehensible.

23. Franklin W. Knight and Peggy K. Liss, eds., *Atlantic Port Cities: Economy, Culture, and Society in the Atlantic World, 1650–1850* (Knoxville: University of Tennessee Press, 1991); Jacob M. Price, "The Economic Function and Growth of American Port Towns in the Eighteenth Century," *Perspectives in American History* 8 (1974), 123–86.

24. Henry Glassie, *Folk Housing in Middle Virginia: The Structural Analysis of Historic Artifacts* (Knoxville: University of Tennessee Press, 1975).

25. Compare, for example, the Georgian and Federal period merchant housing of Portsmouth with that of Charleston, South Carolina. Along Charleston's East Bay Street, overlooking the city's commercial waterfront were situated Georgian merchants' housing, such as Gabriel Manigault's mansion. On the exterior, the mansions of Portsmouth and Charleston are regionally distinct in terms of the architectural and commercial societies in which they stood; on the interior, these houses reflect trans-Atlantic connections in which community is defined materially in matters of architectural finish and tasteful furnishings. Architectural interiors in the most formal rooms of the house articulate the continuity and community of Atlantic mercantile culture.

26. Candee, *Building Portsmouth,* 99; Peyton R. Freeman to Thomas Bailey, Rockingham County, N.H., Deeds, vol. 209 (1815): 307–8; Jonathan Folsom, John Abbot, and Langley Boardman agreement with Thomas D. Bailey, Rockingham Co., N.H., Deeds, vol. 209 (1815): 308–9.

27. I am indebted to Johanna McBrien, who kindly shared her research on Langley Boardman's furniture making and real estate speculation activities. See Johanna McBrien, "The Portsmouth Furniture Industry, 1798–1840," (M.A. thesis, University of Delaware, 1992).

28. In Marblehead, for example, gable-fronted houses fall into two functional categories: first, there are those that front side yards and are entirely residential; second, there are buildings with ground-floor or cellar commercial premises and upper-story living accommodations. Like the single houses and combination dwelling-with-lower-floor shops of Charleston, these buildings represent the combined appropriation of building forms associated with rural, village, and urban landscapes.

Chapter 18

From Roadside Camps to Garden Homes: Housing and Community Planning for California's Migrant Work Force, 1935–1941

Greg Hise

The Farm Security Administration (FSA) and its predecessor, the Resettlement Administration, planned and managed thirteen labor camps for California's seasonal agricultural workers between 1936 and 1941. Central to this program was the integration of physical planning with social reform. This study examines the comprehensive planning principles, rationalization of building practice, and social policy the FSA promoted. Engineers and architects employed by these agencies designed rural communities that could be constructed quickly and efficiently at minimum cost. The FSA staff drew on formal precedents enunciated by planning theorists, such as Clarence Perry, Henry Wright, and Clarence Stein, and the social policy formulated by housing reformers, including Edith Elmer Wood and Catherine Bauer, to provide migrant field hands and their families safe and sanitary living environments.[1]

The FSA's broader objective was the creation of a cooperative social order. Its failure at the latter, an experiment in "guided democracy," has been well documented in histories of the Depression and Dust Bowl migration.[2] By extension, the camps themselves have been interpreted as failures. However, during five years of design research, professionals at the Region IX Engineering Office (headquartered in San Francisco) developed a sophisticated prototype for the creation of new communities. The FSA utilized their plans and the construction techniques they perfected throughout the western states, from Washington and Idaho to Colorado, Arizona, and Texas. And even though this evolu-

tion in rural new town design was cut short by the World War II defense emergency, the innovations FSA staff developed were continued and, in some cases, accelerated after the agency and many of its key personnel were drafted to meet the increasing demand for industrial war-worker communities in California.

In terms of social reform and social planning, the FSA camp program can be seen as the rural counterpart of the Progressives' better-known response to the industrial city, a lineage that can be traced back to settlement workers and the community center movement. Like the Progressives, the FSA addressed the needs of a disadvantaged and dispossessed labor force: agricultural workers were perceived as casualties of unregulated corporatism and unrestrained capitalism. Improved living conditions, environmental reformers believed, would provide the foundation on which new social relations could be structured. The FSA constructed their strategy around rationalized, minimum house types, standardized site plans, and the completion of model camps. Each of these elements had direct ties to a Progressive Era precedent, the California Commission on Immigration and Housing (CCIH), which Governor Hiram Johnson empowered in 1915 to establish codes and enforce standards. In fact, the FSA program advanced a number of CCIH policies, and key players, from the administration, design staff, and field personnel, shared the Progressives' conviction that reconfiguring spatial relations would in turn condition social relations.[3]

The creation of new communities, the emphasis on community planning, and the experiments with construction technologies carried out in California were all consistent with the national program of the Resettlement Administration (1934–36). Through its Division of Subsistence Homesteads, this agency pioneered federal intervention into rural living conditions and the direct provision of improved housing. The Resettlement Administration's better-known Greenbelt program, and the three new town projects undertaken in Maryland (Greenbelt), Wisconsin (Greendale), and Ohio (Greenhills) in 1935, served as "demonstrations of a new and highly improved technique of land-use and town planning."[4]

Within this context, two factors made the California program unique. Nationally, the Resettlement Administration's mandate was to assist low-income farm families.[5] In California, however, relief workers confronted a different problem. The rural poor were not marginal farmers but the lowest strata in a highly mechanized and productive system of industrial agriculture. Through the work of reformers and labor advocates, the Resettlement Administration eventually extended its mandate to include these itinerant farm laborers. The FSA communities marked the first time the federal government acknowledged the housing needs of this previously "invisible" work force.[6]

Unlike the subsistence homestead projects and the Greenbelt new towns, community building for rural relief in California had to address the needs of a mobile and fluctuating population. The seasonal rise and fall in absolute numbers and the continual turnover of residents—the second factor that distinguished the California program from those of other parts of the country—presented the

Fig. 18.1. Orange Pickers' Camp, Farmersville, Tulare County, California, November 1938. (Courtesy, Library of Congress/ USOWI Collection.)

we can readily discern the formal repertoire environmental reformers had advanced during the preceding two decades.

In March 1935, Paul Taylor, field director for the California Division of Rural Rehabilitation, submitted an application to the State Emergency Relief Administration requesting one hundred thousand dollars to erect forty camps for the "forgotten men, women, and children of California." Taylor formulated his request following fieldwork that included surveys of squalid, unhealthful roadside camps and "Hoovervilles"—a term whose popularity attests to the association of economic hardship and deprivation with the Hoover administration.[7] Photographer Dorothea Lange accompanied Taylor and poignantly rendered these living conditions (fig. 18.1). Taylor's proposal outlined an across-the-board aid package that would improve housing for a vast number of destitute families regardless of country or state of origin, length of residency in California, or future potential for rehabilitation to the consuming class. Taylor knew these camps could not be self-liquidating; he proposed labor in lieu of rent and argued that precisely where the need was greatest—due either to extreme seasonality of crops or severity of climate—was where the largest amount of aid should be extended.[8]

In response to Taylor's request, the state of California began constructing migrant camps at Arvin and Marysville in September 1935. These initial settlements became the foundation for the FSA program (fig. 18.2). Both camps opened later that year and each housed a hundred families. The plan was extremely simple, consisting of little more than tent sites improved by the addition of tie rails and three "sanitary units" or "utility" buildings, all organized around a central community facility and anchored by an orthogonal street system. The sanitary units contained services including washrooms and showers, laundry facilities, and flush toilets; one unit for every forty tents was standard. Entry was by a single gate adjacent to the camp office. From this vantage point FSA staff could

Fig. 18.2. FSA Migrant Camps in California. (Drawing by Lisa Padilla.)

Region IX staff with a different planning and design problem than either the homestead or Greenbelt initiatives.

In response to these demands, FSA designers devised an overarching formal typology: a permanent institutional core surrounded by impermanent dwellings. The challenge they faced in the early camps was to integrate these two elements. At first the diagram itself served as the site plan. But as the program expanded to encompass permanent housing and the staff's technical expertise increased, the FSA planners continually assessed and reworked the site plan. By 1941 at Woodville—the Region IX showcase of a model rural new town—

Fig. 18.3. FSA Camp, Brawley,
California. Note tent platform,
arbor, and storage unit.
(Courtesy, Library of
Congress/USOWI Collection.)

monitor residents and visitors alike. The following
year, the state turned over Marysville and Arvin to
the Resettlement Administration. The agency's *Final Budget* of March 30, 1936, specified the addition
of tent platforms and shade arbors, additional sanitary units, an assembly room and nursery, recreational facilities and playground, and landscaping.[9]

Immediately after taking on the two demonstration state camps, the Resettlement Administration
began four additional projects at Shafter, Winters,
Coachella, and Brawley. A photograph taken at
Brawley illustrates improvements made to the Spartan conditions at Arvin and Marysville (fig. 18.3).
However, even with the addition of a storage unit
and arbor, and the elaboration of the community
building, these initial camps aligned with the populist vision first advanced by progressives such as
Paul Taylor and Carey McWilliams. They envisioned

these settlements as key components of a relief
program and intended them to house the largest
number of migrants possible at a cost low enough
to allow construction throughout the state.[10]

In many respects the site planning and physical
plant of these camps followed the codes and standards the CCIH enacted and enforced through the
State Labor Camp Act (1915).[11] The camps provided
sanitary, impermanent housing laid out in neat
rows, a straightforward diagram of programmatic
requirements. Each shelter was a repetitive module that satisfied the short-term needs of a rotating
population of farm-working families. The camp
personnel occupied the only year-round dwelling,
located at the camp entry, to allow for monitoring
and control. In other words, the state, and later the
federal government, responded to the Dust Bowl
migration by instituting a relief program that, at

least initially, was overlaid onto an existing program of labor reform.

Consistent with the CCIH's emphasis on educating private growers, the first camps undertaken by the Resettlement Administration were justified to a hostile electorate as models that large-scale producers could emulate. What made the FSA settlements different, however, was not their tidy rows of tents or gravel walks and streets, but their social planning. This community focus was evident in the permanent, centralized communal facilities that served to stabilize camp life, to organize the floating pool of workers for potential employment or state relief, and to introduce the migrants to "modern" standards of health and hygiene.[12]

Two factors explain the FSA's attention to social planning and the inclusion of permanent community facilities. The first was an ongoing demographic shift in the work force. Although the Dust Bowl migration did not begin in earnest until 1933—and only reached its peak during the years from 1935 to 1938—it was clear during the 1920s that the seasonal agricultural labor force was changing. Then, in 1929, the first deportation drives and forced repatriation of Mexican "nationals" accelerated this transition.[13]

The rising percentage of native-born, white families altered the state and federal governments' response to the plight of agricultural migrants. According to Carey McWilliams, the roots of this change can be traced to the rapid expansion of cotton acreage in the San Joaquin Valley immediately after the First World War. According to a report filed by the CCIH's Supervisor of Camp Inspection: "The labor supply for cotton this season [1925] consists of a majority of Mexicans, the balance being American and Negro cotton pickers from Oklahoma and other southern states who are coming into the Valley in answer to advertisements placed in southern papers."[14]

Secondly, unlike the peripatetic "foreigners" whom they replaced, the "American" family groups came to California with every intention of remaining beyond the planting and harvest seasons. Farm-working families began to occupy private camps for prolonged periods, and Okies and Arkies flooded the state's auto camps and battened down for the winter.[15]

An editorial in the *San Francisco News* placed the change squarely with the influx of families from the drought-afflicted states.

> It took a riot [at Wheatland] in which a district attorney, a sheriff, and two strikers were killed to arouse California to the need of cleaning up conditions for migratory laborers in 1913 when the picking was done almost entirely by single men. Growers provided camps for them, and the State Immigration and Housing Commission enforce[d] standards. Today a different problem exists. The harvesting is done by whole families instead of by single men, and individual growers can no longer provide adequate camps. So the families squat by the side of the road or in vacant fields.[16]

A housing survey of Tulare County relief clients conducted by the California State Relief Administration offers a graphic depiction of the conditions Okies and Arkies encountered. Tulare is at the center of the San Joaquin Valley, in the south-central cotton belt identified by McWilliams. Southwest migrants' familiarity with the crop made Tulare a destination of choice. Okies were a majority of the thirty-seven thousand individuals (35 percent of the county's residents) receiving assistance. Representative of cases in the administration's report was a family of thirteen residing in a Farmersville camp. Their shelter consisted of two tents pitched together. The surveyor recorded conditions as: "Three rickety beds with straw mattresses lined the rear and one side; in front stood a wood stove with box shelves nearby. A plank served as a table. A two-foot aisle ran down the middle; here two boys slept. There was only a dirt floor, no electricity, and water was hauled from a pump nearby. Two outhouses served the entire camp of twelve families."[17] In other words, the Dust Bowl influx overlaid a new set of factors onto an existing problem. Both the demographic and temporal shifts dramatically altered the direction of housing and community building for rural workers.

According to the best statistical analyses the FSA could generate, in the late 1930s California agriculture required between a hundred and seventy and two hundred thousand seasonal workers. At this time, the number of families following the crops reached upwards of a hundred and twenty-five thousand.[18] These young family groups required expanded community services, and the FSA camp managers responded by instituting a variety of programs. They encouraged the formation of an elected camp council and urged residents to participate in civic affairs and attend council meetings. The FSA sponsored reading groups, sewing clubs, and community newspapers. Residents initiated additional programs. They established "good neighbors" clubs to acculturate newcomers, child welfare committees to impress on recent arrivals the importance of personal health and hygiene, and recreational committees to promote athletics and sponsor competitive events.

The architectural embodiment of this cooperative system and the visual focus of the camp layout was the community center. At the community center, camp council meetings were held, classes were offered by agricultural extension personnel and home management specialists from the Bureau of Home Economics (USDA), and large social events, such as plays and Saturday night dances, occurred. At first, the assembly site was nothing more than an enlarged shelter, a platform that was covered when needed. As the importance of the centers for community life became apparent, the FSA design staff secured approval for permanent structures. At this point the community buildings achieved new symbolic significance through their contrasting construction, but they remained a large, flexible space that could be readily adapted by the residents for a variety of functional needs.[19]

It was at Westley, which opened in November 1938, that the Region IX staff took the first steps toward construction efficiencies, standardization, and scale economies. The metal shelters were one product of that effort (fig. 18.4). These units were designed as a more durable substitute for cotton tents and were intended to provide improved protection from inclement weather. Manufacturers delivered the shelters in five panels. At the site a crew of six could assemble a finished structure in ten minutes. Each unit included a covered porch and a storage area with built-in shelves. In addition, the FSA provisioned each family with two iron beds, two iron benches, and a kerosene stove. Tennessee Coal and Iron Company produced and delivered these efficient, ready-to-assemble units at a cost of $150. They were affordable, long lasting, and easy to erect.[20] However, while the metal shelters provided a much-needed improvement over makeshift canvas tents, they were, as one resident described them, "little more than an experiment."[21]

Then, beginning in 1938 at Arvin, the Region IX office decided to retrofit the California projects with small, single-family cabins or "garden homes." (fig. 18.5). These 240-square-foot dwellings contained a kitchen, bath with shower, dining area, and cot. Two additional beds occupied a sleeping porch that could be closed off for winter occupancy. These units rented for $8.20 a month furnished including utilities. The total construction figure of $550 fixed the rent. Because hard costs (services and grading) accounted for most of the final cost, the FSA staff decided to double the square-footage for all the garden homes constructed after Arvin.[22]

The FSA followed the garden homes by appending two-story, multifamily housing blocks to the existing settlements. As the complexity of the labor camps' programmatic requirements and the staff's experience and expertise increased, the FSA's planning for and production of permanent housing evolved. The drive for efficiency and low cost was operational at every level. FSA engineers strove to develop building and unit designs of maximum

Fig. 18.4. Metal Shelter, FSA Camp, Visalia, California, March 1940. (Courtesy, Library of Congress/USOWI Collection.)

Fig. 18.5. Garden Home, FSA Camp, Arvin, California, 1938. (Courtesy, Library of Congress/USOWI Collection.)

flexibility within a rational kit of parts. They organized housing production as a series of operations that could be performed economically and efficiently by teams of workmen. Pre-engineering set the stage for horizontal building practices, and workmen created on-site shops for the production of multiple subassemblies that were then distributed to individual building lots. From programming through site analysis to interior finishes, the later camps displayed a remarkable degree of co-ordination.

In their 1943 study *The History of Prefabrication,* Alfred Bruce and Harold Sandbank singled out the FSA projects as essential laboratories for quantity production. "The FSA, during the period prefabrication was growing to maturity, sponsored the development of whole communities of low-cost homes using varied types of construction in what might be called an actual field laboratory of prefab housing. It has placed an emphasis on both low-cost and mass-scale production, attempting to develop complete plans for communities based on mass-scale operations." The authors concluded that the FSA, along with the Tennessee Valley Authority, had been the "stimulation for the actual use of prefabrication in direct efforts to provide and erect low-cost homes."[23]

The same drive to lower costs and improve efficiency that generated pre-engineering and rationalized building operations led to a reworking of the camp plan as well. At Westley, the orthogonal grid that ordered the first camps was replaced by a new geometry: a double-loaded hexagon. FSA designers offered a rationalist explanation for their choice of a hexagonal plan. They determined this configuration allowed for a more efficient layout of service lines and other infrastructure. The hexagon also offered a reduction in the built site area since the shelters, which followed the pattern of access roads, could be laid out more economically. This permitted planners to dedicate a higher percentage of land to pedestrian circulation, recreation, and shared, open space.[24]

While the functional benefits that accrued from this plan were significant, the most efficient plan—favored by the FSA staff—was a circular scheme. The circle is a planning ideal with deep historical roots. Both as a diagram and when plotted on the ground, the circle invokes a complex symbolic language resonant of centripetal forces. Centrality, or at least prominence, was precisely what the FSA camp managers desired; the hexagon created a dominant and convenient locale for community facilities.

As a planning device, the circle, or, in this case, a modified circle, also served to graduate and rank importance through relative distance from the center. It is important to note that at Westley, shelter was zoned by type for the first time. The inner ring of the double-loaded hexagon was reserved for metal shelters while tent platforms formed the outer ring. The suggestion is that longer-term occupants would locate along the inner ring, and, as the camp population thinned, a more stable core of residents would remain clustered around the community center.

Yuba City (completed in February 1940) was the first project planned with permanent housing from its inception (fig. 18.6). At Yuba City, FSA planners sited the multifamily units to take advantage of the shade offered by an existing cypress grove. They arranged each of the twelve sixplexes in an orderly east-west orientation to maximize exposure to prevailing breezes.[25] However, it is evident from the aerial photograph that even though Yuba City was programmed for permanent housing from its conception, the camp contained two independent spatial orders. On the one hand, the shelters and tent sites were organized in the familiar hexagonal configuration around the community center and shared facilities. The permanent housing, on the other hand, was organized according to climatic concerns and centered on the cypress grove.

The plan's dual foci had important parallels with emerging FSA policy. Whereas the early camps were predicated on the provision of relief—through improved shelter conditions and access to state relief programs—and were intended to address the needs of the largest number of migrants possible, the introduction of permanent housing signaled a policy shift. Now the FSA directorship began to focus its attention on transforming agricultural laborers and their families from a seasonal, migrant work force to a fixed population that supplemented wage work in growers' fields with domestic production for self-sufficiency. The multifamily units and garden cottages were essential components for that effort.

Only after the Region IX staff turned their attention to the design of permanent satellite communities did an integrated, comprehensive master plan result. This was the planners' stated objective at Woodville, a model rural new town. In his article on the FSA's planning evolution, the architect Vernon DeMars suggested that an observer could

Fig. 18.6. FSA Camp, Yuba City, California. (Courtesy, Library of Congress/USOWI Collection.)

see the "general pattern [that] agricultural workers housing will take in the future" at Woodville. Moreover, the project demonstrated the "important task of testing new patterns, unencumbered by the millstone of land values or restrictions imposed by existing land patterns."[26]

According to DeMars, Woodville was conceived as the "nucleus for a new small town." At this point, FSA settlements were no longer seen as way stations, and the problem became how to develop a rural node that could function as a self-contained community and, at the same time, have the infrastructure and facilities in place to serve as a nucleus for the future development of a complete new town.[27]

At Woodville, the FSA designers adhered closely and, in some cases, overtly to the planning principles advanced by environmental reformers. The site plan reveals these attributes and illustrates how the Region IX planners integrated the need for temporary housing and community services with the new directives of a permanent settlement (fig. 18.7).[28] As constructed, the community occupied eighty acres of a 160-acre parcel. The site is in Tulare County, seven miles from the town of Porterville and ten miles from Highway 99, on the northwest corner formed by the intersection of a north-south artery—state route J27—and an east-west feeder—Tulare County Avenue 160. The FSA planners forecast J27 would become a major thoroughfare. Given this, they elected to locate the major entry off J27, but developed two strategies to mitigate traffic's detrimental effects on the community. First, they designated a permanent greenbelt paralleling the roadway for the entire stretch of the community to "discourage the establishment of stores [and businesses] opposite the entry." Second, they set the major axis of the nascent community perpendicular to the road to "point the direction of future growth."[29]

Within this transit armature, the Region IX staff located 313 housing units. Note, however, that unlike the Yuba City site plan, at Woodville the hous-ing was zoned by type within an integrated and hierarchically organized master plan. The two types of temporary housing, tent platforms and metal shelters, were located in the northwest quadrant, farthest from the entry. Contrary to the overall regularity generated by orthogonal planning at the early camps or the strict geometry of the hexagonal model at Westley and Yuba City, the tents, and particularly the shelters, were arrayed with greater variety. The gridded tent sites lay along a series of minor streets that fed into a cul-de-sac. Shared services fronted the two blocks formed by the street abutting the cul-de-sac. The metal shelters shared this studied informality and were further elaborated by the inclusion of minor pedestrian spurs. Rather than addressing the street, the shelters opened out to shared common space. The common was formed by restricting services and vehicular access to the cul-de-sacs. Although the FSA stated its intention to "retire" the impermanent units and replace them with permanent housing, the overall planning of these shelters displayed a considerable degree of care and integration with the permanent units and the community center.

If we turn to the multifamily apartments and garden homes, the links to neighborhood unit principles and planning strategies identified with Clarence Perry, Henry Wright, and Clarence Stein are discernible. For example, the FSA site planners elected to situate the multifamily units at the point of contact between the new community and the surrounding landscape. This particular strategy can be traced back to Grovesnor Atterbury and Frederick Law Olmsted Jr.'s plan for the Russell Sage Foundation's Forest Hills Gardens (1910). At Woodville, the apartments retain the heliotropic orientation noted at Westley. Their siting, sixty degrees off the east-west axis, allowed for private backyards and public lawns as well as convenient access to the residents' allotment gardens.

The garden homes were arranged along cul-de-sacs on eighth-acre plots. In an interview, DeMars acknowledged the debt to Stein and Wright's de-

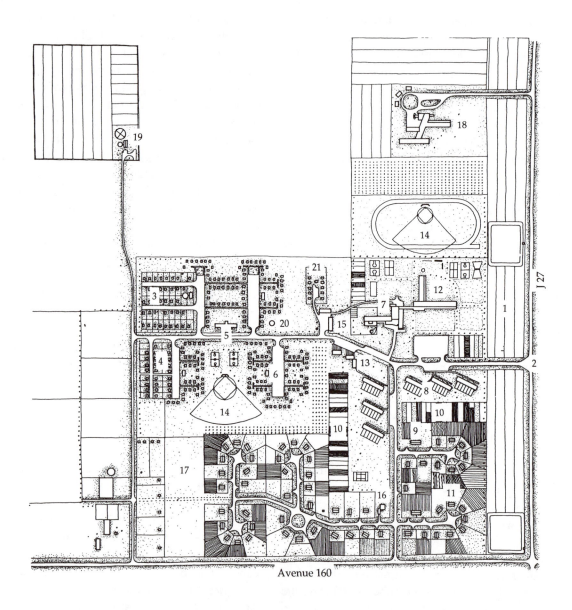

Legend:

1. Greenbelt
2. Entry
3. Tent Slabs
4. Metal Shelters
5. Central Utility
6. Comfort Station
7. Community Center
8. Six-Family Row Houses
9. Duplexes
10. Allotment Gardens
11. Garden Homes
12. School
13. Store
14. Baseball Diamond
15. Gatehouse
16. Manager's House
17. Future Homes
18. Future Hospital
19. Sewage Disposal
20. Water Tower
21. Isolation Unit

Fig. 18.7. Site Plan, FSA Camp, Woodville, California. (Roger Montgomery/Peregrine-Smith Books.)

sign for Radburn, New Jersey (1929). In addition, the relatively large lots display the influence of the national subsistence homestead program and large-scale California projects, such as the FSA's agricultural cooperative at Mineral King. It was generally assumed that individual family gardens would provide for both sustenance and a supplemental income. Together, the thirty-six apartments and thirty-seven garden homes formed the southeast quadrant. On the plan, the anticipated extension of these units to the southwest was clearly indicated.

The highly articulated community center, school, and cooperative store—flanked to the south by the apartments—a grouping which the FSA referred to simply as "the center," formed the hub around which the housing-types were organized (fig. 18.8). The centrality of the school and the community center cluster resonated with the formal dictates of neighborhood unit planning. The social program did as well. The complex included space for adult education, home economics classes, and a library. Adults and children could participate in and attend performances at the community stage or larger assembly hall. In addition, there was a nursery school, a clinic, and the camp offices.[30] The lineage of all these functions can be traced to the Progressive Era community center movement. Playfields, including a baseball diamond, were sited directly adjacent to the elementary school. (An additional diamond was located just south of the central utility building between two cul-de-sacs of metal shelters.) Recreation was an essential ingredient for the balanced community package.

Woodville exemplified rational and comprehensive community planning. Therefore, it is informative to analyze its physical and social programs in the explicit terms and conditions identified by environmental and social reformers. At the community scale, Woodville was bounded by an arterial street (Avenue 160) and a county highway (J27) that provided ease of access. With the inclusion of a landscaped buffer, the community's edges were clearly articulated. Internally, the FSA designers

Fig. 18.8. FSA Camp, Woodville, California. (Courtesy, Library of Congress/USOWI Collection.)

adopted formal and visual strategies to reinforce a "sense of belonging" and promote the individual's identification with the neighborhood. They achieved comprehensibility at multiple scales. At the master plan level, functional segregation and clearly defined land-uses—distinctive housing-types, a commercial core, community facilities, and recreation—encouraged legibility. And, while these distinct uses were clearly articulated, at the same time they were coordinated and fit within the dictates of a coherent, overall scheme.

One strategy the planners applied was a hierarchical and highly specialized circulation system. From the pedestrian foot spurs that led residents between the cul-de-sacs and minor streets into a common green to the main collector lined by the cooperative store, school, community center, and medium-density housing that channeled residents out to the highway, we recognize the dictates of superblock planning. At Woodville, site planning for infrastructure and services, the street pattern, and the location of housing followed these principles. The site planners applied them skillfully and structured the circulation system to heighten the focus on the community center and school.

The FSA planners promoted Woodville as a model for new satellite communities. According to DeMars, it was "endowed not only with the necessities but many of the amenities of living." Woodville lacked one important element considered essential for satellite development, however: proximity to diverse sources of steady employment. Yet DeMars and others remained optimistic: "Perhaps the decentralization of industry will really come, and a balance may be achieved between work in the factory and work in the field. Perhaps with the availability of cheap electric power [from the Colorado River project], raw materials could be processed at their source into finished products."[31]

Even though the constitutive elements that formed Woodville—the impermanent tents and metal shelters, the lightly constructed apartments, and the five-hundred-square-foot garden homes—could be dismissed as inconsequential, taken as a whole the project was significant. Through a model rural community such as Woodville, the FSA planners interpreted and reconfigured the formal vocabulary of modern community planning and, in turn, inserted themselves into the ongoing discourse. At Woodville, the ideals formulated and promoted by a broad cross section of social and environmental reformers, government agencies, and business leaders—all of whom turned their attention to questions of housing for wage earners and the proper spatial relationship between housing and the workplace during the economic crises of the 1920s and 1930s—were put into practice.

Although the FSA program in California was grafted onto a broader and, in many respects, antithetical national mandate, and even though the communities constructed could never house more than ten thousand of the approximately a hundred and fifty thousand farm workers in the state, the FSA experiment did have an impact. These rural settlements served, much as their promoters and sponsors had argued, as an unparalleled opportunity to test and refine the hypotheses and proposals of planners and reformers. Their models might have remained just that. But the exigencies of the Depression and the particular configuration of the federal government's response to this crisis created the context for applying the formal, technical, and social programs formulated during the preceding two decades. And once the California projects were completed, they offered a visible representation of low-cost satellite community-building. Moreover, the federal sponsorship of these experiments legitimized modern community planning and industrialized housing.

Notes

I want to thank Paula Fass and James Gregory for critiquing an earlier version of this essay. Following the Vernacular Architecture Forum annual meeting in Lexington, Kentucky, Elizabeth Cromley, Paul Groth, Richard Longstreth, Dell Upton, Richard Walker, and an anonymous reader offered helpful suggestions for revisions. In *Mass-Housing and Community Planning in California, 1920–1950* (Baltimore: Johns Hopkins University Press, forthcoming 1995) I place the FSA camp program in the context of post–World War II urban expansion.

1. Environmental and social reformers produced a vast literature that examined community planning and housing. I consulted the manuscripts and reprints in the Edith Elmer Wood Papers, The Avery Library, Columbia University, and the Catherine Bauer Wurster Papers, The Bancroft Library, University of California, Berkeley. See also Clarence Perry, *The Neighborhood Unit, Monograph I* in *Neighborhood and Community Planning,* Vol. 7 of the *Regional Survey of New York and Its Environs* (New York: Committee on Regional Plans of New York and Its Environs, 1929), and Clarence Stein, *Toward New Towns for America* (Cambridge, Mass.: MIT Press, 1951). Useful interpretive studies are Roy Lubove, *Community Planning in the 1920s* (Pittsburgh: University of Pittsburgh Press, 1963), Gertrude S. Fish, ed., *The Story of Housing* (New York: Macmillan, 1979), and Nathaniel S. Keith, *Politics and the Housing Crisis Since 1930* (New York: Universe Books, 1973).

2. See especially Walter J. Stein, *California and the Dust Bowl Migration* (Westport, Conn.: Greenwood Press, 1973) and "A New Deal Experiment with Guided Democracy: The FSA Migrant Camps in California," Canadian Historical Association, *Historical Papers: 1970* (Toronto: University of Toronto Press, 1970).

3. In "How New Deal Agencies are Affecting Family Life," M. L. Wilson, the first director of the Subsistence Homestead program, wrote: "Somehow, or in some way, the attitudes and lives of the families who occupy these communities must be integrated so as to provide a new and different view of life and a new and different set of values." Cited in Paul K. Conkin, *Tomorrow a New World: The New Deal Community Program* (New York: Da Capo Press, 1976), 102.

4. See Conkin, *Tomorrow a New World* for a history of the subsistence homesteads. On the Greenbelt communities, see Joseph L. Arnold, *The New Deal in the Suburbs: A History of the Greenbelt Town Program, 1935–1954* (Columbus: Ohio State University Press, 1971), and Stein, *Toward New Towns for America.*

5. To accomplish this, the administration implemented three major programs: the extension of credit to help offset the boom and bust cycles of small farming; the resettlement of destitute families on productive land; and land conservation projects (either retiring or reforesting submarginal acreage).

6. Some members of the Resettlement Administration staff viewed the marginality of the California program as an asset. In a letter to Gardner Jackson, Jonathan Garst noted: "[W]e are however in a wonderful position. We can be legionnaires and still radical in this state. We wrap the constitution about us and wave the American flag. . . . I think that the main reason [for our support] is that you can illustrate the poverty of a migratory worker better than you can in the case of a textile worker in Massachusetts or in North Carolina." Garst to Jackson, Sept. 2, 1936, in box 31, Jackson Papers, FDR Library.

7. As head of the California Division of Immigration and Housing (DIH), McWilliams knew firsthand the squalid living conditions in California's roadside camps and Hoovervilles. Because the DIH inspected private camps, he was aware of their frequently oppressive conditions. In testimony to the LaFollette committee, he stressed the coercion employers exercised through foremen, contractors, and ranch managers. However, the DIH hesitated to enforce the law and to condemn employer housing, fearing it would force migrants into illegal and even more unhealthful squatter settlements. Many growers' camps included company stores, and laborers were paid in scrip, an added infringement. In fact, it was the boast of the Herman Baker Camp in Madera County that no one who

worked there left with their earnings. For McWilliams' testimony, see the clippings contained in carton 3, folder 89, of the Farm Security Administration-San Francisco Collection, Bancroft Library, University of California, Berkeley (hereafter cited as FSA-SF Collection), especially "LaFollette Committee Resumes Hearings Here, Studies Migrant Problem," *San Francisco News,* Jan. 24, 1940. For the Baker Camp report, see United States Department of Agriculture, Resettlement Administration, "Labor Camp Schedule," Aug. 25, 1936, carton 3, folder 77, FSA-SF Collection. On the DIH position, see "Completion Report: Marysville, Exhibit A: Social and Economic Justification," in Farmers Home Administration, Washington National Records Center, Record Group 96 (hereafter cited as WNRC-RG96), box 209, folder LR-89-CF-25, Project Records, 1935–40.

8. "Establishment of Rural Rehabilitation Camps for Migrants in California," memo dated Mar. 15, 1935, to Harry E. Drobish, Director of Rural Rehabilitation, Lot 898, Prints and Photographs Division, Library of Congress. Drobish subsequently sent the document to Frank Y. McLaughlin, administrator, California State Emergency Relief Administration.

9. In addition to a detailed analysis of project expenses—the bottom line a miserly $384 per unit—the report concluded: "Family incomes will be derived from migratory agricultural employment as at present. No provision has been made for liquidating the cost of this project" WNRC-RG96, "Region IX: California, RF-CF-25 and RF-CF-26," box 209, folder LR-89-CF-25, Project Records, 1935–1940.

10. In a Feb. 5, 1937, editorial, the *San Francisco News* argued that the Arvin and Marysville camps were "invaluable" and served "as demonstrations of what can and should be done. . . . That is why they have been so bitterly fought by reactionary influences intent on keeping migratory farm workers in a state approaching peonage."

11. See the State Labor Code, *Labor Camp Act: Sections 2410–2425, Article 4* (1915), and the California Department of Industrial Relations, "Employee Housing: Labor Camps: Minimum Requirements," n.d.

12. In John Steinbeck's fictional account of the Okie migration, *The Grapes of Wrath* (New York: Viking, 1939), the first thing the Joad women did when they arrived in the "Government Camp" was to wash up where you "get in a little stall-like, an' you turn handles, an' water comes a-floodin' down on you—hot water or col' water, jus' like you want it" (339). In 1940 Charles Todd and Richard Sonkin interviewed Mrs. Becker from Texarkana who described how she learned the hot water and laundering systems from "overseers," and she in turn helped organize a "welfare" group that brought assistance to the needy at private camps. The FSA camps also served as agents of acculturation through health-care clinics and offered many residents their first chance to benefit from up-to-date appliances. Todd-Sonkin Recordings, American Folklife Center, Library of Congress. Interview with Mr. and Mrs. J. W. Becker, tape #4145-56A/B, Aug. 16, 1940, Shafter, Calif.

13. On the repatriation of Mexican workers, see Camille Guerin-Gonzales, "Cycles of Immigration and Repatriation: Mexican Farmworkers in California Agriculture, 1900–1940," (Ph.D. diss., University of California, Riverside, 1985).

14. Report dated Oct. 1, 1925, cited in McWilliams, "The Housing of Migratory Labor." James N. Gregory analyzed the complexities of this migration in *American Exodus: The Dust Bowl Migration and Okie Culture in California* (New York: Oxford University Press, 1989). In "Migration Chains" (chap. 1), he documents the "tumbleweed circuit," a round-trip route familiar to southwest migrants prior to the drought.

15. According to the California Department of Agriculture, 71,047 "refugees" entered the state between June 1935 and June 1936. An estimated 75 percent of these originated from the "drought states." See W. F. Baxter, "Migratory Labor Camps," *The Quartermaster Review* (July–Aug. 1937): 3. California growers promoted the myth that field hands recruited from Mexico were "homing pigeons" and "birds of passage" in order to pacify nativists' fears that immigrant workers would become permanent "guests."

16. *San Francisco News,* Aug. 10, 1935. In time, the in-migrants became the focus of intense scrutiny, suspicion, and hate, a pattern of behavior and attitudes that had shaped the response to immigrant field workers from Mexico and Asia and led to the exclusionary acts. In other words, although there had always been a mobile, seasonal work force in California, what was new during the 1930s was that the so-called Okies and Arkies represented an internal migration, and this complicated the response.

17. Donald W. Johnston and Clarence J. Glacken, "A Social Survey of Housing Conditions Among Tulare County Relief Clients: April–June, 1939," State Relief Administration, Tulare County, Calif., quote, 22. This was not an isolated case chosen to dramatize inadequate housing and poor living conditions. Twenty percent of the 3,100 households surveyed lived in tents, chicken coops, pump-houses, or trailers. Sixty-three percent of those rented. The Farmersville family paid $4.00 a month ground rent—they were fortunate. The survey mean stood at $10.50 a month—35 percent of a farm worker's average yearly salary of $350.00

18. Border inspectors from the state department of agriculture reported over 90 percent of the in-migrants as "caucasians." More than 75 percent of these came from four states—Oklahoma, Texas, Arkansas, and Missouri. Family groups entering FSA camps had, on average, just over four members. Three-quarters of the men were between the ages of twenty and forty-four; children under ten years of age predominated (they made up more than 50 percent of the children). The yearly income of these families ranged from $400.00 to $450.00. By 1940, the average length of stay in an FSA settlement reached one year. The figures on California migrants are drawn from Jonathan Garst, "A Study of 6655 Migrant Households Receiving Emergency Grants," (1939); Baxter, "Migratory Labor Camps"; California State Chamber of Commerce, "Migrants: A National Problem and Its Impact on California," State Chamber of Commerce, Sacramento, Calif., 1940. For quantitative assessments of FSA camp residents, see the "Monthly Narrative Report[s]" in box 21, folder PR-89-183, WNRC-RG96.

19. For the residents' multiple uses of the community centers, see the camp newspapers. For example, the weekly schedule of camp activity listed in *The Hub* (Visalia) included sewing classes, scout meetings, movies, and a burial fund meeting. See also the *Migratory Clipper* (Arvin), "Weekly Meeting of the Camp Council"; the *Woodville Community News* (Woodville), "Adrift on the Land," an evening meeting "to discuss our experiences roaming the country in search of better means"; and a 1939 Christmas program with Hollywood celebrities reported in the *Migratory Clipper.*

20. FSA, Contract and Construction Docket Files, 1929–1946, Farmers Home Administration, Record Group 96, National Archives-Pacific Sierra Branch, box 10. Initially, the Construction Division of the Resettlement Administration (and later the FSA) undertook camp construction. Later, contracts were put out to bid. See the FSA administrator's statement in the 1938 *Annual Report* (1939).

21. *Voice of the Agricultural Migrant,* Yuba City, Mar. 29, 1940, 10–11. For more on the improved standard of the metal shelters over tents, see "The Joyous Thought of a Metal Shelter," *Voice of the Agricultural Migrant,* Mar. 8, 1940, 4.

22. For rent rates, see the FSA's "Monthly Narrative Report[s]."

23. Alfred Bruce and Harold Sandbank, *A History of Prefabrication* (New York: John B. Pierce Foundation, 1943), 14. Others saw FSA housing as a model for low-cost dwellings in radically different settings. Rex Thomson, the superintendent of Charities in Los Angeles, petitioned Supervisor John Anson Ford to consider building a hundred units based on the Arvin garden homes for residents of the Olive View Sanatorium. Thomson included a photo of the Arvin housing with his request. Thomson to Ford, Feb. 9, 1938, box 65, folder 14aa, John Anson Ford Collection, Huntington Library.

24. Author interview with Vernon DeMars, Oct. 14, 1988.

25. This configuration represented a specious reworking of the *Zeilenbau* planning principles developed by German Modernist architects. German Modernists aligned apartment blocks in a strict north-south orientation to

maximize sun exposure. The inversion of these principles in California's Central Valley offered scant relief from the heat characteristic of this agricultural area. In fact, it was precisely because of these often oppressive conditions that landscaping became such a high priority in the FSA camps. Author interview with Garrett Eckbo, Nov. 18, 1988.

26. DeMars, "Social Planning for Western Agriculture," *Task* 2 (1941): 5–9.

27. I was alerted to the changing conception of FSA settlements by Vernon DeMars, who stated that the "change in site plan reflected a changing conception of community" (interview, Oct. 14, 1988). Talbot F. Hamlin also noted this shift in his assessment of the FSA: "What started out to be a mere matter of furnishing shelters for wandering laborers and their families became a matter of building highly developed communities with permanent populations" Hamlin, "Farm Security Architecture: An Appraisal," *New Pencil Points* (Nov. 1941): 709–20.

28. Woodville opened during the first week of July 1940. The settlement was sited in a region of cotton, grape, asparagus, and citrus production. From September to April—the peak of the agricultural season—1,240 persons on average resided at Woodville. See "FSA Opens New Migrant Town Near Porterville," *Oakland Tribune,* July 5, 1941, and "Press Release: Porterville," n.d., carton 8, folder 325, FSA-SF Collection. For an overview of the first year at Woodville, see the anniversary edition of the *Woodville Community News,* June 15, 1942.

29. Landscape planning for the greenbelt buffer called for a row of fruitless mulberries paralleling the roadway, two reservoirs, and an alfalfa ground cover. In addition to the mulberry boundary, the plan called for sycamores, Chinese elms, and Arizona ash. In total, over twenty-four hundred trees and fifty species, chosen to provide shade and privacy, were planted throughout the site. According to Eckbo, trees grew quickly in this climate if adequately watered (interview, Oct. 25, 1988). The quotes are from DeMars, "Social Planning," 9.

30. The *Woodville Community News* is the best source for community programs. Each issue contained four to six pages devoted to the residents' diverse interests, including meeting minutes, an update on clinic services, nursery and grammar school news, and meeting times for the sewing club, adult classes, and library. Residents based the cooperative store on Roachdale principles, and the *News* ran articles devoted to the cooperative movement and the benefits residents could achieve by patronizing their own store.

31. DeMars, "Social Planning." Roger Montgomery offered a similar perspective on Woodville and the FSA planning evolution in "Mass-Producing Bay Area Architecture," in *Bay Area Houses,* 2d ed., ed. Sally Woodbridge (Salt Lake City: Peregrine Smith Books, 1988). Montgomery focused his account on the ways in which the Bay Area tradition informed the formal attributes of social architecture and how the FSA experiment in turn broadened both the architectural discourse and the range of architectural practice.

Select Bibliography

Andrew, David S. *Louis Sullivan and the Polemics of Modern Architecture: The Present Against the Past*. Urbana: University of Illinois Press, 1985.

Attfield, Judy, and Pat Kirkham, eds. *A View from the Interior: Feminism, Women, and Design*. London: Women's Press, 1989.

Axelrod, Alan, ed. *The Colonial Revival in America*. New York: W. W. Norton, 1985.

Bauman, Richard. *Let Your Words Be Few: Symbolism of Speaking and Silence Among Seventeenth-Century Quakers*. Cambridge: Cambridge University Press, 1983.

Bacon, Margaret Hope. *Mothers of Feminism: The Story of Quaker Women in America*. San Francisco: Harper & Row, 1986.

Benedict, Burton. *The Anthropology of World's Fairs: San Francisco's Panama Pacific International Exposition of 1915*. London and Berkeley: Lowie Museum of Anthropology, 1983.

Bernstein, Rebecca Sample, and Carolyn Torma. "Exploring the Role of Women in the Creation of Vernacular Architecture." In *Perspectives in Vernacular Architecture, IV*. Edited by Thomas Carter and Bernard L. Herman. Columbia: University of Missouri Press, 1991.

Blackmar, Elizabeth. *Manhattan for Rent, 1785-1850*. Ithaca: Cornell University Press, 1989.

Bluestone, Daniel. *Constructing Chicago*. New Haven: Yale University Press, 1991.

Blumin, Stuart M. *The Emergence of the Middle Class: Social Experience in the American City, 1760-1900*. Cambridge: Cambridge University Press, 1989.

———. *The Urban Threshold: Growth and Change in a Nineteenth-Century American Community*. Chicago: University of Chicago Press, 1976.

Borsay, Peter. *The English Urban Renaissance: Culture and Society in the Provincial Town, 1660-1770*. Oxford: Clarendon Press, 1989.

Bose, Christine E., Philip L. Bereano, and Mary Malloy, "Household Technology and the Social Construction of Housework." *Technology and Culture* 25 (1) (Jan. 1984): 53-82.

Boys, Jos. "Is There a Feminist Analysis of Architecture?" *Built Environment* 10 (1) (Nov. 1984): 25-34.

Brown, Elisabeth Potts, and Susan Mosher Straud, eds. *Witnesses for Change: Quaker Women Over Three Centuries*. New Brunswick, N.J.: Rutgers University Press, 1989.

Buckley, Cheryl. "Made in Patriarchy: Toward a Feminist Analysis of Women and Design." *Design Issues* 3 (2) (Fall 1986): 3-14.

Butler, David M. "Quaker Meeting Houses in America and England: Impressions and Comparisons." *Quaker History* 79 (2) (Fall 1990): 93-104.

Chapman, William. "Slave Villages in the Danish West Indies: Changes of the Eighteenth and Early Nineteenth Centuries." In *Perspectives in Vernacular Architecture, IV*. Edited by Thomas Carter and Bernard L. Herman. Columbia: University of Missouri Press, 1991.

Chappell, Edward A. "Acculturation in the Shenandoah Valley: Rhenish Houses of the Massanutten Settlement." *Proceedings of the American Philosophical Society* 124 (1980): 56.

Chiarappa, Michael J. "The Social Context of Eighteenth-Century West New Jersey Brick Artisanry." In *Perspectives in Vernacular Architecture, IV*. Edited by Thomas Carter and Bernard L. Herman. Columbia: University of Missouri Press, 1991.

Clarke, Nina Hammond. *History of the 19th-Century Black Churches in Maryland and Washington, D.C.* New York: Vantage Press, 1983.

Cowan, Ruth Schwartz. "The 'Industrial Revolution' in the Home: Household Technology and Social Change in the Twentieth Century." *Technology and Culture* 17 (1) (Jan. 1976): 1-23.

————. *More Work for Mother: The Ironies of Household Technology from the Open Hearth to the Microwave*. New York: Basic Books, 1983.

Cromley, Elizabeth Collins. *Alone Together: A History of New York's Early Apartments*. Ithaca: Cornell University Press, 1990.

————. "A History of American Beds and Bedrooms." In *Perspectives in Vernacular Architecture, IV*. Edited by Thomas Carter and Bernard L. Herman. Columbia: University of Missouri Press, 1991.

Darnton, Robert. *The Great Cat Massacre: And Other Episodes in French Cultural History*. New York: Vintage Books, 1984.

Davis, Susan D. *Parades and Power: Street Theatre in Nineteenth-Century Philadelphia*. Philadelphia: Temple University Press, 1986.

Doerflinger, Thomas. *A Vigorous Spirit of Enterprise: Merchants and Economic Development in Revolutionary Philadelphia*. New York: W. W. Norton, 1987.

Earle, Carville V., and Ronald Hoffman. "Staple Crops and Urban Development in the Eighteenth-Century South." In *Perspectives in American History,* 10. Edited by Donald Fleming and Bernard Bailyn. Cambridge, Mass.: Harvard University Press, 1976.

Fenske, Gail, and Deryck W. Holdsworth. "Corporate Identity and the New York Office Building." In *The Landscape of Modernity: Essays on New York City, 1900-1940*. Edited by D. Ward and O. Zunz. New York: Russell Sage, 1992.

Frisch, Michael H. *Town into City: Springfield, Massachusetts, and the Meaning of Community, 1840-1880*. Cambridge, Mass.: Harvard University Press, 1972.

Gad, Gunter, and Deryck W. Holdsworth. "Corporate Capitalism and the Emergence of the High-Rise Office Building." *Urban Geography* 8 (3) (1987): 212-31.

Gardner, Carol Brooks. "Analyzing Gender in Public Places: Rethinking Goffman's Vision of Everyday Life." *The American Sociologist* (Spring 1989): 42-56.

Genovese, Eugene D. *Roll, Jordan, Roll: The World the Slaves Made*. New York: Random House, 1972.

Glassie, Henry. *Folk Housing in Middle Virginia: The Structural Analysis of Historic Artifacts*. Knoxville: University of Tennessee Press, 1975.

————. "Eighteenth-Century Cultural Process in Delaware Valley Folk Building." *Winterthur Portfolio* 7 (1972): 29-57.

————. *Pattern in the Material Folk Culture of the Eastern United States*. Philadelphia: University of Pennsylvania Press, 1969.

Greene, Jack P. "Independence, Improvement, and Authority: Toward a Framework for Understanding the Histories of the Southern Backcountry during the Era of the American Revolution." In *An Uncivil War: The Southern Backcountry during the American Revolution*. Edited by Ronald Hoffman, Thad W. Tate, and Peter J. Albert. Charlottesville: University Press of Virginia for the United States Capitol Historical Society, 1985.

————. *Pursuits of Happiness: The Social Development of Early Modern British Colonies and the Formation of American Culture*. Chapel Hill: University of North Carolina Press, 1988.

Haraven, Tamara D. "The History of the Family and the Complexity of Social Change." *American Historical Review* 96 (1) (February 1991): 95-124.

Harper, R. Eugene. *The Transformation of Western Pennsylvania, 1770-1800*. Pittsburgh: University of Pittsburgh Press, 1992.

Hayden, Dolores. *The Grand Domestic Revolution: A History of Feminist Designs for American Homes, Neighborhoods, and Cities*. Cambridge, Mass: MIT Press, 1981.

Henretta, James A. "Families and Farms: *Mentalité* in Pre-Industrial America." *William and Mary Quarterly* 3d ser., 35 (1978): 3-32.

Herman, Bernard L. *Architecture and Rural Life in Central Delaware, 1700-1900*. Knoxville: University of Tennessee Press, 1987.

Hershberg, Theodore, ed. *Philadelphia: Work, Space, Family, and Group Experience in the Nineteenth Century*. New York: Oxford University Press, 1981.

Hofstra, Warren R. "Land, Ethnicity, and Community at Opequon Settlement, Virginia, 1730-1800." *Virginia Magazine of History and Biography* 98 (1990): 423-48.

———. "Land Policy and Settlement in the Northern Shenandoah Valley." In *Appalachian Frontiers: Settlement, Society, & Development in the Preindustrial Era*. Edited by Robert D. Mitchell. Lexington: University Press of Kentucky, 1990.

Hooks, Bell. *Talking Back. Thinking Feminist, Thinking Black*. Boston: South End Press, 1989.

Hudson, Kenneth. *Food Clothes and Shelter*. London: Baker, 1978.

Jackson, John B. *Discovering the Vernacular Landscape*. New Haven: Yale University Press, 1984.

———. "The Domestication of the Garage." In *The Necessity For Ruins and Other Topics*. Amherst: University of Massachusetts Press, 1980.

Jackson, Kenneth T. *Crabgrass Frontier: The Suburbanization of the United States*. Oxford: Oxford University Press, 1985.

Jackson, Peter. "The Cultural Politics of Masculinity: Towards a Social Geography." *Transactions, Institute of British Geographers* N.S. 16 (1991): 199-213.

James, Sydney V. *A People Among People: Quaker Benevolence in Eighteenth Century America*. Cambridge, Mass.: Harvard University Press, 1963.

Jensen, Joan. *Loosening the Bonds: Mid-Atlantic Farm Women, 1750-1850*. New Haven: Yale University Press, 1986.

Kerber, Linda. "Separate Spheres, Female Worlds, Woman's Place: The Rhetoric of Women's History." *Journal of American History* 75 (1) (June 1988): 32-37.

Kesseler, Suzanne, and Wendy McKenna. *Gender: An Ethnomethodological Approach*. New York: John Wiley, 1978.

King, Anthony D., ed. *Buildings and Society: Essays on the Social Development of the Built Environment*. London: Routledge & Kegan Paul, 1980.

———. *The Bungalow: The Production of a Global Culture*. London: Routledge & Kegan Paul, 1984.

Kniffen, Fred B., and Henry Glassie. "Building in Wood in the Eastern United States: A Time-Place Perspective." *Geographical Review* 56 (1966): 40-66.

———. "Folk Housing: Key to Diffusion." *Annals of the Association of American Geographers* 55 (1965): 553.

Knight, Franklin W., and Peggy K. Liss, eds. *Atlantic Port Cities: Economy, Culture, and Society in the Atlantic World, 1650-1850*. Knoxville: University of Tennessee Press, 1991.

Kostof, Spiro. *The City Shaped: Urban Patterns and Meanings Through History*. London: Thames and Hudson, 1991.

Kulikoff, Allan. "The Transition to Capitalism in Rural America." *William and Mary Quarterly* 3d ser., 46 (1989): 120-44.

Kwolek-Folland, Angel. "The Elegant Dugout: Domesticity and Moveable Culture in the United States, 1870-1900." *American Studies* (Fall 1984): 21-37.

———. "The Useful What-Not and the Ideal of 'Domestic Decoration.'" *Helicon Nine* 8 (1983): 72-82.

Lane, Belden C. *Landscapes of the Sacred: Geography and Narrative in American Spirituality*. New York: Paulist Press, 1988.

Lears, T. J. *No Place of Grace: Antimodernism and the Transformation of American Culture, 1880-1920*. New York: Pantheon Books, 1981.

Levy, Barry. *Quakers and the American Family: British Quakers in the Delaware Valley, 1650-1765*. New York: Oxford University Press, 1988.

Lloyd, Bonnie. "Woman's Place, Man's Place." *Landscape* 20 (1) (Oct. 1975): 10–13.

Longstreth, Richard. *On the Edge of the World: Four Architects in San Francisco at the Turn of the Century*. New York: Architectural History Foundation, 1983.

Lupton, Ellen, and J. Abbott Miller. *The Bathroom, The Kitchen and the Aesthetics of Waste: A Process of Elimination*. Cambridge, Mass.: MIT List Visual Arts Center, 1992.

MacDonald, Sally, and Julia Porter. *Putting on the Style: Setting Up Home in the 1950s*. London: Geffrye Museum, 1990.

Marietta, Jack D. *The Reformation of American Quakerism, 1748-1753*. Philadelphia: University of Pennsylvania Press, 1984.

Marling, Karal Ann. *George Washington Slept Here: Colonial Revivals and American Culture, 1876-1986*. Cambridge, Mass.: Harvard University Press, 1988.

May Bridget A. "Progressivism and the Colonial Revival: The Modern Colonial House, 1900-1920." *Winterthur Portfolio* 26 (Summer/Autumn 1991): 107-22.

McMurry, Sally. *Families and Farmhouses in Nineteenth Century America: Vernacular Design and Social Change*. New York: Oxford University Press, 1988.

———. "Women in the American Vernacular Landscape." *Material Culture* 20 (1) (1988): 33-49.

Merchant, Carolyn. "Gender and Environmental History." *Journal of American History* 76 (4) (Mar. 1990): 1117-21.

Merrill, Michael. "Cash is Good to Eat: Self-Sufficiency and Exchange in the Rural Economy of the United States." *Radical History Review* 3 (1977): 42-69.

Meyerowitz, Joanne. *Women Adrift: Independent Wage Earners in Chicago, 1880-1930*. Chicago: University of Chicago Press, 1988.

Mills, David S. "The Development of Folk Architecture in Trinity Bay." In *The Peopling of Newfoundland*. Edited by J. J. Mannion. St. John's: Memorial University of Newfoundland, 1977.

Mitchell, Robert D. *Commercialism and Frontier: Perspectives on the Early Shenandoah Valley*. Charlottesville: University Press of Virginia, 1977.

———. "The Formation of Early American Culture Regions: An Interpretation." In *European Settlement and Development in North America*. Edited by J. R. Gibson. Toronto: University of Toronto Press, 1978.

Moore, Willard B. "The Preferred and Remembered Image: Cultural Change and Artifactual Adjustment in Quaker Meeting Houses." In *Perspectives in Vernacular Architecture, II*. Edited by Camille Wells (Columbia: University of Missouri Press, 1986).

Nabokov, Peter, and Robert Easton, *Native American Architecture*. New York: Oxford University Press, 1989.

Neil, Robert. *Chestertown, Maryland: An Inventory of Historic Sites*. Chestertown: Town of Chestertown, 1981.

Newton, Milton. "Cultural Preadaptation and the Upland South." *Geoscience and Man* 5 (1974): 143-54.

Noble, Allen G., ed. *To Build in a New Land: Ethnic Landscapes of North America*. Baltimore and London: Johns Hopkins University Press, 1992.

Nobles, Gregory H. "Capitalism in the Countryside: The Transformation of Rural Society in the United States." *Radical History Review* 41 (1988): 163-77.

Oakes, James. *The Ruling Race: A History of American Slaveholders*. New York: Knopf, 1975.

Olson, Sherry H. *Baltimore: The Building of an American City*. Baltimore: Johns Hopkins University Press, 1980.

Pocious, Gerald. "Architecture on Newfoundland's Southern Shore: Diversity and the Emergence of New World Forms." In *Perspectives in Vernacular Architecture*. Edited by C. Wells. Annapolis: Vernacular Architecture Forum, 1982.

Portner, Sherry B., and Harriet Whitehead. *Sexual Meanings: The Cultural Construction of Gender and Sexuality*. New York: Cambridge University Press, 1981.

Price, Jacob M. "The Economic Function and Growth of American Port Towns in the Eighteenth Century." *Perspectives in American History* 8 (1974): 123-86.

Purser, Margaret. "All Roads Lead to Winnemucca: Local Road Systems and Community Material Culture in Nineteenth-century Nevada." In *Perspectives in Vernacular Architecture, III*. Edited by Thomas Carter and Bernard L. Herman. Columbia: University of Missouri Press, 1989.

Raboteau, Albert J. *Slave Religion: The "Invisible Institution" in the Antebellum South*. New York: Oxford University Press, 1978.

Rediker, Marcus. *Between the Devil and the Deep Blue Sea: Merchant Seamen, Pirates, and the Anglo-American Maritime World, 1700-1750*. New York: Cambridge University Press, 1987.

Reps, John. *Cities of the American West: A History of Frontier Urban Planning*. Princeton: Princeton University Press, 1979.

Rodriguez, Sylvia. "Art, Tourism, and Race Relations in Taos: Toward a Sociology of the Art Colony." *Journal of Anthropological Research* 45 (Spring 1989): 77-99.

Rothenberg, Winifred B. "The Emergence of a Capital Market in Rural Massachusetts, 1730-1838." *Journal of Economic History* 45 (1985): 781-808.

———. "The Emergence of Farm Labor Markets and the Transformation of the Rural Economy: Massachusetts, 1750-1855." *Journal of Economic History* 48 (1988): 537-66.

———. "The Market and Massachusetts Farmers, 1750-1858." *Journal of Economic History* 41 (1981): 283-314.

Rotundo, E. Anthony. *American Manhood: Transformations in Masculinity from the Revolution to the Modern Era*. New York: Basic Books, 1993.

Russett, Cynthia. *Sexual Science: The Victorian Construction of Womanhood*. Cambridge, Mass.: Harvard University Press, 1989.

Sanday, Peggy. *Female Power and Male Dominance: On the Origins of Sexual Inequality*. New York: Cambridge University Press, 1981.

Scott, Joan W. "Gender: A Useful Category of Historical Analysis." In *Gender and the Politics of History*. New York: Columbia University Press, 1988.

Smith, Billy G. *The "Lower Sort": Philadelphia's Laboring People, 1750-1800*. Ithaca: Cornell University Press, 1990.

Smith, Julia Floyd. *Slavery and Rice Culture in Low Country Georgia*. Knoxville: University of Tennessee Press, 1985.

Sobel, Mechal. *The World They Made Together: Black and White Values in Eighteenth-Century Virginia*. Princeton: Princeton University Press, 1987.

Soderlund, Jean. *Quakers and Slavery: A Divided Spirit*. Princeton: Princeton University Press, 1985.

Spain, Daphne. *Gendered Spaces*. Chapel Hill: University of North Carolina Press, 1992.

St. George, Robert Blair. "'Set Thine House in Order': The Domestication of the Yeomanry in Seventeenth-Century New England." In *Common Places*. Edited by Dell Upton and John Michael Vlach. Athens: University of Georgia Press, 1983.

Stanton, Phoebe. *The Gothic Revival and American Church Architecture: An Episode in Taste, 1840-1856*. Baltimore: Johns Hopkins University Press, 1968.

Starr, Kevin. *Americans and the California Dream, 1850-1915*. New York: Oxford University Press, 1973.

Stilgoe, John R. *Borderland: Origins of the American Suburb, 1820-1939*. New Haven: Yale University Press, 1988.

Teaford, Jon C. *The Municipal Revolution in America: Origins of Modern Urban Government, 1650-1825*. Chicago: University of Chicago Press, 1975.

Tolles, Frederick B. *Meeting House and Counting House: The Quaker Merchants of Colonial Philadelphia, 1682-1763*. New York: W. W. Norton, 1963.

Trinder, Barrie. *The Making of the Industrial Landscape*. London: Dent, 1982.

Turner, Victor, ed. *Celebration: Studies in Festivity and Ritual*. Washington, D.C.: Smithsonian Institution Press, 1982.

Twombley, Robert C. "Saving the Family: Middle Class Attraction to Wright's Prairie House, 1901-1909." *American Quarterly* 27 (1) (Mar. 1975), 57-72.

Ulrich, Laurel Thatcher. *Good Wives: Image & Reality in the Lives of Northern New England Women, 1650-1750*. New York: Knopf, 1982.

Upton, Dell, ed. *America's Architectural Roots: Ethnic Groups That Built America*. Washington, D.C.: National Trust For Historic Preservation, 1986.

———. *Holy Things and Profane: Anglican Parish Churches in Colonial Virginia*. Cambridge, Mass.: MIT Press, 1986.

———. "New Views of the Virginia Landscape." *Virginia Magazine of History and Biography* 96 (1988): 441-42.

———. "Outside the Academy: A Century of Vernacular Architecture Studies, 1890-1990." In *The Architectural Historian in America*. Edited by Elisabeth Blair MacDougall. Washington: National Gallery of Art, 1990.

———. "Pattern Books and Professionalism: Aspects of the Transformation of Domestic Architecture in America, 1800-1860." *Winterthur Portfolio* 19 (2-3) (Summer-Autumn 1984).

———. "The Power of Things: Recent Studies in American Vernacular Architecture." *American Quarterly* 35 (1983): 270-74.

———. "Vernacular Domestic Architecture in Eighteenth-Century Virginia." In *Common Places: Readings in American Vernacular Architecture*. Edited by Dell Upton and John Michael Vlach. Athens: University of Georgia Press, 1986.

———. "White and Black Landscapes in Eighteenth-Century Virginia." In *Material Life in America 1600-1860*. Edited by Robert Blair St. George. Boston: Northeastern University Press, 1988, 357-69.

Vanek, Joann. "Household Technology and Social Status: Rising Living Standards and Status and Residence Differences in Housework." *Technology and Culture* 19 (3) (July 1978): 361-75.

———. "Time Spent in House Work." *Scientific American* (Nov. 1974): 116-20.

Vickers, Daniel. "Competency and Competition: Economic Culture in Early America." *William and Mary Quarterly* 3d ser., 47 (1990): 3-29.

Vlach, John Michael. "Afro-American Housing in Virginia's Landscape of Slavery." In *By the Work of Their Hands: Studies in Afro-American Folklife*. Ann Arbor: UMI Research Press, 1991.

———. "The Shotgun House: An African Architectural Legacy." In *Common Places: Readings in American Vernacular Architecture*. Edited by Dell Upton and John Michael Vlach. Athens: University of Georgia Press, 1983.

Wade, Richard C. *The Urban Frontier: The Rise of Western Cities, 1790-1830*. Cambridge, Mass.: Harvard University Press.

Warner, Samuel Bass. *The Private City: Philadelphia in Three Periods of Its Growth*. Philadelphia: University of Pennsylvania Press, 1968, 2d edition, 1987.

Weaver, William Woys. "The Pennsylvania German House: European Antecedents and New World Forms." *Winterthur Portfolio* 21 (1986): 243-64.

Weisman, Leslie Kanes. *Discrimination by Design: A Feminist Critique of the Man-Made Environment*. (Urbana: University of Illinois Press, 1992.

Weiss, Marc A. *The Rise of the Community Builders: The American Real Estate Industry and Urban Land Planning*. New York: Columbia University Press, 1987.

Wilson, Christopher. "New Mexico in the Tradition of Romantic Reaction." In *Pueblo Style and Regional Architecture*. Edited by Nicholas C. Markovich, Wolfgang F. E. Prieser, and Fred G. Sturm. New York: Van Nostrand Reinhold, 1990.

Woods, Mary. "The First American Architectural Journals: The Profession's Voice." *Journal of the Society of Architectural Historians* XLVIII (June 1989).

Wright, Gwendolyn. *Building the Dream: A Social History of Housing in America*. New York: Pantheon, 1981.

———. *Moralism and the Model Home: Domestic Architecture and Cultural Conflict in Chicago, 1873-1913*. Chicago: University of Chicago Press, 1980.

Zelinsky, Wilbur. *The Cultural Geography of the United States*. Englewood Cliffs, N.J.: Prentice-Hall, 1973.

Zunz, Olivier. *Making America Corporate 1870-1920*. Chicago: University of Chicago Press, 1990.

Contributors

ANNMARIE ADAMS is a member of the faculty of the School of Architecture at McGill University, Montreal, where she teaches architectural history and studio courses. She has completed a book manuscript about health and feminist issues in British housing in the late nineteenth century, and she recently guest-curated an exhibition at the Canadian Centre for Architecture on a related North American topic.

SUSAN MULCHAHEY CHASE received a B.A. in economics from Michigan State University, an M.A. in American studies from the University of Michigan, and a masters of industrial and labor relations from Cornell University. She is a doctoral candidate in the College of Urban Affairs and Public Policy, University of Delaware, where her research has focused on the use of restrictive deed covenants in the suburbs created around Wilmington, Delaware, between 1900 and 1941.

ELIZABETH COLLINS CROMLEY is the author of *Alone Together* as well as essays on domestic space, resort architecture, urban parks, and aspects of apartment design. Past president of the Vernacular Architecture Forum, she is a member of the faculty of the School of Architecture at the State University of New York at Buffalo.

SUSAN GARFINKEL is a doctoral candidate in the American Civilization program at the University of Pennsylvania where she has focused on material culture studies. She also holds M.A. degrees in folklore and folklife from the University of Pennsylvania and early American culture from the University of Delaware and the Winterthur program. Her dissertation explores the intersection of theology and the plan and function of Quaker meeting houses in Philadelphia.

BERNARD L. HERMAN teaches architectural history at the University of Delaware where he is a member of the art history department and where he has long been associated with the Center for Historic Architecture and Engineering. His publications include *Architecture and Rural Life in Central Delaware 1700–1900* and, most recently, *The Stolen House*.

GREG HISE is an urban historian and assistant professor in the School of Urban and Regional Planning at the University of Southern California. His research and writing focus on the twentieth-century expansion of American cities. A forthcoming book examines modern community planning, mass housing, and the post–World War II urban region.

WARREN R. HOFSTRA is associate professor of history at Shenandoah University in Winchester, Virginia. He holds M.A. and Ph.D. degrees from Boston University and the University of Virginia respectively. In addition to teaching in the fields of American social and cultural history, he directs the Community History Project of Shenandoah University. Hofstra has published in the fields of material culture, geography, archaeology, economic history, and social history and is currently engaged in an extended research project on settlement, social evolution, and material life in the early Shenandoah Valley.

Deryck W. Holdsworth received his graduate degrees from the University of British Columbia, Vancouver, Canada, and his undergraduate training at the University of Newcastle, England. He is currently an associate professor of geography at Pennsylvania State University. His publications include *Historical Atlas of Canada, III: Addressing the Twentieth Century,* which he co-edited, *Reviving Main Street,* which he edited, *The Parking Authority of Toronto, 1952–87,* and articles on the skyscraper, prefabricated housing, pattern book housing, and suburban development.

Carter L. Hudgins is executive director of the Historic Charleston Foundation. He holds a Ph.D. in history from the College of William and Mary and is the author of essays in historical archaeology, material culture, and historic preservation policy.

Jan Jennings is an associate professor in the department of design and environmental analysis at Cornell University. Her current research focuses on gender issues and consumerism in popular architecture. A former Forman Fellow at the Winterthur Museum (1991), Jennings is the editor of *Roadside America: The Automobile in Design and Culture* and co-author of *American Vernacular Interior Architecture, 1870–1940* and *American Vernacular Design, 1870–1940.* She has served as a member of the board of the Vernacular Architecture Forum, as president of the Society for Commercial Archeology, and was the first director of the city of Tulsa's Historic Preservation Office.

Karen Koegler is a geographer who has taught at the University of Kentucky since 1983. She also holds degrees in historic preservation, library science, and art history and has published articles on a variety of issues in the field of historic landscapes, including place names, preservation issues, and childhood spaces. An analysis of western Pennsylvania's vernacular stone houses was the primary focus of her dissertation.

Peter E. Kurtze is an architectural historian and a historic preservation consultant in private practice in Baltimore, Maryland. He specializes in research and documentation of historic properties and teaches at the University of Maryland and at Goucher College. A former employee of the Maryland Historical Trust, Kurtze is longtime secretary of the Vernacular Architecture Forum.

Angel Kwolek-Folland is an associate professor of history at the University of Kansas where she teaches courses in women's history, gender studies, and material culture. She received her Ph.D. in U.S. history from the University of Minnesota where she specialized in the history of women. She maintains research and teaching interests in architectural history and material culture studies and has published essays in *American Studies, Helicon Nine,* an anthology edited by Ava Baron entitled *Work Engendered: Toward a New History of Men, Women, and Work,* and in the forthcoming *The Material Culture of Gender/The Gender of Material Culture.* A full-length work, *Engendering Business: Men and Women in the Corporate Office, 1870–1930,* is forthcoming.

William D. Moore is a doctoral candidate in the American and New England studies program at Boston University where he is writing his dissertation about the architecture and material culture of Masonic temples in New York State from 1870 to 1930. He is currently director of the Chancellor Robert R. Livingston Masonic Library & Museum in New York City. He received his B.A. in folklore and mythology from Harvard College.

DIANE SHAW is a doctoral candidate in architectural history at the University of California at Berkeley where she is writing a dissertation on the urban and social design of nineteenth-century small cities in New York state. She holds a B.A. in history from Smith College and an M.A. in American studies from George Washington University. She has worked as an architectural historian for the city of Baltimore, the Maryland Historical Trust, the National Trust for Historic Preservation, and the Historic American Buildings Survey.

PAMELA H. SIMPSON holds a Ph.D. in art history from the University of Delaware. She is the Ernest Williams II Professor of Art History and head of the art department at Washington and Lee University in Lexington, Virginia. She has worked as a consultant and surveyor for the Virginia Department of Historic Resources and is co-author of *The Architecture of Historic Lexington*. She has also served as a board member and second vice-president of the Vernacular Architecture Forum.

ABIGAIL A. VAN SLYCK earned a Ph.D. in architectural history from the University of California at Berkeley. She is currently an assistant professor of architecture and women's studies at the University of Arizona and serves on the board of directors of the Vernacular Architecture Forum. She is the author of a forthcoming book, *Free to All: Carnegie Libraries and American Culture,* and articles on the history of American libraries in the *Journal of the Society of Architectural Historians* and in the *Working Papers* series of the Southwest Institute for Research on Women. In 1993, she was awarded a Fulbright research grant to work on a comparative study of Carnegie libraries in New Zealand and the United States.

JOHN MICHAEL VLACH is professor of American civilization and anthropology at George Washington University. Vlach's previous publications include *Back of the Big House: The Afro-American Tradition in Decorative Arts, Charleston Blacksmith,* and the collection of essays *Common Places,* which he co-edited with Dell Upton.

MICHAEL ANN WILLIAMS teaches folklore at Western Kentucky University. Past editor of the Vernacular Architecture Forum's newsletter, she is also the recipient of the 1993 Abbot Lowell Cummings Award for her book *Homeplace*.

CHRISTOPHER L. YIP teaches in the School of Architecture at the California Polytechnic State University at San Luis Obispo. He has degrees in architecture and architectural history from the University of California at Berkeley and specializes in issues of Chinese American architecture.

M. JANE YOUNG is a folklorist who teaches in the American Studies program at the University of New Mexico. She is the author of one book, *Signs from the Ancestors: Zuni Cultural Symbolism and Perceptions of Rock Art,* and co-editor of *Feminist Theory and The Study of Folklore.* Her current research explores gender and tradition and the relationship between verbal and visual art.

Index